324.
6
KLI

The Comp  ns

D1331117

Volumes of a Collaborative Research Program Among
Election Study Teams from Around the World

Series editors: Hans-Dieter Klingemann and Ian McAllister

UWE BRISTOL
WITHDRAWN
LIBRARY SERVICES

The Comparative Study of Electoral Systems (CSES) is a collaborative program of research among election study teams from around the world. Participating countries include a common module of survey questions in their post-election studies. The resulting data are deposited along with voting, demographic, district, and macro variables. The studies are then merged into a single, free, public dataset for use in comparative study and cross-level analysis.

The set of volumes in this series is based on these CSES modules, and the volumes address the key theoretical issues and empirical debates in the study of elections and representative democracy. Some of the volumes will be organized around the theoretical issues raised by a particular module, while others will be thematic in their focus. Taken together, these volumes will provide a rigorous and ongoing contribution to understanding the expansion and consolidation of democracy in the twenty-first century.

Further information on CSES activities can be obtained from:

CSES Secretariat
Center for Political Studies
Institute for Social Research
The University of Michigan
426 Thompson Street
Ann Arbor, Michigan 481042321
USA

CSES web site: http//:www.cses.org

The Comparative Study of Electoral Systems

Edited by Hans-Dieter Klingemann

UWF Bristol
FR-4 8918
-6 MAR 2012
ACE
Library Services

OXFORD
UNIVERSITY PRESS

OXFORD
UNIVERSITY PRESS

Great Clarendon Street, Oxford OX2 6DP

Oxford University Press is a department of the University of Oxford.
It furthers the University's objective of excellence in research, scholarship,
and education by publishing worldwide in

Oxford New York

Auckland Cape Town Dar es Salaam Hong Kong Karachi
Kuala Lumpur Madrid Melbourne Mexico City Nairobi
New Delhi Shanghai Taipei Toronto

With offices in

Argentina Austria Brazil Chile Czech Republic France Greece
Guatemala Hungary Italy Japan Poland Portugal Singapore
South Korea Switzerland Thailand Turkey Ukraine Vietnam

Oxford is a registered trade mark of Oxford University Press
in the UK and in certain other countries

Published in the United States
by Oxford University Press Inc., New York

© The several contributors 2009

The moral rights of the authors have been asserted
Database right Oxford University Press (maker)

First published 2009
First published in paperback 2012

All rights reserved. No part of this publication may be reproduced,
stored in a retrieval system, or transmitted, in any form or by any means,
without the prior permission in writing of Oxford University Press,
or as expressly permitted by law, or under terms agreed with the appropriate
reprographics rights organization. Enquiries concerning reproduction
outside the scope of the above should be sent to the Rights Department,
Oxford University Press, at the address above

You must not circulate this book in any other binding or cover
and you must impose the same condition on any acquirer

British Library Cataloguing in Publication Data

Data available

Library of Congress Cataloging in Publication Data

The comparative study of electoral systems / Hans-Dieter Klingemann (ed.).
    p. cm.
  ISBN 978–0–19–921735–9 (acid-free paper)
1. Elections–Cross-cultural studies. 2. Representative government and
representation–Cross-cultural studies. 3. Voting–Cross-cultural studies.
4. Political parties–Cross-cultural studies. I. Klingemann, Hans-Dieter.
JF1001.C572 2009
324.6–dc22

Typeset by SPI Publisher Services, Pondicherry, India
Printed in Great Britain
on acid-free paper by
CPI Antony Rowe, Chippenham, Wiltshire

ISBN 978–0–19–921735–9 (hbk); 978–0–19–964239–7 (pbk)

1 3 5 7 9 10 8 6 4 2

Foreword

If the hallmark of the late twentieth century was the expansion of democracy, the early twentieth-first century looks likely to be characterized by its consolidation and a concern for the quality of the democratic process. In 1900, no country had universal suffrage, although 25 nations had some form of restrictive democratic practices. A century later, around 120 of the world's 192 countries were electoral democracies. By any assessment, democracy has become the political norm in the world—not the exception. This shift in the nature and direction of global political governance is as dramatic as it is profound.

But despite the apparent ubiquity of democracy, not all democracies can be considered equal. They differ widely in the freedom they afford their citizens, in the fairness of their electoral institutions, and in the freedom of political leaders and parties to stand for public office. Perhaps most important of all, not all of the citizens in the new democracies unconditionally support their new political institutions. There is widespread agreement that what ordinary citizens think about democracy and its institutions is a key component of democratization; it is only when the mass citizenry unconditionally embraces democratic principles can democratic consolidation be considered complete and work on the quality of the democratic process begin. On that basis, many democracies have much farther to travel before they can be considered stable and enduring.

The purpose of this series is to understand how public support for democracy—the key element in democratic consolidation—is shaped. The series is based on the Comparative Study of Electoral Systems project that has produced the most sophisticated and systematic dataset dealing with the operation of representative democracy across the world. Established in 1994, the CSES today covers more than 50 countries and involves some 200 collaborators, drawn not just from Europe and North America, but also from South America, Central Asia, the Indian subcontinent, South-East Asia, and the Pacific region. The CSES is unique in combining information on institutional arrangements with survey data relating to citizen attitudes and behavior. This research design allows scholars to test major theories about the performance of electoral institutions. Only through comparative analysis, where citizens are observed in different settings, can the impact of political institutions be properly understood and evaluated.

The first module of the CSES, on which the current volume is based, approaches these questions by examining micro–macro theories of attitude formation and voting behavior. One aspect of this approach involves examining the impact of constitutional and electoral arrangements on political attitudes and vote choice to understand the complex relationship between constitutions, electoral systems, and political performance. A second part of the module examines social cleavages and their importance in structuring party competition, and addresses the ongoing debates about the social underpinnings of party systems. The third part of the module is concerned with public satisfaction with political institutions generally, and democracy in particular. The current first volume focuses on the first and third aspects mentioned.

The second CSES module, completed in 2006, examines accountability and representation and addresses some of the most important theoretical questions in the study of democracy. One part of the module examines the role of elections in accountability and representation, and asks if elections are a mechanism to hold government accountable or if elections are a means to ensure that citizens' views are properly represented in the democratic process. Another part is concerned with engagement and participation in politics and such issues as decreasing turnout and campaign activity. As participation has fallen precipitously in almost all of the advanced democracies, questions have been raised about the health of democracy. And the last part of the module is designed to understand how voters arrive at their political choices within new democracies.

The third CSES module, which is scheduled to be completed in 2011, focuses on the political choices that voters face in an election. This module examines the role of retrospective and prospective evaluations in shaping voter choice, as well as the importance of ideology and government performance. It also examines the consequences when elections do not offer voters salient choices; these consequences can range from declining participation to the rise of extremist parties and even a decline in political support for democracy generally. In addition, the module repeats some of the items in the first and second modules, providing a longitudinal component to democratic performance across a range of new and established democracies.

This series is based around these CSES modules, and the volumes in the series address the key theoretical issues and empirical debates in the study of elections and representative democracy. Some of the volumes will be organized around the theoretical issues raised by a particular module, while others will be thematic in their focus. Taken together, we hope these volumes will provide a rigorous and ongoing contribution to understanding the expansion and consolidation of democracy in the twenty-first century.

Any project of this scale incurs many debts. Generously supported by the American National Science Foundation (NSF), the Center for Political Studies (CPS) at the University of Michigan, United States, has hosted the CSES Secretariat from the very beginning to date. Plenary Sessions (Module 1) were held at the Social Science Research Center Berlin, Germany (WZB, 1994, 1998), the Central European University, Budapest, Hungary (1995); International IDEA, Stockholm, Sweden (Module 2, 2003); and Washington DC, United States (Module 3, 2005). In addition, separate meetings of the various Planning Committees were hosted in Ann Arbor, United States (1995), Berne, Switzerland (1997), Madrid, Spain (1999), Enschede, the Netherlands (2000), Santiago, Chile (2001), Wierzba, Poland (2002), Mexico City, Mexico (2004), Taipei, Taiwan (2005), Seville, Spain (2006), and Bangalore, India (2006). A regional conference met in Cologne, Germany, in April 2007, the last event before closing our account. This list of events testifies for CSES's global attraction. We are grateful and happy to report that important questions on the interplay between political institutions and political behavior which can only be answered by large-scale comparative research find support in a world-wide cooperation not just of individual researchers but also of their various institutions.

Given the scope of CSES it seems difficult to single out and pay tribute to individual collaborators. Though rare, indeed, there is unanimous agreement in the CSES community to name Steven Rosenstone, member of the first Steering Committee. His energy and his ability to argue and convince carried the day in many crucial discussions, paving the way to a CSES that has turned into a flagship of global research on micro–macro theories of political behavior. The CSES community recognizes his seminal contribution.

Hans-Dieter Klingemann
Ian McAllister

Contents

Preface

The Comparative Study of Electoral Systems (CSES) demonstrates the potential of international cooperation for innovative, large-scale social research. In the late 1980s, European scholars recognized that key indicators of their various national election studies could not be compared properly. To improve that situation they formed an International Committee for Research into Elections and Representative Democracy (ICORE) in 1989 in Rimini, Italy, at a Research Session on Electoral Studies, sponsored by the European Consortium for Political Research (ECPR). American scholars responsible for the American National Election Study (ANES) joined this initiative. At another ICORE meeting in Grenoble, France, it was suggested that the project be extended beyond Europe and the United States. This opened the door to start a truly remarkable bid to compare political attitudes and electoral behavior on a global scale. In February 1994, on behalf of ICORE, Curtice, Klingemann, Rosenstone, and Thomassen circulated a stimulus paper proposing to reserve about 10–15 minutes time in postelection surveys to carry a theoretically defined common questions-module. They also suggested a "macro questionnaire" to collect data on those aspects of political institutions that might have an impact on electoral behavior. This call resonated well in the profession. Eighty-five social scientists representing 42 different polities responded to the stimulus paper in writing; 50 social scientists from 31 countries came to the first Plenary Conference of CSES. The meeting was organized shortly before the August 1994 XVI World Congress of the International Political Science Association (IPSA) and hosted by the Social Science Research Center Berlin, Germany (WZB). In January 1995, a Planning Committee—elected in Berlin—met at the Center for Political Studies (CPS), Institute for Social Research (ISR), the University of Michigan, United States. The Planning Committee circulated preliminary recommendations for Module I of CSES in March 1995. In the context of the second CSES Plenary Conference held at the Central European University (CEU), Budapest, Hungary, February 1996, the Planning Committee met again to discuss results of pretests, and design its Final Report (Appendix 1 in this volume). This report specified both the micro and macro indicators (Appendices 2 and 3) constituting the final version of Module 1. The Australian team delivered the first data set, covering the parliamentary election of March 1996. The third CSES Plenary Conference took place in April 1998 and was hosted again by the Social Science Research Center Berlin, Germany (WZB). Fieldwork for Module 1 ended with data collected for the March 2002 election in Portugal. Thus, Module 1 covers a six-year period and 45 elections in 33 countries. The comparative dataset was prepared by the CSES Secretariat, located at ISR, and made available via its website to interested scholars without any embargo. We are grateful to the American National Science Foundation (NSF) for continuing support of the Secretariat.

The current volume is based on the data collected for CSES Module 1. First papers were presented in August 2000 at IPSA's XVIII World Congress, Quebec City, Canada. A follow-up conference was organized by the Social Science Research Center Berlin, Germany (WZB) in February 2002 where all but one of the chapters for this volume were discussed. The editor would also like to thank participants of his Winter 2005 graduate seminar at the University of California, Irvine, United States, for critical assessments of the contributions to this volume. The Social Science Research Center Berlin, Germany (WZB) has supported work on this volume in many ways. We are grateful for this support.

This volume has profited from helpful criticism of a great number of colleagues who were connected to the project at various periods of time but are not represented in this volume. In particular, it profited from the interventions of Gabriel Badescu, Michele Claibourn, Gary W. Cox, Juan Diez Nicholas, Susanne Fuchs, Marta Lagos, Pedro R. Laylo Jr., Linda Luz Guerrero, Radoslaw Markowski, Ekkehard Mochmann, Virginia Sapiro, Hossein Shahla, Paul Sum, and Bojan Todosijevic. We are in their debt. Above all, however, the contributions of Steven Rosenstone, member of the Steering Committee for Module 1, deserve praise. Without his great academic, organizational, and social skills, CSES and this volume would not have seen the light of day.

English-language editing and all technical work involved in the preparation of the manuscript for this book was under the apt control of Nora

Onar. Sarah Argles, Dominic Byatt, Claire M. Croft, Louise Sprake, Lizzy Suffling, and Emma Tuck were understanding and highly professional partners at OUP.

Hans-Dieter Klingemann

Berlin
May 2008

About the Contributors

Bernt Aardal is Research Director, The Norwegian Election Studies, Institute for Social Research, Oslo, and Adjunct Professor of political science at the University of Oslo, Norway.

Andrew Appleton is Associate Professor of political science at Washington State University, Pullman, WA, United States.

Susan A. Banducci is Associate Professor of political science at the University of Exeter, United Kingdom.

André Blais is Professor of political science at the Université de Montréal, Canada.

John Curtice is Professor of political science at the University of Strathclyde, United Kingdom.

Ingunn Opheim Ellis is Senior Researcher at Urbanet Analyse AS, Oslo, Norway.

Elisabeth Lesley Gidengil is Professor of political science at McGill University, Montréal, Canada.

Ashley Grosse is Vice-President of special projects at YouGov Polimetrix, Palo Alto, CA, United States.

Thomas Gschwend is Professor for quantitative methods at the University of Mannheim, Germany.

Sören Holmberg is Professor of political science at Göteborg University, Sweden.

David A. Howell is Assistant Director of the Center for Political Studies, and Director of Studies of the Comparative Study of Electoral Systems at the University of Michigan, Ann Arbor, MI, United States.

Jeffrey A. Karp is Associate Professor of political science at the University of Exeter, United Kingdom.

Hans-Dieter Klingemann is Professor of political science at the Free University of Berlin and Director emeritus of the Social Science Research Center Berlin, Germany.

Henk van der Kolk is Assistant Professor of political science at the University of Twente, the Netherlands.

Martin Kroh is Senior Researcher, Socio-Economic Panel Study (SOEP), German Institute for Economic Research (DIW), Berlin, Germany.

Ola Listhaug is Professor of political science at The Norwegian University of Science and Technology, Trondheim, Norway.

Karen Long Jusko is Assistant Professor of political science at Stanford University, Palo Alto, CA, United States.

Ian McAllister is Professor of political science at the Australian National University, Canberra, Australia.

Richard Nadeau is Professor of political science at the Université de Montréal, Canada.

Neil Nevitte is Professor of political science at the University of Toronto, Canada.

Yoshitaka Nishizawa is Professor of political science at Doshisha University, Kyoto, Japan.

Hermann Schmitt is Senior Researcher at the University of Mannheim, Germany.

W. Phillips Shively is Professor of political science at the University of Minnesota, Minneapolis, MN, United States.

Jacques J. A. Thomassen is Professor of political science at the University of Twente, the Netherlands.

Gábor Tóka is Associate Professor of political science at the Central European University, Budapest, Hungary.

Bernhard Weßels is Senior Researcher at the Social Science Research Center Berlin, Germany.

List of Figures

List of Tables

List of Tables

Part I

Introduction

1

The Impact of Political Institutions:

A Contribution of the "Comparative Study of Electoral Systems" (CSES) to Micro–Macro Theories of Political Attitude Formation and Voting Behavior

Hans-Dieter Klingemann[1]

Introduction

Over the past decade (neo-) institutionalism has become the dominant paradigm in political science. The big questions about the emergence and impact of institutions have been brought back on the agenda. While this paradigmatic shift is widely acknowledged, a closer look reveals that the discipline had never stopped dealing with political institutions. Constitutions, election laws, party systems, and related sets of rules and regulations have continuously been studied, serving as dependent or independent variables in theory formation. Yet, surprisingly, one aspect of political institutions has been persistently overlooked: the comparative study of the impact of institutions on individual political behavior. If one defines institutions as a set of rules, which express an idea about what is good or how things should work and which influence actors' behavior (North 1990), the crucial question arises: Do institutions really do what they purport to do? For example, let us take the proportionate influence vision of democracy on one hand, and the majority control vision on the other. Does the first really contribute to a better representation of the many, as is often claimed? Does the latter really guarantee accountability and more effective government? Whether institutions do

3

what they are supposed to do can only be shown by demonstrating their influence on the behavior of actors. Institutions cannot act by themselves. They do so through the behavior of individual or collective actors. The Comparative Study of Electoral Systems (CSES), established in 1994, was set up to deal with the question of the impact of institutions on political behavior. It is one of the first studies to address the question by generating comparative micro- and macro-level data to study electoral behavior empirically across a broad range of institutional contexts.

The purpose of the Comparative Study of Electoral Systems (CSES) is twofold. The project is designed to, first, empirically assess how institutions governing the conduct of elections constrain the beliefs and behaviors of citizens. Second, it seeks to understand how these institutions impact the nature and quality of democratic choice as expressed through popular elections (CSES Planning Committee 1996). These research questions go beyond the prevailing micro-level approaches to electoral behavior because expectations about micro-level vote choice are systematically related to institutional settings in which vote choice takes place. This approach to electoral behavior seeks to discover under which conditions individual-level vote choice is influenced by electoral institutions. Accordingly, the CSES Planning Committee has explored related research questions such as: What mechanisms govern the relation of the electoral system, party system, age of democracy, and electoral participation? Is there a difference in candidate orientation under conditions of proportional representation or plurality vote? Does divided control of government obscure accountability in presidential systems? Are citizens taking advantage of electoral institutions that allow strategic voting? Does evaluation of effectiveness and support for democratic institutions differ in consolidated democratic regimes and those that have undergone a transition from autocracy to democracy?

In this volume we deal with these and other research topics in four sections: electoral participation (Part III), political parties, candidates, and issues (Part IV), expressive and instrumental voting (Part V), and political support (Part VI). The two chapters of Part II describe our project as an undertaking in "big" social science and locate the methodological challenges facing data collection. They provide the necessary background information to relate results obtained by the substantive analyses. Schmitt and Weßels (2005) have suggested a taxonomy[2] to order the possible causal relationships of micro-characteristics of voters and macro-characteristics of electoral institutions. This taxonomy distinguishes three

Table 1.1. Causal relationships of micro–macro analyses

1 Relations of micro-level dependent and macro-level independent variables
2 Relations of micro-level independent and macro-level independent variables
3 Strength of relations of micro-level dependent and micro-level independent variables under different conditions of macro-level variables

different types of relationships, two of which—one and three—are tested most prominently in the contributions to this volume (Table 1.1).

Data collection for CSES Module 1 extends over a six-year period. It started in March 1996 and ended in March 2002. The final release of CSES Module 1 includes 33 countries. The survey has been fielded twice in Hong Kong (1998, 2000), Mexico (1997, 2000), Peru (2000, 2001), Russia (1999, 2000), and Spain (1996, 2000). While all samples allow estimates representative for the national electorates of the various countries, sample design allows for the representation of specific regions in Belgium (Flanders, Walloon), Canada (Quebec), Germany (West Germany, East Germany), and Great Britain (Scotland).

The study focuses on parliamentary and presidential elections, not countries. In addition to 27 parliamentary elections and four presidential elections, joint parliamentary and presidential elections have been held in seven countries. This adds up to a total of 45 electoral contests of which 34 concerned parliaments and 11 the election of a president. In some chapters in this volume, party-list vote and candidate vote are analyzed separately. This means that we distinguish between these two different types of voting in the 13 electoral systems which combine party-list and candidate vote. Table 1.2 provides an overview of the possible "cases." Note that (a) the direct election of the prime minister in Israel is classified as a presidential election; (b) Hong Kong has never been an independent state and its electoral system is more complex than indicated; and (c) the election of April 2000 in Peru was rigged by Alberto Fujimori. It should also be noted that not all analyses presented could be based on the same number of cases—mostly because of missing variables or different designs.

A Summary of Substantive Results

Electoral Participation

The two chapters of Part III focus on *nonvoting*. However, research interests are different. Nevitte et al. (Chapter 4) start with a micro-model designed

Table 1.2. Elections covered by CSES Module 1

Time of election	Country	Elections for parliament	Candidate vote	Party-list vote	Elections for president	Regional sample
02.03.1996	Australia	Parliament	Candidate			
03.03.1996	Spain a	Parliament		Party list		
12.03.1996	Taiwan	Parliament	Candidate	Party list	President	
03.04.1996	Romania	Parliament		Party list	President	
29.05.1996	Israel	Parliament		Party list	President	
01.06.1996	Czech Republic	Parliament		Party list		
12.10.1996	New Zealand	Parliament	Candidate	Party list		
20.10.1996	Japan	Parliament	Candidate	Party list		
05.11.1996	USA	Parliament	Candidate		President	
10.11.1996	Slovenia	Parliament		Party list		
01.05.1997	Great Britain	Parliament	Candidate			Scotland
02.06.1997	Canada	Parliament	Candidate			Quebec
06.07.1997	Mexico a	Parliament	Candidate	Party list		
15.09.1997	Norway	Parliament		Party list		
21.09.1997	Poland	Parliament		Party list		
21.12.1997	Lithuania				President	
11.03.1998	Denmark	Parliament		Party list		
29.03.1998	Ukraine	Parliament	Candidate	Party list		
06.05.1998	The Netherlands	Parliament		Party list		
10.05.1998	Hungary	Parliament	Candidate	Party list		
24.05.1998	Hong Kong a	Parliament	Candidate	Party list		
20.09.1998	Sweden	Parliament		Party list		
28.09.1998	Germany	Parliament	Candidate	Party list		West Germany East Germany
08.05.1999	Iceland	Parliament		Party list		
13.06.1999	Belgium	Parliament		Party list		Flanders Walloon
24.10.1999	Switzerland	Parliament		Party list		
12.12.1999	Chile				President	
19.12.1999	Russia a	Parliament	Candidate	Party list		
12.03.2000	Spain b	Parliament		Party list		
26.03.2000	Russia b				President	
09.04.2000	Peru a	Parliament		Party list	President	
13.04.2000	South Korea	Parliament	Candidate	Party list		
02.07.2000	Mexico b	Parliament	Candidate	Party list	President	
10.09.2000	Hong Kong b	Parliament	Candidate	Party list		
06.01.2001	Thailand	Parliament	Candidate	Party list		
08.04.2001	Peru b	Parliament		Party list	President	
09.09.2001	Belarus				President	
17.03.2002	Portugal	Parliament		Party list		
		33	34	17	30	11

Note: a: First survey carrying Module 1; b: Second survey carrying Module 2.

to explain nonvoting by individual-level socioeconomic characteristics. Subsequently, macro-variables are introduced to test their impact on the explanatory power of the micro-variables. Banducci and Karp (Chapter 5), on the other hand, begin by observing that turnout tends to be higher in elections governed by proportional representation (PR). This relationship is well documented in the research literature. However, little is known about why this is the case. The authors propose that PR systems have an effect on political efficacy, that is, on the belief that personal involvement makes a difference to what happens in politics.

With respect to macro-level variables, Chapter 4 demonstrates, first, that electoral system, party system, and age of democracy are systematically related to nonvoting. The greater the disproportionality between votes and seats, the more likely it is that citizens will abstain from voting. Moreover, nonvoting is higher for citizens of new democracies compared to citizens of old, consolidated democracies. This is as hypothesized. However, the effect of type of party system does not behave as expected when controlling other contextual factors. In party systems with a high number of effective parties, citizens are not more but less likely to vote. Chapter 4 next shows that the explanation of nonvoting by socioeconomic characteristics of respondents in a pooled analysis combining 33 elections in 29 countries can be improved by adding macro-variables to the equation. As far as electoral institutions are concerned, electoral systems with greater district magnitude push nonvoting down while a higher number of effective parties tends to increase nonvoting. Finally, the chapter proposes a micro-model relating nonvoting with age, education, marital status, and household income which is independently estimated for all 33 elections. An explanation of the variation in strength of relationships is attempted by type of electoral system (district magnitude), type of party system (effective number of parties) as well as a country's wealth (GDP) and income distribution (Gini coefficient). Results show that there is no impact of electoral institutions as well as income distribution. However, the strength of the individual-level association of income and nonvoting covaries with wealth; the higher the level of a country's wealth, the lower the impact of income on nonvoting. Overall, the authors are not very impressed by the effect of the institutional (or economic) context on nonvoting. They stress that individual-level socioeconomic status variables seem to affect nonvoting the same way, regardless of contextual variation. Nevertheless, the analysis shows at least one politically important effect of the macro-context: citizens living in wealthier countries have a better chance to participate in elections regardless of their income situation.

Why is turnout higher in elections governed by PR? This is the major question tackled in Chapter 5. The authors propose that PR systems have a positive effect on political efficacy which in turn affects voters' inclination to participate in an election. This should be particularly true for supporters of small parties who suffer most from election laws causing a high degree of disproportionality between votes and seats. In their analysis, Banducci and Karp first explore the micro- and macro-determinants of political efficacy. Results show that there is a positive link between political efficacy and voting under electoral systems that translate votes into seats proportionally. The analysis then proceeds to explain turnout by selected micro- and macro-variables. Micro-variables include different types of party preference (preference of small parties, no single party preferred, no party preference), gender, age, and education. Type of electoral system (PR systems, mixed systems, degree of disproportionality), party system (*n* of parties in parliament), type of government (*n* of parties in government), and age of democracy (old vs. new democracies) are chosen as macro-variables. Participation in election is estimated by a logistic regression jointly taking into account all micro- and macro-variables cited above (except degree of disproportionality because of multicollinearity). Political efficacy is added as the key individual-level independent variable, as are closeness of the election and compulsory voting as macro-variables. The authors summarize the effects of these macro-variables on nonvoting as follows:

> ... a citizen's likelihood of voting increases from .62 when there are the fewest parties in parliament to .84 when the maximum are represented. The number of parties in government also has a negative effect on both efficacy and participation suggesting that a greater number of parties in government depresses turnout indirectly by leading to a decreased sense of efficacy and directly by failing to create an incentive for parties to mobilize voters.

In addition, substantial differences in voter participation are found between old and new democracies with nonvoting increasing in new democracies, and electoral rules, such as compulsory voting, which improves the odds of voting as it should. Most importantly, however, the analysis successfully demonstrates how a feeling of political efficacy is shaped by the electoral and party system and subsequently influences the citizen's decision to vote.

Political Parties, Candidates, and Issues

All six chapters of Part IV are concerned with *political parties, candidates, and issues*. While their substantive focus is different, they share the interest in micro–macro explanations of electoral behavior.

Schmitt (Chapter 6) discusses two different conceptualizations of party identification. The traditional version of party identification emphasizes the affective orientation toward a particular political party (single-party identification: S-PID). It is expected that this type of party identification not only determines attitudes toward other political objects but also causes voting behavior. An alternative conceptualization of party identification has been proposed by Dutch researchers. In the Netherlands, larger groups of voters identified with more than one political party (multiple-party identification: M-PID). Schmitt's contribution to this volume tries to answer three questions: (1) How widespread is the phenomenon of M-PID; (2) how is M-PID facilitated or restricted by particular macro-contexts; and (3) how important is M-PID as compared to S-PID for the prediction of vote choice? It is assumed that M-PID develops because citizens are identifying with ideological tendencies, not with specific political parties. This assumption leads to three propositions about the impact of macro-contexts which are of particular concern to this summary of results: (1) The greater the effective number of parties that are ideologically close, the greater the likelihood of M-PIDs (format of the party system); (2) electoral systems which require voters to choose between parties rather than individual candidates tend to produce S-PIDs; and (3) the longer people are exposed to a particular set of party alternatives, the more likely it becomes that they identify with one party only (S-PID). The latter expectation is tested by comparing types of party identification in old and new democracies. Results show that M-PID is not just a marginal phenomenon. Across countries on average 10 percent of the respondents report to be close to more than one party, ranging from a high of 22 percent in Norway to a low of 1 percent in the Netherlands and South Korea. Neither party system format nor electoral system has the expected effect on M-PID. There is, however, a clear relation of S-PID and age of democracy. There are very few voters with M-PIDs in old democracies while such voters are much more numerous in new democracies. The less experience with elections, the more widespread is M-PID. Thus, electoral experience seems to be an important factor leading to S-PID. How important is M-PID as an individual-level determinant of vote choice (party preference) as compared to S-PID? Results of country-specific analyses taking into account social structural variables (age, gender, union membership, church attendance, education, living environment) and traditional party identification, as well as left–right distance between respondents' left–right self-identification, subjective left–right placement of political parties, and evaluation of party leaders, all lead to the same conclusion: S-PID has a much higher impact on party preference than M-PID. These results support the traditional conceptualization of party identification. However, the effect of the macro-context reveals that in periods of political transition, multiple-party identification may be a first step on the road to single-party identification.

Chapters 7 and 8 deal with different aspects of candidate orientation. Holmberg (Chapter 7) is interested in citizens' familiarity with local candidates standing for election. Curtice and Shively (Chapter 8) list and discuss normative arguments made by protagonists of different types of electoral systems regarding the role of elected representatives. Most of these studies assume that political parties, not local candidates, are important for voter representation in parliament. Although empirical evidence is scarce, theories of representative democracy continue to regard the local candidate as a most important vehicle of political representation.

Holmberg presents data on local candidate recognition in 23 countries. Descriptive results show that—across countries—on average 55 percent of those eligible to vote remember the name of candidates who ran in their constituency in the last parliamentary election. This is a nontrivial proportion. It speaks for the likelihood of candidate effects on voting behavior. Between-country variation of candidate recognition is high. Candidate recognition ranges from above 90 percent in Japan, Thailand, and South Korea to below 20 percent in Mexico and Belarus. As far as macro-level variables are concerned, it is assumed that plurality or majority electoral systems embody higher incentives to seek candidate knowledge than proportional electoral systems. Gender, age, education, voting, contact with politics and politicians, as well as general political knowledge are hypothesized to affect candidate recognition on the individual level. On the macro level, three different types of electoral systems are expected to make a difference. At first sight, the observed differences seem to correspond to expectations: candidate recognition is high in plurality and majority systems (59 percent; six countries) as well as in semi-PR systems (60 percent; nine countries), and it decreases substantially in PR-mix and PR-list systems (47 percent; eight countries). However, both the bivariate and the multivariate analyses demonstrate a higher impact of most individual-level characteristics of citizens. In fact, in a logistic regression combining respondents from 18 countries, the type of electoral system contributes second lowest to the explanation of candidate knowledge with only the effect of gender being smaller. Contact with politics and politicians, voting, education, general political knowledge, and age—in that order—show higher effects than the electoral system. Thus, regarding macro-variables, the author concludes: "Candidate recognition is affected by how the electoral system is designed. Plurality-majority systems lead to higher levels of candidate familiarity than PR-list systems. But the difference is not large. The election system matters, but it does not matter much."

The analysis by Curtice and Shively deals with normative arguments related to different types of electoral systems accorded to the role of elected representatives. Which type of electoral system provides greater incentives for representatives to act as citizen intermediaries? The authors propose that advocates of single-member plurality election systems have more convincing arguments than the protagonists of other election systems. After all, candidates for election or reelection running under the rules of a single-member plurality system are highly dependent on support from their local constituency. In addition to this basic proposition, it is expected that the constraints of single-member constituencies give representatives a better feeling for what ordinary people think. And finally it is hypothesized that the single-member plurality system should be positively related to satisfaction with the way democracy works. Bottom-up democratic procedures, the authors argue, should be conducive to a higher degree of satisfaction with the democratic process. In the empirical analysis, these hypotheses are tested considering four individual-level variables (contact with an elected representative; remembering names of candidates standing for election in the local district; voters' evaluation of representatives' knowledge of what ordinary people think; satisfaction with the way democracy works) and four macro-level variables (type of electoral system; ratio of representatives to citizens; GDP; length of time a country has been a democracy). Classification of electoral systems is custom-tailored to the research question at hand. A first division contrasts electoral systems with (1) some single-member constituencies and (2) all multimember systems. In the first group (1.1), systems which distribute all seats in single-member constituencies are distinguished from (1.2) systems which mix single-member constituencies and party-lists. In the second group, electoral systems are separated from each other when (2.1) representing systems which offer no choice among candidates and (2.2) systems which do. It is the "all single-member constituency system" which receives the highest attention in the subsequent analysis. Simple description shows that "contacting" and "remembering candidates" behave as expected. Citizens in single-member plurality electoral systems report to have more contacts and remember more candidates running in their constituency. On the other hand, evaluation of whether politicians know what ordinary people think, and evaluation of satisfaction with the way democracy works, do not produce the expected results. Subsequently, the individual-level variables ("contact with elected representatives," "remembering names of candidates standing for election in the local district," "voters' evaluation of representatives," "knowledge of what ordinary people think," and "satisfaction of the way democracy works") are related to the four macro-level variables described above. Results can be summarized without much difficulty: Not a single test satisfies the hypothesized relations fully. The authors conclude:

> By way of contrast, there is little evidence to suggest that living in a multi-member district is any more desirable than living in a single-member one. So far as the criteria that we have been considering and the indicators of those criteria that we have been able to deploy are concerned, we are simply forced to conclude that there is nothing to choose between single- and multimember districts with regard to the intimacy of representation. This goes against much intuition and the tenaciously held beliefs of advocates for individual representation, but our evidence suggests that neither side has much of a case. This particular debate about electoral systems at least simply appears to be a blind alley and it certainly provides no grounds for preferring one electoral system over another.

Economic voting is the topic of Nishizawa (Chapter 9). He investigates whether an incumbent government that has performed well regarding the state of the economy during its term is rewarded by voters on Election Day, or, if the reverse is true, the government is punished by voters' strengthening the opposition parties or their candidates. Thus, the dependent variable is the individual vote for a party of the incumbent government; the main independent individual-level variable is the evaluation of the country's economic performance during the past 12 months. It is assumed that institutional macro-variables mediate and shape the possibility for voters to assign responsibility for the economic situation. Two hypotheses are tested: (1) economic performance evaluation has a greater impact on the incumbent government in parliamentary as compared to presidential systems; (2) economic performance evaluation has a stronger effect on the incumbent government in plurality electoral systems. The major argument for the first proposition emphasizes that prime ministers have better control over policy decisions than presidents. Thus, the impact of responsibility should be greater in parliamentary systems. The major argument for the latter hypothesis consists of the assumption that plurality electoral systems provide the best way to ensure accountability. The third, and the last, macro-level variable considered indicates economic development (OECD vs. non-OECD countries). Although previous research results are inconclusive it is assumed that—by and large—citizens in new democracies should be more sensitive to economic performance of governments as compared to citizens in economically developed countries.

Logistic regression (with interaction terms) is used on a pooled cross-national data set which includes the three macro-variables described above. In addition to the main individual-level independent variable (evaluation of economic performance during the past 12 months), six other individual-level variables are introduced as controls: (1) evaluation of the current state of the economy, (2) satisfaction with the way democracy works in the country, (3) closeness to any incumbent party, (4) degree of liking of incumbent parties as compared to opposition parties, (5) household income, and (6) education. On the macro level, country dummies are included to pick up any country-specific variation left unaccounted for by the more specific variables. Results confirm the initial propositions. The author concludes: "Parliamentary incumbents are more susceptible to voters' evaluation of the economy than are the presidential incumbents. Also, incumbents in plurality elections are more vulnerable to voters' evaluation of the economy than are their counterparts in PR elections." And thirdly: "The economy seems to be a prime concern of voters particularly in countries whose welfare safety-net is underdeveloped."

Ideological voting is discussed by Kroh (Chapter 10). He proposes that citizens vote for parties and candidates that best represent their ideological interests. Thus, ideological proximity is the main individual-level independent variable and it is measured as the distance between self-location of a respondent on an 11-point left–right self-placement scale and the perceived positions of political parties on the same scale. It is often said that in order to understand the substantive meaning of abstract ideological concepts such as left and right, voters need to be politically sophisticated (in this case indicated by levels of education) as well as politically knowledgeable (in this case measured by a three-item knowledge scale). To control for alternative possibilities to reach a voting decision, party identification and candidate evaluations are included in the analysis. At the macro level, party system complexity is considered to have an effect on the probability of ideological voting. Party system complexity is measured by four indicators: effective number of parliamentary parties, effective number of government parties, ideological polarization, and ideological concentration (consensus about party placements). It is expected that the higher the level of party system complexity, the lower the effect of ideological proximity on voting. A high number of political parties would increase party system complexity because the more parties compete on the ideological dimension, the more difficult it is for voters to be informed about each party's ideological position. A large number of government parties, on the other hand, should ease ideological voting because voters have a tendency to relate to coalition governments as a single political object. Ideological polarization and concentration indicate clarity of ideological positions. Thus, a high degree of ideological polarization and concentration should decrease party system complexity and facilitate ideological voting.

The effect parameters of individual-level regressions constitute the key dependent variables in a multilevel conditional logit regression. The database consists of 33,968 respondents and 30 contextual, macro-level units of different levels of party system complexity. Results confirm expectations. On the individual level, small ideological left–right distances increase ideological voting. Thus, ideological proximity affects party choice (even when controlling for party identification and candidate-liking). Second, higher levels of political sophistication and political knowledge increase the probability of ideological voting. On the macro level, ideological voting increases in two contexts. This occurs first when party system complexity is low (i.e. ideological voting increases with a lower number of effective parties in parliament and a higher number of effective parties in government). It also occurs when there is a low level of interparty overlap and a high level of ideological concentration of parties. The latter findings demonstrate that ideological voting is facilitated or restricted by the degree of complexity of the political supply-side.

The last chapter of Part IV by Klingemann and Weßels (Chapter 11) asks how individual-level determinants of three different types of vote choice are influenced by two macro-characteristics of the political environment: degree of differentiation of political supply and degree of effectiveness of electoral institutions. The following types of vote choice are considered: party-list vote, candidate vote, and president vote. Party-liking, candidate-liking, and generalized issue distance (defined by self-location of respondents and locations of parties on a left–right scale) are selected as the individual-level independent variables. A "stacked" data set is used to estimate logit models that explain each of the three individual-level dependent variables (party-list vote, candidate vote, president vote). All micro-level effects confirm expectations. However, the authors are not interested in interpreting these already well-known findings on the micro level. Rather, they focus on an explanation of the variation of the effects of the micro-level predictor variables under varying degrees of differentiation of political supply and effectiveness of electoral institutions. Results clearly indicate that individual-level determinants of electoral choice are affected by differing macro-contexts. Depending on the object of choice (party, candidate, president), there seems to be a trade-off in the utility of the three evaluative criteria (party-liking, candidate-liking, generalized issue distance) which is conditioned by differing degrees of differentiation of supply and effectiveness of electoral institutions. The more complex the choice situation and the more effective electoral institutions translate choices into preferred outcomes, the more voters focus on the criteria which seem to be most useful—party-liking in the case of party-voting, candidate-liking in the case of candidate-voting, and—with some qualifications—presidential voting. Parallel to the increase in the impact of these core criteria for vote choice, the predictive power of the other evaluative criteria diminishes. Thus, voters reduce complexity by emphasizing one particular evaluation criteria and de-emphasizing the others. The authors conclude that voters seem to be able to adapt their decision criteria for electoral choice to the broader characteristics of their political environment.

Expressive and Instrumental Voting

Expressive and instrumental (strategic) motivations of voting and political involvement are taken up in the two chapters of Part V.

Is political involvement driven by instrumental or expressive motivation? This is the prime question Tóka addresses in Chapter 12. He discusses three different modes of political involvement: the decision to vote (turnout), the development of partisanship (party choice), and the search for political information (information processing activities). Instrumental models of political involvement assume that voters are interested in the political consequences of election outcomes (e.g. government policies). Expressive models, on the other hand, expect that citizens experience a reward which is intrinsic to the activity itself. These different assumptions imply different explanations and predictions of the various modes of political involvement. In the literature there seems to be agreement that turnout is best explained by expressive motivations (e.g. sense of citizen duty). But voters' choice between political parties in elections, on the other hand, is thought to follow the logic of the instrumental model.

Furthermore, it is argued that expressive rationality does not necessarily lead to a well-reflected vote choice and may have negative collective consequences. Thus, the more impact expressive motives have, the stronger the need for representative as compared to direct democracy.

The three dependent variables are measured as follows: (1) Information about turnout is based on the respondent's report to have voted in the last election (yes/no). (2) Party preference (choice) is based on party identification (yes/no). (3) Acquisition of political information (info) adds the number of correct responses to three country-specific political knowledge questions. The investment (or instrumental) value of the vote and the consumption (or expressive) value of the vote are the two major independent variables at the individual level. The investment value of the vote is based on a like–dislike question of the major parties and expresses the range of ratings given by each respondent to the different parties on an 11-point scale. The consumption value of the vote is also based on the like–dislike scores of political parties. It is defined as the highest rating given by each respondent to any one of the parties evaluated.

Three individual-level hypotheses are tested: (1) Turnout with expressive roots should be positively influenced by intrinsic rewards. (2) The costs and the intrinsic rewards involved in the development of a party preference should lead to a mixed model combining instrumental and expressive motivations. (3) The motivation to acquire political information should be mainly influenced by the perceived utility difference between different election outcomes. Three macro-level conditions are expected to have an impact on these individual-level relationships: constitutional design, the electoral system, and the party system. These are the hypotheses: (1) Constitutional design: Expressive voting should be higher in elections where national office is not at stake (measured by a scale rating legislative elections in terms of their de facto impact on the composition of the executive). (2) Electoral system: The greater the disproportionality between votes and seats generated by the electoral system, the more citizens should care about wasted votes and act strategically. Thus, instrumental voting should be higher in plurality elections. (3) Party system: Expressive voting should be observed in multi-party systems which encourage sincere voting (voting for a party which best matches one's own preferences), and where the consequences of the vote for government formation and policies are hard to predict. Thus, the greater the number of political parties, the greater the probability of expressive voting.

Data analysis proceeds in two steps. In the first step, all three individual-level dependent variables are submitted to country-specific logistic regression analyses testing the impact of instrumental and expressive value of the vote (controlling for a set of socio-demographic individual-level variables). In the second step, the regression coefficients obtained for the 96 regression equations are correlated with the three macro-characteristics of the electoral contexts described above (constitutional design, electoral system, party system). The individual-level results show that for the decision to vote and the acquisition of party preference, the expressive account receives stronger support than the instrumental explanation. This is in line with expectations. However, the development of a party preference seems to be driven even more by expressive motivations than turnout. Expressive motivations have a significant positive effect on party preference in 32 out of 34 elections while instrumental motivation has a similar effect in only 17 out of the 34 electoral contests. Hence, party preferences appear to develop even more on expressive motivations than on turnout. Political information processing, on the other hand, is not equally affected by expressive motivation, but rather by instrumental ones in 22 out of the 27 cases (for which all necessary data are available). This result indicates that political learning is rooted in instrumental motivation. The final hypothesis tested in the chapter suggests that choice between parties at elections for expressive or instrumental reasons is caused by electorally relevant characteristics of political macro-contexts. An inspection of the 18 possible correlation coefficients shows that none of the macro-variables reaches statistical significance at the .05 level. Thus, Tóka's analysis does not lend support to the idea that a particular macro-context would alter the relative impact of expressive as compared to instrumental motivation on voting behavior. The author suggests that expressive voting seems to be an inevitable feature of mass democracy, rather than a characteristic of particular institutional contexts.

Gschwend (Chapter 13) relates district magnitude and strategic voting. First, a theory is proposed to explain how voters form expectations about the election outcome in their electoral district. Based on this theory, a new indicator is developed to measure strategic voting. Second, hypotheses are tested regarding the relationship between strategic voting and the strategic voting incentives implied in district magnitude. Third, and last, arguments are presented how to best model district magnitude effects.

Most theories of voting behavior start with the assumption that voters cast a vote for their most preferred party or candidate (sincere voting). However, it is also well known that voters deviate from this rule if they feel that their most preferred party choice is not viable politically. This type of voting behavior is called strategic. Thus, a strategic voter is someone who votes for a less preferred party if the expected probability that this party will gain a seat is higher than the expected probability that the most preferred party will gain a seat in that constituency. Early on Duverger (1954) has shown that the expected probability that any given party is viable is higher in proportional representation (PR) systems as compared to plurality systems. This expectation should be valid nation-wide. However, Leys (1959) and Sartori (1968) suggest that there may be a sizeable within-nation variation of the effect of electoral institutions across constituencies. For example, a party that is small on the national level may well have regional strongholds. This leads to the proposition that the probability of strategic voting depends on the nature of the district and not the nation as a whole—even in PR systems. The larger the district magnitude is, the higher is the probability of strategic voting. This proposition is tested by Gschwend for the first time using individual-level data and primary electoral districts as the unit of analysis.

The dependent variable consists of the fraction of all voters in an electoral district casting a strategic vote. To construct the dependent variable, voters' preference rankings of parties (like–dislike scales) that actually field lists or candidates in a particular electoral district are taken into account. The party ranked first is considered the respondent's sincere vote choice. In a second step, the viability of a party is established. Single-member district parties coming in first or second in the last election and multimember district parties which have gained at least one seat meet the viability criteria. Employing a heuristic that takes into account past election results is certainly easier for voters to apply than calculating expected probabilities. Strategic voting is assumed if a voter casts the ballot not for the party that is highest on the individual preference scale but for a less preferred but viable party. The number of voters who want to avoid wasting a vote in a district is then expressed as a proportion of all voters in this district. District magnitude across all elections varies between one and 48 in the 1,949 constituencies included in the study. In the 35 PR-tiers, district magnitude ranges from four to 656. Results support the well-known general expectation: the lower the district magnitude, the higher the degree of strategic voting. The functional form of the relationship between district magnitude and the frequency of strategic voting is disputed in the literature. Some authors suggest relying on a generalized linear model; others propose a generalized additive model to avoid any parametric restrictions for district magnitude as the sole predictor of the expected frequency of strategic voting at the district level. Comparing results obtained by these different approaches leads to the following conclusion:

> as long as the district magnitude of the electoral districts is not greater than 50, it does not make a big difference whether "district magnitude" or "log (district magnitude)" is used, as long as there is an appropriate link function that permits out-of-bound predictions. Depending on how the relationship between district magnitude and the frequency of strategic voting is modeled, one can expect on average 6–8 percent strategic voters in single-member districts, while for electoral districts with a district magnitude greater than 10 one should not expect more than about 2 percent strategic voters.

These results provide empirical evidence that the level of strategic voting at the district level is related to district magnitude. The higher the district magnitude at the district level, the lower the level of strategic voting. This is the first time that this has been shown to hold across different types of electoral systems.

A last set of questions raised in Part VI focuses on the impact of different electoral institutions on *support of democratic processes and institutions*. Chapters 14 and 15 address the major issues involved. Listhaug, Aardal, and Opheim Ellis discuss the relation of institutional variation and three specific attitudinal dimensions of democratic system support. Thomassen and van der Kolk deal with the problem of performance of democratic institutions and generalized support of democracy in old and new democracies.

Listhaug, Aardal, and Opheim Ellis (Chapter 14) propose a broad definition of political support encompassing the whole range of individual-level attitudes toward the political system and its various parts. In their analysis, they distinguish between the following three areas: regime performance (satisfaction with the way democracy works), external efficacy, defined as citizens' perceptions of responsiveness of the political system (Do political parties/politicians care about what ordinary people think?), and evaluation of the government/opposition mechanism of democratic systems (Does it make a difference who is in power?). It is expected that levels of political support—evaluation of regime performance, degree of external efficacy, and the functioning of the interplay between government and opposition—can be explained by a combination of micro- and macro-level variables. Three hypotheses are proposed at the micro level: (1) The partisan- or policy-distance hypothesis: Voters for winning parties should show a higher level of support than those who vote for losing parties. (2) The performance hypothesis: Citizens who evaluate the performance of the economy positively should show a higher level of support than those who evaluate the performance of the economy negatively. (3) The political parties as linkage to the political system hypothesis: Citizens who identify with a political party should show a higher level of political support than those who do not identify with a political party. Gender, age, and education are introduced as individual-level control variables.

The micro-level hypotheses are mostly confirmed. However, they are not the main focus of the analysis. Rather, special attention is given to the impact of macro-level characteristics. Listhau, Aardal, and Opheim Ellis test the impact of macro-characteristics on the micro-level dependent support variables. The first set of macro-characteristics they introduce includes political institutions that differ in their emphasis on accountability and representation (type of executive; type of electoral system; degree of disproportionality). If citizens display a high concern for a broad representation of group interests and policy positions, support is expected to be stronger in countries with parliamentary rather than presidential systems, and in countries with proportional rather than majoritarian electoral systems. If citizens value accountability, the opposite should be true. Institutions that are believed to maximize representation (parliamentarism, PR, high proportionality) should produce higher input support (external efficacy) under the condition that citizens value representation. If citizens value accountability, the same should be true if they live in presidential regimes, systems with majoritarian voting, or electoral systems producing strong disproportionality between votes and seats. The second set of macro-variables consists of political rights and civil liberties. It is expected that the more strongly political rights and civil liberties are institutionalized, the higher the level of political support. The authors qualify this relationship for citizens living in new democracies. If experiences with the past autocratic system have been negative, citizens' evaluations of the new democratic system (e.g. perceptions of efficacy; how much it matters who is in power) may be more positive than one might expect in light of the deficiencies of the present system.

The following three macro-level variables are used as controls: gross domestic product, level of inequality, and degree of ethnic conflict. It is expected that wealth, low inequality, and a low degree of ethnic conflict increase levels of political support. Results obtained by a combined micro-macro multivariate analysis (ca. 50,000 respondents; ca. 30 countries) show that effects of the macro-variables indicating political institutions on individual-level political support are insignificant. The authors conclude: "Basically we find a lack of empirical effects of conventional electoral institutions on attitudes."

In the last chapter, Thomassen and van der Kolk (Chapter 15) discuss the impact of old and new democracies on micro-level relationships between political support ("satisfaction with the way democracy works") and political effectiveness. It is expected that a political system's day-to-day policy output is evaluated by the citizenry and translated into different degrees of system support. In the analysis, effectiveness is operationalized in terms of perceived economic performance ("Would you say that over the past 12 months, the state of the economy in 'country' has gotten better, stayed about the same, or gotten worse? (if gotten better: Would you say much better or somewhat better?) (if gotten worse: Would you say much worse or somewhat worse?"). The major micro-level hypothesis is supported by the empirical results; that is, the higher the degree of perceived (economic) effectiveness, the higher the degree of political support. It is expected that this relationship is modified when controlling for the macro-level effect of old well-established democracies on the one hand, and new democracies on the other hand because they differ in terms of their "reservoir of goodwill" which shields against short-term negative development. Age of democracy is operationalized by distinguishing democratic regimes that existed before 1950 and those established after 1989 (with Spain put in an intermediate position). Satisfaction with democracy should be higher in old and lower in new democracies while the effect of performance evaluation should be stronger in new as compared to old democracies. These expectations are confirmed by multivariate analyses. Satisfaction with the way democracy works is higher in old and lower in new democracies and the effect of people's perception of the state of the economy on their satisfaction with democracy is stronger in new democracies (and Spain) than in the established democracies. However, differences between old and new democracies are small. Economic performance seems to affect old democracies as well, although not to a similar degree.

The Impact of Political Institutions

All the chapters summarized analyze the impact of political institutions on individual-level attitudes and behavior. Electoral system (10), party system (8), and age of democracy (5) are the preferred indicators. Thirty-two propositions have been tested, 12 of which were rejected. Variations

Table 1.3. The impact of political institutions on individual political attitudes and behavior

	Dependent variable	Expectations about the impact of political institutions	Macro-level hypothesis: confirmed/not confirmed
Electoral participation Chapter 4: Socioeconomic status and nonvoting	Nonvoting	Electoral system (district magnitude): The greater the potential discrepancy between the proportion of votes received by a party and the distribution of seats for parties, the more likely the citizens will abstain from voting when the effects of other contextual factors are controlled.	Confirmed
		Party system (effective number of parties): Citizens in party systems where there are more effective parties will be less likely to abstain from voting than citizens in party systems with fewer parties.	Not confirmed
		Age of democracy: Citizens of new democracies will be more likely to abstain from voting than citizens of consolidated democracies, when the effects of other contextual factors are controlled.	Confirmed
	Strength of the country-level relationships between age, education, marital status, household income, and nonvoting	Impact of electoral system (district magnitude) and party system on strength of country-level relationships between age, education, marital status, and nonvoting	Not confirmed Not confirmed
Chapter 5: Electoral systems, efficacy, and voter participation	Voter participation	Electoral system: Voter participation should increase in PR systems and in election systems with compulsory voting.	Confirmed
		Party system (*n* of parties in parliament): Voter participation should increase with higher number of parties in parliament.	Confirmed
		Coalition government (*n* of parties in government): Voter participation should decrease with higher number of parties in government.	Confirmed
		Age of democracy: Voter participation should be higher in old and lower in new democracies.	Confirmed
	Political efficacy as an intervening variable	PR systems promote the feeling of political efficacy. This is regarded as the main reason why PR systems have a positive impact on voter participation.	

Political parties, candidates, and issues

Chapter 6: Multiple-party identifications?	Multiple- vs. single-party identification (type of party identification)	Electoral system: PR systems cultivate "single" identifications with unique, concrete parties while plurality systems do not.	Not confirmed
		Party system: The greater the number of ideologically close parties competing for one's vote, the greater the likelihood of holding multiple-party identifications.	Not confirmed
		Age of democracy: The longer citizens deal with a particular set of party alternatives, the more likely they are to identify with one, and just one, of the party options.	Confirmed
Chapter 7: Candidate recognition in different electoral systems	Candidate recognition	Electoral system: Plurality-majority systems should lead to higher levels of candidate recognition than PR-list systems.	Confirmed
Chapter 8: Who represents us best? One member or many?	Perceived quality of political representation	Electoral system: There should be differences between single- and multimember districts with regard to the perceived quality of political representation.	Not confirmed
Chapter 9: Economic voting: Do institutions affect the way voters evaluate incumbents?	Vote for an incumbent party vs. vote for an opposition party	System of government: Economic performance evaluation should have a greater impact on the incumbent government in parliamentary as compared to presidential systems.	Confirmed
		Electoral system: Economic performance evaluation should have a greater impact on government in plurality as compared to proportional electoral systems.	Confirmed
Chapter 10: The ease of ideological voting: Voter sophistication and party system complexity	Strength of country-level ideological proximity voting	Citizens vote for parties that match their ideological views (individual-level ideological proximity hypothesis).	Confirmed
		Four indicators of party system complexity:	
		Party system: The greater the number of effective parties, the lower the level of ideological voting.	Confirmed
		Ideological polarization: The higher the level of ideological polarization, the higher the level of ideological voting.	Confirmed
		Ideological concentration: The higher the level of ideological concentration, the higher the level of ideological voting.	Confirmed
		The greater the number of effective government parties, the higher the level of ideological voting.	Confirmed
		Thus, the general hypothesis of party system complexity is confirmed: Ideological voting increases when party system complexity is low.	

(cont.)

Table 1.3. (*Continued*)

	Dependent variable	Expectations about the impact of political institutions	Macro-level hypothesis: confirmed/not confirmed
Chapter 11: How voters cope with the complexity of their political environment. Differentiation of political supply, effectiveness of electoral institutions, and the calculus of voting	Strength of country-level relationships between (1) party-list vote, (2) candidate vote, (3) president vote, and party-liking, candidate-liking, and generalized issue-distance	Party system: The higher the degree of differentiation of political supply, the more voters focus on the criteria which seem to be most useful in their specific political environment (party-liking in case of party-list voting; candidate-liking in case of candidate-voting).	Confirmed
		Electoral system: The more effective electoral institutions translate individual choices into preferred election outcomes, the more voters focus on the criteria which seem to be most useful in their specific political environment (party-liking in case of party-list voting; candidate-liking in case of candidate-voting).	Confirmed
Expressive and instrumental voting			
Chapter 12: Motivation of turnout, partisanship, and political learning	Strength of country-level relationships between voting (turnout), development of partisanship (choice), and	Electoral system: Instrumental voting should be higher in elections governed by electoral systems generating a high degree of disproportionality.	Not confirmed
		Party system: The greater the number of political parties, the greater should be the probability of expressive voting.	Not confirmed
	political knowledge (info) and indices of expressive and instrumental motivations for political involvement	Impact of legislative elections on the composition of the executive: Expressive voting should be higher in elections where national office is not at stake.	Not confirmed
Chapter 13: District magnitude and the comparative study of strategic voting	Strategic voting (aggregated fraction of the total number of voters in a voting district)	Party system: The lower the district magnitude, the higher the degree of strategic voting disregarding type of electoral system.	Confirmed

Political support			
Chapter 14: Institutional variation and political support	Indicators of political support: Political efficacy	System of government: Citizens who have a high concern for broad representation of group interests and policy positions, political support should be more represented in parliamentary rather than presidential systems.	Not confirmed
	Who is in power makes a difference	Electoral system: The same expectation should hold for proportional rather than majoritarian electoral systems.	Not confirmed
	Satisfaction how democracy works	Political rights and civil liberties: The stronger political rights and civil liberties are institutionalized in a country, the higher should be the level of political support.	Not confirmed
Chapter 15: Effectiveness and political support in old and new democracies	Satisfaction with the way democracy works	Age of democracy: Satisfaction with the way democracy works should be higher in old democracies because old democracies have had a greater opportunity to build up a reservoir of good will.	Confirmed
	Strength of country-level relationships between satisfaction of the way democracy works and political effectiveness (perception of the state of the economy)	Age of democracy: Satisfaction with the way democracy works should be more strongly related to political effectiveness in new than in old democracies.	Confirmed

in strength of country-specific individual-level predictors of political participation and vote choice are related to different macro conditions in five chapters. Ultimately, the results are mixed. They are assembled in Table 1.3. Effects of individual-level socioeconomic characteristics on nonvoting seem to be unrelated to electoral institutions (Chapter 4). There are also no effects of electoral institutions on individual-level associations between expressive and instrumental predictors on political involvement (Chapter 12). On the other hand, low party system complexity is reported to increase the odds of ideological voting (Chapter 10); effective electoral institutions as well as differentiation of political supply impact on the association between party-list vote, candidate vote, and president vote (as individual-level dependent variables) and party-liking, candidate-liking, and generalized issue-distance (as individual-level independent variables; Chapter 11); and the age of democracy modifies the relation of economic performance and support of democracy (Chapter 15).

Overall most propositions involving political institutions find supporting empirical evidence. A closer look, however, reveals that it is equally true that most of the effects of political institutions on political attitudes or electoral behavior are rather modest. This is observed by many authors of this collection. Holmberg expresses this conclusion succinctly: "The electoral system matters, but not much."

Comparisons of results are difficult. As we have already mentioned before, most of the analyses are based on a different number or type of countries and elections. Similar macro-indicators such as electoral system or party system have been operationalized differently. And, last but not the least, different techniques of data analysis were utilized. As shown by Howell and Long Jusko in Chapter 3, there is much potential for future improvement.

However, two results deserve special mention. First, political efficacy has been singled out by Banducci and Karp as the individual-level intervening variable that explains the positive effect of PR systems on voter participation (Chapter 5). Second, Gschwend has demonstrated that strategic voting is related to district magnitude regardless of type of electoral system (Chapter 13). These two questions have been asked for a long time. Now they have been answered convincingly.

Do institutions make a difference? With respect to this general research problem, results prove that they (mostly) do. Effects are not always as strong as expected and not always in the direction of the normative goals embedded in the respective institution. Future research on the interplay of institutions and individual political behavior based on the growing database of CSES will further our knowledge. By better understanding the intended and unintended consequences of political institutions, we may better understand how to ease or restrict the relationships between voters and parties, represented and representatives, citizens and the state in the normatively desired direction.

Notes

1. I owe thanks to Bernhard Weßels who critically read this chapter.
2. This taxonomy was first presented by Weßels in 1998 at the CSES Conference in Berlin.

Part II

The Project

2

"Big Social Science" in Comparative Politics:

The History of the Comparative Study of Electoral Systems

Ashley Grosse and Andrew Appleton

Introduction

This chapter presents a case study of "big social science" in the field of comparative politics. The particular case reviewed, the Comparative Study of Electoral Systems (CSES) is a collaborative program of research among election studies conducted in representative democracies around the world. The project is unique and rich with important lessons for the collaborative researcher. This case study contributes insights into the unique challenges of multinational data collections. The chapter is organized in three parts. First, reviewing the original impetus for the project, it provides a narrative history of CSES from its beginnings at the International Committee for Research into Elections and Representative Democracy (ICORE) in 1994. Second, the chapter identifies two contrasting "ideal type" models of cross-national collaborative research, of which CSES represents one variety. The distinguishing characteristics of these models are outlined, and the advantages and disadvantages of each explored. Finally, the chapter addresses the challenges that have faced CSES during the organization and completion of Module 1.

CSES is no longer in its infancy. As witnessed by the increasing number of papers and publications that depend upon the data set, political scientists have begun to recognize its potential for yielding significant comparative results about individual values and behavior across national contexts. With Module 2 completed and Module 3 in the field, more data will soon be forthcoming. For the first time, researchers will be able to construct the kind of longitudinal, cross-level causal statements envisaged by W. Phillips Shively in what he terms macro–micro, or Type IV, analyses.[1]

It may be claimed that the greatest virtue of the project is its efficiency as "big science." It is predicated on a simple notion, namely, the coordination of national election studies conducted in postelection modules according to uniform standards and submission of these to a secretariat for inclusion in the comparative data set. The efforts of first the ICORE and then the CSES planning committees to develop, implement, and refine both common modules and standards of data gathering qualify CSES as an experiment in "big (social) science," comparable to other important cross-national survey research projects. CSES collaborators are responsible for securing their own funding. Although the Planning Committee sometimes makes efforts to identify sources of support for underfunded electoral projects, the bulk of both the resources and the labor devoted to CSES is decentralized.

The latest edition of Russell Dalton's classic, *Citizen Politics: Public Opinion and Political Parties in Advanced Industrial Democracies* (2005) in some ways represents an overview of the aspirations of those studying political values and behavior in cross-national context. As in previous editions, Dalton makes copious use of three data sources: the Eurobarometer, the European Values Study/World Values Survey (EVS/WVS), and the International Social Survey Program (ISSP). To these is now added a fourth: CSES. For example, in the comparison of left–right self-placement in 10 democracies, the author prefers to use the scaled data offered by CSES to the alternatives offered in these other data sets (Dalton 2005: 118–21). This, we contend, illustrates both the promise of CSES to provide standards for comparative research and also highlights some of the potential challenges that face the project as it moves toward maturity.

In this chapter, we provide an overview of CSES in comparative context. Part narrative history of the genesis and implementation of the project (section "Introduction"), part comparison of critical features of CSES with other cross-national survey research projects that are also considered "big science" (section "Narrative history"),[2] our study aims to discern some of the unique features of CSES that set it apart from other such projects, as well as address questions about the challenges that may face CSES as an institution in the coming years.

Narrative History

The formal beginnings of CSES can be traced back to ICORE, and even further back to the European Consortium for Political Research (ECPR) Research Session on Electoral Studies held in Rimini in 1989. At the 1989 ECPR session, John Curtice, Co-Director of the British General Election Study (University of Strathclyde), identified a significant paradox in European electoral research. While electoral studies were one of the most developed and integrated subdisciplines in political science, the field lacked a similarly developed program of cross-national research. National election studies in Europe were remarkably successful but purely national endeavors. What Curtice and others found remarkable was that although there were a growing number of prestigious national election studies, coming out of the tradition known as the "Michigan School," there was no organized effort to profit from their shared theoretical and methodological features.[3] Logistical barriers such as a common language, different questionnaires, research designs, and varying standards of documentation hindered comparative electoral research.

The establishment of ICORE came out of the ECPR session as a bid to develop further opportunities for comparative research into European electoral behavior. The committee was composed of the directors of several established European election studies. ICORE's first order of business was to create a European Elections Database archiving all the national election studies documented in English at the Eurolab of the Zentralarchiv für empirische Sozialforschung in Cologne. This database facilitated publication of *The European Voter* (2005), edited by Jacques Thomassen. This book represents the only systematic effort to make use of data generated by six national election studies (Denmark, Germany, the Netherlands, Norway, Sweden, and the United Kingdom). Thus, ICORE created a platform for real intellectual progress in designing a program that would facilitate comparative electoral research. These primary tasks and the creation of truly coordinated election studies would be the impetus for organizing the research network known as the Comparative Study of Electoral Systems.

In 1994, ICORE organized the first conference on CSES with a steering committee composed of Jacques Thomassen (University of Twente), Chair of ICORE, Steven Rosenstone (University of Michigan), Hans-Dieter Klingemann (Wissenschaftszentrum Berlin für Sozialforschung), and John Curtice (University of Strathclyde). "The central purpose of the conference [was] is to bring together social scientists and directors of national election studies, who [were] are interested in such an international effort, to specify the research agenda, study design, and instrumentation that will permit the coordinated, international, comparative study of electoral systems in 1996 and beyond" (Thomassen et al. 1994: 13). In preparation for that first conference, the Steering Committee of ICORE circulated to directors of election studies in 63 consolidated and emerging democracies a stimulus paper calling for an internationally collaborative program of cross-national research. The stimulus paper laid out several general themes around which a collaborative effort might be organized, a rough study design, and a schedule for the planning process. In particular, the stimulus paper identified the following three themes: the impact of electoral institutions (parliamentary vs. presidential systems of government, the electoral rules that govern the casting and counting of ballots, and political parties and party systems), the nature of political and social cleavages and alignments, and perceptions of the legitimacy of democracy. All three themes would find an intellectual home in the CSES modules and all are represented in this volume. Response to the stimulus paper was enormous. Eighty-five social scientists from 44 different polities responded with comments and suggestions that were summarized and circulated once again. Electoral researchers in Europe, the Americas, and Asia expressed their enthusiasm for the project design and signed on to carry a common battery of questions in a postelection study as their contribution to the furthering of cross-national research.

The first CSES meeting in Berlin in the fall of 1994 produced a general agreement on a set of principles, processes, and standards that would guide the project. The study planning began almost immediately. A planning committee was identified and three months later the American National Election Study hosted a planning meeting in Ann Arbor for the committee to make proposals on the content of the questionnaire that would become Module 1.

From the beginning, the intention was to create an inclusive research project. All country collaborators were invited to participate in setting the substantive agenda for the study, designing the questionnaire module, and specifying the demographic and macro-level data to be collected with the latter part being a real innovation to large-scale cross-national survey research. The first planning meeting circulated its recommendations for comments and suggestions to all collaborators. To ensure that the project remained a community good, a second planning conference of all collaborators was organized in the spring of 1995 that took place once again in Ann Arbor. At the meeting, participating collaborators asked the American National Election Study, with financial support from the US National Science Foundation, to serve a two-year term as Secretariat for the project. The project was underway.

During the summer and fall of 1995, collaborators in seven polities—Belarus, Costa Rica, Hungary, the Netherlands, Romania, Spain, and the United States—conducted pilot studies of the CSES module. Several items were also piloted in the Philippines, Japan, and South Africa. Collaborators prepared and disseminated pilot study reports for discussion at a second planning meeting held in December 1995 in Budapest organized by Gábor Tóka of the Central European University. Forty colleagues from 29 polities attended the conference. Participants representing 29 different national election studies engaged in an exhaustive review of the project's plan, evaluating the questionnaire module, the measurement of voter turnout and vote choice, the background data to be collected, the guidelines outlining standards for data quality, the norms regarding the archiving and disseminating of the data, and the macro-level data to be collected.

The CSES research network was in agreement that common data collection should begin as early as 1996. Allowing for staggered elections around the world, the window for data collection would continue for four or five years. The final module included 16 questions, estimated as 10 minutes of interviewing time (Appendix 2). Collaborators were also asked to submit a completed questionnaire on the electoral laws, institutional arrangements, and electoral data relevant to the particular election in which individual level data was collected (Appendix 3). This information turned out to be an innovation and of great help to contextualize results of the micro-level analyses.

Finally, the first module was fielded after 39 elections across 33 countries (Australia, Belarus, Belgium-Flanders, Belgium-Walloon, Canada, Chile, the Czech Republic, Denmark, Germany, Great Britain, Hong Kong (1998, 2000), Hungary, Iceland, Israel, Japan, Korea, Lithuania, Mexico (1997, 2000), the Netherlands, New Zealand, Norway, Peru (2000, 2001), Poland, Portugal, Romania, Russia (1999, 2000), Slovenia, Spain (1996, 2000),

Sweden, Switzerland, Taiwan, Thailand, the United States, and Ukraine). Six countries were able to run the module in more than one post-national election study between 1996 and 2001, allowing for more data points.

CSES in Comparative Perspective

In this section, we turn to a comparison of CSES with three other large-scale, cross-national survey data collection projects: the European Values Study/World Values Survey (EVS/WVS), the International Social Survey Program (ISPP), and the Eurobarometer[4]. By placing CSES alongside the other forms of collaborative cross-national research, we intend to illuminate both the similarities that CSES shares with them and the specificities that mark CSES as a unique experiment in cross-national, "big social science."

Age

The first point of comparison between these projects is that of age and longevity. CSES is the youngest of the four enterprises (Eurobarometer, EVS/WVS, ISSP). The first CSES modules were implemented in Australia, Spain, and Taiwan in early 1996. By 2002, Module 1 was fielded in 33 nations. By way of comparison, the first Standard Eurobarometer was administered in 1970, initially under the heading of European Communities Studies.[5] The first wave of the EVS/WVS was completed in 1981, and the first module of the ISSP was administered in 1985 in Germany, Great Britain, Italy, and the United States, and in 1986 in Australia and Austria.

However, a planning process that displays further important variation preceded the fielding of each of these survey instruments. In the case of the Eurobarometer, the genesis for the idea lay back in the 1950s and was very much a part of the postwar enthusiasm for positive social science ushered in by the behavioral revolution. In fact, the roots of the collaboration lay in the friendship between Jacques René Rabier and Jean Monnet that had been nurtured in the late 1940s—Jacques René Rabier became the spokesman for Jean Monnet when he was appointed as the first president of the High Authority of the European Coal and Steel Community. As the European Economic Community (EEC) took root in the late 1950s, the idea of a social scientific survey that would track citizen attitudes toward the policies and institutions of the new body was proposed by Rabier in conjunction with Jean Stoetzel (whom Rabier had met during resistance activities in World War II), and a pilot study was implemented in 1962.[6] The EEC Commission agreed to sponsor a set of surveys in the six member countries beginning in 1970 (conducted by Rabier, with close advice from Ronald Inglehart and other interested social scientists). In 1973, with the enlargement of the EEC to nine member states, this fledgling survey instrument was transformed into the standard Eurobarometer. The European Commission's (EC) Eurobarometer unit also conducted the Central and Eastern Eurobarometer from 1990 to 1997, and launched the Candidate Countries Eurobarometer in 2001 (initially under the header of the Applicant Countries Eurobarometer), with a pilot study in 1999–2000.[7]

Up to this point we have used the term "European Values Study/World Values Survey (EVS/WVS)" to refer to what is often just called the "World Values Survey (WVS)." In fact, EVS and WVS are two independent organizations. The EVS has its secretariat and coordination center at Tilburg University in the Netherlands and is supported by its own foundation. The EVS data set is currently prepared by the Zentralarchiv für Empirische Sozialforschung (University of Cologne, Germany) which is also responsible for data dissemination. The WVS—which had been hosted for a long time by the Institute for Social Research (University of Michigan)—has recently relocated its secretariat to Stockholm. The JD-Systems Group in Madrid is responsible for the preparation of the data set and acts as the WVS's main data archive.

The WVS grew out of the EVS which, as noted above, was first administered in 1981. The EVS was inspired by much of the work on value-change in advanced industrial societies that had taken place in the 1970s. The initial EVS was conceived by a team of sociologists of religion from the University of Tilburg headed by Ruud de Moor and executed by such pollsters as Gordon Heald, Juan Linz, Elisabeth Noelle-Neumann, Jacques René Rabier, and Hélène Riffault and conducted in 10 European countries (later extended to an additional 14 including Canada and the United States). The EVS evoked such interest that it led to the implementation of a second wave of surveys, a development very much inspired by the work of Ronald Inglehart. This second wave was designed to be administered worldwide, thus giving birth to the first wave of the WVS. While organizationally independent, EVS and WVS share a substantive interest in value research. EVS describes its program as an exploration of the moral and social values underlying European social and political institutions and government conduct (e.g. Halman, Luijkx, and van Zunder 2005). However, EVS explicitly limits its activities to Europe and the WVS has a global interest. It mostly organizes and coordinates surveys outside Europe. Nonetheless, in the 1990 and 1995 waves, the WVS made a special effort to include the Central and Eastern European countries. The emphasis in 1999 and 2000 was to bring in African and Islamic societies. Both EVS and WVS have their own independent steering committees which are responsible for questionnaire development. In the past, EVS and WVS have coordinated questionnaire development. This has turned out to be a difficult process and it is hoped that common interests and collaboration will prevail in the future. However, EVS and WVS have negotiated a cooperation agreement to exchange surveys fielded by members of their various networks. The common data set is prepared by the JD-Systems Group.

The ISSP grew out of collaboration between the Allgemeine Bevölkerungsumfrage der Sozialwissenschaften (ALLBUS) of the Zentrum für Umfragen, Methoden, und Analysen (ZUMA) in Mannheim and the General Social Survey (GSS) of the National Opinion Research Center (NORC) of the University of Chicago.[8] In 1982 and again in 1984, the Zentrum für Umfragen, Methoden und Analysen (ZUMA), and NORC fielded a common set of questions which provided the intellectual and practical basis for the extension of this form of collaboration cross-nationally. The ISSP was formed in 1984, in conjunction with the Social and Community Planning Research (SCPR) center of Great Britain and the Research School of Social Sciences of Australian National University, through a grant from the Nuffield Foundation. The ISSP has designed and implemented a series of 10 modules, seven of which have been fielded on repeat occasions.[9] By the end of 2001, the ISSP had grown to 38 members, with the secretariat for the organization first based at NORC, USA, and since 2003 at the Norwegian Social Science Data Services, Bergen University.

As described above, CSES is thus the youngest of these cross-national survey research ventures, with its roots in the efforts of ICORE in the late 1980s and early 1990s. However, the participation of key members of the CSES team (such as Hans-Dieter Klingemann, Marta Lagos, Yilmaz Esmer, and Juan Diez-Nicholas) in certain of these other projects should be noted. In addition, other leading researchers with no connection to CSES (e.g. Jacques René Rabier, Ronald Inglehart, and Hélène Riffault) were involved in the design and implementation of more than one of these projects.

Survey Design

The different origins and mission of these ventures in "big social science" has also been manifest in their design and mode of operation. On one end of the spectrum stands the Standard Eurobarometer which comprises a standardized set of questions asked face-to-face in all member countries of the European Union. The Eurobarometer design incorporates a longitudinal set of value-orientation questions, of questions on social and political attitudes, standard measures of SES, and study-specific modules dealing with information on topical issues requested by institutions of the EU. Today, contracted survey research companies administer each Eurobarometer simultaneously in 27 countries. The longitudinal approach has enabled the construction of a "cumulative" file that contains longitudinal data on 105 key variables.[10]

The EVS/WVS also comprises a standardized questionnaire that is fielded in quasi-identical format in participating countries. However, the wide variation of national contexts (economic, political, social) arising from the disparate characteristics of the countries in which it has been fielded has necessitated a much greater need to grapple with issues of concept definition and concept stretching. In addition, it was difficult to coordinate the research programs of EVS and WVS. The EVS/WVS has been carried out in waves, each wave spreading across approximately three years. The mode has been face-to-face, although there are some exceptions (e.g. in New Zealand, it was conducted by mail). The design of EVS/WVS allows for both spatial and longitudinal comparison on core questions.

The ISSP design incorporates core modules into a broader survey instrument that is being fielded in member countries. The core modules are developed in one language (British English) by the planning committee and then translated into the native tongue. ISSP permits members to administer their module either face-to-face or through self-completion. In addition, it sponsored a mode experiment in 1996–7, in which seven countries fielded a common module (role of government) by both their usual mode and another. The design of ISSP attempts to strike a balance between longitudinal comparison (across similar modules over time), spatial comparison (the same module across national contexts), and issue coverage (different modules). A distinguishing characteristic of ISSP is that it allows to conduct two or more modules in the very same year and, in borderline cases, for the simultaneous inclusion of several modules even in one national survey. For example, four of the five original modules (social support, social equality, family and gender, and work) were fielded in Ireland in 1989; the third module on attitudes toward government, the second on work, and the second on religion were all fielded in Bangladesh in 1998.

CSES, like ISSP, has been organized on a modular basis. The point of departure for CSES, as noted in the original 1994 ICORE planning document prepared by Jacques Thomassen, Steven Rosenstone, Hans-Dieter Klingemann, and John Curtice,[11] is the "substantial amount of overlap in themes (and in many cases the questions)" of preexisting election studies in different countries around the world. However, as the authors quickly note, there is "a big difference between overlap in themes and survey questions and fully comparable, coordinated, data collections." The second major element that distinguishes CSES from ISSP is the desire to link the individual to the institutional context of political action. Three main axes of institutional design (regime type, electoral rules, and political parties) were identified in the planning document as constituting one of the major data-collection innovations of this collaborative research effort. Finally, unlike ISSP (or, indeed, Eurobarometer and EVS/WVS), CSES studies are uniquely event dependent. Country studies are constrained by the timing of elections (fixed in some participating countries while oscillating between predictability and unpredictability in others). Whereas Eurobarometer has been conducted multi-annually, EVS/WVS in waves up to four years, and ISSP either annually or biennially (depending on the frequency of member countries' social surveys), CSES is by necessity an asynchronous enterprise linked to the country-specific electoral cycle.

With regard to mode, the bulk of CSES country studies have been conducted face-to-face. For example, Module 1 was administered face-to-face in 21 countries, self-administered in three, through a combination of telephone and mail in two, and a combination of face-to-face and telephone in two other countries. Similar patterns of survey mode exist for Modules 2 and 3. The modular design of CSES will permit longitudinal comparison across many core items. However, compared to ISSP, CSES has an inevitably restricted number of data points as a consequence of its dependency upon election events.

Institutional Support

Of the four projects under review, the Eurobarometer is the project with the highest level of institutional support. With its origins in the postwar predilection for positivist political science, Eurobarometer quickly became a tool of public policy and as such gained high-level support within the European Commission. While the actual survey research is conducted by commercial opinion research companies, the core funding for Eurobarometer comes from the European Union. The Eurobarometer is centrally managed by the Public Opinion Analysis unit of the European Commission, since 2001 in the framework of the Directorate General for Press and Communication (the old DG 10).

However, the strong historical link between Eurobarometer and the academic community, a function of the origins of the survey, is evident in a number of ways. First, the core value questions embedded in the Eurobarometer surveys over almost three decades correspond to the demands of research-oriented social scientists interested in questions of value-orientations and value-change. Second, the main figures that led the Eurobarometer, such as Jacques René Rabier, Karlheinz Reif, or Anna Melich, were members of academia before they made the transition to officials of the Commission. Third, the data produced by Eurobarometer is routinely deposited in academic data archives with the ICPSR and the Zentralarchiv für Empirische Sozialforschung being the main repositories. Fourth, the Eurobarometer has, on occasion, incorporated batteries of questions prepared by academic researchers. For example, James Gibson and Gregory Caldeira added an important set of questions focusing upon public opinion toward the European Court of Justice. However, the practice of carrying additional modules has been suspended for the foreseeable future. Finally, the National Science Foundation of the United States awarded a grant to Ronald Inglehart and the University of Michigan to prepare a cumulative, longitudinal set of data covering surveys between 1970 and 1992. The Mannheimer Zentrum für Europäische Sozialforschung (MZES) and the Zentralarchiv für Empirische Sozialforschung have produced the latest and most expansive versions of the trend files.

The EVS/WVS has been coordinated by their respective boards composed of leading survey researchers in academia. In general, funding for country studies has been sought from local agencies, although the Volkswagen Foundation and the Wissenschaftszentrum Berlin für Sozialforschung have supported fieldwork in about 20 Central and Eastern European countries. In addition, the National Science Foundation of the United States provided grants for surveys in Egypt, Iran, Jordan, Pakistan, and Bangladesh. The EVS/WVS has coordinated the design of each questionnaire and the preliminary analysis of data gathered through a series of plenary meetings that have been held subsequent to the completion of each of the four waves so far.

As mentioned above, EVS and WVS do their own data preparation and dissemination. Joint files of each wave as well as a cumulative file have been prepared by the JD-Systems Group under the direction of Jaime Diez-Medrano. Members of the EVS/WVS networks are promised access to data from other country studies in exchange for the provision of the information gathered from their own surveys. Thus, one of the distinguishing features of WVS is the lag between data production and dissemination outside of the EVS/WVS community. Currently, the first, second, and third waves are available through the ICPSR, the Zentralarchiv für Empirische Sozialforschung, and other data archives.

As EVS/WVS has expanded, particularly outside polities that have been able to join large-scale comparative survey projects asking politically sensitive questions, key actors have been instrumental in finding local collaborators and aiding their integration. Of particular note are the contributions of Hans-Dieter Klingemann, who has been co-principal investigator in a sizeable number of Eastern European and former Soviet Union countries, and of Ronald Inglehart, who is acknowledged as the intellectual impetus behind survey efforts in many of the non-Western cases. Another good illustrative example is that of Vietnam. The 2001 World Values Survey for Vietnam was conducted by the Institute for Human Studies in Hanoi, under the direction of Pham Minh Hac, substantially aided by Russell J. Dalton and Nhu-Ngoc Ong of the Center for the Study of Democracy at the University of California, Irvine.

The ISSP has an established secretariat at NORC in Chicago for which limited funding for data preparation, coding, and cleaning has been provided by the National Science Foundation of the United States. However, the main task of merging the data into a cross-national data set has been performed by the Zentralarchiv für Empirische Sozialforschung, University of Cologne, in collaboration with the JD-Systems Group in Spain (since 1996). The ISSP has placed a substantial burden of the data preparation and cleaning upon contributing country institutions, with well-defined rules about the format in which data have to be submitted.

The ISSP holds yearly plenary sessions to which representatives from all member countries are invited. Members of research working groups are elected at the plenary meeting and shoulder the responsibility for the preparation of drafts for new modules. The ISSP has also formed a working group on methodology. In a limited number of cases, national studies are carried out by more than one participating institution (e.g. work in France is done by a consortium consisting of Centre de recherche en économie et statistique, Centre d'information des données socio-politiques, Observatoire Français des conjonctures économiques, and Laboratoire d'analyse secondaire et de méthodes appliquées en sociologie, all involved in the study). ISSP has developed rules that prohibit the incorporation of more than three new members per year.

As noted in the first part of this chapter, CSES grew out of ICORE. While CSES has a much more limited scope, being concentrated in the area of election studies, the project has a broadly decentralized structure that accommodates the interests of divergent member countries. The secretariat, based at the Institute for Social Research at the University of Michigan, has been partially supported by the National Science Foundation of the United States. As described elsewhere in this volume, data coordination and cleaning has been largely undertaken by the secretariat, after initial preparation by country collaborators.

The main coordination of CSES modules is undertaken by the Planning Committee, elected at the plenary session of the consortium. The aim of the organization is to hold planning meetings every year (organized and funded by local hosts), and plenary sessions once every three years. In addition to the elected members of the Planning Committee, there is provision for outside consultancy from experts in the field (e.g. Gary Cox, who was instrumental in the development of the macro-questionnaire, or Ekkehard Mochmann, who was the expert on socioeconomic background data and on problems of data archiving). One of the unique features of CSES has been the elaboration of the macro-data questionnaire (which permits cross-level causal analysis, in conjunction with the information allowed for by the modular design), gathered through the completion of a standardized questionnaire sent to all project collaborators. This macro-data questionnaire turned out to be of great help in the design of micro–macro analyses.

As noted above, the secretariat at the Institute for Social Research, University of Michigan, has shouldered the responsibility for final data cleaning and dissemination. While collaborators have been provided with a standardized codebook, problems of data errors, inconsistent coding, missing data, and data ambiguities have been dealt with by the secretariat (in consultation with the Planning Committee), drawing upon expertise garnered from the preparation of the American National Election Study. The CSES has developed and maintained a web site that provides rapid and open access to the data submitted by contributors. There are few restrictions upon the provision of this data to the non-CSES academic community.

Discussion

One of the obvious points to make is that "big science" is alive and well in comparative research, albeit perhaps facing challenging times. Just as comparativists discovered the rich intellectual vein to be tapped from the coordination of survey research across national contexts, public funding bodies discover the constraints imposed by the new fiscal environment. With Eurobarometer as a possible exception, each of the three other projects has had to adapt to the challenges of mounting a carefully planned and coordinated research program in the face of fiscal austerity. Particularly salient in the case of ISSP or the EVS/WVS—perhaps to a lesser extent for CSES—has been the role that seed money and external grants from nonpublic sources have played in stimulating the research endeavor. However, resource inequalities between members of the projects or limited public university funding are all challenges faced by those engaged in large-scale comparative research. We will return to this point in the discussion below of the specific challenges facing CSES.

The structure of these social scientific projects also reflects to some degree the particular differences manifest between them. EVS/WVS, with global aspirations and a unique survey to administer, relies upon an in-built data-sharing incentive structure to encourage collaboration. ISSP, on the other hand, dependent as it is upon an extremely tight coordination process for the production of field-worthy modules within short time periods, has a much more rigidly defined and circumscribed structure. Eurobarometer, as befits the nature of this essentially public enterprise, is fairly centralized in its operations. CSES, the newest arrival, falls somewhere between EVS/WVS and ISSP. CSES has no selective incentives to encourage participation (the incentives are more purposive in nature, a sense of "belonging" to a research community), nor does it have the same degree of rule-boundedness that ISSP has developed. However, the origins of CSES in preexisting national election studies, which necessarily meant a higher degree of convergence between studies than in ISSP, may have made some of the problems encountered by ISSP moot.

Evident, too, in this overview of large-scale, cross-national survey research is the strength of certain national social scientific research traditions. The presence of the same set of national research establishments at the creation of these projects (Germany, the United States, the United Kingdom, and to a certain extent Australia, the Netherlands, and Sweden) speaks eloquently to the nexus between public and academic, social but scientific research traditions that have been forged in those countries.

Again, an interesting variant is the Eurobarometer. While it is a product of the positivist-institutionalist thinking of Rabier, shared by his close collaborator and superior, Monnet, the project was in some respects atypical of the French research tradition of the era. It was finally brought to fruition in 1970 with close collaboration of both American and German academics. While this is not to negate the undeniable contributions of other member countries, nor to argue for a national-hegemonic social science paradigm, there is surely something intrinsically compelling about the common understandings and aspirations concerning the promise of "big science" that pervaded social scientific departments in the core countries cited above.

Finally, the experience of these four research projects also highlights the importance of individuals in the inception and promotion of the ideas. When resources are neither abundant nor guaranteed, the role of individual investigators willing to take risks and stake professional capital is quite remarkable in hindsight. Charles Tilly (1975) asked the now famous question, what separates successful states from those that disappeared? In the same manner, we might ask what separates successful attempts at cross-national social scientific research partnerships from those that fail to achieve their promise? And the answer to both questions may be (in part), a successful supply of entrepreneurs.

Challenges to CSES, Lessons of CSES

In this final section we address some of the key challenges facing CSES. We also intend to point out some of the advantages of the CSES over other forms of collaborative cross-national research that may prove to be instructive for future research ventures of this kind.

Clearly, the major source of preoccupation for any cross-national survey research venture of the different kinds described above is funding. In principal, the simple formula "for each country, its own funding" is one that avoids questions of seeking research support outside the country of study. It also has an aura of equality (at least in one variant of democratic theory). Yet, at the outset of the CSES project, concern was expressed over the cost of implementing election studies in poorer countries. Oscar Hernandez of the Universidad de Costa Rica argued: "Strong support is needed from ICORE so that social scientists within each country have access to international agencies in securing funds for the survey. Local funding will be difficult to find in many countries." Marta Lagos of

MORI in Chile suggested "some kind of centralized support in order to present the project to different foundations." Yet this source of centralized support, however desirable, has not been readily forthcoming, and an inevitable tension remains between those countries with higher levels of public support for survey research (strongly correlated, one suspects, with a rich tradition in this area) and those countries that are struggling to implement these kinds of studies for the first time. Unfortunately, higher standards of data collection require increasing amounts of funding and exponentially increasing expertise, conditions not always guaranteed to secure the participation of less resource-rich countries.

A more acute manifestation of the larger problem is the standardized cleaning and archiving of data. For those engaged in rigorous cross-national survey research, the Achilles heel of such collaborative projects may lie at the stage when data is cleaned, merged, and archived. After the intense and rigorous debates that precede the construction of a valid and reliable survey instrument, the "behind the scenes" work of data archiving is one that has received less ready attention. Funding is one outstanding question no matter how decentralized the enterprise: Who pays? Who bears responsibility? In the short term, CSES secured funding from the National Science Foundation of the United States to undertake a substantial portion of this work. However, the merging and archival process is only as good as the instrumentation and documentation of each component survey. Where problems have arisen, the CSES secretariat and country contributors have negotiated solutions on ad hoc bases. Absent an incentive structure of the kind embedded in the EVS/WVS, or the rigid mandates of ISSP, it is difficult to see how it could be otherwise.

The second aspect that bears upon the data merging and archiving process is that of the goal stated by Steven Rosenstone of "the democratization of democracy studies." In part normative, in part institutional, the commitment to fast, open, and egalitarian data access inevitably conflicts with the technocratic impulse to maintain data under embargo until it is deemed by the research community to be error free. Clearly there is a trade-off here between the fast provision of data and quality control. To date, no clear equilibrium point has been identified by the CSES team. Indirectly, the pressure to release data quickly may force collaborators to compromise the quality of the data, while on the other hand, the slow release of data may render the utility of the data less important, and also diminish the overall value of the CSES project.

A further area of challenge for CSES may be to strike the balance in each module between (necessary) parsimony and a set of questions that captures the key concerns of those studying electoral dynamics across a range of sometimes quite disparate states. In the comments invited by the initial ICORE steering committee, one cannot fail to be struck by the divergence between scholars of elections and parties in even "most-like systems" as to what constitutes the most important potential objects of study. Adding in comments made by observers from other countries, the danger is of the proverbial Tower of Babel. From general questions of concept-stretching, extension, and intension, to more specific ones about the validity and reliability of cross-national measures proposed, the questions that faced CSES then, as now, are those that comparative research has grappled with for approaching half a century.

At the outset of this chapter, we noted that the promise of Modules 2 and 3 is to usher in the possibility of macro–micro causal analyses. This may be one of the most exciting aspects of CSES in the years to come, and it is certainly one that distinguishes it from the other aforementioned data gathering projects. Yet the potential for such cross-level analyses brings an additional set of challenges. Beyond issues of data validity and reliability that lie outside the scope of this discussion, the macro-level data is time-sensitive. Unlike the micro-level data in CSES, the macro data constitute repeated observations of the same case. Variation is to be expected across observations (more so for some variables than others), yet the temporal dimension is reduced by the observational strategy. It is not implausible to suggest that, when considering potential macro–micro explanations for a specific phenomenon, the *timing* of the variation in macro variable X may account for as much variance in micro variable Y as the *range* of variation in X. Thus, the temporal dimension afforded by the CSES design also poses a challenge to the construction of the macro-level data set.

Conclusion

In conclusion, CSES has achieved a degree of institutionalization over the last decade that merits the consideration of the project as a successful experiment in big social science. Looking back over the initial calls to action issued in 1989 at ECPR in Rimini, the constitution of ICORE, the formation of the planning committee, the Berlin conference of 1994, or the fielding of Module 1, it is clear that the seemingly simple notion that disparate national election studies could and should achieve some measure of coordination across studies, has reached fruition. In doing so, CSES has sometimes opted to tread the path well trod by other cross-national survey research projects. At other times CSES has chosen to innovate and invent. Taking stock at this juncture, it is evident that much has been accomplished but much remains to be done.

What is of great comfort to the cross-national social scientist is that, despite sometimes quite divergent approaches, there is a core set of principles and practices that run across the four projects that we have included in this chapter. Part of the maturation of a discipline is the emergence of common concepts, definitions, methods, and norms. It may be argued that these projects cumulatively represent an important building block in that regard. Whether they have come to constitute *sui generis* a research paradigm in the study of political behavior is perhaps more contentious, but such a claim on the part of the protagonists in these enterprises should neither surprise nor shock.

Notes

1. NSF funding proposal 2001 (available at http://www.cses.org).
2. The other projects that we will use for comparison purposes are: Eurobarometer, European Values Study/World Values Survey, and the International Social Survey Program. The European Social Survey (ESS), funded by the European Commission's fifth framework program, the European Science Foundation, and national sources, was still in its infancy at the time of writing. ESS covers most European countries. It was fielded in 2002/3 for the first time and is repeated biannually. The ESS has now become a flagship among the "big social science" survey projects.
3. In fact, there was a substantial amount of overlap in themes, concepts, and actual questions in election studies in Europe.
4. As mentioned in n. 2, this is not an exhaustive list of such projects, nor is it a random sample. However, together with CSES, these survey-based data collection efforts are among the most frequently used and cited by students of comparative political participation. They represent sometimes overlapping, sometimes contrasting models of "big science" in comparative research and as such provide a useful counterpoint to compare and contrast with the *modus operandi* of the Comparative Study of Electoral Systems. It may also be noted that several researchers have been involved with more than one of these projects. For a comprehensive review of comparative survey research, see Miki Caul Kittilson (2007).
5. In 1973, it was still a "European Communities Study," later sometimes referred to as Eurobarometer 0. Standard Eurobarometer 1 (Spring 1974) was lost; the first available Standard Eurobarometer was Number 2 (Autumn 1974). This explains the usual confusion about the starting year in the literature.

Thanks to Meinhard Moschner, Zentralarchiv für Empirische Sozialforschung, University of Cologne, for this clarification.

6. This information is based upon a personal communication with Karl-Heinz Reif. The actual title of the study was "Attitudes towards Europe—Five Countries Study 1962" drafted for the Press and Information Service of the European Economic Community.

7. There are a few other projects that have been undertaken by the Public Opinion Analysis Sector of the European Commission, such as "Flash Eurobarometer," the Continuous Tracking Surveys, and the Top Decision-Makers Eurobarometer of 1996. For more information, see the Eurobarometer-related parts of the GESIS web site.

8. www.issp.org

9. The modules on "Environment, and National Identity," have been fielded twice. "Social Equality, Family and Gender, Work, and Religion" have been fielded three times; the module on "Attitudes towards Government" has been fielded four times.

10. The original Inglehart trend file covered the period 1973–92, and included 52 variables. This has been supplanted by the Mannheim trend file from 1970 to 2002 (latest version 2.0) with an expanded variable list compiled by Hermann Schmitt. More information on this file can be found at: http://www.gesis.org/en/data_service/eurobarometer/standard_eb_trend/trendfile.htm

11. Available at http://www.cses.org/plancom.htm

3

Methodological Challenges: Research Opportunities and Questions for the Future

David A. Howell and Karen Long Jusko

Introduction

At a critical juncture in the development of the Comparative Study of Electoral Systems (CSES) project—the completion of the first module, and launching of the second and third—it is useful to highlight areas of methodological interest arising from the unique design of the study. Researchers analyzing the CSES data would benefit from a more complete understanding of, and guidance concerning the methodological implications of the study's research design. To this end, this chapter is intended to stimulate interest in using the CSES for methodological research and the study of design effects, to examine the completeness and quality of relevant information currently collected by the study, and to identify ways in which the collection of such information can be improved.

Our examination of methodological and design issues is not intended to question the validity of conclusions reached through analysis of the data. Despite the differences in study administration that we outline, there is no evidence that findings from analysis of the data are anything but robust. We expect that the cross-national variation in the administration of the project quite likely just obscures systematic patterns, adding to their natural variance. It is difficult to imagine circumstances in which variation in features of the election studies' implementation would manufacture patterns where none exist. Therefore, while it is helpful to be attentive to the implications of cross-national variation in the administration of the module, one can still confidently proceed in the comparative analysis of electoral processes using CSES data.

Our discussion begins with a review of the study's research design. Thereafter, we outline a number of implementation issues the effects of which are worth understanding in order to draw proper inferences from the data. Throughout, we highlight and describe launching points in the CSES data and documentation for further investigation. We conclude with a series of forward-looking suggestions for preparing users to consider the impact of these issues when conducting their own analyses.

The CSES Research Design

The CSES Module 1 data release of August 4, 2003, contains information from 39 election studies conducted in 33 different countries. The project is in all respects a collaborative effort. As described in the previous chapter, an elected Planning Committee, composed of scholars and survey researchers from throughout the world, receives input and provides governance. While a central operation collects, merges, and manages the deposited data sets, each participating investigator is responsible for securing independent funding for their individual election study, fielding the survey in their own country using sound methods, and depositing the results in a complete and timely fashion. In return, the CSES provides valuable exposure for the individual election studies, a chance to examine themselves in a comparative context, and expertise in data processing, distribution, and archiving.

The power of the CSES research design lies in the multilevel compilation of electoral data. Micro-level public opinion survey data, collected through a common survey module developed by the CSES Planning Committee, are the core of the project. The project requires that these data be collected in national postelection studies, and requests that they be supplemented with basic demographic and voting items. Added later are district-level and macro-level (i.e. system-level) information that is provided by collaborators and collected from other publicly available resources. This powerful design allows multilevel analyses of electoral behavior across a range of institutional and political–economic environments. In short, the CSES project situates voters in their political environments, and provides a means to assess the impact.

Differences in administration are primarily confined to the micro-level survey data. Early on, the CSES Planning Committee established a set of guidelines for collaborators in hopes of maximizing comparability and minimizing measurement error across the individual election studies. Nonetheless, many collaborators face real constraints (resources, timing, and cultural, among others) that induce variation in the methods by which the survey is administered in each national setting. Such variation leads to interesting questions: Which of these variations do analysts need to consider when using CSES data? What can CSES do to improve comparability, or at least awareness of noncomparability, in the administration of the election studies?

The CSES Sample Design and Data Collection Report

Most of the information available to identify variation in administration is gathered from the CSES Sample Design and Data Collection Report (sometimes abbreviated as "Design Report"), which the project requests to be completed and deposited for each election study.

The CSES Design Report was developed with two goals in mind: to capture important details of the sample and administration of each election study, and at the same time not prove overly burdensome for a collaborator to complete. Fortunately, the majority of election studies (30 of 39; 77 percent) submitted a Design Report with their data deposit. Most of the other election studies provided alternate forms of documentation from which similar information could be obtained. In examining the Design Reports, it seems that the documents often do capture much of the critical information concerning individual election study design and implementation. In fact, we used information from the Design Reports to prepare most of the tables in this chapter. However, as we reviewed them, we discovered a number of general, repeating issues.

One concern is that many Design Reports suffered from significant item nonresponse. In some instances, the person completing the report was not a member of the organization that collected the data, and so the answers were from second-hand sources or unknown altogether. In other situations, the collaborator was not aware up front that a Design Report was required which meant some of the information was lost or never collected in the first place, as it was not known it would later be needed.

We can also hypothesize that occasionally the person chosen to complete the report may have had limited expertise in survey administration and was unfamiliar with the terminology used. Or perhaps the information requested was sometimes difficult to obtain and left blank to save effort. To the extent possible, we suggest that new collaborators be made aware of the Design Report requirements as soon as possible upon their recruitment, so they can arrange to collect the relevant data and have the answers at hand when the report is compiled. Additionally, we would suggest that collaborators complete their Design Report as close to the end of the data collection period as possible to reduce loss of information and problems with recall, and thus decrease missing information and increase accuracy.

Another issue was language difficulties. By agreement, CSES project communications and products are in English. However, not all documentation submitted to the CSES Secretariat was translated into English, reducing the accessibility of the information to the CSES staff and user community. We also suspect that in some instances, language barriers complicated the completion of the Design Report and occasionally led to skipped questions or inaccuracies due to misinterpretation. This highlights a need to use very clear language and instructions, perhaps providing definitions for core concepts and further clarification in instructions to assist in proper interpretation and accuracy.

CSES Election Study Administration Guidelines

The final report of the CSES Module 1 Planning Committee established nine "aspired to standards for data quality and comparability" (hereafter referred to as "CSES Standards") for the administration of CSES modules by national election study teams (CSES Planning Committee 1996, Appendix 3.1). As these standards provide a useful framework for discussion, and for organizing future research, they are summarized for reference in Figure 3.1.

Through the rest of the chapter, we consider how well each of these standards has been adhered to, using information provided to the CSES staff upon the deposit of micro-level survey data sets. Further, drawing on recent research, we identify ways in which cross-national differences in the administration of the module may manifest themselves in the data.

**Aspired to Standards for Data Quality and Comparability
(CSES Planning Committee, 1996)**

1. **Mode of interviewing**: Interviews should be conducted face-to-face, unless local circumstances dictate that telephone or mail surveys will produce higher quality data.

2. **Timing of interviewing**: We strongly recommend that collaborators in the Comparative Study of Electoral Systems conduct their interviews in the weeks following their national election. Out of concern for data quality, data collection should be completed in as timely a fashion as possible. In the event of a runoff election, interviewing shall be conducted after the first round election. The date of interview shall be provided for each respondent.

3. **Placement of module in post-election questionnaire**: The questionnaire module should be asked as a single, uninterrupted block of questions. We leave it to each collaborator to select an appropriate location for the module in his national survey instrument. Collaborators should take steps to ensure that questions asked immediately prior to the questionnaire module do not contaminate the initial questions in the module. Collaborators are also free to select an appropriate place in their survey instrument to ask the turnout, vote choice, and demographic questions.

4. **Population to be sampled**: National samples should be drawn from all age-eligible citizens. When non-citizens (or other non-eligible respondents) are included in the sample, a variable should be provided to permit the identification of those non-eligible respondents. When a collaborator samples from those persons who appear on voter registration lists, he should quantify the estimated degree of discrepancy between this population and the population of all age-eligible citizens.

5. **Sampling procedures**: We strongly encourage the use of random samples, with random sampling procedures used at all stages of the sampling process. Collaborators should provide detailed documentation of their sampling practices...

6. **Sample Size**: We strongly recommend that no fewer than 1,000 age-eligible respondents be interviewed.

7. **Interviewer training**: Collaborators should pretest their survey instrument and should train interviewers in the administration of the questionnaire. The Planning Committee will provide each collaborator with documentation that clarifies the purposes and objectives of each item and with rules with respect to probing don't-know responses.

8. **Field practices**: Collaborators should make every effort to ensure a high response rate. Investigators should be diligent in their effort to reach respondents not interviewed on the initial contact with the household and should be diligent in their effort to convert respondents who initially refuse to participate in the study. Data on the number of contact attempts, the number of contacts with sample persons, and special persuasion or conversion efforts undertaken should be coded for each respondent.

9. **Strategies for translation (and back-translation)**: Each collaborator should translate the questionnaire module into his or her native language(s). To ensure the equivalence of the translation, collaborators shall perform an independent re-translation of the questionnaire back into English. Collaborators engaged in translation of the questionnaire module into the same language (e.g. Spanish, French, English, German, and Portuguese) should collaborate on the translation.

Figure 3.1. Aspired to standards for data quality and comparability

Source: CSES Planning Committee (1996).

Mode of Interviewing

CSES Standard:

> Interviews should be conducted face-to-face, unless local circumstances dictate that telephone or mail surveys will produce higher quality data.

As reported in Table 3.1, there is some variation in the mode in which the CSES module was administered. In 27 of the 39 elections (69 percent) analyzed, the CSES module was administered through face-to-face interviews. In six of the 39 elections (15 percent), the CSES module was administered through self-completion or mail-back surveys. In four elections, the module was administered through telephone interviews (10 percent). Finally, in two cases, the mode of interview was mixed within the sample.

In several cases, the CSES module was part of a larger study in which several modes of interview were used. Table 3.1, therefore, also reports whether the election studies included in Module 1 are identified as single-panel studies (simply "postelection studies") or whether the studies include a preelection component. Additionally, there are several cases in which two postelection surveys were administered to the same panel of respondents through different modes. To the extent that different modes of interview affect who is likely to participate in a survey, analysts using the CSES data may benefit from knowledge of the larger survey environment in which respondents are situated.

With the findings of previous experimental research, we may be able to anticipate some of the effects of the different interview modes in the CSES. The American National Election Study (ANES) has investigated the effects of survey mode through several split sample experiments (Bowers and Ensley 2003; Green, Krosnick, and Holbrook 2001; Wessel, Rahn, and Rudolf 2000). The evidence is remarkably consistent in the American context where, first, telephone and face-to-face samples differ with regard to the demographic compositions. For example, telephone surveys underrepresent the socially disadvantaged. Although some of this bias results from coverage error, Green, Krosnick, and Holbrook (2001) suggest that the bias results from systematic nonresponse. Second, the quality of responses also differs across modes of interview. Telephone responses are more susceptible to satisficing and social desirability biases. These systematic patterns are consistent with research conducted in other settings (Tourangeau, Rips, and Rasinski 2000). Similarly, self-administered questionnaires may yield samples and data qualities systematically different

Table 3.1. Mode of interview

Mode of CSES module	Study type
Face-to-face (*n* = 27)	
Belarus (2001)[a]	Postelection study
Chile (1999)	Postelection study
The Czech Republic (1996)	Preelection and postelection panel study
Denmark (1998)	Postelection study
Hong Kong (1998)	Postelection study
Hong Kong (2000)	Postelection study
Hungary (1998)	Preelection and postelection panel study
Japan (1996)	Preelection and postelection panel study
Korea (2000)	Postelection study
Lithuania (1997)	Postelection study
Mexico (1997)	Postelection study
Mexico (2000)	Postelection study
The Netherlands (1998)	Preelection and postelection panel study
Norway (1997)	Postelection study
Peru (2000)	Postelection study
Peru (2001)[a]	Postelection study
Poland (1997)	Postelection study
Portugal (2002)[a]	Postelection study
Romania (1996)	Postelection study
Russia (1999)	Preelection and postelection panel study
Russia (2000)	Preelection and postelection panel study
Slovenia (1996)	Postelection study
Spain (1996)	Postelection study
Spain (2000)	Postelection study
Taiwan (1996)	Postelection study
Thailand (2001)	Preelection and postelection panel study
Ukraine (1998)	Postelection study
Mail/self-completion (*n* = 6)	
Australia (1996)	Postelection study
Belgium-Flanders (1999)	Postelection study (face-to-face and mail/self-completion)
Belgium-Walloon (1999)[a]	Postelection study (face-to-face and mail/self-completion)
Canada (1997)	Preelection and postelection panel study (telephone and mail/self-completion)
Great Britain (1997)	Postelection study
New Zealand (1996)	Postelection study
Telephone (*n* = 4)	
Germany (1998)	Postelection study
Iceland (1999)[a]	Postelection study
Israel (1996)	Postelection study
Switzerland (1999)	Postelection study
Mixed mode within sample (*n* = 2)	
Sweden (1998)	Postelection study (face-to-face and telephone)
United States (1996)	Pre- and postelection panel study (face-to-face and telephone)

[a] Denotes election studies that are included in the August 4, 2003, release of the CSES data set.

Source: CSES Module 1 election study documentation and materials.

from either face-to-face (Richman et al. 1999) or telephone interviews. It is reasonable to expect, therefore, that the different survey environments created by the various modes of interview used in the CSES studies result in important differences both in who participates in a study, and the responses they are likely to give.

Timing of Interviewing

CSES Standard:

> We strongly recommend that collaborators in the Comparative Study of Electoral Systems conduct their interviews in the weeks following their national election. Out of concern for data quality, data collection should be completed in as timely a fashion as possible. In the event of a runoff election, interviewing shall be conducted after the first round election. The date of interview shall be provided for each respondent.

Like mode of interview effects, considerable research efforts have been devoted to understanding the effect of the timing of survey administration on both sample and data quality. This research suggests that there are at least two ways in which timing of an election study may affect the quality of the collected survey data. First, the timing of the study may affect the quality of the sample. Heberlin and Baumgartner (1978), and more recently Yammarino, Skinner, and Childers (1991), find that topic saliency is an important determinant of participation in a study. By consequence, it is reasonable to expect that participation rates may be higher when the election study is administered in close proximity to the election. Further, election studies may systematically underrepresent those less interested in politics (Brehm 1993). Second, survey timing may affect the quality of responses as well. For example, accurate reporting of voting behavior may be threatened by both memory decay and desire to present oneself well. When a respondent is uncertain about past events, the desire to present oneself in a favorable light may affect what aspects of the past are remembered. Belli et al. (1999) find that elapsed time compounds these biases in their analysis of vote overreporting. Of the 39 studies in the CSES data set, almost all provide information sufficient to calculate the number of days that transpired between the election and completion of the fieldwork. As reported in Table 3.2, most studies began within two weeks of the end of the election (25 of 39; 64 percent) and finished within two months of the end of the election (24 of 39; 62 percent). All but four studies were completed within six months of the

Table 3.2. Distance between election end and data collection period in days

Election study	Date of election end[a]	Election end to data collection start (days)[b]	Election end to data collection end (days)[c]
Spain (2000)	March 12, 2000	1	9
Hungary (1998)	May 10, 1998	4	11
Poland (1997)	September 21, 1997	8	16
Spain (1996)	March 3, 1996	6	16
Japan (1996)	October 20, 1996	1	17
The Czech Republic (1996)	June 1, 1996	5	18
Mexico (2000)	July 2, 2000	5	18
Ukraine (1998)	March 29, 1998	3	18
Germany (1998)	September 28, 1998	0	19
Portugal (2002)	March 17, 2002	6	22
Mexico (1997)	July 6, 1997	8	23
Switzerland (1999)	October 24, 1999	1	24
Belarus (2001)	September 9, 2001	15	27
Peru (2000)	April 9, 2000	26	29
Romania (1996)	November 3, 1996	23	30
Lithuania (1997)	December 21, 1997	23	31
Chile (1999)	December 12, 1999	23	37
Korea (2000)	April 13, 2000	29	40
Russia (1999)	December 19, 1999	6	43
Iceland (1999)	May 8, 1999	16	46
Thailand (2001)	January 6, 2001	9	54
United States (1996)	November 5, 1996	1	58
The Netherlands (1998)	May 6, 1998	0	59
Canada (1997)	June 2, 1997	1	62
Sweden (1998)	September 20, 1998	1	62
Israel (1996)	May 29, 1996	45	70
New Zealand (1996)	October 12, 1996	1	73
Norway (1997)	September 15, 1997	0	76
Russia (2000)	March 26, 2000	14	76
Great Britain (1997)	May 1, 1997	0	89
Denmark (1998)	March 11, 1998	26	97
Hong Kong (1998)	May 24, 1998	8	113
Australia (1996)	March 2, 1996	0	114
Hong Kong (2000)	September 10, 2000	0	153
Taiwan (1996)	March 12, 1996	81	183
Belgium-Walloon (1999)	June 13, 1999	80	289
Belgium-Flanders (1999)	June 13, 1999	80	298
Slovenia (1996)	November 10, 1996	325	362
Minimum		0	9
Mean		23	73
Median		6	45
Maximum		325	362

[a] In the case of elections spanning multiple days, the latest date was used.

[b] Where there were discrepancies between the field start as stated in the Design Report and the earliest interview completion date in the data, the earliest postelection date was used.
[c] Where there were discrepancies between the field end as stated in the Design Report and the latest interview completion date in the data, the latest date was used.

Source: CSES Module 1 election study documentation and materials.

election, and all interviews were conducted within a year of the election. Note also that the length of the field period varies considerably among the CSES countries. Some studies were in the field less than two weeks, while others were conducted over substantially longer periods of time. When examining the effects of time lag between election and interview, it would be interesting to also investigate whether there were any effects due to the differing length of field periods (a starting point might be respondent characteristics and response differences). We suspect that one area for improvement in the Design Report would be to provide definitions concerning what is meant by the "beginning" and "ending" dates of the field period. So often did we find discrepancies between the field dates and the range of dates for completed interviews that we thought there must be some varying interpretations of what constitutes the begin and end of a data collection period. It would be useful to indicate whether the range of dates is intended to be for the panel in which the core CSES module was administered or for the study overall (as some election studies had multiple panels or waves). It would also be helpful to include a note asking collaborators to describe discrepancies between the two sources of the information.

Placement of Module in Postelection Questionnaire

CSES Standard:

> The questionnaire module should be asked as a single, uninterrupted block of questions. We leave it to each collaborator to select an appropriate location for the module in his or her national survey instrument. Collaborators should take steps to ensure that questions asked immediately prior to the questionnaire module do not contaminate the initial questions in the module. Collaborators are also free to select an appropriate place in their survey instrument to ask the turnout, vote choice, and demographic questions.

In addition to the mode of interview, and the timing of a particular study, other differences in the ways in which the CSES module is administered may have implications for cross-national comparison. For example, as seen in Table 3.3, the studies differ as to whether the CSES module was included in a larger study as a continuous block of questions, or the questions were dispersed throughout the larger study. Insights from experimental and survey research are helpful in identifying ways in which differences in module placement and question-ordering may affect cross-national comparison. First, some attitudes may be particularly susceptible

Table 3.3. Question ordering and placement

Election	Administration of the CSES module				Administration of item: Q5 "Political parties are necessary"			
	Included as continuous block?	Placement of module	Survey items distributed over panels	Survey items distributed over modes	Included in the survey	Differences in question wording/introduction	Preceded by CSES item Q4	Proceded by CSES item Q6
Germany (1998)	Yes	Beginning	No	No	Yes	No	Yes	Yes
Hong Kong (1998)	Yes	Beginning	No	No	Yes	No	Yes	Yes
Hong Kong (2000)	Yes	Beginning	No	No	Yes	No	Yes	Yes
Israel (1996)	Yes	Beginning	No	No	Yes	Yes	Yes	No
Mexico (2000)	Yes	Beginning	No	No	Yes	No	Yes	Yes
Peru (2000)	Yes	Beginning	No	No	Yes	No	Yes	Yes
Portugal (2002)	Yes	Beginning	No	No	Yes	No	Yes	Yes
Romania (1996)	Yes	Beginning	No	No	Yes	No	Yes	Yes
Spain (2000)	Yes	Beginning	No	No	Yes	No	Yes	Yes
Ukraine (1998)	Yes	Beginning	No	No	Yes	No	Yes	Yes
Hungary (1998)	Yes	Middle	No	No	Yes	No	Yes	Yes
New Zealand (1996)	Yes	Middle	No	No	Yes	No	Yes	Yes
Norway (1997)	Yes	Middle	No	No	Yes	No	Yes	Yes
Poland (1997)	Yes	Middle	No	No	Yes	No	Yes	Yes
Russia (1999)	Yes	Middle	No	No	Yes	No	Yes	No
Switzerland (1999)	Yes	Middle	No	No	Yes	No	Yes	Yes
Canada (1997)	Yes	End	No	No	Yes	No	Yes	Yes
Great Britain (1997)	Yes	End	No	No	Yes	No	Yes	Yes
Sweden (1998)	Yes	End	No	No	Yes	No	Yes	Yes
United States (1996)	Yes	End	No	No	Yes	No	Yes	Yes
Korea (2000)	Yes	—	No	No	Yes	—	—	—
Lithuania (1997)	Yes	—	No	No	Yes	No	Yes	Yes
Mexico (1997)	Yes	—	No	No	Yes	No	Yes	Yes
Spain (1996)	Yes	—	No	No	Yes	No	Yes	Yes
Australia (1996)	No	—	No	No	Yes	No	Yes	No
Belgium-Flanders (1999)	No	—	Yes	Yes	Yes	No	Yes	No
Belgium-Walloon (1999)	No	—	Yes	Yes	Yes	No	Yes	No
The Czech Republic (1996)	No	—	No	No	Yes	Yes	Yes	Yes
Denmark (1998)	No	—	No	No	Yes	No	Yes	No
The Netherlands (1998)	No	—	—	No	Yes	No	Yes	No
Peru (2001)	No	—	No	No	Yes	No	Yes	Yes
Russia (2000)	No	—	No	No	No	—	—	—
Slovenia (1996)	No	—	No	No	Yes	No	Yes	No
Thailand (2001)	No	—	Yes	No	No	—	—	—

Notes: These data are based on the English translations of the survey instruments and other documentation provided by the collaborators.

to carryover effects of previous questions. For example, Bartels (2000) finds that changes in levels of efficacy can be attributed, in large part, to changes in the question ordering of core ANES items. When the item is preceded by questions about government waste, corrupt politicians, and the influence of big business on government, levels of faith in the electoral process were considerably less than when the question was preceded by a general question on government responsiveness. Second, however, some attitudes are less vulnerable than others to carryover effects. McAllister and Wattenberg (1995) find no significant impact of question reordering on party identification in either the British Election Survey or American National Election Study. These "results are consistent with the notion that party identification is one of the more enduring and stable components of mass political behavior in both presidential and parliamentary systems" (McAllister and Wattenberg 1995: 259). To the extent that CSES items measure "enduring" elements of political attitudes and activities, variance in question ordering may contribute little to cross-national variation. As noted above, the CSES module was often included in a larger study. A third concern, therefore, arises from when in this larger study the CSES module was administered. The quality of responses may be compromised by respondent fatigue, for example. Conversely, however, by a later point in the questionnaire the respondent and interviewer may have developed rapport that makes for more focused attention from the respondent (Bradburn and Sudman 1991; Tanur 1983–4). To evaluate cross-national variation in the placement of the CSES module within larger studies, we used the materials provided by the collaborators to answer the following questions: Was the CSES module included as a continuous block of questions? Where was the CSES module included in the larger study? Were the CSES items distributed over different panels of the study? Were the CSES items distributed over different modes? Finally, we consider how consistently a particular CSES item (Q5 in the micro questionnaire, shown below) was administered.

Q5. *Some people say that political parties are necessary to make our political system work in [country]. Using the scale on this card (where ONE means that political parties are necessary to make our political system work, and FIVE means that political parties are not needed in [country]), where would you place yourself?*

In 24 of the 34 studies for which such information is available, the CSES module was administered as an uninterrupted block of questions.

In several cases, however, the CSES items were distributed over different waves of the study, and in a few instances, these panels relied on different modes of data collection. In nearly half of the election studies in which the module was administered as an uninterrupted block, it was carried at the beginning of the postelection wave of the study. In the remaining studies, the module was often embedded in the middle of the larger survey, and in four studies, the module was included at the end of a larger battery of survey items. As Table 3.3 reports, the test question, Q5, seemed to be administered fairly consistently across the studies. Q5 was preceded by CSES item Q4 in the countries for which this information is available. However, there are several cases in which CSES item Q6 did not follow Q5. Furthermore, in a few instances the back-translations of the election study surveys indicate differences in question wording for Q5.

Population to be Sampled, Sampling Procedures, and Sample Size

CSES Standard:

- *National samples should be drawn from all age-eligible citizens. When non-citizens (or other non-eligible respondents) are included in the sample, a variable should be provided to permit the identification of those non-eligible respondents. When a collaborator samples from those persons who appear on voter registration lists, he should quantify the estimated degree of discrepancy between this population and the population of all age-eligible citizens.*

- *We strongly encourage the use of random samples, with random sampling procedures used at all stages of the sampling process. Collaborators should provide detailed documentation of their sampling practices . . .*

- *We strongly recommend that no fewer than 1,000 age-eligible respondents be interviewed.*

Perhaps the greatest design variation introduced into the CSES project is derived from the characteristics of the samples themselves. Survey errors are often conveniently categorized into two groupings: sampling error and non-sampling error. Sound, research-based sampling methods are of utmost importance in reducing measurement error in the data collected. Because of the variation of methods in use by CSES studies, the authors suspect that sampling variation may end up making a greater overall contribution to measurement error than error of nearly any other sort. This, of course, would be an extremely valuable topic to investigate, both out of academic interest, and also as information for the CSES user community.

A properly implemented sample design, with an appropriate sample size and correction for selection biases, is an excellent framework for querying and understanding the political opinions and needs of the public. However, it is relevant that while participation in a survey does not consume many respondent resources, implementing a proper survey requires a large outlay of resources on the investigator's part (Verba 1995*a*). Several CSES Design Reports hint at resource constraints when collaborators decide how to create and pursue their sample. We mention this not out of concern that such data are in use, but to motivate further research into the differences in survey and sample design so that the CSES user community can be well informed about the implications of these differences for their own analyses.

The core of any sound sampling technique is to undertake a physical process of some sort that assigns the desired probabilities to potential respondents (Kish 1965). There are many sampling techniques that are adequate for accomplishing this goal as long as assumptions are known and accounted for through weighting or other corrections. It is essential to remember, however, that the implementation of a sample design can just be as important, or perhaps even more so, in obtaining quality data (Traugott 1987). While the exhaustiveness with which collaborators document their sampling techniques varies, the CSES showed good foresight in devoting an entire section of the Design Report to the topic. The section asks for information that details demographic characteristics of both the sample and the population being studied. With the information provided, we can make some strides in identifying differences in sampling techniques and perhaps even begin to roughly estimate sampling error across the many studies. It is unfortunate, however, that the sampling section of the Design Report is rarely filled out to completion. In the long term, CSES would benefit from recontacting collaborators to obtain sampling information that is currently absent, and continuing to stress to collaborators the importance of filling out the report in its entirety.

A variety of sampling methods and variants thereof were applied by the CSES component studies such that there are too many to list here, though we will mention a few. A number of the CSES studies are panels—longitudinal surveys with a sampling frame that is maintained and supplemented as necessary with additional, new cases that refresh depleted portions of the panel (due to attrition and other reasons) and preserve the representative status of the sample. Other studies draw on altogether new samples. There are advantages to each in different situations (Kish 1965). The sampling frames can be drawn and improved using a variety of advanced statistical and probabilistic techniques.

The way in which the Design Report collects sampling data does not, in our view, adequately gather information about panel respondents that appeared in data collections preceding the current one. For example, the sample for the United States election study of 1996 included a set of panel respondents that had been interviewed previously in both 1992 and 1994. While the Design Report gathers information concerning attrition within the current year's election study, it does not well gather attrition information for panel respondents carried forward from past studies.

Another sampling option, used most commonly in telephone operations, is random-digit dialing (RDD). In countries where large portions of the population have telephones, as in the United States where better than 90 percent of the population have phones, RDD is a feasible option (Schumann and Kalton 1985). Yet it should be weighed that persons without telephones are thus altogether excluded from the sample frame, and can potentially have fairly different characteristics than those with phones. In countries where the amount of households with phones is low, this effect is exacerbated. Other issues concerning phone samples are the inclusion or exclusion of unlisted numbers, inclusion or exclusion of cellular numbers, sampling households that have only cell phones and no land lines, phone number mobility, and overrepresenting households that have more than one telephone line.

Another source of sample frames is electoral registers and postal address files. Survey research in Great Britain (as is the case in its contribution to CSES) often creates its sample from one of these two data sources. While each method can be more appropriate in different situations, at least some research shows preference for postal address files, asserting that they are cheaper to implement and more easily stratified (Lynn and Taylor 1995). Voting registries sometimes have an additional disadvantage in that they do not capture those persons who are eligible to vote by age, but are not registered to do so.

For CSES, there are three sampling issues particularly worthy of mention as they are being treated with some variation across participant countries. One is the definition of a non-sample line; there is some inconsistency in how non-sample lines are identified, if at all, across studies. A second issue is the use of replacement and quota techniques, and the effects thereof. The third issue is that a handful of data sets have a somewhat high estimate of "eligible population excluded," as shown in Table 3.4. At least two studies state that 15 percent or more of the population is excluded from their sample. In regards to using random sampling methods, those who completed Design Reports generally self-identified their use of random methods of some sort, though it would be useful to identify differences in application of those methods.

Additionally, as can be seen in Table 3.4, each study (with one exception) was able to obtain interviews with 1,000 or more respondents. Using the information on population, sampling procedures, and realized sample size, we attempt to calculate a response rate for each election study (Table 3.4). This proved to be more difficult than we first thought. First, there was significant item nonresponse to the numbers requested, in particular to the numbers for nonresponse and non-sample. Techniques for addressing non-sample were also inconsistent. For example, Slovenia seemed to be the only election study using replacement to explicitly factor it out of its response rate calculation, while others considered there to be no non-sample due to replacement (leading to higher response rates). Another suggestion we have for the Design Report is to provide clarification where it instructs in the response rate section to provide numbers "to first wave if a panel study." In at least one instance a collaborator misinterpreted this as a reason to skip the section altogether, presumably because they did not conduct a panel study. Others interpreted this instruction as being the first wave within the current election study, when in fact some or their entire sample had participated in a prior election study. It would be a useful exercise to review skip patterns across the entire Design Report, to identify items that can be misinterpreted, but also to better clarify which sections apply to which scenarios. For instance, many sections of the report were applicable for some modes of interview but not others, and the applicability was not often clearly stated. This led to some confusion in the Design Reports submitted. Some sections were probably especially confusing to answer for surveys that were mixed mode.

Overall, while the numbers are not necessarily arrived at comparably across election studies, the average response rate where we can calculate it is over 60 percent for the group. It is important to understand response rates for their impact on data quality, though high (or low) response rates do not necessarily indicate low (or high) nonresponse error (Keeter et al. 2000). As a practical matter, it is also important to know

Table 3.4. Response rates by election study

Election study	Eligible population excluded (estimate) (%)	First wave of election study				Panel attrition		Actual CSES records (from data)
		Sample lines issued [a]	Non-sample [b]	Completed interviews [c]	Calculated response rate [c/(a − b)] (%)	Panel attrition [d] (%)	Calculated CSES records [c^a(1 + d)]	
Australia (1996)	0	3,000	95	1,798	61.9	0.0	1,798	1,798
Belarus (2001)	0	—	—	—	—	—	1,000	1,000
Belgium-Flanders (1999)	<1	3,418	—	2,179	63.8	0.0	2,179	2,179
Belgium-Walloon (1999)	<1	—	—	—	—	—	1,960	1,960
Canada (1997)	—	8,748	1,071	3,949	51.4	−53.1	1,851	1,851
Chile (1999)	30	—	—	—	—	—	1,173	1,173
The Czech Republic (1996)	1–2	3,038	—	1,589	52.3	−22.7	1,229	1,229
Denmark (1998)	—	3,644	194	2,001	54.9	0.0	2,001	2,001
Germany (1998)	—	6,000	2,066	2,019	51.3	0.0	2,019	2,019
Great Britain (1997)	—	6,540	726	3,615	62.2	−14.7	3,084	2,897[a]
Hong Kong (1998)	0	2,800	999	1,000	55.5	0.0	1,000	1,000
Hong Kong (2000)	0	2,500	999	674	44.9	0.0	674	674
Hungary (1998)	2–4	3,892	57	2,400	62.6	−36.5	1,525	1,525
Iceland (1999)	—	—	—	—	—	—	1,631	1,631
Israel (1996)	15	3,895	—	1,091	28.0	0.0	1,091	1,091
Japan (1996)	—	—	—	1,535	—	−13.6	1,327	1,327
Korea (2000)	—	—	—	—	—	—	1,100	1,100
Lithuania (1997)	—	2,152	—	1,009	46.9	0.0	1,009	1,009
Mexico (1997)	—	2,230	—	2,033	91.2	0.0	2,033	2,033
Mexico (2000)	—	2,615	—	1,766	67.5	0.0	1,766	1,766
The Netherlands (1998)	1	4,207	0	2,101	49.9	0.0	2,101	2,101
New Zealand (1996)	8.47	7,403	356	4,080	57.9	0.0	4,080	4,080
Norway (1997)	—	2,958	—	2,055	69.5	0.0	2,055	2,055

Peru (2000)	7	3,560	—	1,102	31.0	0.0	1,102	1,102
Peru (2001)	—	5,797	1,533	1,118	26.2	0.0	1,118	1,118
Poland (1997)	0	2,800	160	2,003	75.9	0.0	2,003	2,003
Portugal (2002)	4.6	1,600	—	1,303	81.4	0.0	1,303	1,303
Romania (1996)	3	1,496	0	1,175	78.5	0.0	1,175	1,175
Russia (1999)	4.4	3,074	52	1,919	63.5	-4.0	1,842	1,842
Russia (2000)	4.4	3,074	52	1,919	63.5	-8.9	1,748	1,748
Slovenia (1996)	5	2,100	—	1,529	72.8	0.0	1,529	2,031[b]
Spain (1996)	<1	1,321	21	1,212	93.2	0.0	1,212	1,212
Spain (2000)	—	1,274	—	1,208	94.8	0.0	1,208	1,208
Sweden (1998)	—	—	—	—	—	—	1,157	1,157
Switzerland (1999)	2-3	8,870	2,558	3,257	51.6	0.0	3,257	2,048[c]
Taiwan (1996)	2	—	—	1,200	—	0.0	1,200	1,200
Thailand (2001)	—	—	—	—	—	0.0	1,081	1,081
Ukraine (1998)	—	—	—	—	—	—	1,148	1,148
United States (1996)	—	2,605	198	1,714	71.2	-10.5	1,534	1,534
Total								62,409

[a] The final data file for Great Britain is reduced to contain only verified electors. Additionally, after processing, the final Great Britain file contained less cases than the interim file their Design Report was based on.

[b] The Slovenia response rate numbers are based on a basic sample, without replacement units. The final Slovenia data file contains more records because it includes replacement cases. Slovenia altogether removed oversampled records before depositing its data file, resulting in less records.

[c] Switzerland

Source: CSES Module 1 election study documentation and materials.

response rates so that analysts can confidently report them to journals that require such information prior to publishing works using a particular data set.

Weights present in the CSES data file are those that were provided by collaborators with their data deposits, generally in the categories of sample, demographic, and political weights. The CSES staff then created additional derivative weights from the deposited ones. The first derivative weight centers the weight for each polity weight around the value "1" so that the average respondent within a polity has a weight of 1. The second derivative weight makes a sample size adjustment such that each election study component contributes equally to the analysis, regardless of the original sample size.

Collaborators submitted weight variables that correct for a number of different factors, as shown in Table 3.5. While 54 percent of election studies provided one or more weight variables, less than a third of them correct for each of three major sources of sampling error listed (disproportionate probability of selection, matching population demographics, and nonresponse). There are rare instances in election study reports where text seems to indicate that a weight is necessary or available, but no weight was provided with the data deposit. Without a weight in these instances, it is questionable whether inferences can be drawn about the nation as a whole. Thus, it should probably be a future priority of the project to engage in discussions with collaborators who do not provide correction weights with their data deposits. There is also inconsistency to be addressed in cross-national comparisons where one country corrects its data in one way and another does not. Perhaps the CSES should consider recommendations for weighting procedures that not only are comparable corrections provided by each election study, so that the weights could be

Table 3.5. Weights and corrections

Answer	Is a weight present?		Corrects for disproportionate probability of selection?		Weighted to match demographics?		Corrects for nonresponse?	
	n	%	n	%	n	%	n	%
Yes	21	54	8	21	12	31	7	18
No	18	46	10	26	6	15	11	28
Missing	0	0	21	54	21	54	21	54
Total	39	100	39	100	39	100	39	100

Source: CSES Module 1 election study documentation and materials.

more consistently presented. This may also have the side advantage of making the process of weighting the merged data set a simpler and more comprehensible one for analysts. Analysts could become comfortable in using the weights without having to deduce the methods used in producing a particular weight, because they would know that it is consistently prepared appropriate to the standard guidelines of the study.

Interviewer Training

CSES Standard: *"Collaborators should pretest their survey instrument and should train interviewers in the administration of the questionnaire. The Planning Committee will provide each collaborator with documentation that clarifies the purposes and objectives of each item and with rules with respect to probing don't-know responses."*

In his book *Survey Research Methods*, Floyd Fowler (1984: 115) clearly and concisely states that at minimum interviewer training should focus on the specifics of a study and also cover these five more general areas of information:

1. Procedures for contacting respondents and introducing the study.
2. The conventions that are used in the design of the questionnaire with respect to wording and skip pattern instructions so that interviewers can ask the questions in a consistent and standardized way.
3. Procedures for probing inadequate answers in a nondirective way.
4. Procedures for recording answers to open-ended and closed questions.
5. Rules and guidelines for handling the interpersonal aspects of the interview in a non-biasing way.

By casual observation, it seems that the "interviewer training" fields in the CSES Design Report are well populated relative to other sections of the questionnaire. It would be a reasonably easy task to assess this information using Fowler's five rules of interviewer training as a standard, in order to quantitatively evaluate interviewer training overall, with the results used to provide feedback to individual collaborators on interviewer training, perhaps even offering some sort of assistance or access to materials.

While there is much information available from the collaborators concerning their interviewer training, the issue of whether each study is adequately pretesting its instruments is not well addressed. It may be the case that pretesting is not often occurring, perhaps due to budgetary or time constraints. The CSES community would benefit, however, from more detailed evaluation of how the items included in the modules are being perceived in the field.

Field Practices

CSES Standard:

> Collaborators should make every effort to ensure a high response rate. Investigators should be diligent in their effort to reach respondents not interviewed on the initial contact with the household and should be diligent in their effort to convert respondents who initially refuse to participate in the study. Data on the number of contact attempts, the number of contacts with sample persons, and special persuasion or conversion efforts under-taken should be coded for each respondent.

It is useful to make a distinction between unit nonresponse (refusal to be interviewed altogether) and item nonresponse (refusing to answer a particular question or series of questions). While both are important, unit nonresponse is more an issue of questionnaire design and interviewer training, and so here we focus on unit nonresponse.

Incentives to respondents appear to be helpful in reducing unit nonresponse (Tanur 1983–4). Incentives benefit response rates for both face-to-face and telephone interviews, at no apparent expense to the quality of the resultant survey data (Singer, Groves, and Corning 1999). Incentive data is well captured in the CSES Design Report, though we suggest improvements in three areas. The first is that the Design Report asks about incentives "prior to study/pre-study" when in fact many incentives are provided during or after a study and may be excluded due to the wording. The second is that when the report asks about respondent payments, it might better differentiate between incentives paid upon completion, or upon first contact (before completion). Third, the incentive strategies asked about are respondent-centered; while there is an "other" category, it would be useful to ask about incentive structures that are not specific to the respondent—incentive pay given to interviewers per completion, and so on (Table 3.6).

When asked if during the field period, interviewers varied the time of day that they called, 17 answered "yes," with three "no" answers, and 19 missing. Refusal conversion is an important strategy in survey implementation. High refusal rates reduce reliability of results due to

Table 3.6. Incentive strategies

Did study use listed strategies?	Sent letter		Sent pay		Sent token gift		Other action	
	n	%	n	%	n	%	n	%
Yes	12	31	1	3	3	8	3	8
No	19	49	30	77	28	72	28	72
Missing	8	21	8	21	8	21	8	21
Total	39	100	39	100	39	100	39	100

Source: CSES Module 1 election study documentation and materials.

missing data, and contribute to bias when the characteristics of those refusing are unique in the population (Martin 1983). To demonstrate, it has been asserted that in face-to-face and telephone surveys, those who refuse political science and public opinion surveys tend to be less educated, and those who refuse economic surveys tend to have high incomes (Fowler 1984). As shown in Table 3.7, less than half of the election studies indicated that they pursued refusal conversion. However, it seemed to us that even some of these may not qualify as formal refusal conversion, as may have been the intent of the question. For example, some studies answered that "yes" they employ refusal conversion, but then answered "no" to all of the refusal conversion techniques that followed (including "other"). Providing clarification as to the CSES definition of refusal conversion may be in order. In some cases any attempt at persuasion by the initial interviewer—in other words, the respondent attempting to refuse the interview and the original interviewer persuading them to continue—seemed to be identified as a refusal conversion attempt. Others held the stricter definition of refusal conversion being where the respondent

Table 3.7. Refusal conversion strategies

Did study use listed strategies?	Made refusal conversion effort		Sent letter		Sent pay		Referred to more experienced interviewer	
	n	%	n	%	n	%	n	%
Yes	18	46	5	13	0	0	10	26
No	11	28	16	41	22	56	10	26
Missing	10	26	18	46	17	44	19	49
Total	39	100	39	100	39	100	39	100

Source: CSES Module 1 election study documentation and materials.

refused the initial interviewer, and further action was undertaken outside of the original interviewer's attempts at persuasion. Also of interest is that in some election studies, interviewers were specifically instructed to accept a refusal without any persuasion at all, which might be useful to capture as part of the Design Report. Further, earlier versions of the Design Report skipped over the refusal conversion section for those that answered "no" to the first question. This skip was removed in later versions, which we find to be a beneficial change. In some instances after the change, collaborators answered "no" to refusal conversion (perhaps because persuasion was disallowed by the original interviewer) but then indicated new contact attempts for refusal cases. The latter information would have been lost had the skip patterns of the original Design Report been strictly followed. This, in combination with errors resulting from skip patterns elsewhere in the instrument, leads us to believe that the use of skip patterns within the Design Report should be minimized. Skip patterns in respondent interviews are helpful in reducing overall interview length. However, skip patterns in the Design Report do not seem to reduce the completion time enough to justify the potential for error that is induced by their presence.

Of the 18 studies that attempted refusal conversion, 10 indicated passing the case on to a more experienced interviewer, five indicated sending follow-up letters, and none offered additional payment to persuade the individual to change their mind. Of course, the amount of missing data in these questions (nearly 50 percent) makes it difficult to understand the overall distribution for the group. One could improperly guess that the missing data is more likely to be election studies that did not conduct refusal conversion, when in fact it is probably just as likely that the missing data was from those who did not have the time available to fill out the Design Report either completely, or at all.

Strategies for Translation (and back-translation)

CSES Standard:

> Each collaborator should translate the questionnaire module into his or her native language(s). To ensure the equivalence of the translation, collaborators shall perform an independent re-translation of the questionnaire back into English. Collaborators engaged in translation of the questionnaire module into the same language (e.g. Spanish, French, English, German, and Portuguese) should collaborate on the translation.

In the 39 election studies included in the CSES Module 1 data release, there were 27 or more unique languages into which the module was translated, excluding variations of English. In some cases, a single election study required producing multiple translations other than English—Israel (Arabic, Hebrew, Russian), Lithuania (Lithuanian, Russian), Switzerland (German, French, Italian), Taiwan (Chinese Hakka, Chinese Mandarin, Taiwanese), and Ukraine (Russian, Ukrainian). Further, if in the case of the same language translations being required in multiple election studies—notably Dutch, French, German, Russian, and Spanish—investigators chose not to collaborate on the translation, there could be a total of as many as 38 translations that produced the data for the current release. It would be a worthwhile exercise to compare questionnaires by language across multiple studies and to evaluate the consistency of the instrument used.

For the most part, collaborators have been quite good about providing CSES with their native-language version(s) of the questionnaire. Of issue, however, is the retranslation of these questionnaires back into English. To do so provides valuable feedback on the correctness of the translation, and is an indicator of comparability in question wording.

As is extensively detailed in survey methodology literature, and as discussed previously, maintaining question wording is crucial to comparability and the reduction of measurement error. With factual questions small changes in definition can produce substantially different responses, and with opinion-based questions, subtle changes, even those that are nearly imperceptible, can make for markedly different results (Kalton and Schumann 1982). To facilitate research on this subject and accuracy in translation, the CSES community might consider investing further resources in providing accurate and detailed translations of the survey instruments used in the field.

Preparing Users to Consider Methodological Issues in Their Analyses

At this juncture, we have discussed a variety of methodological and design topics relevant to the collection of CSES micro-level data. The use of comparison as a basis for inference is the foundation of CSES, and for this reason it is to the benefit of both the study and its user community to reduce measurement error wherever possible. The first and best way to do so is through concerted attention to the implementation of proven survey methodologies, accompanied by a thorough documentation of individual election study designs. Reducing design effects, or at least accounting for them, may increase the chance of finding an interesting result, and may also reduce the chance of being misled by an incorrect one. The CSES is a unique and powerful data set, capable of addressing many important questions that no other current data set can, and deserves our continued attention to these issues.

With the goal in mind of generally making CSES users more aware of the methodological and design issues that are useful to consider in their analyses, a number of initiatives are suggested or already underway, including:

- verifying that all election study documentation submissions are indeed available for download via the CSES web site;
- continuously improving the CSES Sample Design and Data Collection Report in order to better capture the information most salient to analysis;
- assertively recontacting collaborators in order to fill gaps in knowledge concerning individual surveys, and to obtain documents or information that is missing from the study's country archive;
- creating cross-national summary tables containing comparisons of study methods;
- archiving and distributing collaborator contributions that are not directly related to CSES, but may be helpful to its user community;
- considering an expansion of the documentation for recommended survey methods, definitions, and instructions that are provided to collaborators;
- actively soliciting feedback on improvements to the CSES data file and documentation; and,
- encouraging researchers to conduct and share methodological and design effects research, perhaps via the CSES web site, so that analysts can consider the issues in their own analyses.

Conclusion

The unique, collaborative study design of the Comparative Study of Electoral Systems presents many interesting opportunities for methodological and design effects research. A rich set of information is already available to methods researchers through the CSES Sample Design and Data Collection reports completed by collaborators and provided on the CSES web page. Questions from the report can be used to examine effects due to variation in: mode of interview, proximity in time between surveys and the elections they cover, placement of the module in each study's questionnaire, question ordering, sampling, response rates, weighting, interviewer training, field practices, translation, and question wording. Our efforts here are intended to stimulate interest in these issues as they pertain to the CSES. As important as conducting such research is, it is perhaps of even more importance to distribute the results to CSES users in such a way that they may account for the issues in their own analyses. The CSES user community will undoubtedly pursue initiatives to further this goal.

Appendix 3.1

CSES Module 1:
Sample Design and Data Collection Report

Country (date of election):

Type of election (e.g. presidential; parliamentary; legislative):_____

Organization that conducted the survey field work:_____

Investigators responsible for data collection

Name: ....   Name: ....

Affiliation: ....   Affiliation: ....

....

Address: ....   Address: ....

....

....

....

....

Fax: ....   Fax: ....

Phone: ....   Phone: ....

E-mail: ....   E-mail: ....

Name: ....   Name: ....

Affiliation: ....   Affiliation: ....

....

Address: ....   Address: ....

....

....

....

....

Fax: ....   Fax: ....

Phone: ....   Phone: ....

E-mail: ....   E-mail: ....

Languages used in interviews: (Please provide copies of all survey instruments, and translation for those that were not conducted in English).

....

....

A. Study Design

☐   Post-election study
☐   Pre-/Post-election panel Study
Date post-election interviewing began:..
Date post-election interviewing ended:..

If Panel Study:
Date pre-election interviewing began:..
Date pre-election interviewing ended:..

Mode of (post-election) interview:
    ☐ In person, face-to-face
    ☐ Telephone
    ☐ Mail or self-completion supplement

B. Sample Design and Sampling Procedures

1. Eligibility requirements

    a) Age: Minimum............ Maximum............

    b) Citizenship: Yes ☐ No ☐

    c) Other requirements:

2. Sample frame:

    a) Were any regions of the country excluded from the sample frame?
    No ☐ Yes ☐:..
    ....
    ....

    b) Were institutionalized persons excluded from the sample?
    No ☐ Yes ☐:..
    ....
    ....

    c) Were military personnel excluded from the sample?
    No ☐ Yes ☐:..
    ....
    ....

    d) If interviews were conducted by telephone:
    What is the estimated percentage of households without a phone: ___%

    Were unlisted telephone numbers included in the population sampled?
    No ☐ Yes ☐

    Were substitution methods used for unproductive sample points? No ☐ Yes ☐:..
    ....
    ....

    e) Were other persons excluded from the sample frame: No ☐ Yes ☐:.........................
....
....

    f) Estimated total (a + b + c + d + e) percentage of the eligible population excluded from the sample frame: ___ %

3. Sample selection procedures:

    a) What were the primary sampling units? Were the primary sampling units randomly selected? No ☐ Yes ☐ (please describe):
....
....
....

    b) Were there further stages of selection? No ☐ Yes ☐ (please describe):
....
....
....

    c) How were individual respondents identified?
....
....
....

    e) Under what circumstances was a sample line designated non- sample?
    (Check all that apply)
        ☐ Non-residential sample point
        ☐ All members of household are ineligible
        ☐ Housing unit is vacant
        ☐ No answer at housing unit after .... callbacks
        ☐ Other, explain:...
        ....

    f) Were non-sample replacement methods used? No ☐ Yes ☐ (please describe):
....
....
....

For surveys conducted by telephone:
Was the sample a random digit dial sample? Yes ☐ No ☐
Was the sample a listed sample? Yes ☐ No ☐
Was the sample a dual frame? No ☐ Yes ☐ with ..... % list frame and ...... % RDD

For surveys conducted by mail:
Was the sample a listed sample? Yes ☐ No ☐ (please describe):...
....
....

4. Compliance

    a) Prior to the study was:

        a letter sent to respondent? No ☐ Yes ☐ (please include with deposit)

        payment sent to respondent? No ☐ Yes ☐, in the amount of:....................................

        a token gift sent to respondent? No ☐ Yes ☐ (please describe):

        ....

        ....

        ....

        any other incentives used? No ☐ Yes ☐ (please describe):

        ....

        ....

        ....

    b) During the field period

        How many contacts were made with the household before declaring it non-sample?..

        How many contacts were made with the household before declaring it non-interview?..

        Maximum number of days over which a household was contacted:........................

        Did interviewers vary the time of day at which they re-contacted the household? No ☐ Yes ☐ (please describe):..

    c) Refusal conversion

        Was an effort made to persuade respondents who were reluctant to be interviewed? No ☐ Yes ☐ (please describe):..

        ....

        ....

        Were respondents who were reluctant to be interviewed sent a letter persuading them to take part? No ☐ Yes ☐ (please describe/include with deposit):

        ....

        ....

        Was payment offered to respondents who were reluctant to take part? No ☐ Yes ☐, in the amount of:..

        Were respondents who were reluctant to take part turned over to a more experienced interviewer? Yes ☐ No ☐

        What was the maximum number of re-contacts used to persuade respondent to be interviewed?..

        ....

        Were any other methods used to persuade respondents reluctant to be interviewed to take part? No ☐ Yes ☐ (please describe):..

        ....

        ....

5. Response rate (to first wave if a panel study)

    Total number of sample lines issued: ....

        Number of refusals: ....

        Number never contacted (no-contact): ....

        Other non-response: ....

        Number of lines of non-sample: ....

    Total number of completed interviews: ....

    Response rate: ....

Panel attrition (NOTE: Complete only if CSES questionnaire is administered as part of a 2-wave panel study):

Total number of respondents in Wave I of the study: ....

Number of Wave I respondents re-interviewed
in wave containing CSES Module: ....

Percent total panel attrition: ....

Panel attrition by age and education: (% re-interviewed):

18–25	.... %	None	.... %
26–40	.... %	Incomplete primary	.... %
41–65	.... %	Primary completed	.... %
65 & over	.... %	Incomplete secondary	.... %
		Secondary completed	.... %
		University incomplete	.... %
		University degree	.... %

6. Sample weights

    a) Are weights included in the data-file? No ☐ Yes ☐ (please describe their construction): ....

    ....

    ....

    ....

    ....

    ....

    b) Are the weights designed to compensate for disproportionate probability of selection at the person or household level? No ☐ Yes ☐ (please describe):

    ....

    ....

    ....

    c) Are the weights designed to match known demographic characteristics of the population? No ☐ Yes ☐ (please describe): ....

    ....

    ....

    d) Are the data weighted to correct for non-response? No ☐ Yes ☐ (please describe):

    ....

    ....

7. a) Please describe the interviewers (age, level of education, and years of experience):

    ....

    ....

    ....

    ....

    ....

    b) Description of interviewer training:

    ....

    ....

    ....

    ....

    ....

XIV. Comparison of sample to population

Characteristic	Population Estimates	Sample Estimates	
		Unweighted	Weighted
Age			
18–25			
26–40			
41–66			
65 and over			
Education			
None			
Incomplete Primary			
Primary Completed			
Incomplete Secondary			
Secondary Completed			
Post-Secondary Trade/Vocational			
Incomplete University			
University Degree			
Gender			
Male			
Female			

Part III

Electoral Participation

4

Socioeconomic Status and Nonvoting: A Cross-National Comparative Analysis

Neil Nevitte, André Blais, Elisabeth Gidengil, and Richard Nadeau

Introduction

Most empirical research on electoral behavior is based on voting (or nonvoting) patterns in a single country, often in a single election. This chapter draws on the CSES data set to examine the extent to which socioeconomic status (SES) factors explain nonvoting in 23 countries (and 33 elections).[1] The 23 countries included in the analysis are: Canada, the Czech Republic, Denmark, Germany, Hong Kong, Hungary, Japan, Israel, Korea, Mexico, the Netherlands, New Zealand, Norway, Poland, Romania, Russia, Slovenia, Spain, Switzerland, Taiwan, Ukraine, the United Kingdom, and the United States.[2] The investigation proceeds in three stages. The first stage uses CSES individual-level data to probe variations in the extent to which SES factors do, or do not, increase nonvoting. The second stage introduces contextual factors as controls, and explores whether and to what extent key SES variables remain significant predictors after a variety of macroeconomic and institutional variables are taken into account. The third stage examines whether the contextual factors affect the relationship between SES factors and nonvoting.

Socioeconomic Status and Nonvoting

Nonvoting is an individual, micro-level phenomenon (Lane and Ersson 1990). Citizens make a conscious decision to vote or abstain. Fortunately, most people vote. Even in countries with high proportions of nonvoters, the majority of citizens vote in national elections. The exceptional behavior examined here is *nonvoting*. To explain nonvoting it is sensible to begin with the individual characteristics of nonvoters. Electoral rules and institutional arrangements undoubtedly do have some effect on levels of turnout. But if "turnout" could be wholly explained by such structural factors, then there would be no discernible patterns in the individual-level characteristics of nonvoters. The weight of evidence is however, that nonvoters are concentrated in particular pockets of society.

Individual-level explanations of electoral behavior typically emphasize the role of motivational factors, resources, and organizational mobilization in predicting nonvoting (Dalton 1996; Franklin 1996; Oppenhuis 1995; Verba, Schlozman, and Brady 1995). Verba, Schlozman, and Brady (1995) succinctly capture the three core individual-level explanations for nonvoting. They argue that people do not participate because: (1) they do not want to, (2) because they cannot, or (3) because nobody asked them to participate.

The first individual-level explanation, the idea that *people do not participate because they do not want to,* places the emphasis on the role of attitudes toward politics, and particularly the role of psychological engagement, in predicting participation. Individuals who do not participate are those who have little interest in politics, because they believe that the action will not make a difference, or simply they believe that participating is not important.

The second general explanation, namely that *people do not participate because they cannot,* places the emphasis on the extent resources play a role in the distribution of political participation. Involvement in politics requires resources—time to take part in activities, money to contribute, and skills to be effectively engaged in various channels of participation (Verba, Nie, and Kim 1978). The uneven distribution of resources within populations means that participation is more difficult for some people than for others (Oppenhuis 1995).

Finally, participation is not solely an individual phenomenon. The notion that *people do not participate because nobody asked them* places the emphasis on the idea that people are mobilized to participate in politics. The social networks of people play an important role in creating incentives for people to participate. Contact with political parties (Wielhouwer and Lockerbie 1994), involvement within groups (Leighley 1990; Pollock 1982; Rogers, Barb, and Bultena 1975), attending church, or even being employed, provide people with a social network in which they can be asked to participate. The CSES data contain a set of items that allows us to explore systematically these three individual-level explanations of participation.

The Impact of Age

A substantial body of research indicates that there is a robust correlation between age with electoral turnout[3]: voting generally increases with age (Crewe 1981; Dalton 1996; Franklin 1996; Powell 1986; Topf 1995).[4] The prevailing explanation for the relationship between age and voting is that psychological engagement increases with age. As one begins to pay taxes, or becomes a parent or homeowner, the effects of government policy become apparent, and so politics becomes a more central concern (Dalton 1996; Oppenhuis 1995). The evidence is that age is a significant predictor of nonvoting and appears to be related to the motivations, or the desire, to vote. Older people vote more because they want to, and because they are more motivated to do so (Wolfinger and Rosenstone 1980).

H_A: A1 *Nonvoting is negatively associated with age, after other SES factors are taken into account.*

The Impact of Education

Education is also an important predictor of voting (Dalton 1996; Franklin 1996; Oppenhuis 1995; Teixiera 1992; Topf 1995; Verba 1995a). The impact of education on voting behavior is usually characterized in two ways. First, citizens with higher levels of formal education are more likely to have been socialized to embrace those civic norms that place a higher value on participation (Nie, Junn, and Stehlik-Barry 1996). Second, with higher levels of formal education, citizens gain cognitive skills and the accumulation of these skills has the effect of lowering the costs of, and lowering barriers to, participation (Blais 2000; Verba, Nie, and Kim 1978; Wolfinger and Rosenstone 1980).

H_A: A2 *Nonvoting is negatively associated with education, after other SES factors are taken into account.*

The Impact of Religious Involvement

Religious involvement is also associated with political participation. In the American setting, the frequency of attendance at religious services has frequently been shown to be a significant predictor of American voting behavior (especially Teixiera 1992; Verba 1995b; Verba, Schlozman, and Brady 1995; Wolfinger and Rosenstone 1980). Franklin (1996) also finds that frequent attendance of religious services decreases the likelihood of nonvoting in British, German, and French elections. Religious involvement is usually related to participation in three ways. First, there is evidence indicating that "frequent churchgoers have a stronger sense of voting duty" than those who do not (Oppenhuis 1995); people who attend church participate more because they feel it is important to do so. Second, religious involvement encourages the civic skills that make most forms of political participation easier (Miller and Wattenberg 1984; Verba 1995b; Verba, Schlozman, and Brady 1995); people who attend church participate more because they have more resources. And finally, churchgoers are a part of a network that mobilizes people to participate; church is a place where people are asked to participate in politics (Blais 2000; Verba, Schlozman, and Brady 1995).

In some countries, where parties identify with particular religious communities, deeply religious voters are encouraged to express their support for those parties, and under those circumstances levels of nonvoting among "politically represented" religious communities are lower.

H_A: A3 *Nonvoting is negatively associated with the frequency of attendance of religious services, after other SES factors are taken into account.*

The Impact of Income

With respect to household income, the consistent finding is that those with low levels of income, net other factors, are more likely than their wealthier counterparts to abstain from voting (Blais 2000; Kleppner 1982; Teixiera 1992; Wolfinger and Rosenstone 1980). Wolfinger and Rosenstone (1980) argue that voters who are insecure in their basic needs are less interested in politics; they have more pressing concerns. Consequently, they are less likely to vote than those in higher secure income brackets.[5] People with low income, in other words, have limited resources.

H_A: A4 *Nonvoting is negatively associated with household income, after other SES factors are taken into account.*

The Impact of Marital Status

There is some evidence indicating that marital status has an impact on voting behavior (Blais 2000; Teixiera 1992; Wolfinger and Rosenstone 1980). Single, divorced, or widowed individuals are less likely than married people to vote. In their case, the prevailing explanation is that married people are more settled than those who are not and they have stronger political attachments to their communities. With deeper community attachments, married people may feel a deeper obligation to vote (Blais 2000; Wolfinger and Rosenstone 1980).

H_A: A5 *Nonvoting is negatively associated with marriage, after other SES factors are taken into account.*

The Impact of Union Membership

Findings from cross-national research consistently indicate that union affiliation decreases the incidence of nonvoting (Dalton 1996; Franklin 1996). Although levels of unionization have declined somewhat in many advanced industrial states, the effect of union membership on individual-level participation is linked to mobilization in two ways: first, union members are encouraged to vote by their union organization, and second, union members may develop attachments to political parties that are affiliated with the union to which they belong (Dalton 1996).

H_A: A6 *Nonvoting is negatively associated with union affiliation, after other SES facilitating factors are controlled.*

The Impact of Gender

Gender is also a common predictor of voting behavior (Dalton 1996; Oppenhuis 1995; Powell 1986; Topf 1995; Wolfinger and Rosenstone 1980; Worcester 1983), and the typical finding is that women are less likely to vote than men. Some scholars argue, however, gender differences are largely attributable to age, education, and occupational composition differences of the two groups. When these are taken into account, gender differences in voting behavior disappear (Crewe 1981; Norris 1991; Wolfinger and Rosenstone 1980). Dalton's analysis (1996) presents evidence indicating that, women are somewhat less likely to vote than men. But, in some countries such as Denmark and the Netherlands, the reverse pattern appears to hold (van der Eijck and Oppenhuis 1990; Oppenhuis 1995).

H_A: A7 *Women are less likely to vote than men, after other SES facilitating factors are controlled.*

The Impact of Employment Status

Employment status has been conceptually linked to political participation, including voting behavior, in two different ways. Like marital status, being in the full-time paid workforce is sometimes taken to signify a measure of stability that is sufficient to encourage the development of political attitudes. Employment promotes the acquisition of attitudes that favor participation. Employment is also linked to learning politically relevant skills such as letter writing and attending meetings, skills that facilitate political participation (Verba 1995b). In short, people who are employed participate more because they want to and have more resources.

H_A: A8 *Nonvoting is negatively associated with being employed, after other SES facilitating factors are controlled.*

The Impact of Place of Residence

Voting behavior is also influenced by whether or not voters live in *rural or urban regions* (Oppenhuis 1995; Wolfinger and Rosenstone 1980). The effects of urban living appear to vary cross-nationally. American voters in rural areas, suburbs, or cities vote more frequently than do those in mid-sized towns (Verba and Nie 1972). European voters living in cities are, by contrast, less likely to vote than those in rural areas (Oppenhuis 1995).

H_A: A9 *Nonvoting is associated with region of residence, after other SES factors are taken into account.*

The Impact of Minority Community Status

Finally, our examination of the impact of socio-demographic factors includes consideration of whether the individuals are members of a minority community.[6] Members of minority communities, especially in countries where political parties represent certain ethnic identities, may be more likely to participate in electoral politics (Ackaert, Winter, and Swyngedouw 1996; del Castillo 1996).[7] One might suppose that where the barriers to the formation of political parties are comparatively low, for instance in some proportional representation (PR) systems, or in countries where minority communities are geographically concentrated, minority community status might encourage voting. On the other hand, where barriers to the formation of political parties are somewhat higher, minority communities feel excluded from the political process, and so are less likely to vote than members of the ethnic majority (Ackaert, Winter, and Swyngedouw 1996). There may also be differences in the socioeconomic resources of majority and minority language communities. There are thus a variety of reasons for expecting that minority status may influence nonvoting.

H_A: A10 *Nonvoting is negatively associated with minority community status, after other SES facilitating factors are controlled.*

Approach and Methods

These hypotheses are explored using directly comparable measures and standardized coding schemes. The key empirical research questions in the first stage of the analysis are: Which hypotheses consistently hold up in multiple national settings? And, which do not? Following standard practices the direct effects of these SES factors on nonvoting in each country are estimated using logistic regression, and we rely on the Cox and Snell coefficient of determination (R^2), rather than the Nagelkerke R^2, to compare how well SES accounts for the variance in nonvoting.[8]

Findings

The Relationship Between SES and Nonvoting

Table 4.1 reports the basic SES model for each country singly because we are interested in exploring the extent to which there are consistent cross-national patterns between SES and nonvoting. Following standard procedure, Table 4.1 reports the estimated effect of each SES factor on nonvoting (log-odds).

The primary finding is that there is evidence of common patterns. SES indicators are significantly related to nonvoting in almost every country regardless of substantial variations in economic performance and political and institutional arrangements. Yet there are significant cross-national differences in the extent to which SES explains the variance in nonvoting. On average, SES explains about 6 percent of the variance in nonvoting; these factors explain the most variance in the United States (17 percent), and the least in Chile (0.5 percent).

(1) Age has significant and consistent effects in about two-thirds of the elections included in this analysis (24 out of 32 elections)[9]: Belarus, Canada, the Czech Republic, Germany, Hungary, Japan, Lithuania, Mexico (1997 and 2000), the Netherlands, New Zealand, Norway, Poland, Russia (1999 and 2000), Slovenia, Spain (1996 and 2000), Sweden, Switzerland, Taiwan, Ukraine, the United Kingdom, and the United States. In all 24 significant cases, the likelihood of nonvoting decreases with age.

Table 4.1. Impact of socioeconomic variables on nonvoting in 33 elections

	Belarus[p]		Canada		Chile[p]		The Czech Republic		Denmark		Germany	
	B	S.E.	B	S.E.	B	S.E.	B	S.E.	B	S.E.	B	S.E.
Age	−0.57	0.15**	−0.66	0.10**	−0.02	0.11	−0.58	0.15**	−0.22	0.17	−0.49	0.14**
Education	−0.30	0.17	−0.38	0.10**	0.12	0.15	−0.37	0.13**	−0.02	0.16	−0.91	0.21**
Income	0.05	0.09	−0.23	0.06**	−0.12	0.08	−0.10	0.09	−0.18	0.14	−0.08	0.09
Marital status (married)	−0.54	0.22*	0.07	0.16	n.a.		−0.47	0.22*	−0.40	0.33	−0.78	0.24**
Church attendance	−0.02	0.19	n.a.		n.a.		−0.29	0.21	n.a.		−0.32	0.17
Place of residence												
Town	1.04	0.52*	n.a.		n.a.		0.39	0.29	0.20	0.37	0.38	0.37
Suburb	n.a.		n.a.		n.a.		0.92	0.31**	n.a.		0.41	0.29
City	0.35	0.28	−0.18	0.17	n.a.		0.49	0.41	0.10	0.39	0.54	0.33
Union	−0.13	0.24	0.08	0.16	n.a.		−0.64	0.25*	−0.48	1.11	−0.16	0.24
Gender (women)	−0.08	0.22	−0.19	0.15	−0.20	0.18	−0.13	0.22	0.10	0.26	0.16	0.21
Employment status												
Part time	0.45	0.47	0.08	0.31	n.a.		0.30	0.39	0.50	0.52	0.02	0.32
Full time	0.19	0.28	0.18	0.18	n.a.		0.08	0.25	0.09	0.33	−0.08	0.26
Religious denomination												
Specific to country											−2.50	0.43**,[1]
											−2.18	0.42**,[2]
											−2.24	0.45**,[3]
Linguistic minority												
Specific to country												
N	874		1,671		1,031		1,111		1,714		3,490	
Cox and Snell R²	6.4%		4.8%		0.5%		5.3%		0.8%		5.4%	

	Hong Kong (1998)		Hong Kong (2000)		Hungary		Israel		Japan		Korea	
	B	S.E.	B	S.E.	B	S.E.	B	S.E.	B	S.E.	B	S.E.
Age	-0.23	0.13	-0.32	0.19	-0.53	0.11**	-0.38	0.21	-0.79	0.14**	-0.15	0.11
Education	-0.39	0.15**	-0.29	0.19	-0.74	0.12**	-0.29	0.21	-0.14	0.14	-0.14	0.13
Income	-0.06	0.07	0.06	0.09	-0.10	0.06	-0.06	0.13	-0.24	0.07**	0.00	0.07
Marital status (married)	-0.44	0.22*	-0.13	0.28	-0.29	0.14*	-0.07	0.34	n.a.		n.a.	
Church attendance	-0.07	0.18	0.26	0.22	-0.36	0.11**	-0.31	0.22	n.a.		n.a.	
Place of residence												
Town	-0.29	0.53	0.85	1.34	-0.29	0.14*	-0.07	0.47	n.a.		-0.08	0.20
Suburb	-0.35	0.54	-1.67	1.27			n.a.		n.a.		-0.33	0.18
City	-0.23	0.52	-0.81	0.66	-0.30	0.24	0.94	0.51	n.a.		-0.89	0.33**
Union	-0.17	0.22	-0.35	0.33	-0.64	0.20**	0.06	0.32	-0.37	0.32	0.60	0.42
Gender (women)	0.03	0.18	0.01	0.24	-0.29	0.14*	0.41	0.35	-0.20	0.21	0.19	0.16
Employment status												
Part time	-0.22	0.30	0.02	0.42	0.44	0.25	0.13	0.41*	-0.09	0.37	-0.14	0.31
Full time	-0.12	0.21	0.12	0.28	0.19	0.19	-0.92	0.40	0.01	0.25	-0.01	0.17
Religious denomination Specific to country							2.82	0.96**,a				
Linguistic minority Specific to country												
N	763		380		2,788		1,226		1,874		1,100	
Cox and Snell R^2	2.7%		3.6%		11.2%		7.2%		5.5%		1.9%	

(cont.)

Table 4.1. (Continued)

	Lithuania[p]		Mexico (1997)		Mexico (2000)		The Netherlands		New Zealand		Norway	
	B	S.E.	B	S.E.	B	S.E.	B	S.E.	B	S.E.	B	S.E.
Age	-0.59	0.15**	-0.48	0.08**	-0.29	0.10**	-0.35	0.13**	-0.96	0.14**	-0.70	0.10**
Education	-0.21	0.15	-0.32	0.08**	-0.32	0.10**	-0.40	0.10**	-0.40	0.11**	-0.24	0.10*
Income	-0.01	0.10	-0.12	0.06*	0.06	0.06	-0.15	0.08	-0.07	0.08	-0.19	0.08*
Marital status (married)	-0.89	0.25**	-0.08	0.13	-0.33	0.15*	-0.26	0.21	-0.81	0.19**	-0.30	0.20
Church attendance	n.a.		-0.16	0.06*	-0.17	0.08*	-0.44	0.15**	-0.18	0.14	-0.15	0.09
Place of residence												
Town	-0.25	0.29	0.08	0.24	-0.20	0.22	0.05	0.32	0.18	0.31	-0.09	0.18
Suburb	n.a.		n.a.		n.a.		0.11	0.27	-0.31	0.31	-0.14	0.19
City	-0.30	0.29	-0.18	0.23	0.14	0.20	0.08	0.34	-0.19	0.28	-0.49	0.21*
Union	n.a.		0.18	0.20	-0.56	0.20**	-0.74	0.22**	-0.20	0.22	-0.27	0.14
Gender (women)	0.59	0.23*	-0.01	0.15	-0.16	0.16	-0.04	0.21	-0.10	0.19	0.39	0.15**
Employment status												
Part time	0.07	0.36	-0.22	0.30	-0.26	0.58	0.84	0.25**	-0.10	0.27	0.25	0.23
Full time	-0.22	0.29	-0.16	0.16	0.15	0.17	0.40	0.26	0.12	0.25	0.07	0.19
Religious denomination												
Specific to country			-0.43	0.19*,1	-0.56	0.23*,1	-1.05	0.37**,3	-0.85	0.32**,5		
							-0.93	0.41*,4	-1.03	0.37**,6		
Linguistic minority												
Specific to country												
N	902		3,444		3,975		1,633		7,346		1,934	
Cox and Snell R^2	5.2%		4.5%		3.8%		5.1%		3.5%		7.4%	

	Peru[p]		Poland		Romania		Russia (1999)		Russia[p] (2000)		Slovenia	
	B	S.E.	B	S.E.	B	S.E.	B	S.E.	B	S.E.	B	S.E.
Age	-0.11	0.17	-0.58	0.08**	-0.16	0.10	-0.61	0.11**	-0.77	0.12**	-0.44	0.13**
Education	0.25	0.13*	-0.69	0.09**	-0.34	0.12**	-0.44	0.10**	-0.36	0.12**	-0.36	0.13**
Income	0.00	0.23	-0.09	0.04*	-0.15	0.07*	-0.02	0.06	0.00	0.07	-0.11	0.07
Marital status (married)	n.a.		-0.36	0.11**	-0.33	0.16*	-0.41	0.15**	-0.67	0.18**	-0.50	0.21*
Church attendance			-0.79	0.10**	0.06	0.12	-0.30	0.12*	-0.07	0.15	0.02	0.15
Place of residence												
Town	0.03	0.47	-0.41	0.14**	0.42	0.25	-0.24	0.41	0.56	0.38	-0.16	0.22
Suburb	n.a.		-0.01	0.20	-0.07	0.24	0.29	0.20	0.11	0.23	-0.02	0.40
City	-0.59	0.42	-0.37	0.14*	0.17	0.20	0.62	0.18**	0.35	0.22	-0.11	0.23
Union			-0.30	0.15*	-0.36	0.20	-0.31	0.16	-0.09	0.20	-0.48	0.20*
Gender (women)	0.32	0.24	-0.42	0.11**	-0.18	0.15	-0.20	0.15	0.10	0.18	-0.11	0.17
Employment status												
Part time	-0.11	0.31*	0.00	0.18	0.24	0.28	0.16	0.28	0.35	0.29	0.20	0.33
Full time	-0.56	0.27	0.05	0.14	-0.34	0.20	0.17	0.19	-0.34	0.22	0.36	0.24
Religious denomination												
Specific to country							-0.75	0.34*,3			-0.88	0.31**,1
Linguistic minority												
Specific to country												
N	1,096		1,772		2,148		3,122		1,470		932	
Cox and Snell R²	1.0%		13.8%		6.2%		5.6%		5.3%		6.4%	

(cont.)

Table 4.1. (*Continued*)

	Spain (1996)		Spain (2000)		Sweden		Switzerland		Taiwan		Thailand[p]	
	B	S.E.	B	S.E.	B	S.E.	B	S.E.	B	S.E.	B	S.E.
Age	−0.67	0.19**	−0.61	0.16**	−0.46	0.18**	−0.64	0.08**	−0.53	0.21*	−0.02	0.10
Education	0.13	0.17	−0.12	0.13	−0.75	0.18**	−0.59	0.08**	−0.24	0.20	−0.19	0.11
Income	−0.04	0.11	−0.09	0.09	−0.10	0.10	−0.22	0.05**	0.13	0.10	−0.29	0.07**
Marital status (married)	0.27	0.28	−0.25	0.21	−0.74	0.23**	−0.30	0.12*	−0.74	0.29*	n.a.	
Church attendance	n.a.		n.a.		−0.53	0.20**	−0.48	0.11**	−0.26	0.22	n.a.	
Place of residence												
Town	0.84	0.30**	0.35	0.26	0.20	0.29	0.18	0.15	−0.67	0.41	n.a.	
Suburb	0.00	0.53	0.33	0.44			n.a.		−0.42	0.37	n.a.	
City	−0.05	0.36	0.35	0.24	−0.05	0.42	0.32	0.15*	−0.33	0.34	n.a.	
Union	0.20	0.38	−0.03	0.33	−0.47	0.25	−0.23	0.14	−0.46	0.28	n.a.	
Gender (women)	−0.13	0.28	−0.17	0.22	−0.22	0.23	−0.54	0.13**	−0.02	0.27	0.02	0.15
Employment status												
Part time	−0.17	0.35	0.04	0.30	0.42	0.31	0.19	0.17	−0.64	0.51	n.a.	
Full time	−0.17	0.35	0.35	0.25	0.15	0.31	0.38	0.15*	−0.12	0.33	n.a.	
Religious denomination												
Specific to country	−1.23	0.60*[1]	−2.72	0.53**[1]			0.41	0.14**[b]			−0.35	0.18*[7]
			−2.50	0.59**[3]								
Linguistic minority												
Specific to country											1.01	0.19**[c]
N	833		756		1,022		1,577		1,892		2,120	
Cox and Snell R^2	4.0%		9.8%		6.6%		16.2%		4.0%		3.9%	

	Ukraine		United Kingdom		United States	
	B	S.E.	B	S.E.	B	S.E.
Age	−0.58	0.12**	−0.61	0.08**	−0.67	0.10**
Education	−0.14	0.12	−0.15	0.07*	−0.82	0.10**
Income	−0.01	0.06	−0.13	0.05**	−0.20	0.06**
Marital status (married)	−0.12	0.17	−0.36	0.12**	−0.47	0.15**
Church attendance	−0.33	0.14*	−0.37	0.09**	−0.39	0.09**
Place of residence						
Town	0.67	0.23**		n.a.	−0.01	0.36
Suburb	n.a.			n.a.	−0.27	0.36
City	0.53	0.24*		n.a.	−0.43	0.37
Union	−0.32	0.17	−0.20	0.12	−0.35	0.18
Gender (women)	−0.25	0.17	−0.01	0.12	0.03	0.14
Employment status						
Part time	0.36	0.23	−0.23	0.16	0.23	0.22
Full time	−0.09	0.22	−0.03	0.15	0.10	0.19
Religious denomination						
Specific to country			−0.50	0.18**,5	−0.66	0.28*,3
Linguistic minority						
Specific to country						
N	1,998		2,582		2,782	
Cox and Snell R^2	6.2%		5.9%		16.9%	

* $p < 0.05$; ** $p < 0.01$; [1]Catholic; [2]Protestant; [3]No religion; [4]Calvinist; [5]Episcopalian; [6]Presbyterian; [7]Buddhist; [a]Arabic; [b]French; [c]Other; Table reports logit estimates (log-odds).

H_A: A1 *Confirmed. Nonvoting is negatively associated with age, after the SES facilitating factors are controlled.*

(2) Education also has a consistent and significant effect on nonvoting in 19 out of the 33 elections under consideration, namely, Canada, the Czech Republic, Germany, Hong Kong (1998), Hungary, Mexico (1997 and 2000), the Netherlands, New Zealand, Norway, Poland, Romania, Russia (1999 and 2000), Slovenia, Sweden, Switzerland, the United Kingdom, and the United States. Nonvoting is substantially more frequent among those who have little education and these results are consistent with other research findings (Blais 2000; Dalton 1996; Franklin 1996; Oppenhuis 1995; Topf 1995; Verba, Nie, and Kim 1978).

H_A: A2 *Confirmed. Nonvoting is negatively associated with education, after the SES facilitating factors are controlled.*

(3) Religious attendance is significant in 11 of 23[10] elections included in this analysis: Hungary, Mexico (1997 and 2000), the Netherlands, Poland, Russia (1999), Sweden, Switzerland, Ukraine, the United Kingdom, and the United States. As expected, those who attend religious services frequently are less likely to abstain from voting than those who never attend (Verba 1995*b*). Nonetheless, there is no clear pattern between religious identification and nonvoting. In some countries, those with a religious identification are less likely to abstain from voting than those with no religious identifications; countries where this holds are Mexico (Catholic), New Zealand (Episcopalian and Presbyterian), Slovenia (Catholic), and the United Kingdom (Episcopalian). But in other countries, the relationship is the reverse; it is the people with no religious identification who are less likely to abstain from voting, notably in Russia and the United States. Finally, in some countries both people with a particular religious identification and those with no religious identification are less likely to abstain than the rest of the population. This phenomenon is found in Spain (Catholic and no religious identification), in Germany (Protestants, Catholic, and people with no religion), and in the Netherlands (Calvinists and people with no religious identification). These results suggest that it is attending religious services rather than religious identification that is associated with nonvoting.

H_A: A3 *Confirmed. Nonvoting is negatively associated with the frequency of attendance of religious services, after the SES facilitating factors are controlled.*

(4) Household income (measured in quintiles) has statistically significant influence on nonvoting in 11 of the 33 elections included in this

analysis: Canada, Japan, Mexico (1997), Norway, Poland, Switzerland, the United Kingdom, the United States, Romania, Peru, and Thailand. High-income citizens are consistently less likely to be nonvoters than those in the lowest income quintile in 10 of the 11 elections. The exception is Peru where people with higher income vote less. The relationship between income and nonvoting is less uniform than in the case of age, education, and attendance to religious services, but is still considerable. These results also confirm findings from other research (Dalton 1996; Oppenhuis 1995; Wolfinger and Rosenstone 1980).

H_A: A4 *Confirmed. Nonvoting is negatively associated with household income, after the SES facilitating factors are controlled.*

(5) Being married decreases the likelihood of nonvoting in 18 elections (out of 29), a substantial effect[11] which is evident in Belarus, the Czech Republic, Germany, Hong Kong (1998), Hungary, Lithuania, Mexico (1997), New Zealand, Poland, Romania, Russia (1999 and 2000), Slovenia, Sweden, Switzerland, Taiwan, the United Kingdom, and the United States.

H_A: A5 *Confirmed. Nonvoting is negatively associated with marriage, after the SES facilitating factors are controlled.*

Support for the remaining hypotheses is much less systematic. For instance, no systematic patterns emerge in the way rural or urban residence influences nonvoting. Union affiliation decreases the likelihood of nonvoting in six of the CSES countries (the Czech Republic, Hungary, Mexico (2000), the Netherlands, Poland, and Slovenia). Men are significantly more likely to vote than women in some countries (Hungary, Poland, and Switzerland), though less likely to vote in Norway and Lithuania. And there is no clear relationship between nonvoting and employment status.

H_A: A6–9 *Not confirmed as a cross-national pattern.*

(10) The influence of minority status is also somewhat unclear. It is reasonable to suppose that members of minority communities might feel excluded from the political system, and so be less likely to vote. There is evidence consistent with that interpretation in the case of Israel where Arabic speaking Israelis are significantly less likely to vote than others. The same is observed among French speakers in Switzerland. But, in other countries with significant communal minorities (e.g. Canada, New Zealand, Romania, Spain, Taiwan, and Ukraine), identification with a minority community has no significant effect on nonvoting after other

SES factors are controlled. And in Spain, the CSES data indicate that minority status does not appear to influence nonvoting, a finding that is contrary to past research (del Castillo 1996).

The initial basic finding from the individual-level data is that SES does matter in determining nonvoting behavior in a variety of contextual settings. Given these results, two significant questions arise: Are these patterns sustained when the effects of contextual factors are controlled? And to what extent does SES influence nonvoting, net the effects of economic, historical, and institutional variables?

The Impact of Contextual Factors

So far, the analysis has relied entirely on individual-level data, but there are strong reasons to suppose that system-level characteristics are related to levels of turnout. First, there is the argument that economic conditions affect levels of nonvoting. For example, Powell (1982) speculates that in countries with poorly performing economies, citizens may be less preoccupied about politics and less likely to vote; they have more pressing concerns. At the same time, "the human development that accompanies [economic] modernization should enhance political participation" (Powell 1982: 37). Similarly, the distribution of wealth within a society could have some effect on voter turnout. In countries with a large wealth gap and where most wealth is concentrated in a small segment of the population, individuals in the lowest income groups may feel relatively powerless and so less inclined to vote. It is not clear whether aggregate wealth, or its distribution, is related to turnout in a linear way (Blais and Dobrzynska 1998), but there are at least two dimensions of aggregate economic conditions that warrant investigation.

H_A: B1a *Aggregate wealth is negatively associated with nonvoting, when the effects of other contextual factors are controlled.*[12]

H_A: B1b *The distribution of wealth is positively associated with nonvoting, when the effects of other contextual factors are controlled.*[13]

Second, there are historical factors to consider. Consolidated democracies are routinely distinguished from the newer ones, and the CSES includes nine countries that qualify as "new" in the sense that they have held their first "free and fair" elections relatively recently: Belarus, the Czech Republic, Hungary, Lithuania, Poland, Romania, Russia, Slovenia, Taiwan, Ukraine, Peru, Chile, and Thailand. The extent to which elections in these settings really do qualify as fair and free is of course debatable, but it is plausible to suppose that citizens in consolidated democracies have had a more sustained and continuous experience with the "habit" of voting than is the case for citizens in regimes with a briefer electoral history of open electoral competition.

H_A: B2 *Citizens of new democracies will be more likely to abstain from voting than citizens of consolidated democracies, when the effects of other contextual factors are controlled.*[14]

A third system-level characteristic that has been linked to levels of voter turnout concerns the impact of electoral rules.[15] A substantial body of empirical evidence indicates that electoral systems operating under proportional representation (PR) rules, experience lower levels of nonvoting (Blais and Carty 1990; Blais and Dobrzynska 1998; Franklin 1996; Jackman 1987; Jackman and Miller 1995; Powell 1986). Single member, simple plurality (SMSP) systems, by contrast, are usually associated with higher levels of nonvoting. The widely accepted principle is that SMSP systems are more likely than PR systems to produce outcomes where there is a greater discrepancy between the proportion of votes received by a party and the distribution of the seats for parties. And so, SMSP systems are more likely to be perceived as producing "unfair" outcomes, more "wasted votes," and so discourage voting (Blais and Dobrzynska 1998). From this logic, we would expect the following:

H_A: B3 *The greater the potential discrepancy between the proportion of votes received by a party and the distribution of seats for parties, the more likely the citizens will be to abstain from voting, when the effects of other contextual factors are controlled.*[16]

The conventional wisdom once was that PR systems experience higher voter turnout because PR rules produce more parties, and a greater number of political parties present voters with a wider selection of electoral choices (Karp and Banducci 1999). But the empirical evidence supporting the claim is far from clear. Indeed, Jackman and Miller (1995) suggest that the presence of many parties is associated with lower turnout, probably because multiparty systems increase the likelihood of coalition outcomes, outcomes that are negotiated by elites, rather than decided by voters directly. Lijphart (1999) argues that it is the effective number of parties and not the absolute number of parties that is most vital because it is the effective number of parties that more adequately captures the viable choices available to voters. The CSES data allow us to evaluate the impact of the number of parties on voter turnout net the effects of electoral rules.

H$_A$: B4 *Citizens in party systems where there are more effective parties will be less likely to abstain from voting than citizens in party systems with fewer parties.*

Combining Contextual and Individual-Level Explanations

All of the contextual factors are significant predictors of nonvoting (Table 4.2 reports the results). With respect to the economic context, there are two findings: There is evidence confirming earlier research (Blais and Dobrzynska 1998; Powell 1982) which indicates that as the levels of aggregate wealth increase, the likelihood of nonvoting decreases. Furthermore, the log-odds estimate for the effects of the distribution of wealth, 0.036 suggests that as the distribution of wealth becomes more unequally distributed, the likelihood of nonvoting increases. This result is also consistent with our expectation that nonvoting *increases* as the gap between rich and poor widens.[17]

H$_A$: B1a *Confirmed. Aggregate wealth is negatively associated with nonvoting, when the effects of other contextual and SES factors are controlled.*

H$_A$: B1b *Confirmed. The distribution of wealth is positively associated with nonvoting, when the effects of other contextual and SES factors are controlled.*

The model described above does not include the number of years the countries have had free elections. This variable is excluded because of

Table 4.2. Impact of contextual factors on nonvoting

	B	S.E.
Economic context		
GDP	−0.014	0.002***
Gini coefficient	0.036	0.003***
Institutional context		
District magnitude	−0.002	0.000***
Effective number of parties	0.139	0.011***
Age	−0.128	0.017***
Education	−0.315	0.019***
Income	−0.033	0.013***
Married	−0.538	0.033***
% of correct prediction	84.5	
Nagelkerke R^2	6.4%	
N	54,217	

*** $p < 0.001$.
Table reports logit estimates (log-odds).
OLS unstandardized B coefficients.

multicollinearity problems; the number of years with free elections is highly correlated with the wealth of the country (Pearson correlation = 0.82). Consequently, it is difficult to isolate the impact of GDP on non-voting while controlling the democratic history of countries. When the model is run with a variable that measures the number of years with free elections (instead of GDP), we observe that the longer a country has had free elections, the lower is nonvoting, and that supports our hypothesis (results not shown). The substitution of GDP with number of years with free elections does not alter the influence of the other contextual factors.

H_A: B2 *Confirmed. Citizens of new democracies are more likely to abstain from voting than citizens of consolidated democracies, when the effects of other contextual and SES factors are controlled.*

According to Table 4.2, the magnitude of electoral districts also influences nonvoting. The greater the district magnitude, the lower are the levels of nonvoting.

H_A: B3 *Confirmed. Citizens of countries with large district magnitude will be less likely to abstain from voting than are citizens in systems with small district magnitude, after the effects of other contextual factors are controlled.*

The CSES data also indicate that the number of effective parties seems to matter to nonvoting. The likelihood of nonvoting increases as the effective number of parties increases. The direction of the relationship observed does not appear to be caused by the presence of the variable that measures the magnitude of electoral district: even when district magnitude is removed from the analysis, the greater the effective number of parties the higher is nonvoting (results not shown).

H_A: B4 *Not Confirmed. Citizens in party systems where there are more effective parties are more likely to abstain from voting than citizens in party systems with fewer parties.*

Together, these contextual factors confirm that economic conditions, district magnitude, and the effective number of parties do have some influence on an individual's decision to vote or abstain. Furthermore, a long experience with the opportunity to vote seems to encourage voting.

The results also indicate that most of the SES factors have significant influences on nonvoting, and they work in the expected direction, even when contextual factors are controlled. First, older citizens are much less likely to abstain from voting than younger citizens. Second, those with higher levels of formal education are significantly less likely than others to abstain from voting. Third, the odds of nonvoting decrease substantially as income rises. Finally, those who are married are less likely to abstain from voting. The primary finding, then, is that SES, and particularly age, education, marital status, and household income, continue to influence nonvoting, regardless of levels of aggregate economic wealth, electoral history, electoral rules, and number of parties (see also Blais 2000).

The Impact of Contextual Factors on Individual-Level Explanations

The analysis has focused on the impact of two different sets of factors separately: the individual-level explanations and the contextual explanations. The next logical step is to explore whether there are significant interactions between these two sets of factors. The present section examines how the contextual factors influence the way socioeconomic factors shape nonvoting. Here, the two most intriguing questions are: "Why do SES factors play a significant role in some countries but not in others?" and "Can the contextual factors explain why SES factors are significant predictors of nonvoting in some countries but not in others?" This last section explores how all five contextual factors affect the relationship between age, education, income, and marital status with nonvoting.

To explore these questions requires a different research design. The focus of analysis shifts from individual- to country-level analyses. The logic of inquiry is to examine whether the strength of the relationship between the socioeconomic factors and nonvoting varies with the contextual factors. The number of cases now becomes 27.[18] The log-odds estimates in Table 4.1 serve as the value of the dependent variables. For instance, the first dependent variable is the strength of the impact of age on nonvoting. For each of the 27 elections examined, the variable "impact of age" takes the values of the estimated log-odds coefficient for age in Table 4.1.

As shown in Table 4.3, the magnitude of electoral districts, the effective number of parties, and the wealth of a country, as well as the distribution of wealth within the country, have no impact on the strength of the relationship between nonvoting and age, education, and marital status.

The contextual factors do not affect the relationship between these three socioeconomic factors and nonvoting.[19] However, the relationship between individual income and nonvoting reveals a significant pattern:

Table 4.3. Interaction effect between individual and contextual factors

	Age		Education		Income		Married	
	B	S.E.	*B*	S.E.	*B*	S.E.	*B*	S.E.
GDP	−0.005	0.005	−0.004	0.006	−0.008	0.002***	0.002	0.007
Gini coefficient	0.005	0.006	0.004	0.007	0.001	0.002	0.007	0.009
District magnitude	0.000	0.001	0.000	0.002	0.000	0.001	0.001	0.002
Effective number of parties	−0.013	0.033	−0.012	0.041	−0.022	0.011	0.017	0.046
Constant	−0.587	0.282*	−0.381	0.343	0.082	0.095	−0.722	0.415
Adjusted R^2	−0.040		−0.114		0.481		−0.074	
N	28		29		29		26	

*** $p < 0.001$.
Table reports OLS unstandardized coefficients.

the impact of individual income on nonvoting is negatively affected by the wealth of a country. The wealthier the country, the weaker is the impact of income on nonvoting. Put differently, the wealthier the country, the more rich and poor people vote in similar proportions. Inversely, the poorer the country, the more rich and poor people vote in different proportions.[20] One possible explanation for this finding might be that in poorer countries, the income gap between rich and poor people is greater than in wealthy countries. But the plausibility of that explanation is undermined by the fact that the model takes into account the distribution of wealth within countries and it turns out that this variable is not significant.

Conclusion

This analysis reevaluates a variety of hypotheses concerning the relationship between SES and nonvoting. One central finding is that SES influences nonvoting in a wide variety of economic, political, and institutional settings. Citizens who have weaker resources, motivations, or opportunities to be mobilized by other people are less likely to vote than others. That finding corroborates a number of other cross-national research results (Dalton 1996; Franklin 1996; Oppenhuis 1995; van der Eijck and Franklin 1996; Verba, Schlozman, and Brady 1995).

The CSES data indicate significant cross-national variations in the strength and patterns of the linkages between SES and nonvoting; no single SES indicator works in exactly the same way in all national settings. But five SES indicators—age, education, religious attendance, marital status, and income—exhibit common effects; they are significant predictors of nonvoting and the direction of their effect is constant in multiple settings. In addition, contextual factors such as aggregate wealth, district magnitude, and the number of effective parties do appear to have a significant impact on voter turnout. And finally, the impact of income on nonvoting seems to be greater in poorer countries than in richer ones.

But there are a number of findings, and non-findings, that clearly merit much closer investigation with an expanded CSES data set. First, the evidence of the relationship between communal pluralism and voter turnout is unclear, and the question of whether communal minority membership, defined by language, religion, or ethnicity, and voter turnout cannot be adequately settled with the data from these cases. The effects of wealth distribution on nonvoting also warrants further investigation. Second, the extent to which the effects of SES factors are cross-nationally consistent is striking. The absence of interaction effects is also striking. Only one out of a possible 16 interactions turns out to be significant. In effect, the same SES variables affect nonvoting in the same way regardless of the contextual variations.

Notes

1. Note that two countries are excluded (Australia and Belgium) because they have compulsory voting with enforcement mechanisms.
2. The surveys for Chile, Lithuania, Peru, and Thailand did not include a question that asked respondents directly whether they have voted or not, asking only for what party they voted: For these elections, the nonvoting variable equals 1 for people who specify for what party they have voted and equals 0 otherwise.
3. In some cases it has been shown that when age is controlled, the effects of other SES predictors become insignificant (Norris 1991; Wolfinger and Rosenstone 1980).
4. Niemi and Barkan (1987) show that the reverse effect may hold in transitional democracies such as Kenya and Turkey. Under some political circumstances, younger people may be more trusting of electoral politics, and consequently are more likely to vote. In consolidated democracies, there is some evidence of a curvilinear relationship between age and nonvoting: nonvoting is more frequent among the young and the elderly than among the middle-aged, though it generally decreases with age (see Milbrath and Goel 1977; Wolfinger

and Rosenstone 1980). Aside from the impact of infirmity, others attribute the higher levels of nonvoting among older cohorts to lower levels of education (Verba and Nie 1972; Wolfinger and Rosenstone 1980).

5. To avoid the complications posed by absolute income levels, the CSES measure of income is categorized into quintiles for each country.

6. Here "language spoken at home" is used to indicate identification with a linguistic community (i.e. Quebecois in Canada). Only those cases where linguistic minorities exceed 5 percent of the respondents are included in this analysis.

7. del Castillo (1999) finds that turnout for national elections from 1977 to 1993 differs considerably among Spain's minority communities. Further, del Castillo notes that the presence of such nationalist parties as the Basque National Party encourage turnout, even in the European Elections, where these parties are not likely to have a significant chance to win offices. Ackaert, Winter, and Swyngedouw (1996) report that both the turnout rate and voting behavior vary across the minority communities in Belgium. The differences are attributed to variations in the party system, and to differences in the salience of elections.

8. Usually, the Nagelkerke R^2 is reported as a measure of explained variance when using logistic regression models. The Nagelkerke measure builds upon Cox and Snell, by reporting the proportion of the total possible explained variance attributable to the specified model (the maximum value for a Cox and Snell R^2 is dependent on the specifications of the model and especially the distribution of the sample). Under some circumstances, the Nagelkerke measure can be misleading. For example, the Nagelkerke R^2 value for this model for Australia is 16 percent, as opposed to the Cox and Snell measure, 2 percent. As it turns out, the maximum R^2 for Australia is only 11 percent. The maximum R^2 value varies considerably among the countries included in this study (because the characteristics of the national samples with regard to nonvoting vary considerably); it is very difficult to interpret the relative strengths of the models in explaining variance in nonvoting. Further, as in the case of Australia and a few other countries, the Nagelkerke R^2 reports large proportions of explained variance when there is little variance to explain. When logistic and OLS models are compared, the Cox and Snell R^2 consistently matches the adjusted R^2 in relative strength with cross-national comparison. For that reason, the Cox and Snell R^2 may be a more reliable measure for cross-national comparisons. When the merged model is used, the maximum R^2 value is constant across the models, and the Nagelkerke R^2 is reported.

9. For Peru, the age of respondents is not available.

10. This item is not included in the CSES data for Canada, Chile, Denmark, Japan, Korea, Lithuania, Peru, Spain (1996 and 2000), and Thailand.

11. This item is not available for Chile, Japan, Korea, and Thailand.

12. The variable used here measures the GNP per capita. *Source:* World Development Indicators, World Bank.

13. The variable used here measures the Gini Index. *Source:* World Development Indicators, World Bank.
14. The variable used here measures the number of years with free elections in keeping with Inglehart (1990).
15. This follows Blais and Dobrzynska's modification (1998) of Powell.
16. The variable used here measures the magnitude (number of representatives) of electoral districts.
17. The current model does not include "attendance to religious services" because this variable was not available in too many countries. Its inclusion in the model would have dramatically reduced the number of cases and thus limited our ability to verify the impact of contextual factors. The results do not change significantly when the variable is included in the model: all the conclusions stated still hold. The model also shows that the impact of attendance to religious services is overall a significant factor in predicting nonvoting. Note, that because the maximum R^2 value is constant across both models, and reliable comparisons can be made, the Nagelkerke R^2 value is reported as a measure of explained variance.
18. Six elections cannot be included for this last section because of missing information for one or many of the variables: Hong Kong (2000), Mexico (1997, 2000), Russia (1999), Taiwan, and Thailand.
19. The models described above do not include the number of years the countries have had free elections. This variable is excluded because of multicollinearity problems (the number of years with free election is highly correlated with the wealth of the country—Pearson correlation = 0.82). The models for age, education, and marital status are not different if we include number of years with free elections and exclude the GDP variable.
20. Not surprisingly, the number of years with free elections also has an impact on the strength of the relationship between individual income and nonvoting. The greater the number of years with free elections, the smaller the impact of individual income on nonvoting. We decided to include the wealth of the country instead of number of years with free elections for statistical reasons; the model with GDP has a higher fit than one with the number of years of free elections. In addition, there is intuitively a stronger association between GDP and the impact of income on nonvoting because both GDP and individual income refer to wealth.

5

Electoral Systems, Efficacy, and Voter Turnout[1]

Susan A. Banducci and Jeffrey A. Karp

Introduction

One of the least disputed conclusions to emanate from the research on electoral systems and turnout is that countries with proportional representation (PR) have higher voter turnout. Some estimate that PR systems have a turnout advantage as high as 12 percent (Franklin 1996). There is, however, disagreement over the mechanisms by which PR produces higher turnout. Some believe that PR helps to foster higher turnout by increasing a citizen's perception that his or her vote matters in an election. Because plurality elections give all the spoils to the single candidate who receives the most votes, the potential decisiveness of a vote for a minor party or noncompetitive candidate is minimized. On the other hand, in PR systems, where the proportion of votes gained by a party is more closely related to the share of seats that a party receives, all votes could potentially be decisive in determining the number of seats a party gains in parliament. Past research therefore, has assumed that the disproportionality between seats and votes in plurality systems instills in voters a sense that their vote is wasted if not cast for a viable candidate. This lack of efficacy is believed to contribute to comparatively lower rates of participation in plurality systems than in PR systems.

Another view emphasizes the importance of political parties in offering voters a choice. Multiparty systems are more likely to occur under PR rules and in these systems there is a greater likelihood that parties will strive to distinguish themselves ideologically (Katz 1980). If parties fail to offer a clear choice to voters, as is hypothesized with regard to two-party systems, voters are more likely to abstain (Downs 1957). Thus, voters who have more options to choose from may display greater levels of political efficacy and may be more motivated to vote on election day than in cases where there is no perceived choice.

These explanations hinge on the role of efficacy. The extant comparative literature, however, has relied almost entirely on aggregate data to examine the influence of electoral systems on political participation (for an exception see Karp and Banducci 2008). It, therefore, has never explicitly measured "vote efficacy," the feeling that one's vote is potentially decisive. With the collection of cross-national election studies under the Comparative Study of Electoral Systems (CSES), it is now possible to examine how attitudes are shaped by electoral rules and how these attitudes influence turnout. In this chapter we address three issues in the extant literature on participation, efficacy, and electoral systems: first, the evidence regarding the influence of macro-level factors; second, how proportional representation enhances efficacy; and third, the role of political minorities. We then develop a model to examine the relationship between electoral systems, voter efficacy, and turnout using CSES Module 1.

Macro-Level Factors

Most empirical studies that attempt to measure the impact of institutional arrangements on turnout do so by employing aggregate data across a number of countries with different electoral systems (see, e.g., Blais and Dobrzynska 1998; Franklin et al. 2004; Jackman 1987; Powell 1986). These studies find that disproportionality reduces turnout (Blais and Dobrzynska 1998; Jackman 1987; Jackman and Miller 1995). This finding is consistent with the assumption that an unequal translation of votes into seats diminishes some people's sense of political efficacy leading them to abstain. Disproportionality may also influence participation in other ways. Disproportional outcomes may affect participation by shaping the strategies of parties and their candidates. Parties may campaign more actively when their chances of gaining representation improve (Jackman 1987).

Another feature of the electoral system that has the potential to influence both efficacy and turnout is the nature of the party system. Multipartism has been found to have both a negative (Jackman 1987; Jackman and Miller 1995) and a positive (Ladner and Milner 1999) effect on turnout.

Jackman (1987) infers that in multiparty systems where coalition governments are the norm, citizens are discouraged from voting when the formation of government is decided by political elites rather than by election outcomes. Therefore, as the number of parties and likelihood of coalition governments increases, efficacy and the probability of voting will decline. On the other hand, a positive relationship between the number of parties and turnout is consistent with the expectation that parties increase turnout by mobilizing voters, strengthening partisan attachments, and offering greater choice. These differing effects of multipartism indicate that a persuasive case can be made for both positive and negative effects. On the one hand, multipartism should promote efficacy and stimulate turnout by strengthening partisanship and offering voters more choice. Yet, voters may also feel less efficacious when coalitions are the norm and governments are determined by party elites.[2]

Multipartism can also positively influence turnout by affecting strength of partisan attachments. The larger number of parties and a tendency not to converge to the ideological center in PR systems should increase the options from which voters can choose and result in fewer abstentions. Moreover, voters are more likely to have strong attachments to parties that cater more specifically to their needs as opposed to catch-all parties that appeal to the median voter. Strength of partisan attachments has been found to be related to the electoral system. In systems that foster extreme parties, voters develop stronger attachments (Bowler, Lanoue, and Savoie 1994). Past research has also shown that voters with strong party attachments are more likely to be interested in politics and more likely to vote (Campbell et al. 1960; Verba, Nie and Kim 1978). Election returns from Swiss communes where majority and PR electoral systems are used suggest that part of the boost in turnout gained in PR systems is from the increased number of parties (Ladner and Milner 1999).

From these aggregate studies, however, it is not clear how the macro-level factors related to the electoral system (such as multipartism and disproportionality) influence political participation. Do more disproportional systems depress voter efficacy due to the higher probability of wasted votes? Does multipartism increase turnout by increasing partisan attachments and efficacy or by increasing mobilization efforts? Or, alternatively, does multipartism reduce turnout by decreasing efficacy because of an increased likelihood of coalition governments and the lack of decisiveness of a vote in determining government composition?

Electoral Systems and Efficacy

The assumption that macro-level factors associated with the electoral systems affect voters' sense of efficacy is largely consistent with the advantages cited by PR advocates. PR advocates often point to its potential for increasing citizen efficacy and engagement in politics as one of the fundamental benefits of PR over plurality or first-past-the-post (FPP) systems. The explanation for why PR would increase efficacy and engagement has tended to focus on the fairness of the system. PR rules can be seen as more "fair" when compared to FPP systems because they reduce the proportion of voters who cast "wasted" votes. By increasing the effective impact of individual votes, PR rules might increase attachment to and trust in a political system (Amy 1993). Consequently, an electoral system that ensures that the fewest votes are wasted will presumably motivate more people to vote. Systems that distort the translation of votes into seats may alienate and discourage small or "minor" party supporters who are not fairly represented (Bowler, Lanoue, and Savoie 1994). Researchers using aggregate data have suggested that this alienation may result in a diminished sense of efficacy and depress turnout (Blais and Carty 1990; Franklin 1996; Jackman 1987; Jackman and Miller 1995; Powell 1986).

Without the use of individual-level data it is difficult to assess the extent to which disproportionality influences turnout indirectly through efficacy. In one study of turnout using the CSES data, Norris (2004) does find that efficacy increases the probability of voting.[3] However, she does not examine whether efficacy varies across electoral systems and other institutional features related to the electoral system.

Role of Political Minorities

Finally, there is little discussion in the literature about which voters will be advantaged or disadvantaged by electoral arrangements but such arrangements may have a differential impact on both voter efficacy and voter participation. For example, large party supporters under plurality rules are not thought to be discouraged from voting by the electoral system. However, it is difficult to distinguish between large and small party supporters in the absence of individual data. Anderson and Guillory (1997) suggest that being a political minority is an important variable when examining the influence of political institutions and satisfaction with democracy. Those supporting parties that were not in government were more likely to be satisfied with democracy in consensual systems that aim to restrain majority rule by requiring or encouraging the sharing of power between the majority and the minority (Lijphart 1984). In contrast, in majoritarian systems, where power is concentrated in the hands of the majority, persons who recall voting for the losing party were more dissatisfied. The implementation of PR in New Zealand after a history of plurality elections also provides evidence that those supporting small parties are more likely to increase in efficacy (Banducci, Donovan, and Karp 1999) and participation (Karp and Banducci 1999) after the transition to a proportional system. Thus, we have reason to expect that the effects of the electoral system on political efficacy are likely to depend on whether a citizen is in the political minority.

Direct and Indirect Effects of Macro-Level Factors on Turnout

The findings from earlier studies suggest that PR should foster higher turnout but are not conclusive when it comes to explaining the mechanisms by which a voter's sense of efficacy may be altered or whose electoral participation is most likely to be affected by the electoral arrangements. Using individual-level data across a large number of countries allows us to test both the direct effects of the factors associated with proportional representation (such as disproportionality and multipartism) on efficacy, and the direct and indirect effects of these factors on turnout. We are also able to examine how minor party supporters are differently affected by the electoral arrangements.

In our analysis of electoral rules, efficacy, and turnout, the direct and indirect effects of disproportionality are central to our expectations and the model. We expect that disproportionality reduces both efficacy and turnout as well as conditions the relationship between minor party preferences and efficacy. When institutional rules make it more difficult for small parties to gain representation, we should expect those who prefer small parties to be more dissatisfied with the political system (i.e. have lower levels of efficacy) and, consequently, to be less likely to vote. Therefore, the effects of preferring a small party on a voter's sense of efficacy will depend on the level of disproportionality that is produced by the electoral system and the difference in efficacy levels of small and large party supporters will be greatest in the most disproportional systems.

To reconcile the contradictory expectations about the effects of multipartism on turnout, we distinguish between the number of parties holding executive power in a coalition government and the number of parties gaining representation in parliament. On the one hand, if voters are sensitive to the potential effect of their vote on government formation, as the number of parties in government increases efficacy will be expected to decrease. On the other hand, increased numbers of parties represented in parliament is expected to enhance efficacy and directly promote participation through greater mobilization efforts on the part of political parties. We might also expect parties that share power in a broad coalition to have less incentive to mobilize voters during an election. Therefore, an increase in the number of parties in government will be directly linked to a decrease in the probability of voting. We thus hypothesize that the number of parties in government will have a negative effect on both efficacy and turnout.

Because we are considering cross-national and individual variation in rates of participation, it is also important to consider the effect of electoral rules that influence the costs and benefits of voting but not efficacy. Examples of rules that facilitate voting are the adoption of mail ballots and scheduling of elections on weekends or holidays (Franklin 1996). Among the most effective rules for stimulating voting is compulsory voting, which regardless of the sanction for noncompliance can impose a small inducement that is enough to neutralize the cost of voting (Lijphart 1997). While such a rule may enhance participation, it is not expected to enhance political efficacy.

Measuring Efficacy and Participation with CSES Data

Part of the difficulty in determining the relationship between electoral systems and turnout is the reliance on proxy variables and aggregate turnout to draw inferences about the interactions between institutions and individual behavior. While aggregate cross-national studies are useful, these hypotheses are best tested with individual-level data. But such an approach requires a sample large enough to include citizens living under different combinations of institutional arrangements. The data must also include relevant variables such as measures of party preference and efficacy that are collected in a comparable fashion. Although there have been several large cross-national surveys, none have contained the appropriate measures to examine voter participation. The World Values Surveys (1981–2005) include a wealth of data from a large number of countries measuring political attitudes and confidence in political institutions. The

International Social Survey Program (ISSP) is another valuable source for cross-national data on political behavior and attitudes. However, since neither of these studies is conducted to coincide with an election, there is no direct measure of whether or not a citizen cast a ballot.[4] Likewise, the Eurobarometer studies that regularly sample citizens in member states of the European Union occasionally ask respondents who they voted for in the last election or who they intend to vote for in a future election.[5] More direct measures of participation are available for the elections to the European Parliament but the electoral rules for electing MEPs do not vary substantially across member states.

The Comparative Study of Electoral Systems (CSES) overcomes these limitations by relying on indigenous teams of researchers to administer a common module of questions directly after a national election. In August 2003, over 25 countries deposited their data with the CSES secretariat.[6] Each country's sample is based on the eligible population of voters, except for Australia and New Zealand where enrolment is compulsory and the sample is based on registered voters. These unique data allow one to examine how institutions constrain individual behavior in ways not previously possible. The diverse sample of countries available in the CSES also offers an advantage over other studies that often rely on data from advanced industrial states. Not only is there greater variation in context but individual-level factors such as socioeconomic status will have a greater range of values (see Nevitte et al., Chapter 4 in this volume).

The sample of countries can be divided into four general types of electoral systems: proportional representation, plurality or first-past-the-post, majoritarian (using the alternative vote), and mixed systems that combine plurality with PR in one chamber.[7] Fourteen of the 22 countries in our sample use PR to determine the overall partisan composition of the lower house. Among these systems, the diversity in electoral arrangements results in substantial variation in the degree to which translation of votes into seats results in proportionality. Among the factors accounting for differences is district magnitude which can have a strong impact on proportionality, with larger districts being associated with greater proportionality (Katz 1997). Two of the countries, the Netherlands and Israel, have a single national constituency electing 150 and 120 members, respectively. Germany, New Zealand, and Mexico also have constituencies where about half of the members in parliament are selected by closed party lists to correct partisan imbalances resulting from the election of electorate candidates by plurality rules. Japan, Hungary, and Ukraine have non-corrective mixed systems, where some candidates are elected in single member districts by either majority (as is the case in Hungary) or plurality (as in the case of Japan) rules, while others in the same chamber are elected by PR. The difference is that the PR component is not used as a corrective.[8]

Some countries also employ thresholds; higher thresholds are designed to keep the smallest parties out of parliament and affect the proportionality of seats to votes. In some cases, the threshold varies depending on whether a single party is standing alone or together with other parties (as is the case in the Czech Republic and Poland). In other cases, the threshold is both local and national as is the case in Germany and New Zealand where parties can enter parliament by either winning a constituency seat or by winning more than 5 percent of the party vote. Electoral formulae can in theory affect proportionality within PR countries, with the *Sainte-Laguë* producing the most proportional outcome while the *d'Hondt* gives a bonus to larger parties (Blais and Massicotte 1996). However, Katz (1997) finds that these formulae make little difference to proportionality.

Among the PR systems, Poland, Slovenia, the Czech Republic, and Spain produce the most disproportional outcomes. These countries have either higher thresholds or small district magnitudes. The small district magnitude in Spain has repeatedly allowed the winning party to get a majority of seats with a plurality of votes (Blais and Massicotte 1996; Gunther 1989). Australia uses the alternative vote for the lower house to achieve a majority. Instead of casting a single vote for a candidate, voters rank their preferences. If no candidate receives a majority, the candidate who receives the smallest number of first preferences is eliminated and the second preferences are then transferred to the other candidates until one candidate receives a majority. In the 1996 election, the system produced more disproportional results than any of the countries with mixed or PR systems (with the exception of Poland), but was more proportional than any of the plurality systems.

Three countries in the sample held their first elections under a system that guarantees more proportional outcomes than the previous electoral system. Ukraine, which previously had used a majoritarian system that required runoffs, adopted a mixed member system in which half of the seats in the legislature are selected by PR and the other selected by plurality rules. New Zealand, which had previously been characterized as a "virtually perfect example of a Westminster system," adopted a mixed system where PR determines the overall partisan composition of parliament (Vowles et al. 1998). Japan replaced its single nontransferable vote (SNTV) system, which severely disadvantaged small parties, with a mixed non-corrective system capable of producing more proportional outcomes (Woodall 2000).[9]

Methods and Measurement

Our expectations about electoral system effects on turnout hinge on the role of efficacy as an intervening variable between the electoral system and the decision to vote. Of the CSES items, the question that measures this aspect of efficacy is: "Some people say that no matter who people vote for, it won't make any difference to what happens. Others say that who people vote for can make a difference to what happens." The variable has a 4-point scale ranging from 1 to 5 with positive values indicating higher levels of efficacy.[10] This question is the most direct measure of evaluations of the efficacy of a vote available and thus of how the electoral system translates votes into seats. In terms of face validity, this question asks respondents to evaluate the meaningfulness of voting, a component of elections as an accountability mechanism. Therefore, it should be the most direct measure of the psychological effect.

If we are interested in distinguishing how disproportionality affects small party supporters differently than large party supporters, we also need an indication of party preferences. The CSES Module 1 includes two measures designed to measure party preference. One measure asks respondents whether they think of themselves as being close to any political party and if so to identify that party (additional parties are coded only if the respondent volunteers). This question, however, presents a problem in classifying respondents as either small or large party supporters as just 45 percent of the sample responded that they were close to a political party. The other measure consists of a series of items that measure evaluations of up to six parties employing a 10-point scale ranging from strongly like to strongly dislike.[11] Using this series of party evaluations, the preferred party can be identified as the party that is most positively evaluated by the respondent. When this method is used to determine party preference, 67.6 percent of the sample evaluate one party more highly than another. About 28 of the sample evaluate more than one party equally while just under 4 percent said that they were unaware or did not know about any of the parties. Using the like–dislike scale allows us to classify a significantly larger proportion of the sample according to party preferences.

Strength of party preference can also be determined by using the value of the most preferred party. High values indicate a strong preference for a party (or parties) while lower values indicate a weaker preference. Less than 1 percent of the sample that evaluated at least one party failed to rank a single party above zero. Since the party like–dislike measure has the advantage of not only identifying the party preferences of more respondents than the party proximity measure but also measuring the strength of that preference, we rely on it for our analysis. If the preference is for one of the two largest parties, the respondent is identified as having a preference for a large party. Generally, parties that receive at least 20 percent of the vote are classified as large parties. For example, in Germany, the CDU and the SPD are classified as large parties, receiving 41 and 28 percent of the vote in 1998, respectively. In some countries, such as Canada, Norway, and Ukraine, just one party received at least 20 percent of the vote. All others are coded as small parties (see Appendix 5.1).

One of the frequently cited limitations with using survey data involves the validity of the responses, particularly with regard to political participation. It is not uncommon in election studies to find that the proportion of respondents who report voting is far greater than the aggregation of election returns. One of the theories commonly advanced to explain this discrepancy is that nonvoters are motivated to give a socially desirable response. It has been assumed that the social desirability bias is a general human trait that affects everyone equally (Blais 2000; Brady, Verba, and Schlozman 1995). But recent research suggests that respondents are also likely to be influenced by the electoral context (see Karp and Brockington 2005). That said, since misreporting occurs primarily among nonvoters, the overall bias between reported and actual turnout in any given country will depend on the proportion of nonvoters. The CSES advised collaborators to ask the question in a way that minimized overreporting.[12] For the purposes of our analysis, nonresponses to this question were assumed to be nonvoters. A comparison of the actual and reported turnout indicates that plurality and mixed systems are more likely to have higher levels of overreporting than PR systems.[13] Therefore, we have weighted the data by actual turnout to correct for these differences. We have also weighted the data to correct for unequal sample sizes across countries.

Differences in Efficacy by Party Preference and Electoral System

We first examine variations in strength of preference, efficacy, and turnout by large and small party supporters and by government and opposition party supporters. Table 5.1 shows the distribution of party preferences by country and electoral system.[14] Not surprisingly, in plurality and majoritarian systems, more citizens prefer large parties than in PR and mixed systems. About a third of the electorate expresses a preference for small parties in PR and mixed systems compared to about one-fifth in

Table 5.1. Distribution of party preferences by country and electoral system

	Most preferred party					
	Large party	Small party	No single preference	Don't know	Strongly like	Strongly dislike
Plurality/majority systems						
Australia	56.3	12.6	29.6	1.5	42.8	2.3
Canada	29.0	47.7	20.9	2.4	17.8	3.6
Great Britain	59.9	18.8	17.9	3.4	34.7	4.0
United States	73.7	6.0	18.9	1.4	21.3	2.0
Total	54.9	21.0	21.9	2.2	29.2	3.0
Mixed systems (non-corrective)						
Hungary	26.5	19.0	50.2	4.4	53.3	5.2
Japan	38.6	20.5	31.1	9.9	11.0	10.7
Korea	50.7	11.3	35.5	2.5	19.0	4.7
Russia	45.4	25.7	24.5	4.3	50.2	5.4
Ukraine	33.0	32.9	29.4	4.8	45.0	11.1
Total	38.8	21.9	34.1	5.2	35.9	7.4
PR systems						
Czech Republic	52.0	30.9	15.9	1.2	53.6	1.4
Denmark	51.5	31.6	16.8	0.1	51.4	0.1
Germany	37.0	33.5	27.0	2.5	45.2	3.4
Israel	47.4	21.4	26.8	4.4	48.7	7.0
Mexico	37.0	35.2	22.0	5.8	38.9	9.4
The Netherlands	12.2	20.5	64.6	2.7	25.6	3.2
New Zealand	43.6	26.7	26.8	2.9	41.8	3.5
Norway	29.7	50.1	19.4	0.8	39.9	0.8
Poland	43.5	26.2	22.2	8.1	47.1	8.8
Slovenia	33.7	24.3	29.6	12.4	29.4	16.3
Spain	58.7	17.6	22.3	1.4	26.0	3.6
Sweden	48.6	28.0	21.1	2.3	37.0	3.0
Switzerland	47.3	20.2	26.4	6.1	30.7	7.2
Total	41.7	28.1	34.1	5.2	39.6	5.3
Total	43.5	25.4	27.2	3.9	36.8	5.4

Notes: Data are weighted to adjust for unequal sample size and overreporting of vote. Each country's sample is approximately 1,250. No single preference indicates those who gave the same score for two or more parties. Don't know indicates those who responded "don't know."

plurality or majoritarian systems. Excluding Canada where only one party counted as a large party, only around 12 percent express a preference for small parties in the remaining plurality systems and Australia. In the mixed systems, more citizens prefer large to small parties though there is considerable variation across countries. In newer democracies that have mixed systems, there are smaller differences between the numbers preferring large and small parties reflecting a less stable party system. PR and mixed systems also have the highest proportion without a single preference suggesting that these systems might encourage multiple party attachments.

As is evident also from Table 5.1, citizens in PR systems have the strongest preferences. In the table, those who gave his or her preferred party a ranking of 9 or 10 on a 10-point scale are coded as strongly liking the party while those who gave a 0 or 1 to their least preferred party are coded as strongly disliking the party. These measures indicate how strongly parties are liked or disliked. Almost 40 percent of those in PR countries strongly liked their preferred party indicating strong preferences and suggesting greater affinity for a party. Only 30 percent in plurality/majority systems express this strong party preference. Together these findings are consistent with expectations that PR systems increase the options for which voters can choose which helps to foster stronger attachments to political parties.

Figure 5.1 reports the proportion of citizens who reported having the highest level of vote efficacy and shows the influence of party preference on efficacy by electoral system. Despite the cultural differences between PR countries in our sample, they have far higher levels of efficacy than those found in plurality systems. While not shown in the figure, Canada has the lowest levels of efficacy of any country in the sample, with just 14 percent placing in the top category of efficacy. Importantly, the differences in levels of efficacy between large and small party supporters are substantial in plurality systems and negligible in all of the other systems. A closer examination of these differences within plurality and majority countries (not reported in the figure) indicates that the difference is largest in the United States and smallest in Canada. This difference is likely due to the fact that the small parties in Canada are regional parties that do gain representation. Nevertheless, those who prefer small parties in each of the plurality and majority countries are less efficacious than those who prefer large parties, evidence which supports our initial hypothesis that these types of systems discourage those who prefer small parties. Lower

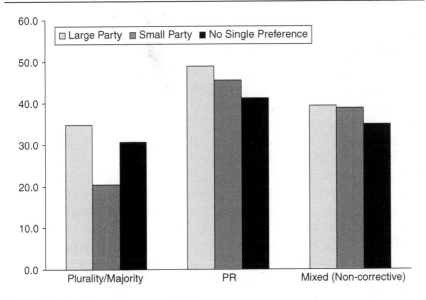

Figure 5.1. Party preferences and efficacy

levels of efficacy are also evident among those not having a single party preference (except in plurality/majority systems).

Micro and Macro Determinants of Efficacy and Turnout

Our initial examination of the data suggests some support for our expectations that the effect of electoral systems on a citizen's sense of efficacy is conditioned by whether or not that citizen supports a small party or large party. We now turn to a multivariate analysis to test whether the relationships observed in the bivariate analysis hold up when controlling for other factors. In this multivariate analysis, two measures are used to capture the effects of the electoral system. To estimate the psychological effect, a measure of the disproportionality of the system is included in the model.[15] Dummy variables for the electoral systems are also used to control for effects associated with the electoral system other than disproportionality. Since our expectation is that disproportionality is likely to disadvantage small parties and more likely to adversely affect small party supporters, we include an interaction term between small party preference and disproportionality. Other dummy variables are used to identify the nature of party preferences leaving those who prefer large parties in the referent category. We also include strength of party preference (as discussed above) which should be positively associated with both efficacy and turnout. For those with no preference, we set strength of preference to the neutral category.[16] We expect those who are older as well as those with higher levels of education (ranging from 1 to 8) to be more efficacious and be more likely to vote. Age, gender, and education are also used in the model as controls.[17]

Along with disproportionality, several other contextual variables are included to test hypotheses discussed earlier.[18] The number of parties gaining over 2 percent of the seats in parliament is used as an indicator of party mobilization.[19] To measure the effects of coalition government, we use the number of parties represented in government. Although increased representation of parties in parliament may lead to broader coalition governments, the two measures are only weakly correlated ($r = 0.20$). There is also a reason to believe that when the outcome is expected to be close, citizens may feel more efficacious and be more likely to participate. Therefore, a control for the closeness of the election is included by taking the difference between the two top vote-getters. The sample includes countries in various stages of democratic development. Therefore, a dummy variable is used for new democracies. Australia, Argentina, Mexico, and one canton in Switzerland have compulsory voting, though these countries differ in how the law is enforced. Since this is one electoral rule that is intended to increase the likelihood of voting, but is not hypothesized to influence efficacy, we include a dummy variable in the turnout model as a control.[20]

Testing the Effect of Macro- and Micro-Level Variables on Efficacy and Turnout

The results of the model for efficacy are reported in Table 5.2.[21] In response to the hypotheses set out earlier, there are two important points that should be noted about the results in Table 5.2. First, confirming our expectations, citizens who prefer small parties are less likely to be efficacious than citizens who prefer large parties at higher levels of disproportionality. The negative interaction term between small party preference and disproportionality indicates that the negative effects of small party on efficacy increase as disproportionality increases. Figure 5.2 helps to illustrate these effects. Specifically, a person who prefers a large party in a system that produces perfectly proportional results has a probability of

Table 5.2. Efficacy model, ordered logit estimates

	Coefficient	Robust standard error
Small party preferred	−0.01	(0.08)
No single party	−0.03	(0.06)
No preference	−0.23	(0.13)
Strength of preference	1.90**	(0.17)
Age (in 10s)	0.03	(0.00)
Education	0.50**	(0.11)
Female	−0.02	(0.02)
Parties in parliament	0.53	(0.88)
Parties in government	−1.23*	(0.53)
New democracies	0.10	(0.23)
PR	−0.04	(0.35)
Mixed	−0.58*	(0.25)
Disproportionality	−0.25	(0.85)
Disproportionality × small party preferred	−0.46*	(0.18)
Close election	0.65	(0.37)
Cut 1	−0.54	(0.90)
Cut 2	0.21	(0.91)
Cut 3	1.14	(0.92)
Cut 4	2.31	(0.94)
Nagelkerke pseudo R^2	0.09	
N	27,440	

* $p < 0.05$; ** $p < 0.01$. Robust errors clustered by country.

0.45 of having the highest level of efficacy. As the system becomes most disproportional, the probability decreases to less than 0.30. As Figure 5.2 reveals, the effects of disproportionality are greatest for those who prefer small parties. In the most disproportional system, a person preferring a large party is 16 percent more likely than a small party supporter to have the highest level of efficacy while there is no difference at the lowest level of disproportionality. The differences between PR and plurality/majoritarian systems are small and nonsignificant when controlling for disproportionality. In another model not reported here, the coefficient for PR doubles and is significant when disproportionality is dropped from the model. This suggests that disproportionality mediates the effects of the electoral system on efficacy.

Second, multipartism appears to have a negative and not a positive influence on efficacy. The number of parties represented in government has a negative impact on efficacy while the number of parties in parliament has no influence on efficacy. This finding is consistent with the expectation that voters will feel they have less influence on determining who is in government when there are broad coalitions but there is no mobilizing influence on efficacy due to a greater number of parties.

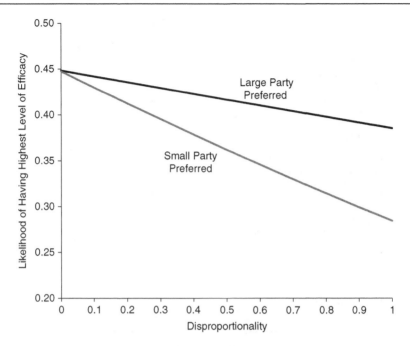

Figure 5.2. Impact of disproportionality on efficacy

Note: Estimates derived from Table 5.2.

We should also note that the strength of party preference has a large and significant effect on efficacy. Those with a greater affinity for a preferred party have a greater sense that their vote makes a difference. Other factors influencing efficacy are the level of formal education, which is among the three most influential variables in the model. We find no significant differences in efficacy between new and old democracies when controlling for these other factors. In elections where the outcome was closer, citizens appear to have a stronger sense that their vote mattered.

Table 5.3 reports the results for the model estimating the impact of these factors on voter participation. We discuss the main findings in Table 5.3 in terms of the effects of efficacy in multiparty and electoral systems on turnout. As expected, the likelihood of voting improves substantially when voters feel their vote makes a difference. Specifically, the difference in the probability of voting between those with the highest level of efficacy and the lowest level of efficacy is 18 percent. Those who prefer small parties are less likely to believe their vote matters (Table 5.2). However, once the level of efficacy is held constant, small party supporters are still less likely to vote than large party supporters. Taken together,

Table 5.3. Participation model logit estimates

	Coefficient	Robust standard error
Small party preferred	−0.16**	(0.05)
No single party	−0.16	(0.08)
No preference	−1.32**	(0.15)
Strength of preference	1.86**	(0.24)
Age (in 10s)	0.22**	(0.00)
Education	1.27**	(0.24)
Female	−0.12**	(0.04)
Parties in parliament	1.43*	(0.69)
Parties in government	−2.37*	(1.14)
New democracies	−0.79*	(0.37)
PR	0.29	(0.42)
Mixed	0.15	(0.53)
Close election	0.80	(0.50)
Compulsory voting	0.99	(0.72)
Efficacy	0.87**	(0.12)
Constant	3.24	(0.54)
Nagelkerke pseudo R^2	0.21	
n	27,206	

$* p < 0.05$; $** p < 0.01$. *Note*: Standard errors adjusted for clustering by country.

these results indicate that the effects of small party preference on voting are somewhat mediated by efficacy but that preference for a small party on its own still depresses the probability of participation. The strongest impact of party preferences is among those who have no preference at all. Voters in this group are 30 percent less likely to vote than those with a preference. This is an equivalent effect as on moving from the youngest to the oldest voter in our sample, and this exceeds the effects of moving from the lowest to the highest levels of education. Figure 5.3 illustrates the impact of party preference and efficacy on turnout by electoral system. Clearly, efficacy has a larger impact on turnout than party preference and the electoral system but, as shown earlier, both party preference and the disproportionality of the electoral system influence efficacy. We therefore must be careful in concluding that the impact of party preference and the electoral system are only minimal when compared to efficacy.

Strength of partisan attachment also has a large influence on the probability of voting; those with the strongest preference are four times more likely to vote than those with the weakest preferences. Therefore, PR systems also increase the probability of voting by fostering stronger partisan preferences (see Table 5.1). As shown in Table 5.2, multipartism in the form of number of parties in government had a negative influence on efficacy, and the results in Table 5.3 show that multipartism, both in terms

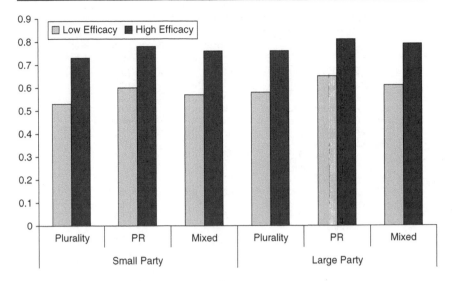

Figure 5.3. Impact of efficacy and party preference on voting by system

Note: Estimates derived from Table 5.3.

of the number of parties in government and in parliament, also directly contribute to participation. The relationship between multipartism and participation is consistent with our expectations. While more parties in parliament does not increase efficacy (see Table 5.2), it does mobilize participation. As Table 5.4 shows, a citizen's likelihood of voting increases from 0.62 when there are the fewest parties in parliament to 0.84 when the maximum are represented. The number of parties in government also has a negative effect on both efficacy and participation suggesting that a greater number of parties in government depresses turnout indirectly by leading to a decreased sense of efficacy, and directly by failing to create an incentive for parties to mobilize voters.

The effects of the control variables in the model also are consistent with expectations. The competitiveness of the election helps to motivate

Table 5.4. Impact of macro-level factors on voting

	Minimum	Maximum
Parties in parliament	0.62	0.84
Parties in government	0.78	0.53
Compulsory voting	0.71	0.87
New democracies	0.78	0.62

Note: Estimates derived from Table 5.3.

voters. While we observed no differences in efficacy between those in new and old democracies, substantial differences remain in voter participation (see Table 5.4). Electoral rules, such as compulsory voting help to improve the odds of voting, though the size of the effect indicates that it is less important than many other factors.[22]

Discussion

The implementation of the CSES project has allowed a test of some of the assumed links between macro-level factors such as electoral systems and individual behavior such as electoral participation. This cross-national and collaborative project is an important step forward in allowing researchers to link these macro- and micro-level characteristics and recognizes that not only do a multitude of factors shape individual political behavior but that some of these factors stem from the context in which individual decisions are shaped or made. This chapter has explored how voter efficacy is both shaped by the electoral system and, in turn, influences the decision to vote. To date most evidence showing a link between electoral systems and turnout could only make assumptions about how electoral systems affected voter efficacy because they were based on aggregate, country-level data.

Regarding the influence of electoral systems on efficacy, this chapter contributes to our understanding of the effects of disproportionality and multipartism. PR systems are less likely to produce disproportionality in the translation of seats to votes. However, such systems are also more likely to produce coalition governments. Importantly, we find that not all voters are equally adversely affected by disproportional outcomes. Namely, the efficacy of those citizens who support small parties (parties most likely to lose under electoral rules that produce disproportionality between seats and votes) is more adversely affected in plurality or majoritarian systems. While there is no gap between small and large party supporters under proportional outcomes, there is a substantial gap in countries where election outcomes are highly disproportional. On the other hand, as the number of parties that form government increases, efficacy declines. Therefore, PR systems enhance efficacy, most effectively among small party supporters by producing proportional outcomes. However, coalition governments which are also a consequence of PR systems tend to reduce voter efficacy, particularly when the size of the coalition is broad.

That macro-level variables can influence attitudes such as voter efficacy takes us a step further in understanding how electoral systems influence voter turnout. We have long known that an individual's assessment of the meaningfulness of his or her vote shapes the decision to vote, and that there is a correlation between proportionality and higher turnout. However, before CSES it was difficult to examine how these macro- and micro-level relationships fit together.

Appendix 5.1: Coding for large and small parties

Argentina
Large parties: Partido Justicialista (PJ/Peronismo), Acción por la
    República/Cavallo
Small parties: Partido Radical (UCR), Frepaso

Australia
Large parties: Liberal, Australian Labor
Small parties: National (Country), Australian Democrats, Greens

Britain
Large parties: Conservative, Labour
Small parties: Liberal Democrats, Scottish National Party, Plaid Cymru

Canada
Large party: Liberal
Small parties: Progressive Conservative, New Democratic Party (NDP), Reform,
    Bloc Quebecois

Czech Republic
Large parties: Czechoslovak Social Democratic Party (CSSD), Civic Democratic
    Party (ODS)
Small parties: Christian Democratic Union-Czech People's Party (KDU-CSL),
    Communist Party of Bohemia and Moravia (KSCM), Civic Democratic Alliance
    (ODA), Civic Democratic Party (ODS), Association for the Republic-Czech
    Republican Party (SPR-RSC)

Denmark
Large parties: Social Democrat (SD), Liberal Party (V)
Small parties: Conservative (KF), Centre Democrat (CD), Socialist People (SF),
    Danish People (DF)

Germany
Large parties: Christian Democratic Union (CDU), Social Democratic Party (SPD)

Small parties: Christian Social Union (CDU), Free Democratic Party (FDP),
Alliance 90 Greens, Party of Democratic Socialism (PDS), Republicans (REP),
German People's Union (DVU)

Hungary

Large parties: Federation of Young Democrats–Hungarian Civic Party
(Fidesz-MPP), Hungarian Socialist Party (MSZP)

Small parties: Independent Smallholders' Party (FKgP), Hungarian Democratic
Forum (MDF), Hungarian Justice and Life Party (MIEP), Alliance of Free
Democratic (SzDSz), Hungarian Communist Workers Party (Munkapart),
Hungarian Democratic People's Party (MDN)

Israel

Large parties: Likud, Avoda

Small parties: Shas, Mafdal, Meretz, Tzomet

Japan

Large parties: Liberal Democratic Party, New Frontier Party

Small parties: Democratic Party of Japan, Social Democratic Party, Japan
Communist Party; New parties: Harbinger, New Socialist Party, Freedom Union

Mexico

Large parties: Partido Accion Nacional (PAN), Partido Revolucionario
Institucional (PRI), Partido de la Revolución Democratica (PRD)

Small parties: Partido del Trabajo (PT), Partido Verde Ecologista Mexicano
(PVEM), Partido Cardenista (PC), Partido Popular Socialista (PPS), Partido
Demócrata Mexicano (PDM)

The Netherlands

Large parties: Labour (PvdA), People's Party for Freedom and Democracy (VVD)

Small parties: Christian Democratic Appeal (CDA), D66, Green-Left (GL),
Political Reformed Party (SGP), Reformed Political Union (GVP), Reforming
Political Federation (RPF)

New Zealand

Large parties: National, Labour

Small parties: Act, Alliance, New Zealand First, Christian Coalition

Norway

Large party: Christian People's Party

Small parties: Center Party, Socialist Left Party, Conservative Party, Labor Party,
Progress Party

Poland

Large parties: Electoral Action Solidarity (AWS), Democratic Left Alliance (SLD)

Small parties: Christian National Union (Z-ChN), Polish Block (BdP), National
Party of Retirees and Pensioners (KPEiR), Self-Defense of the Republic of
Poland (SRP), Freedom Union (UW)

Slovenia
Large party: Liberal Democratic Party (LDS)
Small parties: Slovenian People's Party (NSi), Social Democratic Party (SDSS),
    Christian Democrats (NSi), United List of Social Democrats (ZLSD),
    Democratic Party of Retired Persons (DeSUS)

Spain
Large parties: People's Party (PP), Socialist Party (PSOE)
Small parties: CDS, United Left (IU), Convergence & Unity (CiU), Basque
    Nationalist Party (PNV)

Sweden
Large parties: Sweden's Social Democratic Worker's Party (SAP), Moderate Rally
    Party (M),
Small parties: Left Party (Vp), Centre Party (C), People Party's Liberals (Fpl),
    Christian Democrats (KD)

Switzerland
Large parties: Swiss People's Party (SPS), Social Democrat (SPS), Free Thinking
    Democratic Party (FDP), Christian Democrat (CVP)
Small party: Green Party (GPS)

Taiwan
Large party: Kuomingtang (KMT)
Small parties: Democratic Progressive Party (DPP), Chinese New Party (NP),
    Green Party, China Young Party, Liberal Party

Ukraine
Large party: Communist Party of Ukraine
Small parties: People's Rukh of Ukraine, Socialist Party of Ukraine,
    Social-Democratic Party, People's-Democratic party

United States
Large parties: Democrat, Republican
Small party: Reform Party

Appendix 5.2: Question wording

Voting makes a difference: Some people say that no matter who people vote for, it won't make any difference to what happens. Others say that who people vote for can make a difference to what happens. Using the scale on this card (where 1 means that voting won't make a difference to what happens and 5 means that voting can make a difference), where would you place yourself?

Party Preference: I'd like to know what you think about each of our political parties. After I read the name of a political party, please rate it on a scale from 0 to

10, where 0 means you strongly dislike that party and 10 means that you strongly like that party. If I come to a party you haven't heard of or you feel you do not know enough about, just say so.

Strength of party preference: Range from 0 to 10. Coding described in text.

Religious Attendance: Attendance at religious services. 1. Never; 2. Once a year; 3. Two to eleven times a year; 4. Once a month; 5. Two or more times a month; 6. Once a week.

Education: 1. None; 2. Incomplete primary; 3. Primary completed; 4. Incomplete secondary; 5. Secondary completed; 6. Postsecondary trade/vocational school; 7. University undergraduate degree incomplete; 8; University undergraduate degree completed.

Age: (in years)

Appendix 5.3: Missing values

Age is missing in Argentina; values have been set at the mean (45 years).

Education is missing for Denmark. We imputed educational values for Danish respondents based on a regression equation predicting educational levels in Sweden. We have chosen Sweden as the country on which to base the Danish imputed values because they have similar educational levels and the explained variance in the model predicting Swedish education levels was higher than other countries (adjusted $R^2 = 0.43$). According to OECD statistics, 80 percent of those between the ages of 25 and 64 in Denmark have attained at least upper secondary education compared to 77 percent in Sweden (Organisation for Economic Co-operation and Development 2001, 45–6). Tertiary education has been attained by 16 percent in Sweden and 20 percent in Denmark. The following equation was used to predict education in Denmark:

Education = round (6.0 + (Income* 0.14) + (Mid level professional* −1.3) + (Service* −1.3) + (Skilled manual* −2.0) + (Unskilled manual* −2.3) + (Fulltime employment* 0.33) + (Part time employment* −0.1) + (Not seeking employment* −0.7) + (Student +0.5) + (Retired* −0.8) + (Male* −0.09)).

Notes

1. This chapter is a substantial revision of papers presented at the Annual Conference of the American Political Science Association in Atlanta, GA, September 1–4, 1999, and at the XVIII World Congress of the International Political Science Association, Quebec City, Canada, August 1–5, 2000. This research was partially completed while the authors were postdoctoral fellows at the

University of Waikato, New Zealand. Funding for the first author's work was provided in part by the New Zealand Foundation for Research, Science and Technology (FRST) and the Netherlands Organization of Scientific Research (NWO). Funding for the second author's work was provided by FRST and the European Union's Fifth Framework Programme. The names of the authors are listed alphabetically.

2. Some inconsistencies with regard to the effect of the number of parties may result from how the number of parties is measured. Some studies (Jackman 1987; Jackman and Miller 1995) use the effective number of parties as an indicator of multipartism (Laakso and Taagepera 1979). Blais and Dobrzynska (1998) use both the effective number of parties and the number of parties contesting an election and, while both have a negative relationship with turnout, they find that the number of parties contesting the election performs better than the effective number of parties. However, using the effective number of parties or the number of parties contesting an election as the one indicator of multipartism, may capture both the effect on efficacy of the decisiveness of elections in government formation and the extent of party mobilization efforts, but may not reflect the dynamics of party system effects on efficacy and turnout. The effects of party systems on efficacy and mobilization may be better captured by two variables. First, a citizen's feeling of efficacy, that her vote was decisive in determining a government and policy, may vary by the actual number of parties in government rather than the effective number of parties. After all, the number of coalition partners is arguably a more familiar feature of the party system than the number of effective parties to voters. Additionally, the potential for policy change, which would highlight the effect of voting on policy, has been to decrease as the number of parties in coalition government increases (Tsebelis 1995). Second, the number of parties in parliament may directly influence turnout because as the number of parties increases there will be greater party mobilization efforts.

3. Norris (2004) uses a different measure of efficacy than the one we propose in this chapter. She combines two questions regarding whether a vote makes a difference and whether who is in power can make a difference. Because most of the literature argues that disproportionality and multipartism influence the meaningfulness of a citizen's vote, we rely on the "vote makes a difference" question.

4. The World Values Survey asks which party citizens intend to vote for in the next election and includes a response for those intending not to vote. Given this design there is no measure for party preference of nonvoters.

5. These studies rarely if ever distinguish between voting and party preference.

6. This analysis relies on data from country-level election studies available from the August 2003 official release of Module 1. A single election is used from each country. Three of the countries that were included in this release (Lithuania, Romania, and Belarus) are excluded from this analysis because of missing

values or incomplete information, and due to significant deviations from the standard question wording Thailand has been excluded. Because our focus is on turnout in parliamentary elections, we do not include in our analysis presidential election studies that were deposited (Lithuania, Chile, Peru, and Belarus). Because of an extremely low response rate, Taiwan is not included in the analysis. Because regional election studies were conducted in Wallonia and Flanders, Belgium is not included.

7. At first glance, the CSES may appear to underrepresent the number of plurality countries. The sample includes Canada, the United Kingdom, and the United States. There are, however, few other plurality countries that could have been included (i.e. India and Jamaica).

8. Hungary also has a mixed system where 176 members are elected by majority in single member districts and 152 members are elected by PR. An additional 58 national seats are used to correct some of the distortions that remain (see Blais and Massicotte 1996). Since it is not entirely corrective we classify it as a mixed system.

9. Nevertheless, the first election held in 1996 under the new system continued to produce disproportional results that exceeded that of other mixed systems because few SMDs experienced bipolar competition (Reed 1997).

10. About 3 percent of the total cases are missing of which less than half are coded as "don't know." These missing cases are not evenly distributed across countries. Some of these missing values correspond to missing values on other variables suggesting that the problem is not unique to this variable. Since we cannot be sure why these cases are missing, they have been dropped from the analysis.

11. Collaborators were instructed to ask about all parties represented or likely to be represented in the Parliament (or running in the presidential contest). In circumstances where there are more than six such parties, collaborators were instructed to ask at least about the six most relevant parties, in terms of likely size and importance in coalition formation. If parties only contest elections in part of the country, those parties need only be asked about in those parts of the country where they contest seats.

12. For example the British Election Study asked, "Talking to people about the general election, we have found that a lot of people didn't manage to vote. How about you—did you manage to vote in the general election?" Similarly in Switzerland the question was asked, "On average, about half of the electorate casts a ballot at federal elections. How about you? Did you cast a ballot at the federal elections on October 24?"

13. On average, there is a 20 percent point difference between reported and actual turnout in plurality systems and a 12 percent point difference in PR systems. Among the plurality systems, Canada has a difference of 26 percent points, followed by the United States (21 percent points), and the United Kingdom (13 percent points). Among the PR countries, Mexico and Switzerland have

the highest differences and Israel the lowest. Among the mixed systems, the greatest difference between reported and actual turnout is in Japan, which is a similar difference to that of the United States.

14. Given that we have only one country with a majoritarian system (Australia), we consider plurality and majority systems together since these systems represent one form of democracy while PR systems represent another (Lijphart 1999).

15. This measure is based on the Gallagher (1992) index.

16. The models were estimated with and without no preference (which account for less than 5 percent of the sample) to determine whether this influenced the effects for strength of preference. The effects remained the same.

17. Ethnicity is missing in about half of the countries. Therefore we have excluded it in the analysis.

18. Because each country's level of disproportionality is unique, we do not (nor can we) include separate dummy variables for each country.

19. Unfortunately, Module 1 does not include a measure of party contact or mobilization.

20. Other electoral rules that have been found to influence turnout, such as registration requirements, are not included because they do not vary substantially across the sample of countries. Another rule that is thought to influence turnout is whether an election is held on a Sunday or a holiday (Franklin 1996). We tested this hypothesis and found that turnout was significantly lower in countries with Sunday or holiday voting. It is possible that countries with lower turnout choose to hold elections on Sunday to improve turnout. Or it is possible that idiosyncratic differences in these elections affected the result. Regardless, the inclusion of this variable does not alter the results so it has been omitted.

21. Models have been estimated in Stat using the cluster option so that standard errors are adjusted for clustering at the country level.

22. The effect is lower when all of the countries with compulsory voting are considered together irrespective of how the law is enforced. When considered separately, the impact is greatest for Australia where the level of enforcement is viewed as being stricter than in Mexico.

Part IV

Political Parties, Candidates, and Issues

6

Multiple Party Identifications

Hermann Schmitt[1]

The Concept of Party Identification

Party identification (PID) is a central concept in many models of voting behavior. The basic and now classic notion is from the *American Voter* in which partisanship was conceived as individuals' psychological *identification* with, or affective orientation toward, an important group object in their environment (Campbell et al. 1960: 121). This "psychological party membership" was thought to be acquired through primary political socialization (i.e. parental transmission), and to crystallize into stable alignments as a consequence of growing electoral experience (i.e. repeated voting for the same party; Converse 1969, 1976).

Party identification was regarded as an exogenous variable in models of party choice, coloring attitudes about issues and candidates as they are formed and thus affecting the vote both directly and indirectly (Campbell et al. 1960: 136). Only factors which originated in voters' social-structural location and their socialization experience were causally prior (see Figure 6.1).

Developed in the United States in the mid 1950s, these concepts and indicators were soon applied abroad. This led to the well-known and ongoing debate about the meaning and general applicability of the model. Two very basic objections have been raised against it. First, in some places, PID was found to be less stable than the vote thus violating the *stability assumption* (Thomassen 1976). PIDs were said to encompass more than one party thus violating the *uniqueness assumption* (van der Eijk and Niemöller 1983). Revisionists have since modified the stability assumption. They have shown that PID is endogenous to models of

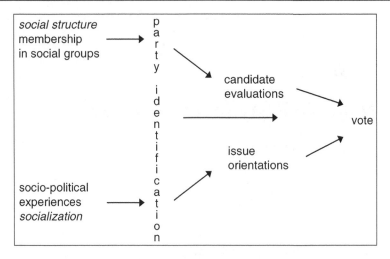

Figure 6.1. The classic social–psychological model of vote choice

vote choice, allowing for non-recursive effects between PID and various other determinants of the vote and the vote itself (e.g. Fiorina 1981; Franklin 1984; Franklin and Jackson 1983; Page and Jones 1979). Party identification is now portrayed as affecting current political evaluations and the vote, and being affected by such evaluations at the same time. Much of the work establishing this revisionist view runs in line with the rational choice paradigm and conceives changes in partisanship as a result of cognitive processes of issue evaluation. Time-series evidence indicates, however, that issue evaluations cannot account for everything, and certainly not for short-term changes in partisanship which should be seen to go back to changing affective or emotional views (Whiteley 1988; see also MacKuen, Erikson, and Stimson 1989). Irrespective of what causes the observed dynamics in partisanship, this round of the PID debate conveys that there is no conceptual need for partisanship to be fundamentally stable over time. It seems important to add, at this point, that the concept tends to become useless (or poorly operationalized as the case may also be) if its indicators are usually found to be more volatile than the vote.

The proclaimed violation of the *uniqueness assumption* however has not been taken up in a comparative way. Van der Eijk and Niemöller (1983: 338) concluded that "... the assumption that voters identify with only one party (if they do so at all) turns out to be false when subjected to an empirical test in the Netherlands" and took this as further evidence for their assertion that party identification theory was not an appropriate tool for the study of Dutch electoral behavior, nor for electoral behavior in European multiparty systems more generally. However, this finding was never replicated. We do not know: (1) how prominent a phenomenon such as multiple party identification is in different political systems, (2) what factors are conducive to it, and (3) what exactly are the behavioral consequences of multiple PIDs. These are the three research questions which this chapter will explore.

Multiple Party Identifications

Possible Sources

When it comes to multiple party identifications, there are at least three different and competing arguments: the Dutch proposition, the electoral systems proposition, and the electoral experience proposition.

The Dutch Proposition (or the Party System Format Proposition)

The first and most radical proposition is that the original theory of party identification is flawed altogether. People simply do not identify with parties, but rather with social groups and, if it comes to politics, with ideological tendencies. In this perspective, identification with a "party" is regarded as a mere reflection of what people really care about.[2] This is called the *Dutch proposition*.

If people do not really identify with parties but essentially with ideological tendencies, and if there are a variety of ideologically similar parties on offer to chose from, then it seems plausible that people, when asked, "identify" with more than one party. In this view, it is the format of the party system that counts. The Dutch proposition therefore leads to a party system format proposition: *the greater the number of ideologically close political parties competing for one's vote, the greater one's likelihood of holding multiple party identifications*.

The Electoral Systems Proposition

Moving on, the second argument maintains that electoral laws have an impact on voter–party relations (Blais and Massicotte 1997). The justification is rather straightforward. Proportional representation systems typically require voters to choose between parties, while plurality and mixed systems tend to require voters to choose between individual candidates (at least in addition to between parties). One might conclude that pure PR systems emphasize the role and importance of political parties, while the variety of plurality systems highlight the role and importance of individual candidates (Lijphart 1968, 1994). *The electoral systems proposition therefore predicts that PR systems cultivate "single" identifications with unique, concrete parties while plurality systems do not.*

Note that this second proposition in a way points in the opposite direction than the first. To the degree that proportional representation "breeds" multiparty systems (Duverger 1951; Farrell 1997), PR should—if the Dutch proposition holds true—lead to identifications with multiple parties rather than with a single party.

The Electoral Experience Proposition

The third argument states that the age of a democratic system is also important and, as a function of its age, the electoral experience of its citizens. This is a variant of Converse's proposition (1969, 1976) on the association between "time and partisan stability." Converse considered the strength of party identification. According to this consideration, younger people enter the adult electorate with only weak party ties. Over time these attachments grow stronger as they gain experience in voting for a party. Testing this learning theory of party identification with data from the Civic Culture Study (Almond and Verba 1963), Converse concluded that in new democracies it takes only a few generations to stabilize partisanship (1969: 143).

In this chapter it is argued that the concentration of partisanship on one and just one party is an essential part of this stabilization process. It might even be that this is the very core of Converse's hypothesis. In turbulent times of regime change, such as the transition from communist rule to liberal democracy in Central and Eastern Europe roughly a decade ago, people are typically strongly involved in politics. Deprived of an intimate knowledge of the new partisan actors on the political scene, they might feel attracted to a number of political parties. The extension of partisanship as indicated by the proportion of identifiers in the citizenry at large might therefore be quickly accomplished, and the intensity of these new partisan attachments might be remarkably strong. If these feelings, however, are not rooted in electoral experiences, they might not turn out to be very stable. As such, *the electoral experience proposition holds that the longer people are dealing with a particular set of party alternatives, the more likely they are to identify with one, and just one, of the partisan options.* This implies that the age of a democratic polity—but also party system changes which alter this particular set of party alternatives—should affect multiple party identifications.

Likely Consequences of Multiple PIDs

The most important consequence of (single) party identification is that people usually vote for the party with which they identify. If voters identify with more than one party, but still have only one vote, this crucial behavioral regularity is likely to be spoiled. One could object that multiple identifications must not be equally strong, and voters might vote for the object of their "main" identification more often than for parties they "also" identify with. While this may be the case, we nevertheless maintain that *single party identifications should have a stronger effect on vote choice than multiple party identifications.*

Database and Methodological Considerations

Database

The database of this research is the first round of studies of the Comparative Study of Electoral Systems (CSES Module 1). Under the auspices of ICORE,[3] this study has produced comparable representative postelection survey data. Fourteen of these surveys could be included in our first step of analysis which mainly confronts proportions of multiple PIDs with structural characteristics of the political systems under study.[4] Twelve surveys could be carried on to our second analytical step in which the relative effect of single and multiple PIDs on vote choices is established.[5] Multiple PIDs were not measured in nine of the 31 CSES surveys and so could not be included in this analysis. The CSES module was administered, finally, in eight political systems which do not, or only very recently, qualify as free democracies. As the development of party identifications is extremely sensitive to the democratic quality of the political system under study, these countries were not included in this study either (Table 6.1).

Table 6.1. 31 CSES Country Studies (Module 1) analyzed and not analyzed

Analyzed in first step	Analyzed in both steps [a]	Not analyzed because relevant data not secured	Not analyzed because not free[b] or free only very recently[c]
Chile	Czech Republic	Australia	Belarus[c]
Czech Republic	Germany	B-Flanders	Hong Kong[c]
Germany	Hungary	Canada	Peru[c]
Hungary	South Korea	Denmark	Romania[d]
South Korea	The Netherlands	Israel	Russia[c]
Lithuania	Norway	Japan	Taiwan[d]
The Netherlands	Poland	Mexico	Thailand[d]
Norway	Spain	New Zealand[b]	Ukraine[c]
Poland	Sweden	United Kingdom	
Slovenia	Switzerland		
Spain	United States		
Sweden			
Switzerland			
United States			
14	11	9	8

Notes: (a) Differences between first-step and second-step countries are due to data availability. For Chile, left–right party placements and party leader rating are lacking. For Slovenia, the strength of party identifications has not been established. (b) While the CSES module was strictly followed in New Zealand, the survey was there conducted as a drop-off to be filled in as a write-in questionnaire. With respect to multiple PIDs, this variation in questionnaire administration produced noncomparable results. (c) "Partly Free" according to Freedom House country ratings. (d) "Free" according to Freedom House country ratings for less than one legislature at the time of the survey.

Methodological Considerations

Party choice is the dependent variable in most analyses of electoral behavior. It is both a nominal and an ipsative variable, as voters in almost all political systems are only allowed to choose one party. From a substantive point of view, this causes two major problems. First, explanatory statements about party choice imply an intraindividual comparison of parties which, in multiparty systems, cannot be observed when only analyzing actual party choice. Second, when analyzing party choice one regularly runs into a problem that arises from (sometimes exceedingly) small numbers of respondents who voted for small parties.

Party Preference as an Alternative Dependent Variable to Vote Choice

These problems can be solved by relying on the electoral attractiveness of, or preference for, a political party as the dependent variable. This variable is a characteristic that can be measured for all parties, irrespective of their particular traits and irrespective of the political system in which they are located. One way of doing this is asking voters directly. Respondents to the European Election Studies of 1989, 1994, and 1999, for example, have all been asked: "Please tell me for each of the following how probable it is that you will ever vote for this party?" Afterwards they were presented with the names of the relevant (in the Sartorian sense) parties in their system. This instrument overcomes the restrictions of the more usually employed question about actual voting behavior, which does not allow respondents to report the extent of their electoral preferences for all parties. Moreover, the 10-point scale used allows a continuous expression of these preferences, rather than a merely dichotomous one.

These "probability to vote" questions were not included in the CSES questionnaire. Fortunately, they can be substituted by another measure that is derived from the more conventional like–dislike scales. While these like–dislike scales constitute another albeit less direct approach to the electoral attractiveness of political parties, they do not in their original form amount to a straightforward measure of party preference. Too many other considerations have an impact on one's liking or disliking of a party, in addition to its electoral attractiveness.

We will therefore transform these like–dislike scores into "party preference points" (PPPs). This is done by comparing for each respondent the like–dislike scores of each possible pair of relevant parties[6] and by attributing a preference point for the "winner" of each comparison (i.e. the party with the superior like–dislike score). In the case of ties, a preference point shall be given to each of the two parties under comparison. The resulting PPPs range from 0 to $<$max $n>$, whereby $<$max $n>$ is the number of relevant parties in the system minus 1. "0" is the score for the party that was defeated in each comparison and is preferred least, and $<$max $n>$ is the score of the party that has been preferred over all others.

The whole approach rests on the assumption that respondents will eventually vote for the party which they prefer most, that the second-highest preference score appears as second choice, and so on. This view is well founded. It can be shown that over 90 percent of those who prefer one party over all others (i.e. with $<$max $n>$ of PPPs) vote for this party.[7] This suggests that party preference scores are reasonably accurate reflections of actual vote intentions. As a consequence, by analyzing the former one arrives at valid conclusions about the latter.

The Simultaneous Analysis of Preferences Toward Relevant Choice Options in an Election

These preferences would normally be represented in a data matrix as different variables, one for each party, which cannot easily be analyzed simultaneously. It is even more interesting to examine determinants of party preference in general rather than those for a specific party. Analyzing these preferences one by one would obscure individual-level interparty variation, as such a design focuses exclusively on the variation between individuals. An adequate analysis of these scores requires a research design in which interparty (intraindividual) and interindividual variance is accounted for simultaneously. This can be realized by rearranging the original data into a so-called stacked form, viewing each preference score given by a voter as a separate case to be explained. In this way, each respondent is represented by a number of cases in the stacked data set—as many as the number of parties for which s/he gave a preference score, or for which such a score can be derived. The stacked data set can be analyzed in the same way as any normal rectangular data matrix.[8] The dependent variable is the preference score; appropriate identifiers allow characteristics of individual respondents and of parties to be added as explanatory or control variables. The independent variables have to be defined in an appropriate manner before they can be included in the analysis, but once this has been done, the stacked data matrix allows examination of the dependent variable using familiar and straightforward methods of analysis, such as multiple OLS regression.[9]

Findings

These methodological considerations will only be relevant in the second part of the analysis, when we try to determine the relative effects of single versus multiple PIDs on party preferences in 11 democracies. Beginning with the fundamentals, this section first inspects the frequency and importance of the phenomenon of multiple PIDs.

The Frequency and Importance of the Phenomenon

Van der Eijk and Niemöller report from their Dutch studies in the early 1980s that "multiple identifications occur frequently" (1983: 338): they found about half of all identifiers, and about one-third of all voters admit

Table 6.2. Number of parties with which voters identify (figures are percentages)

Country	Close to no party	One party	Two parties	Three parties	More than one	Missing cases
Norway	16	62	12	10	22	0
Czech Republic	19	62	12	7	19	2
Hungary	37	46	12	5	17	0
Sweden	15	69	10	6	16	11
Lithuania	50	36	9	5	14	11
Poland	32	56	10	2	12	5
Slovenia	78	10	7	5	12	7
Germany	35	55	1	9	10	1
Chile	62	31	7	0	7	0
Switzerland	32	62	5	1	6	1
Spain	37	57	5	1	6	1
The Netherlands	28	71	1	0	1	0
South Korea	65	34	1	0	1	9
United States	22	78	0	0	0	1
Mean proportion	38	52	6	4	10.2	3

Source: Comparative Study of Electoral Systems (1st module 1996–2000).

to multiple PIDs. These findings cannot be replicated. Relying on the Dutch CSES data, there is hardly anyone in the Netherlands who identifies with more than one party (Table 6.2). Together with the United States, the Netherlands constitute the bottom of the frequency distribution of multiple PIDs. This discrepancy with earlier work seems to result from instrument effects.[10]

This is not to say that the overall phenomenon is as marginal as it is in the Netherlands. Judging from our sample of 14 nations under investigation, we find an average of about one in 10 voters, and of one in six party identifiers, identifying with more than one party. This is clearly more than an ephemeral incident: multiple PIDs must be regarded as a relevant facet of partisanship. Norway occupies the pole position in this regard (with 22 percent of all respondents identifying with more than one party), closely followed by the Czech Republic (19 percent). Low proportions of missing data testify that the respondents had no problems in answering the question.

One in five Norwegians holds multiple PIDs, and one in four Norwegian partisans identifies with more than one party: Norway displays the highest proportion of multiple PIDs measured in this study. It is therefore worthwhile to inspect the Norwegian situation more closely before proceeding to test the four propositions. Table 6.3 displays the "additional" party identifications of Norwegians organized according to

Table 6.3. Multiple identifications with whom: the case of Norway (figures are row percentages, and *n* of cases)

Main identification	All identifications						
	1	2	3	4	5	6	*n*
1 Left Socialists[b]	68[a]	17	6	8	1	0	139
2 Labour Party[c]	11	68	8	3	6	4	656
3 Christian Peoples Party[d]	5	6	72	12	3	2	197
4 Centre Party[e]	8	5	15	66	4	1	149
5 Conservatives[f]	0	9	15	1	65	11	288
6 Progress[g]	1	8	4	3	13	82	170

Source: Comparative Study of Electoral Systems (1st module 1996–2000). (a) Read: while 68 percent of Left-Socialist identifiers do not identify with any other party, 17 percent also identify with the Labour Party, and so on. (b) *Sosialistisk Venstreparti* (c) *Det Norske Arbeiderparti* (d) *Kristelig Folkeparti* (e) *Senterparti* (f) *Høyre* (g) *Fremskrittspartiet*.

their "main" party identification. The major additional identification of Left Socialist identifiers, for example, is (of course) the Labour Party. But there are other Left Socialists who feel close to the Christian People's Party and even to the Centre Party. Identifiers of Labour "also" sympathize with Left Socialists, as with the Christian People's Party and the Conservatives. And sizeable numbers of the adherents of the Conservative Party have sympathies with the Christian People's Party, the Progress Party, and with Labour. What becomes apparent is that the walls which separate Norwegian political parties are not very high. Substantial proportions of partisans identify with not just the one or two parties in close ideological vicinity, but also with ideologically rather distant parties.

Do Multiple PIDs Increase with the Number of Relevant Parties in Multiparty Systems?

The classification of party systems according to the number of relevant parties operating therein is a demanding task (Sartori 1976) and diverts us from our object of inquiry. For the purposes at hand, we will merely distinguish between two classes of party systems: one with few and another with many parties. Parties differ from one another, and some are more important than others. We therefore refrain from counting the sheer number of parties represented in national parliaments and establish instead, for each country under investigation, the "effective" number of parties (Laakso and Taagepera 1979).[11] The scores of the 14 countries studied are given in Table 6.4.

Table 6.4. Effective number of parties (ENP) in the most recent election of members of the national parliament

Slovenia	6.1
Switzerland	5.8
Lithuania	5.6
Czech Republic	5.2
Chile[a]	5.1
The Netherlands	5.1
Norway	5.1
Poland	4.5
Sweden	4.5
Hungary	4.4
Germany	3.3
Spain	2.8
South Korea	2.8
United States	2.1

Source: Calculations provided by Bernhard Weßels. (a) Parliamentary election of 1997.

These scores range from 2 for the United States to 6 for Slovenia which is a fairly broad range indeed. To arrive at two equally strong classes of party systems, countries are subdivided into those with less than 5 (i.e. a few), and those with more than 5 (i.e. many) "effective" parties. The *party system format proposition* predicts that we should find higher proportions of multiple PIDs in party systems with many effective parties. Figure 6.2 displays the result of an initial test.

Germany, Spain, South Korea, and the United States are characterized both by low numbers of effective parties, and by low proportions of PIDs. Norway, the Czech Republic, Hungary, Lithuania and Slovenia, on the other hand, come up with many effective parties and elevated proportions of multiple PIDs. Taken together, eight out of 14 countries support the *party system format proposition*, while six countries, among them the Netherlands, do not follow the predicted pattern. This certainly is all but strong support for the proposition. We conclude that while being weakly related to the frequency of multiple PIDs, the format of the party system is certainly not the driving force behind them.

Are Single PIDs More Frequent in Proportional Representation (PR) Systems?

The electoral systems proposition holds that pure PR systems promote identifications with single, specific parties while mixed and plurality systems do not. This argument can be tested by relating the electoral system effective parties:

few = less than 5   many = more than 5[a]

multiple party identifications:		
few	Germany Spain South Korea United States	Chile The Netherlands Switzerland	7
many[b]	Hungary Poland Sweden	Norway Czech Republic Lithuania Slovenia	7
	7	7	14

Figure 6.2. Multiple party identifications and the format of party systems

Notes: (a) We take the median of the distribution of ENPs as a division line and define those countries with an ENP below 5 as low, and those above 5 as high. (b) We take the median of the distribution of proportions of multiple PIDs (cf. Table 6.1) as a division line and define those countries with 11 percent or more as having many and those with less as having few.

to the relative prevalence of single PIDs in all PIDs, that is, by holding the overall level of partisanship constant. Figure 6.3 displays the result of this analytic exercise.

The results indicate that concentration of partisanship on one single party (which is what "the relative prevalence of single PIDs" actually means) does not depend on the electoral system, at least not according to our admittedly crude classification. Seven countries—Hungary, Lithuania, Chile, Poland, the Netherlands, Switzerland, and Spain—support the proposition while seven others contradict it. Whereas electoral systems are known for their important effects on all sorts of things such as the translation of votes into seats or the level of electoral participation, they seem to leave the development of partisanship unaffected.

Are Multiple PIDs More Frequent in New Democracies?

It is Converse's argument that partisanship takes time to stabilize. Time in this context is shorthand for electoral experience. The quality of electoral

	not PR[a]	pure PR	
single party identifications: relatively few	Hungary Lithuania Chile	Czech Republic Norway Sweden Slovenia	7
relatively many[b]	Germany South Korea United States	Poland The Netherlands Switzerland Spain	7
	6	8	14

Figure 6.3. Multiple party identifications and the electoral system

Notes: (a) Classification of electoral systems according to Blais and Massicotte (1997). (b) We first compute the proportion of single PIDs in all PIDs, then take the median of this distribution of relative proportions as a division line and classify countries with 84 percent single PIDs in all PIDs or more as having relatively many and countries with less as having relatively few.

experience is important here: the more often people vote in free and fair elections, the greater their likelihood to develop party identification. And the more often they vote for one particular party, the stronger their attachment with it will grow. Political conjunctures and particular events also make their imprint on the partisanship of specific generations, but life cycle effects caused by growing electoral experience prevail by far (Converse 1969, 1976; also Cassel 1999). We have argued that the concentration of partisanship on a single, specific party is an important aspect of this stabilization process if not the very core. If this holds, we should find more multiple PIDs in new democracies than in older ones. Figure 6.4 shows that there is something to this argument.

According to Converse and his focus on the stabilization of partisanship, democracies grow old pretty fast (1969). We therefore classify only the postcommunist systems of Central and Eastern Europe and South Korea as "new democracies," and compare them with all the rest of the country studies (including Chile and Spain which, arguably, are not yet "old" democracies).[12] All five of so defined "new democracies" are characterized by "many" multiple PIDs. On the other hand, seven in nine old democracies are characterized by "few" multiple PIDs while there are

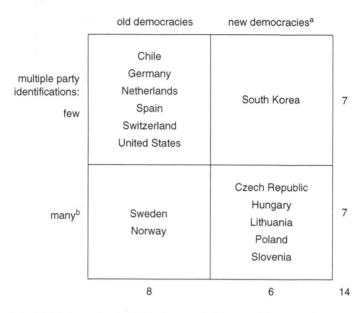

Figure 6.4. Multiple party identifications and the age of democratic party systems

Notes: (a) "New" democracies are established after the breakdown of communism in Central and Eastern Europe, while "old" democracies operate for a longer period of time. (b) We take the median of the range of proportions of multiple PIDs (cf. Table 6.1s as a division line and define those countries with 11 percent or more as having many and those with less as having few).

"many" in two. The deviant cases are Norway and Sweden. All in all, the electoral experience proposition is supported by 12 of the country studies.

At this point one wonders about the deviant cases. Why is it that partisanship in the new democracy of South Korea is highly concentrated, while it is so strangely dispersed in the old Scandinavian democracies of Norway and Sweden? With respect to South Korea, one obvious answer is that democracy in this country is not really new. Ever since the Korean Civil War in the years after the World War II, South Korea oscillated between military rule and liberal democracy. This means that the basic structure of party alternatives is deeply engraved in the public's mind. Thus, South Korean partisanship could develop over many years. However, political oppositions are only recently decided through the verdict of the electorate which probably explains why the current level of partisanship is rather modest (Nohlen, Grotz, and Hartmann 2001).

Things are different in Norway and Sweden. Democracy in Scandinavia has a long and strong tradition of consensual politics (e.g. Pappi and Schmitt 1994). Consensual democracies are characterized by the fact that opposition parties are usually involved in the definition of governmental policies, and by their high legitimacy (e.g. Luebbert 1986). It seems to make sense under those circumstances that partisanship is less "exclusive" even in an old democracy than it is elsewhere. But if this ancillary explanation is accepted, it is difficult to account for the Netherlands and Switzerland which are commonly known to be at least as consensual as Sweden and Norway. So the true answer as to why multiple PIDs are more numerous in Sweden and Norway is not known.

All in all, however, it may be maintained that electoral experiences are the key predictors of multiple PIDs. The less experienced an electorate, the more frequent are multiple party identifications.

Multiple PIDs as Determinants of Party Preference and Vote Choice

It is time to turn to the question of important behavioral consequences of multiple versus single PIDs. Are multiple PIDs less effective determinants of party choice than single PIDs? To be able to answer this question, one needs to predict party choice of respondents with single and multiple PIDs separately and then compare the findings. The simultaneous analysis of preferences toward relevant parties (described above) is a suitable strategy to do this. It allows for the coding of multiple PIDs of respondents in their respective "party stacks"[13] as well as analysis of cases of respondents with multiple PIDs, and those with single PIDs separately. It is also possible to contrast each case of these party evaluations to those of respondents with no PID.

Within this larger analytic design, we follow two more specific strategies for determining relative effects of PIDs. One is derived from the causal order as presumed by the traditional social–psychological model of vote choice (Figure 6.1). Stepwise regressions are performed with party preference as the dependent variable. Social-structural factors are entered first, and their explanatory power is determined. Next, party identifications are entered and the proportion of additional variance explained is determined, that is, the short-term effects on the vote of perceptions of party leaders and issue orientations.[14] Third, the proportion of additional variance explained is determined (together with the proportion of variance explained overall). In addition to this ΔR^2 strategy, concurrent multiple regressions are run both for single and multiple PIDs in each country (with

Table 6.5. The effect of single vs. multiple PIDs, Part I (figures are ΔR^2 if not indicated otherwise)

Predictors	Single PID against none					Multiple PIDs against none				
	First: Social structure[a]	Then: Party identification	Then: Short-term effects[b]	Explained variance	n of cases[c]	First: Social structure	Then: Party identification	Then: Short-term effects	Explained variance	n of cases
Countries[d]										
Spain	10	19	15	44	2,646	6	2	20	28	2,206
United States	13	19	10	42	2,948	—	—	—	—	—
Sweden	14	16	20	50	4,095	10	7	25	42	3,826
Czech Republic	22	13	18	55	5,986	21	7	22	50	5,817
Norway	19	13	19	52	10,416	17	8	21	47	10,250
The Netherlands	14	12	11	37	7,342	12	0	14	26	6,334
Hungary	23	11	17	52	4,749	21	7	19	47	4,718
Poland	11	11	13	35	6,740	8	5	15	28	6,329
Switzerland	8	11	9	28	7,057	2	2	11	20	6,332
South Korea	16	11	8	35	4,870	13	0	9	22	4,163
Germany	25	10	9	44	7,544	23	4	11	37	6,979
Mean	15	13	13	42		13	4	15	32	

Notes: Unweighted data are analyzed—except for the German case where East–West proportionality was established. The dependent variable is party preference (rather than actual vote choice). A stepwise OLS regression is performed with social structure entering first, party identification second, and short-term effects third. (a) The effect of social-structural factors on party preferences is the predicted preference on the basis of the age and gender of respondents, their union membership, religiosity (church attendance, atheism), education (primary, college), and the immediate living environment (village, town). Atheism has not been established in the Swiss study and could not be included there. A race dummy has been introduced as an additional predictor in the US analysis. For the Korean analysis, all social-structural factors are included which are significantly related to the preference for one of the relevant parties. (b) Short-term effects are issue orientations (measured as left–right distance to party) and evaluations of the party leader. Left–right placements of political parties have not been established in the United States. Thus, for the United States, short-term effects are restricted to party leader effects. Party leader evaluations have not been established for all relevant parties in Switzerland—the party leader of the Green party is missing; short-term effects for the Swiss study are therefore restricted to issue orientations (left–right distances). (c) The unit of analysis is party evaluations of respondents rather than respondents themselves; the corresponding technique of stacked data analysis is explained in the text. (d) Three of the 14 studies analyzed before could not be included in the multivariate analyses due to incomplete data: these are those from Lithuania (direction of party identification not fully established), Slovenia (no strength of party identification established), and Chile (no short-term factors—party leader ratings and left–right self- and party placements—established).

Source: Comparative Study of Electoral Systems (Module 1 1996–2000).

Table 6.6. The effect of single vs. multiple PIDs, Part II (figures are βs if not indicated otherwise)

Predictors	Single PID against none				Multiple PIDs against none			
	Social structure[a]	Party identification	Left–right distance[b]	Party leaders[c]	Social structure	Party identification	Left–right distance	Party leaders
Countries[d]								
United States	0.15	0.29	n.a.	0.37	—	—	—	—
Switzerland	0.17	0.28	−0.31	n.a.	0.18	0.12	−0.34	n.a.
South Korea	0.21	0.26	−0.05	0.29	0.24	0.03	−0.05	0.31
The Netherlands	0.18	0.24	−0.17	0.30	0.21	0.04	−0.18	0.32
Norway	0.20	0.23	−0.22	0.37	0.21	0.14	−0.23	0.39
Sweden	0.17	0.23	−0.35	0.26	0.18	0.14	−0.36	0.28
Poland	0.16	0.21	−0.20	0.28	0.17	0.12	−0.21	0.29
Spain	0.10	0.21	−0.15	0.39	0.13	ns	−0.14	0.41
Germany	0.31	0.20	−0.09	0.30	0.34	0.10	−0.10	0.31
Hungary	0.23	0.17	−0.11	0.44	0.23	0.09	−0.12	0.45
Czech Republic	0.20	0.16	−0.12	0.47	0.21	0.07	−0.13	0.49
Mean	0.19	0.22	−0.19	0.35	0.21	0.07	−0.20	0.32

Notes: ns = not significant below $p = 0.05$. n.a. = not applied (not applicable in the case of Taiwan). Unweighted data are analyzed—except for the German case where East–West proportionality was secured. The dependent variable is party preference (rather than actual vote choice). Results are standardized coefficients from a multiple OLS regression. (a) The effect of social-structural factors on party preferences is the predicted preference on the basis of the age and gender of respondents, their union membership, church attendance (never, frequent), education (primary, college), and the immediate living environment (village, town). Atheism has not been established in the Swiss study. A race dummy has been introduced as an additional predictor in the US analysis. For the Korean analysis, all social-structural factors are included which are significantly related to the preference for one of the relevant parties. (b) Left–right distance is the distance which the respondents perceive between themselves and the party under study. Left–right placements of political parties have not been established in the US study. (c) Party leader evaluations have not been established for all relevant parties in Switzerland and the variable was not used in the respective analysis. (d) Three of the 14 studies analyzed before could not be included in the multivariate analyses due to incomplete data: these are those from Lithuania (direction of party identification not fully established), Slovenia (strength of party identification not established), and Chile (no short-term factors established).

Source: Comparative Study of Electoral Systems (Module 1 1996–2000).

a close eye on tolerance scores to prevent multicollinearity problems). The results of both sets of analyses are displayed in Tables 6.5 and 6.6.

These tables suggest a number of conclusions not all of which are relevant in the context of the present chapter. Concentrating on the research question and starting with the ΔR^2 strategy, our expectations are clearly confirmed: single PIDs unmistakably have a greater impact on party preferences (and ultimately on the vote) than do multiple PIDs. This is true both on average and across the board, in every single country study analyzed. Differences are more than marginal amounting on average to almost 10 percent of the variance explained. Furthermore, short-term factors are found to be somewhat more important for the explanation of party preferences (and the vote) of multiple identifiers, and social-structural factors somewhat less important. This finding suggests that multiple identifiers are less well integrated in their social environment than single identifiers, and more affected by the ups and downs of day-to-day politics, by electoral campaigns, and by political leaders. Again, this is suggested by both average figures and the evidence in every single country analyzed.

Looking at βs rather than ΔR^2s, the relative weight of *both* social structure and short-term factors somewhat increased among multiple identifiers. This results from the concurrent (rather than stepwise) multiple regression technique in which a weaker multiple PID effect raises not only the weight of short-term factors but also that of social-structural traits. The main result however does fully coincide with that of the prior analysis: the relative impact of multiple PIDs on party preferences and the vote is clearly inferior to that of single identifications.

By way of concluding this section, it should be noted that the relative importance of party leaders for the shaping of party preferences and the vote is tremendous. On average, evaluations of political leaders yield by far the single strongest effect on party preferences in both sets of concurrent regressions.[15]

Conclusion

What has been termed the *Dutch proposition* states that people do not identify with political parties but with what they stand for (e.g. social groups and, in the sphere of politics, ideological tendencies). In this view, identifications with political parties are a mere reflection of the real thing.

As a consequence, people may hold multiple party identifications if an ideological tendency is represented by more than one political party.

Analyzing 14 country studies from the first module of the Comparative Study of Electoral Systems, it has been established that multiple party identifications are indeed a relevant aspect of partisanship. Noteworthy proportions of national electorates identify with more than one political party.

The sources for these multiple PIDs, however, are not found to accord with the *Dutch proposition*. The *format of party systems proposition*, which is more or less a sequel of that hypothesis, cannot explain where we happen to find many and where we find only few multiple identifiers. The same goes for the *electoral systems proposition*. What is important is time and electoral experience much as Philip Converse taught us some 30 years ago. The longer people are dealing with a given set of partisan alternatives, and the more often they vote for a particular party, the closer their attachment with this party becomes. It is therefore plausible that multiple identifiers are much more frequent in the new democracies of Central and Eastern Europe than in the older democracies studied. Noteworthy exceptions are the consensual democracies of Scandinavia which are also characterized by numerous multiple identifiers.

If it comes to the behavioral consequences of party identification, multiple identifications are much weaker predictors of party preferences and party choice than identifications with a single party. The first round of studies of the CSES thus seems to demonstrate that it is political parties, and not ideological tendencies, with which people identify.

Notes

1. Earlier versions of this chapter were presented at the conference of the Comparative Study of Electoral Systems at the WZB in Berlin, February 21–24, 2002, and the XVIIIth World Congress of Political Science, Quebec City, August 1–5, 2000. Excellent research assistance by Tanja Binder and, later by Christian Stumpf is gratefully acknowledged. Gary Cox, Cees van der Eijk, and Bernhard Weßels provided helpful and stimulating comments which are much appreciated. Of course, remaining errors of fact or interpretation are all mine.

2. The Dutch proposition actually proposes that people do not identify with political parties but with what these parties stand for, and that if multiple parties stand for the same thing—whatever it may be—then people tend to "identify" with multiple parties. Cees van der Eijk brought this to my attention.

3. ICORE is the acronym of the International Committee for Research into Elections and Representative Democracy. ICORE is the "club" of established National Election Studies.

4. Wherever appropriate weighting factors were provided we use weighted data sets in this first "descriptive" step, to improve the representativity of the samples.

5. The analysis of stacked data matrices is based on unweighted data.

6. In the framework of the present study a party is "relevant" if it managed to win, in the election under study, 5 or more percent of the valid vote. All other parties are disregarded and lumped together in an "other party" category. Only evaluations of and preferences toward relevant parties are considered in the stacked data analysis.

7. This leaves room for tactical voters who vote for a second preference in order not to spoil their vote altogether. This seems to be a rather prominent feature of British voting behavior, but tactical voting is certainly not restricted to plurality systems.

8. Note that the stacking of the data matrix is likely to produce correlated standard errors which might render conventional estimates of statistical significance inappropriate. In cases where such concerns are to be taken more seriously than in this analysis with its "robust" solutions, an appropriate alternative estimation of the significance of effects is the calculation of panel-corrected standard errors.

9. The pioneer study for this approach is van der Eijk, Franklin, and Oppenhuis (1996). Also instructive are Oppenhuis (1995), Schmitt (1998, 2000, 2001), Tillie (1995), and van der Eijk, Franklin, and van der Brug (1999).

10. While the CSES (Module 1) provides ample space for the coding of respondents' spontaneous mentions of more than one party to which they might feel close, it deliberately does not ask directly for multiple PIDs to avoid suggesting to respondents that those might exist. By contrast, the Dutch study asked respondents, in the course of the overall nine questions constituting the PID questionnaire, "Are there any other parties to which you feel attracted?" We believe that the latter way of establishing multiple PIDs activates an affirmative response set and thereby leads to an overestimation of the phenomenon. For full question wordings, cf. the CSES PID questionnaire in the appendix, and van der Eijk and Niemöller (1983: 335) for the Dutch study.

Note that the Dutch NES 1998 which carried the CSES (Module 1) study did not follow the CSES operationalization of the strength of party identifications. With regard to the directional component of PID measures, however, the Dutch CSES study scrupulously applied the master questionnaire; and multiple PIDs are determined on the basis of this directional component. Kees Aarts from the University of Twente provided valuable information on this question. Our interpretation of the 1983 Dutch findings as a methodological artefact seems to be confirmed by the New Zealand branch of CSES (Module 1) study.

There, the survey was administered as a drop-off questionnaire and filled in by the respondents themselves after the main interview. This leads to an interview situation which is about as "suggestive" as the 1983 Dutch face-to-face study was. It does not really come as a surprise, then, that the New Zealand CSES findings come close to the 1983 Dutch findings: 45 percent without PID, 31 percent holding one, 22 percent holding two, and 2 percent holding three PIDs.

11. If v_j is the share of vote of the jth party, then the effective number of parties is $(\sum v_j^2)^{-1}$.

12. The classification of Chile as an "old" democracy in particular might come as a surprise. According to Freedom House, Chile is classified as free "only" since 1990. However, the structure of the party system and public electoral experiences of free and fair elections date back at least to the pre-authoritarian period of mass democracy between 1932 and 1972.

13. While the CSES (Module 1) questionnaire establishes up to three directions of partisanship, the strength component of party identification even in the case of multiple PIDs is only measured for the one party which the respondent feels closest to. To overcome this shortage of information, we assume that the strength of attachment with a possible second or third party is minimal.

14. In the framework of the CSES (Module 1) study, issue effects can be operationalized as left–right distances between self and party. Party competence evaluations which are stronger predictors of party choice were not part of the common questionnaire of the module.

15. A nine-nation study on "Political Leaders and Democratic Elections" is currently exploring the phenomenon in diachronic and cross-nationally comparative analysis. The database is an integrated data-file combining the series of national election studies from Australia, Canada, Germany, the Netherlands, Norway, Spain, Sweden, the United Kingdom, and the United States.

7

Candidate Recognition in Different Electoral Systems

Sören Holmberg

Introduction

Historic as well as present-day constitutional engineers assume that electoral systems play an important role in how democracies function. Electoral systems are serious business—changing an electoral system is tantamount to changing the rules under which democracy is practiced. That electoral systems indeed matter is the general message (Anckar 2002; Powell 2000).

One prominent constitutional engineer, the Institute for Democracy and Electoral Assistance (International IDEA), has specified in what ways different electoral systems are consequential. Their primary importance is the translation of votes into parliamentary seats "because in translating the votes cast in a general election into seats in the legislature, the choice of electoral system can effectively determine who is elected and which party gains power" (*Handbook of Electoral System Design* 1997: 7–8). Other consequences mentioned in IDEA's handbook are: the type of party system (the number and relative sizes of the parties); internal cohesion of parties; the way parties campaign; how political elites behave, "thus helping to determine the broader political climate"; and how parties facilitate or complicate forging of alliances. Furthermore, the IDEA handbook points out how perceptions of fairness in the electoral system "...may encourage losers to work outside the system, using non-democratic...tactics." Finally, demands put on voters may vary, because "the choice of electoral system will determine the ease or complexity of the act of voting."

In light of this long list, it is clear that International IDEA considers the shape and form of electoral systems to be of a crucial importance for the way democracies work. Naturally, IDEA's conviction is self-serving. They try to persuade us that what they are doing is essential and worthy of support. If we look more closely at the nine different ways in which, according to International IDEA, electoral systems can influence the workings of democracy, we observe that political science research supports most of their claims but, in most instances, not very strongly. The nine consequences of the choice of electoral system do not enjoy particularly strong support in empirical studies—to the degree that they have been tested in comparative research at all. Empirical comparative studies on the effects of different election systems are an underexplored research area. We assume—and as institutionally inclined political scientists may also hope—that electoral systems matter.

Majoritarian Versus Proportional

One of the main ideas behind the Comparative Study of Electoral Systems (CSES) project is to alleviate this problem by collecting comparative data relevant to the question of electoral systems' impact. During the years 1996–2000, National Election Study Groups in some 30 countries participated in the project generating individual-level micro data on attitudes and behavior of eligible voters as well as macro data on system characteristics such as election laws, government composition, and national statistics. I will use this unique data set to empirically test to what extent different election procedures really impact the way democracies function. However, my test deals with something much more specific and concrete than any of the nine broad consequences of an electoral system identified by International IDEA.

I focus on whether the choice of election system has any effect on the degree of candidate recognition among voters. The relevant candidates in this context are local candidates in the home districts/constituencies of the voters, not national leaders like presidential candidates or prime ministerial hopefuls. The question is to what extent voters are familiar with the individual candidates from which they are supposed to choose. Clearly, if candidates are unfamiliar to voters, candidate characteristics like political profile, charisma, competence, or which demographic group to which candidates belong cannot influence how voters behave. In such cases other factors like party programs, issues, or party leader popularity may prove to be more important determinants of voters' choice than the type of electoral system. If on the other hand, candidates are known to the voters, the possibility opens up for voters to choose representatives according to candidates' individual competence or trustworthiness instead of by party affiliation. In short, individual candidate effects on the way people vote presumes that the candidates are known by the voters. Name recognition could be seen as a minimal requirement for candidate effects on voting behavior.

The rather obvious hypothesis is thus that election systems of the plurality-majority type create higher levels of candidate recognition than proportional systems. Historically plurality-majority election systems originated in Britain and are used in many Anglo-Saxon countries like the United States, Australia, and Canada. Globally, about one-third of all countries use first-past-the-post systems (FPTP), as they are sometimes called. In FPTP systems, we almost always find single-member districts and the winner is the candidate who garners the most votes. Candidate recognition ought to be fairly high since voters choose between a limited number of individual candidates. Many of the claimed advantages of the FPTP system presuppose that candidates are known to voters. Among these advantages are that FPTP systems retain the link between voters and their elected representatives, allow voters to choose between people rather than between parties, and gives popular independent candidates a shot at election (IDEA *Handbook* 1997: 29). This emphasis on the individual candidate is one of the distinguishing features of plurality-majority systems.

Proportional representation systems (PR) on the other hand, are focused on parties and primarily designed to transform a party's share of the vote into a corresponding share of parliamentary seats. Hence, party proportionality is central in PR systems. Candidates in PR systems are in most cases elected in multimember districts where voters choose between party lists, not between individual candidates. IDEA's *Handbook* identifies a weakening of the link between members of parliament and their constituents as one of the disadvantages of PR systems: "Voters have no ability to determine the identity of persons who will represent them, and no identifiable representative of their town, district, or village; nor do they have the ability to easily reject an individual if they feel he or she has behaved poorly in office" (1997: 66). In PR systems, voter recognition of individual candidates is neither a prerequisite for voting nor an encouraged piece of knowledge. Parties are put center stage, not individual representatives.

Some kind of PR system is used in about half of all democracies. More or less pure list PR systems where parties present a list of candidates and voters choose between parties are most popular (used in 40 percent of all democracies).[1] Various systems where straightforward PR techniques are combined with majoritarian procedures are employed in an additional 10 percent of the world's democracies (1997: 20) These mixed systems roughly fall into two categories—semi-PR systems (as used in Russia and Japan) and mixed member proportional systems (as used in Germany and Hungary). In both cases PR party lists and FPTP district elections are used in parallel, but in semi-PR systems the results of the party-list elections do not compensate for any disproportionalities resulting from the majoritarian district elections. These, however, are the rules of the game in mixed member proportional systems.

Results from 23 Countries

The results in Table 7.1 give us a first bird's eye view of the degree of empirical support for the hypothesis that plurality-majority electoral systems compared to PR systems tend to facilitate higher levels of candidate familiarity among voters. Twenty-three countries from the CSES data set are rank ordered according to the degree of candidate recognition among eligible voters. The measurements are based on answers to an interview question asking respondents: "Do you happen to remember the name of any candidates who ran in your constituency in the last parliamentary election?"[2] Up to three names were coded per respondent and checked for incorrect candidate names.[3] Analysis is, however, restricted to the mentioning of only one correct candidate name. Most respondents who gave names mentioned only one candidate. The electoral system in use in the different countries—plurality, majority, semi-PR, PR-mix, or PR-list—is also indicated in Table 7.1.

The study reveals that the level of candidate knowledge varies a great deal across political systems—from high figures above 90 percent in some Asian countries (Japan, Thailand, and Korea) to a low of only 18 percent in Mexico.[4] The average result for the 23 countries is 55 percent, meaning that a little more than half of the people in the democracies studied can correctly name at least one local candidate in their constituency. This may be considered a fairly decent outcome in the sense that a majority of eligible voters in most cases were familiar with at least one local candidate. Thus, candidate voting is in theory possible not only for

Table 7.1. Candidate recognition among eligible voters

Country	Percentage among eligible voters recalling at least one correct candidate name in response to the question: "Do you happen to remember the name of any candidate who ran in your constituency in the last parliamentary election?"	Electoral system
Japan	94	Semi-PR
Thailand	93	Plurality
South Korea	92	Semi-PR
New Zealand	83	PR-mix
Canada	72	Plurality
Peru	71	PR-list
Russia	70	Semi-PR
Norway	69	PR-list
Hungary	64	PR-mix
Great Britain	60	Plurality
Czech Republic	58	PR-list
Australia	58	Majority
United States	52	Plurality
Switzerland	46	PR-list
Germany	41	PR-mix
Ukraine	39	PR-mix
Poland	38	PR-list
Sweden	37	PR-list
Taiwan	37	Semi-PR
Romania	30	PR-list
Spain	26	PR-list
Mexico	18	PR-mix
Belarus	16	Majority

Comments: The data come from the project *The Comparative Study of Electoral Systems (CSES)* which relies on data from *National Election Studies* in the indicated countries covering the period 1996–2000. All results are unweighted except for Germany, Canada, and Great Britain. The percentage base has been defined as respondents who were asked the question about candidate recognition. Results are checked for wrongful candidate names. Only correctly named candidates are retained in the results. The classification of the electoral systems is done by *International IDEA* in a handbook on *Electoral System Design (1997)*. *Semi-PR* systems falls somewhere in between proportional PR-systems and *plurality-majority* systems; *PR lists* as well as winner-take-all districts are used side by side, although the PR lists do not compensate for any disproportionality within majoritarian districts. *PR-mix* systems combine majoritarian and PR electoral systems as well, but results from the PR list elections compensate for disproportionalities produced by the majoritarian district results.

small knowledgeable groups but also for larger segments of the voting population. Voting for a specific candidate need not be a fringe phenomenon even if most empirical studies so far have shown that the role played by local candidates in garnering votes is rather limited.[5] A quick look at the electoral systems employed in the countries at the top or at the bottom of the rank ordering does not reveal any simple patterns.

Countries using plurality-majority systems are found toward the top (Thailand, 93 percent) as well as toward the middle (United States, 52

Table 7.2. The electoral system matters

Electoral system	Number of countries	Average percentage among eligible voters recalling at least one correct candidate name
Majority/plurality	6	59
PR-mix/semi-PR	9	60
PR-list	8	47

Comment: The results derive from the data in Table 7.1.

percent), and the bottom (Belarus, 16 percent). The same is true for countries where the PR-list system is used. For example, Peru (71 percent) and Norway (69 percent) are ranked fairly high while two PR-list countries like Romania (30 percent) and Spain (26 percent) are near the bottom.

We get a better overview if we sort the countries according to a simple classification of their electoral systems. That has been done in Table 7.2. Three broad types of election systems are distinguished: plurality-majority systems found in six countries, PR-mix or semi-PR systems employed in nine countries, and PR-list systems used in eight countries. The average percentage among eligible voters recalling at least one correct candidate name in the three groups of countries with different election systems reveal a readily observable pattern in support of our hypotheses. Candidate familiarity among eligible voters is on the average lowest in countries where the PR-list election system is used.

In the plurality-majority countries, the average level of candidate recognition is 59 percent, compared to 60 percent in mixed PR/FPTP systems, and only 47 percent in PR-list systems. Some of the countries exhibit extremely high or low levels of candidate familiarity. However, the outcome of our hypothesis test is not dependent on the inclusion of these outliers. If, for example, deviant scoring countries such as Thailand and Belarus are excluded from the analysis of the plurality-majority group; Japan, Korea, and Mexico from the mixed group; and Peru and Spain from the PR-list group, the results are basically the same but actually become somewhat more distinct. The average levels of candidate recognition are now 61 percent for the plurality-majority countries, 56 percent for the countries with mixed election systems, and 46 percent for the PR-list countries.

Thus, it may be concluded that a higher level of knowledge of candidates exists in plurality-majority election systems than in PR-list systems.

The difference is on average 12 percentage points to the advantage of systems based on winner-take-all elections in single-member districts.[6] This is not a major difference, but not a negligible difference either. The electoral system matters. How much it matters can be put in perspective by comparing the election system effect with the effects of some other potentially important factors that help people obtain knowledge of political candidates (West 1995).

Degree of education is one such obvious factor. General political knowledge and exposure to politics are other examples, as is level of political interest. One would expect people with higher education, frequent political contacts, and high degrees of interest in politics to be most knowledgeable about local candidates. Age and gender is also always of interest. Our suspicion is that younger people and women are less knowledgeable about candidates for at least two reasons. Most research findings point to the fact that, first, young persons and women tend, on the whole, to be less experienced and knowledgeable about politics than older people and men. Second, most candidates of whom voters are expected to have knowledge are middle aged or older men. There are relatively fewer young or female candidates with whom young people and women may identify. Hence, our hypothesis is that across all kinds of election systems, men and older people tend to have higher levels of candidate recognition than women and young people. Electoral participation is another interesting factor. Nonvoters would be less motivated to learn about local candidates than voters. After all, if you do not intend to go to the polls why bother to learn the names of local candidates.[7] Consequently, we expect that nonvoting is related to lower levels of candidate familiarity.

General Political Knowledge

All of these factors have a bivariate relationship with the level of candidate recognition in most of the 23 CSES countries studied. Not surprisingly, given that candidate recognition is a form of political knowledge, general political knowledge is the factor with the strongest correlation. The average difference in candidate familiarity between people with low and high general knowledge about politics is 39 percentage points across our selected countries.[8] The direction of the difference was the same in all countries, but the magnitude differed somewhat with the United States exhibiting the largest spread between the level of candidate familiarity among people with a low degree of general political knowledge (among whom 13 percent had some candidate recognition) and people with a high degree (among whom 87 percent could name a candidate), constituting a very large difference of 74 percent.

Education

Formal education is also rather clearly related to the extent of candidate recognition. With one exception, in all of the CSES countries examined people with high education (university level) know more about local candidates than people with low education (secondary level).[9] The average difference in candidate recognition is 20 percent across the 23 countries. Once again we do find the largest difference in the United States. Among Americans with limited education, 24 percent could identify a local candidate. Among university educated Americans, the figure was 73 percent.

Contact with politics and politicians is an obvious source of information and an indicator of involvement. In the CSES module, respondents were asked if during the last 12 months they had been in any contact with a member of parliament. A minority answered affirmatively, on average 12 percent.[10] As expected, people who reported contacts with elected representatives were more familiar with local candidates than people without such contacts. Among the minority with contacts, on average 74 percent could name at least one local candidate while only 53 percent of those with no such contacts demonstrated any form of candidate recognition.[11]

Nonvoters

As expected, and without exception in any country, nonvoters were less knowledgeable about candidates than voters. The difference is sizeable but not dramatic (24 percent). On average, in our CSES countries, 57 percent of voters had some candidate familiarity. The corresponding figure among nonvoters was 32 percent. The United States is one of the countries with the largest difference in candidate knowledge between voters (61 percent) and nonvoters (23 percent).[12]

Age

Moving on to age, it turns out that how old people are is only weakly related to candidate recognition. The relationship has, however, a very familiar pyramid shape, with the highest level of candidate recognition among middle aged people and lower levels among the young and the old. The average candidate knowledge across our CSES countries is 57 percent among the middle aged, and 48 and 52 percent, respectively among young and old people. Age was most clearly related to candidate familiarity in the Anglo-Saxon countries and in Belarus, Russia, and Norway. Young people in countries like Australia, Canada, New Zealand, Great Britain, and the United States—and in Norway, Belarus, and Russia—are especially unfamiliar with local candidates compared to their middle aged and older compatriots. Overall, middle aged people were most knowledgeable in 17 countries, old people in four countries, and young people in one country (Romania).[13]

Gender

As with age, gender differences are rather limited, although the expected pattern was found. Women tend to be somewhat less knowledgeable about local candidates than men. Across the 23 countries, on average 58 percent among men and 52 percent of women could correctly name at least one local candidate. The countries with the largest gender differences are Taiwan, Switzerland, and Romania. Two countries went against the dominant pattern and exhibited higher levels of candidate recognition among women than among men: Japan and New Zealand.[14]

One factor behind these results, that is, that men tend to be slightly more familiar with local candidates than women, could be that the number of female politicians is very limited in many countries. Female voters have few leading women candidates with which to identify. The average proportion of women in parliaments worldwide has been around 12–14 percent in recent years (*International Parliamentary Union* 2001). In the CSES data set local candidates mentioned are identified by gender, which means that one can study to what extent people tend to know about candidates of their own sex and of the opposite sex. That is, it is possible to analyze the extent to which men tend to know about male candidates and women about female candidates (Wängnerud 1993). Furthermore, since up to three candidate names were coded per respondent, it is possible for people to mention male candidates as well as female candidates.

Among respondents who identified candidates, a very substantial majority mentioned male candidates, on average 91 percent, while only

25 percent named female candidates. Given that the number of female politicians is far fewer than the number of male politicians, this result is not surprising even if the difference is significant. There is no doubt that the number of female candidates/politicians affects the extent to which female candidates are recognized by voters. In countries with a relatively high proportion of female MPs, recognition of female candidates is much higher than in countries with few women represented in parliament. For example, in Norway and Sweden, where women make up about 40 percent of the parliament, 57 and 47 percent of all respondents who mentioned a candidate identified a female candidate. By way of contrast, in Romania and Korea, where between 5 and 10 percent of parliamentarians are women, only 3–4 percent of the people who recognized a candidate named a woman. If we generalize this relationship, the rank order correlation across the CSES countries studied between the proportion of women represented in parliament and the proportion of respondents who mention female candidates, there is a very strong correlation indeed, no less than +0.85.[15] The structure of female representation matters for candidate recognition. Male candidates tend to be more recognized because there are more male candidates to recognize.

However, the results have very little to do with the gender of the respondents. On the whole, men and women voters recognize male and female candidates to the same extent. Among respondents who name candidates, 93 percent among men, on average, mention male candidates and 24 percent name female candidates. The corresponding figures for women are similar, 89 percent and 27 percent, respectively. This small difference is as expected. Men tend to notice male candidates somewhat more than women—with a 93 percent versus 89 percent recognition rate, while women have a slight tendency to identify female candidates more frequently. This small but nonetheless real difference means that the lower level of candidate knowledge among women to some degree, although a small degree, can be attributed to the fact that there are so few female politicians in the countries studied.

The Electoral System Matters, But Not Much

Going back to the original question of how to assess the impact of electoral system type on voters' candidate recognition, a fairly clear conclusion can be drawn. Having looked at the simple bivariate effects of several causal factors behind voters' familiarity with candidates, it is clear that the nature of the electoral system is not one of the more important factors. The average increase in candidate knowledge of 12 percentage points that was found between PR-list systems and plurality-majority systems is smaller than many of the other effects discussed, for example, impact of general political knowledge, education, contacts with politicians, and electoral participation. That said, the impact of electoral design is clearly larger than that of age or gender. The conclusion is that the type of election system matters, but not a whole lot.

Testing the relationships multivariately does not change this conclusion in any fundamental way. If, based on the CSES data file of some 30,000 respondents from 18 countries, all the factors behind voters' candidate recognition are regressed, the outcome shows larger effects for factors like political contacts, turnout, education, general political knowledge, and age than for electoral system.[16] The only factor of those included that exhibits a smaller effect than electoral system is gender. And gender has almost no independent effect at all on candidate familiarity. The conclusion stands. Candidate recognition is affected by how the electoral system is designed. Plurality-majority systems lead to higher levels of candidate familiarity than PR-list systems. But the difference is not large. The election system matters, but it does not matter much.

Notes

1. The extent of candidate choice varies across PR systems. On paper, most PR systems include some kind of device that in theory allows voters to vote for a preferred candidate on a party list as well as for a party. The actual effects of these personal vote devices vary across systems, but in most cases they have a limited impact (Bogdanor 1985: 11; IDEA *Handbook* 1997: 89; Holmberg and Möller 1999).

2. In two countries, Peru and Belarus, the data collection was done after presidential elections although knowledge of candidates in the *last* parliamentary elections was asked for.

3. The degree of vigorousness in checking for correct candidate names across the different *Election Studies* may vary. Among the 23 countries in Table 7.1, only 14 report mentioned names as well as mentioned correct names. Two countries only report correct names, while seven countries report both names recalled by respondents regardless of whether those names were correct or not, *and* the correctness in respondents' recollection of names. For the countries which report both sets of data, the proportion of at least one correct candidate name mentioned among all eligible voters is on average 7 percent lower compared

to the proportion who mention any name. Thus, for these 14 countries, 51 percent of eligible voters mentioned at least one candidate name. Upon checking, about one in five of those names turned out to be wrong, meaning that, all in all, 7 percent of the voters gave incorrect candidate names. The proportion of eligible voters who mentioned correct candidate names was 43 percent in this group of 14 countries.

4. Familiarity with national political leaders was on average much higher among eligible voters in the CSES countries. Across 26 countries, on average 97 percent of the respondents expressed a like–dislike sentiment for at least one party leader, with a high of 100 percent for countries like Norway and the United States, and a low of 85 percent for Ukraine. Admittedly, the like–dislike scale questions are easier to answer than the knowledge question about local candidate names.

5. Analyses of the impact of local candidates on the way people vote can be found in Bogdanor (1985), Gilljam and Holmberg (1995), and Klingemann and Weßels (2001).

6. The difference is 15 percentage points if we exclude the extreme cases mentioned in the text.

7. Of course, the causal arrow could be reversed. People who do not know about local candidates have less of an incentive to go to the polls compared to people who know about at least some candidates. However, this pull of local candidates has probably a very limited effect in most cases.

8. The CSES module contains three knowledge items per country. On the basis of the answers to these questions, I have constructed a knowledge index with values running from no correct answer to three correct answers. The average difference in levels of candidate recognition between people with no correct answer and people with three correct answers is 39 percent across the 17 CSES countries where the full analysis is possible.

9. The exception is Japan where the level of candidate recognition among people with primary, secondary, and higher education is 93 percent, 95 percent, and 91 percent, respectively.

10. Twenty-eight countries are included in the calculation. The means are 15 percent among countries with plurality-majority election systems, 11 percent in countries with mixed systems, and 11 percent in PR-list systems. In other words, the results are in accordance with the hypothesis.

11. This time the United States did not show the largest spread. That distinction goes to Poland with a candidate recognition rate of 75 percent among persons with contacts and only 36 percent among people without contacts. The comparable result for the United States is 78 percent and 48 percent, respectively.

12. New Zealand has an even larger spread in terms of candidate recognition between voters (85 percent) and nonvoters (40 percent). However, the proportion of nonvoters in the New Zealand sample is only 4 percent. As always, nonvoters are underrepresented, and more select, in most of the country

samples, meaning that candidate familiarity among interviewed nonvoters in all likelihood exaggerate the true degree of knowledge among nonvoters. Twenty-one countries are included in the analysis.

13. It was not possible to construct a complete age variable in the Peruvian data set. Thus, there are only 22 countries in this analysis. The age trichotomy was defined as *young*: 19–30, *middle aged*: 31–60, and *old*: 61+.

14. In both cases, women scored 1 percent point higher for candidate knowledge than men.

15. Fourteen countries are included in the calculation.

16. OLS as well as logistic regressions were applied. Results based on logistic regression gave the most lucid outcomes. The model, including a variable for election system design, was tested based on the entire data set. The model was also tested within each of the countries, excluding the election system variable. Max-rescaled R^2 vary between 0.06 (Mexico) and 0.29 (United States) across the different countries with a mean of 0.17 (18 countries). Max-rescaled R^2 was 0.16 for the regression based on the full data set. However, max-rescaled R^2 was somewhat smaller if all countries were given the same weight in the analysis (0.11). The sizes of the parameter estimates ("β-values") in the unweighted logistic regression, based on the entire material, follows the order given in the text above starting with MP contacts, followed by turnout, education, general political knowledge, and age, ending with gender.

8

Who Represents Us Best? One Member or Many?

John Curtice and W. Phillips Shively

Introduction

There is one issue which tends to dominate the debate about legislative electoral systems. It centres on the relative merits of "fairness" versus an electoral outcome which produces a clear winner. Advocates of proportional representation argue that the allocation of seats for each party in a legislative body should be as proportional as possible to the votes that they win. This, they argue, ensures that the diversity of views of the electorate is faithfully and fairly reflected in the composition of the legislature. In contrast, advocates of majoritarian systems, such as first-past-the-post, argue that what matters is that elections should produce a clear winner. They argue that this characteristic ensures that it is the electorate rather than some shady backroom deal which determines the partisan color of the next government (Katz 1997; Lijphart 1999; Powell 2000; Schumpeter 1976).

This debate is primarily about the proper relationship between seats and votes across the country as a whole. But, important though it is, it is not the only issue at stake in the debate about electoral systems. There is also an argument about representation and the role of elected representatives. Deputies or MPs may well be elected to represent a particular ideological standpoint. But they may also be expected to act as intermediaries or advocates for individual citizens, representing their views to the state when those citizens have a problem with the operation or policies of some part of the bureaucracy (Bogdanor 1985). After all, if the state is not to become overweening or arbitrary in its working then it may well need the counterweight of politicians acting on behalf of the citizens the democratic state is meant to be serving. What is disputed in the debate about electoral systems is whether some systems give elected representatives a greater incentive to act as citizen intermediaries than do other systems—and if so, which?

This chapter addresses this second, relatively neglected, debate. We begin by examining the theoretical arguments deployed in this debate. In so doing, we focus in particular on the arguments commonly suggested by advocates of majoritarian systems as to why the single member plurality system is more likely to ensure that elected representatives act as intermediaries on behalf of citizens, and why this is conducive to the effective operation of a democracy. As a result of this discussion we are able to develop a model of the relationship between electoral systems and citizens. The model focuses upon politician contact and on the implications such contact supposedly has for attitudes towards and satisfaction with elected representatives in particular and democracy in general. We then proceed to test this model using data from the Comparative Study of Electoral Systems (CSES) project. We conclude by examining the implications of our findings for the debate about electoral systems.

Who Represents Us Best?

The claim in which we are interested is that the single member plurality electoral system makes it more likely that elected representatives will act as citizen intermediaries. The first step in formulating this argument is to note that under single member plurality each and every politician depends for reelection on securing sufficient support from a clearly defined body of voters, that is, their constituents. Every constituent is potentially at least equally important to the representative in this endeavor. Each has a vote that can either be cast for the local incumbent or else for some other candidate. A local representative's fate rests on persuading people to take the former rather than the latter course of action.

No multimember system, it is argued, can make quite the same claim. Under a closed party list system, for example, representatives' fates may well depend on their ability to retain a high position on their party's list rather than on securing the votes of their constituents. That would appear to encourage service to the party rather than service to the citizen. But even under an open party list system, or indeed the Single Transferable

Vote (STV) in multimember constituencies, elected representatives would only appear to have an incentive to heed the concerns of some of their constituents rather than all of them. Under STV, for example, a representative needs just enough votes to satisfy the quota, which, for example, in a typical five-member constituency is but one-sixth of the vote. Meanwhile, given that in open party list systems a vote for a candidate also usually counts as a vote for a party, the question of which individual candidates secure election would appear more likely to be determined by the preferences of the party faithful than the views of the electorate as a whole.

In short, it is argued that the single member plurality system encourages all elected representatives to take heed of the views of all their constituents in a manner that is not replicated by any multimember proportional system. Their reelection depends not just on the judgment of the party faithful, but on that of the electorate at large. As a result, elected representatives have an incentive to develop a reputation as an effective local advocate by taking up the problems of individual citizens, or indeed of the local community as a whole, with governmental officials. To fulfill this role, they may hold local "surgeries" or other events that enable citizens to bring them their problems. They will certainly make themselves available for correspondence. And they may write letters to civil servants, government ministers, or even private organizations on behalf of those who come to them. If the matter appears important enough they may even take the opportunity to raise it in some forum within the legislature.

For the individual representative, the aim of this activity is clear. It is that the development of a reputation as an effective local advocate will, come election time, generate a "personal vote" that may assist in reelection (Cain, Ferejohn, and Fiorina 1987; Jacobson 1997). For the democratic system itself there are said to be two benefits. First it means that when the implementation of public policy runs into difficulties elected representatives are soon made aware that there is a problem. If several constituents present an elected representative with the same issue, they will thereby learn that the relevant public policy is proving unpopular and will start lobbying decision-makers to make a change. Thus the development of public policy is constantly informed by feedback on its performance on the ground. Second, the intermediary work of elected representatives provides a vital mechanism for ensuring that government does not become arbitrary or overbearing. If citizens feel that they have been rendered an injustice in, say, the administration of their social security payments, they know that there is someone to whom they can turn with authority to intercede on their behalf. And of course awareness on the part of bureaucrats that citizens may turn to their elected representatives for help gives them an incentive to ensure that their decisions are not considered arbitrary or overbearing in the first place.

In short, the single member plurality system supposedly encourages elected representatives to remain in contact with citizens and for citizens to feel that there is someone in the political system willing to act on their behalf. The result should be a citizenry that is satisfied with its elected representatives and indeed with the democratic system as a whole, thereby helping to foster the legitimacy of the political system. If correct these claims would certainly be an important argument for using such an electoral system.

Granted, these arguments would appear valid for any single member district system, including the alternative vote or the double ballot runoff, not just single member plurality systems. Indeed, because candidates are more likely to have to appeal beyond their party's own supporters to be elected, the incentive to secure a reputation as an intermediary may be even stronger under such variants (Carey and Shugart 1995). So in reality the argument is about the relative merits of single member versus multimember district electoral systems. But as the presence of at least some multimember constituencies is an essential feature of any proportional system, in practice these claims are highly pertinent to the debate about the relative merits of proportional and majoritarian systems.[1] The only way of combining proportionality with single member districts is through additional (or mixed) member systems, but even they require some members not be elected from single member districts (Shugart and Wattenberg 2001b).

But these claims do not go unchallenged. The concern tends not to be over the importance of the role of elected representatives as citizen intermediaries, albeit reservations are expressed about the dangers of particularism and clientilism where such a role is performed to the exclusion of any other (Shugart 2001). To that extent, and in contrast to the debate about the importance of "fairness versus a clear winner," there is considerable agreement between the two camps about what outcome is desirable. Rather the challenge that is posed to the above arguments is whether single member district systems do in fact provide a greater incentive for elected representatives to act as citizen intermediaries than do at least some kinds of multimember district systems.

First, it is suggested that the incentive provided by single member districts to elected representatives to act as citizen intermediaries is not necessarily as strong as its advocates claim. After all, some representatives represent constituencies that in recent electoral history their party has rarely if ever lost. What need do they have of a personal vote? Instead—in the absence of a system of primaries—their political future would appear to depend on keeping happy the party activists who will decide whether they should be renominated as the party's candidate in the next election. In other words, their position is no different from that of a candidate in a closed party list system, which is arguably what the single member district system is a variety of anyway.

But even the degree to which those representing marginal seats have an incentive to act as citizen intermediaries may be overstated. In theory, they might hope to appeal to all voters for their support on the basis of their work as a local representative. But it is an open question whether most voters will be willing to respond. If their vote is primarily motivated by party, then local work may make little difference. Certainly, there seems little reason why elected representatives should go out of their way to act as intermediaries on behalf of those who prove to be committed supporters of an opposition party (who indeed may well be reluctant to approach an "opponent" in the first place). Indeed it is precisely considerations like these that lead Carey and Shugart (1995) to suggest that where parties control nominations at least the single member plurality system provides relatively little incentive to secure a personal vote than virtually any other (for a somewhat different view, see Shugart 2001).

Consider in contrast the position of an elected representative in a multimember constituency under an electoral system where voters can not only express a preference for a party but also indicate a preference for at least one of the individual candidates nominated by a party (and where the distribution of individual candidate votes clearly has an impact on who is elected). No longer is partisanship a sufficient cue to guarantee the election of any individual representative. To be elected not only does a candidate's party need to do sufficiently well, but an individual candidate has to garner sufficient personal votes to secure one of the seats that may be won by their party. In other words, each individual candidate is in competition with all the other candidates put up by the same party. By definition that competition has to be fought on the basis of the candidates' personal qualities rather than their partisanship. And one of the qualities at least that they might wish to try and sell to the electorate is their ability to act as citizen intermediaries.

175

In short, under multimember constituencies with open lists (or indeed STV) the incentive for elected representatives to act as citizen intermediaries may be thought to be greater than it is under single member district systems (Farrell and McAllister 2006; Marsh 2000). No candidate after all has a safe seat. Every candidate depends on their personal popularity as well as that of their party to secure election. True, they may not have much incentive to act on behalf of those who do not back their party. But if the electoral system is reasonably proportional in its allocation of seats between parties then every major segment of opinion in a constituency ought to have at least one incumbent representative who has an incentive to act in a way that will help garner them personal votes in the next election. So, it is argued there is every reason why citizens living in countries with open list multimember systems should feel satisfied with their representatives and their political system as it is alleged that they are under single member district systems.

These arguments may indeed even be extended to closed party list systems. After all if it is the case that voters value elected representatives who act as intermediaries on behalf of their citizens, then parties have an incentive to put at the top of their lists candidates who have a reputation for performing that role. Otherwise they may fear that voters will prefer to back another list. We may even doubt whether the single member district system is more effective than closed party list systems at providing an incentive to candidates to act as citizen intermediaries.

As such, both proponents of single member district systems and advocates of multimember schemes can provide theoretical arguments as to why their preferred option is likely to represent voters best or at least as well as any other. What evidently is required is that the theories be put to the test. Do single member districts prove in practice to be more effective at promoting contact between citizens and their elected representatives, and does this have a favorable impact on citizens' evaluations of the political process? It is to the task of answering that question that we now turn.

Data

If we are to test these theories adequately, then one requirement is clear: we need to be able to compare the experience and reactions of voters under principal legislatures elected in single member districts with reactions in multimember districts. This requires using data from more than

Table 8.1. Countries and their electoral systems

Some single member		All multimember	
All seats	Mixed	No candidate choice	Some candidate choice
Australia	Germany	Israel	Belgium
Belarus	Hungary	Norway	Chile
Canada	Lithuania	Romania	Czech Republic
Great Britain	Mexico	Slovenia	Denmark
New Zealand[a]	Russia	Spain	Japan[a]
Ukraine[a]	S. Korea	Sweden[b]	The Netherlands
United States			Peru
			Poland
			Switzerland
			Taiwan
			Thailand

Countries are classified according to the electoral system in place at the election prior to the one at which data were collected.

[a]Country switched to mixed system of single and multimember seats at election at which data were collected.

[b]Country switched from closed to flexible lists at election at which data were collected.

one country. After all countries rarely change their electoral systems from one type to the other, and even when they do we can expect a time lag in the reactions of elected representatives and voters to a new system. The first module of the Comparative Study of Electoral Systems project provides us with just the kind of comparative data that we need.

In this paper, we make use of the results of this module for 30 countries.[2] A full list of these, together with details of how we have classified the countries' electoral systems is found in Table 8.1. Our classification is different from that used in much of this book. The most important distinction is between those countries where at least a significant proportion of elected representatives are elected in single member districts and those where all elected representatives are from multimember districts (apart perhaps from the occasional rural or island constituency.) If the arguments of the proponents of single member districts are correct, those living in countries in the first group should be more likely than those in the second to report contact with their elected representatives—and also as a result be more inclined to be satisfied with their representatives and democracy in general.

Within each group however we can make one further important distinction. In the case of those countries with single member districts, we can distinguish between those where all the seats in the principal legislature are elected in single member districts and those where only some are elected in this way. The latter group comprises a variety of so-called mixed systems, in which multimember allocation of seats is either used to "correct" the disproportionalities generated by the overall outcome among single member districts or else is simply held in parallel to the single member contests. If single member districts do indeed have the benefits ascribed to them then we might anticipate that such benefits would be less in evidence in those countries using mixed systems than it is in those with single member districts.[3]

Meanwhile, insofar as those countries that use only multimember constituencies are concerned, we distinguish between those that allow voters the opportunity, however limited, to express at least some preference for one or more individual candidates and those that do not provide any such opportunity. The latter are examples of the archetypal "closed" party list system under which election is solely determined by the order of the candidates on the party list. The former however are not necessarily "open" list systems where the election of a party representative depends entirely on the preferences of the electorate. Most in fact are varieties of "flexible" list systems where the order of a list is determined by each party but this order can be changed if and only if a significant number of voters cast an (optional) personal preference for a candidate placed lower down on a list. Also included in this group are countries that give voters as many votes as there are seats to be elected. Under this sort of system voters can express explicit support for one of the candidates nominated by a party while denying support to any of the others (opting instead to support candidates of other parties). Overall however, if it is indeed the case that allowing voters to choose between candidates of the same party encourages elected representatives to act as citizen intermediaries, as is claimed by advocates of open multimember systems, then we should observe higher levels of contact and higher levels of satisfaction among this group than among those countries with closed lists—and perhaps indeed even than among those with single member districts.[4]

Four of our 30 countries, however, are not straightforward to classify. In Japan, New Zealand, Sweden, and Ukraine, the election at which our CSES data were collected was marked by a change of electoral system. Japan, New Zealand, and Ukraine all adopted a mixed system while Sweden switched from a closed to a more "flexible" list system. Our interest, however, is in the impact that a country's electoral system has had on levels of contact between elections. This suggests that these countries should be classified on the basis of the electoral system that was in place prior to the election at which the CSES data were collected rather than on the basis of the new electoral system. This is the procedure adopted in Table 8.1 and throughout the analysis.

Two other countries raise particular issues. In Mexico, elected representatives are subject to a limit of two terms. This might be thought to reduce the incentive for elected representatives to act as citizen intermediaries because many will not be eligible for reelection. In the United States, party nominations are determined by the outcome of primary elections rather than by the decisions of a small group of party activists. This means that even those elected representatives who represent districts that are safe for their party still have an incentive to perform the role of citizen intermediary because they could be challenged for their party's nominations (Carey and Shugart 1995). We thus also take account of both these possibilities in our analyses.

Indicators and Model

The first module of the CSES provides two indicators of the degree of interaction between elected representatives and their constituents. The first indicator is simply a measure of the degree to which voters have had any contact with an elected representative. Respondents were asked: "During the past twelve months, have you had any contact with a [elected representative] in any way?" Note that the question was designed to tap any form of interaction that respondents themselves defined as meaningful contact. This might range from as much as a personal interview to as little as a direct mail. This means that the contact might not be in the form of the elected representative taking on the role of a citizen intermediary. It also means that the interaction may have been initiated by the representative rather than the citizen. Nevertheless, if single member districts do provide an incentive for elected representatives to interact with their constituents then we would expect to find a higher level of contact reported in response to this question by voters in countries deploying such districts.

The second indicator of interaction between citizen and representative is whether voters are actually aware of the names of any of the candidates standing in their constituency. It has been suggested that elected representatives have an incentive to act as citizen intermediaries due to the prospect of winning votes for personal popularity. Yet it seems unlikely that voters who do not even know who the candidates are could be influenced in how they cast their vote by the personal characteristics or reputations of individual candidates. Accordingly, if personal voting is encouraged by the use of single member districts a higher level of knowledge of candidate names in countries with such districts might be expected. The relevant question reads as follows: "Do you happen to remember the names of any candidates who [ran/stood] in your [lower house primary electoral district] in the last election?" Those who said that they did were asked to give up to three names whose accuracy was checked against the official list of candidates.

The first step of analysis is thus relatively straightforward. It is necessary to examine whether those who live in countries with single member district systems are more likely to report contact with an elected representative and/or to remember the names of those who stood as candidates in their constituency in the last election. These are tests of whether single member districts do indeed encourage more interaction between elected representatives and voters.

Above and beyond demonstrating that single member district systems encourage interaction between elected representatives and voters, it is also important to show that such interaction matters. If the existence of interaction is to be an argument in favor of single member district systems then it is also necessary to demonstrate that such interaction has beneficial consequences for the political system. If so, it can be anticipated that those voters who have had contact with an elected representative will have a higher regard for their elected representatives. In addition it is useful to track down those living in countries with single member districts that have not themselves have had any contact with their elected representatives. If they also have a high regard for their representatives it means that the relatively high level of contacts representatives maintain with their constituencies in general ensures that they are in touch with public opinion. Voters' evaluation of their representatives was measured by asking: "Some people say that [elected representatives] know what ordinary people think. Others say that [elected representatives] don't know much about what ordinary people think. Using the scale on this card, where would you place yourself?" The card was a 5-point scale with the first proposition scoring 1 and the second 5.

If the interaction supposedly encouraged by single member district systems is beneficial for democracy as a whole then it should be possible to show that not only do single member districts lead to higher regard for politicians but to greater satisfaction with democracy in general. To measure satisfaction with democracy respondents were simply asked:

"On the whole are you satisfied, fairly satisfied, not very satisfied or not at all satisfied with the way democracy works in [country]?" Again, there are two possibilities to test. The first is that any higher level of satisfaction with democracy in countries with single member districts is directly attributable to a higher level of citizen/representative interaction. We thus look to see whether those who report contact with an elected representative or those who can accurately name an individual candidate are more likely to be satisfied with democracy than are those who do not.

The second possibility is that single member districts generate a higher level of satisfaction with democracy among all citizens, not just among those who have had contact with their representatives (Anderson and Guillory 1997; Norris 1999c). As in the case of evaluations of elected representatives it may be argued the existence of a high level of citizen/representative interaction also affects the views of those without direct experience. They may, for example, be more satisfied with democracy because they believe that there is someone who would act as an intermediary on their behalf. Or it may be that the interaction which occurs has a sufficient impact on the quality of a country's governance that its citizens are more satisfied. In any event, it becomes necessary to test for the possibility of a direct relationship between satisfaction with democracy and kind of electoral system independently of individual-level processes of citizen/representative interaction.

Of course it would be naïve to believe that a country's electoral system, if an influence at all, will be the only variable impacting elected representatives' contact with citizens or the overall level of satisfaction with democracy. Another obvious possible influence on satisfaction with democracy in particular is the length of time that a country has been a democracy (Norris 1999b). Some of the countries examined here are new democracies, others are long established. To test for the possibility that this may have an influence on satisfaction with democracy (and indeed the other variables in our models) an exogenous variable is included that measures how many years have elapsed since a country last became a democracy. Meanwhile, another possible influence on the variables in our models is the ratio of representatives to citizens (Carey and Shugart 1995). The fewer the number of citizens that a representative has to serve, the more likely it is that any individual citizen will have had contact with that representative. Where it proves to be significant this ratio is also included (logged) in the models.[5] And finally it might be anticipated that both satisfaction with democracy and contact between voters and representatives

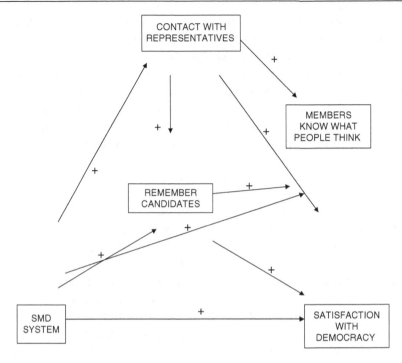

Figure 8.1. The model

are promoted or facilitated by economic wealth. This possibility is tested by including GDP per capita in the models.

Figure 8.1 outlines the full model of supposed benefits of single member districts. Of course it may still be objected that these far from exhaust the possible influences on evaluations of elected representatives or the level of satisfaction with democracy.[6] The trouble is that pursuing this argument too far simply threatens to undermine the claims of advocates of single member districts. If the impact of single member districts on the level of satisfaction with democracy is too small to be discernible without a large number of controls then it is no longer clear that its benefits are of sufficient importance to be a basis on which to choose a country's electoral system. And it is after all the claim of the advocates of single member districts that those benefits are sufficiently strong that they constitute a crucial reason as to why a country should use such districts.

But there are two features of the CSES data that we do have to take into account in our modeling. The first is that the CSES data must surely diverge strongly from the usual assumption that cases have been sampled independently of each other. Two Ukrainian cases obviously will have a great deal in common with each other, for instance, a commonality that neither shares with a Canadian case. In effect, our aggregation of country surveys is a massive, roughly accidental, cluster sample—which must produce strong spatial autocorrelation among our cases. It is true, of course, that standard statistics on cluster samples are used all the time in analyzing individual electorates. The difference is that we regard the dependence between cases within clusters in a normal cluster sample as trivial and ignorable, whereas the clusters in the CSES sample are countries with unique histories, cultures, and institutions.

Our solution to this problem is to deploy probit and linear regression (as appropriate) using robust standard errors with countries as clusters. Robust regression or probit produces exactly the same coefficients as standard regression or probit. But it does produce different standard errors. Unlike standard regression or probit, which proceed from a prior fixed model (the Gaussian assumptions) to assess the amount of uncertainty in the estimation, robust estimation of standard errors builds an empirical estimate of the reliability of the estimated slopes from the intercorrelation of case residuals. This gives it the attractive quality that it does not require the assumption that observations are independent (Greene 2000: 462–5, 488–91, and 505–7).[7] It also does not require that a homoscedastic error structure be specified.

The second feature of the data that needs to be addressed is the sample size for each country which varies significantly. Unless this is corrected for our estimates will be biased towards the pattern found in those countries with the larger samples.[8] The country samples have therefore been weighted equally so that each country contributes equally to the analysis. Since our interest is in assessing the effect of variations in countries' electoral systems, this makes it possible to treat each expression of our independent variable equally.

The Theory in Practice

We have suggested that if the claims of the advocates of single member districts are correct, then those living in countries with at least some single member districts should be more likely to report contact with an elected representative and more likely to recall the name of a candidate from their district in the last election. We also expect that they should be more likely to feel that their elected representatives are in touch with public opinion and more satisfied with the operation of democracy in their country. In Table 8.2, we take a simple look at the extent to which the CSES data support these claims by showing for each country that uses one of our four kinds of electoral system, the proportion giving a positive report on each of our key indicators. The simple mean of each indicator for each kind of electoral system are also shown.

A few points immediately stand out. First, those people living in countries that use only single member districts are on average somewhat more likely to report contact with an elected representative than are those living in countries with other kinds of electoral system, including those with a mix of single and multimember districts. To this extent at least the claims of the advocates of single member districts appear to be upheld, though at the same time their validity does not appear to extend to mixed electoral systems. In contrast, there is little evidence to suggest that those living in countries with single member districts are more likely to be able to name correctly at least one of the candidates standing in their district, let alone be more likely to believe that MPs know what ordinary people think or be satisfied with democracy. Indeed contrary to the claims of advocates of both single member districts and open lists, it is those living in countries with closed multimember lists that are most likely to believe that their elected representatives are in touch with public opinion, even though it is the case that they are least likely to be able to name a candidate correctly. Moreover, we should also note the considerable variance on all four of our indicators between countries with the same electoral system, including in the level of contact reported by those living in countries that only use single member districts. So, even if it is the case that single member districts do on average encourage somewhat higher contact, that influence appears to be small relative to the other factors that evidently must also affect the level of contact.

But this of course is no more than an informal analysis that makes no attempt to model what those other factors might be, let alone assess the statistical significance of the findings. So we now turn to the results of the more formal models. The first of these, displayed in Table 8.3, is an analysis of the influences on the level of contact. This does indeed suggest that influences other than the electoral system make a difference. However, once these have been taken into account, it appears that the electoral system also makes a difference.

The model identifies two significant influences other than the electoral system.[9] The first is the ratio of MPs to the population. Unsurprisingly,

Table 8.2. Contact, recall, and satisfaction

Country	Contacted (%)	Correctly name candidate (%)	Believe MPs know what people think (%)	Satisfied or fairly satisfied with democracy (%)
Some single member				
All single member				
Australia	16	61	15	78
Belarus	9	21	33	47
Canada	22	71	19	73
Great Britain	13	60	19	75
New Zealand	26	83	20	69
Ukraine	8	43	53	9
United States	14	52	24	80
Mean	15	56	26	62
Mixed				
Germany	11	42	21	63
Hungary	7	64	31	42
Lithuania	16	Missing	24	35
Mexico	10	16	24	54
Russia	3	72	35	19
S. Korea	16	98	14	41
Mean	11	58	25	42
All multimember				
No candidate choice				
Israel	16	Missing	31	53
Norway	15	69	32	90
Romania	7	31	43	44
Slovenia	Missing	Missing	37	32
Spain	3	27	33	74
Sweden	11	38	23	71
Mean	10	41	33	61
Some candidate choice				
Belgium	Missing	Missing	29	62
Chile	12	Missing	33	Missing
Czech Republic	8	63	26	61
Denmark	20	Missing	42	89
Japan	8	94	15	63
The Netherlands	5	Missing	28	88
Peru	9	74	30	Missing
Poland	6	39	29	63
Switzerland	19	48	33	75
Taiwan	8	38	19	47
Thailand	17	93	39	77
Mean	12	64	29	69

Contact: % reporting any kind of contact with an elected representative in the last 12 months.

Correctly name candidate: % naming at least one of the candidates standing in their district correctly.

Believe MPs know what people think: % scoring 1 or 2 on 5-point scale where 1 means 'Members of (Congress/Parliament) know what ordinary people think' and 5 means 'Members of (Congress/Parliament) don't know what ordinary people think'.

Table 8.3. Electoral systems and contact (pseudo $R^2 = 0.02$)

	Coefficient	Standard error	z
Electoral system			
All single	0.28	0.13	2.23
Mixed	0.26	0.14	1.83
Multi—some choice	0.22	0.13	1.71
MPs/population ratio	0.46	0.16	1.82
Age of democracy ($\times 100$)	0.38	0.09	4.16
Constant	−1.02	0.21	−4.78

Probit model, robust standard errors to take into account autocorrelation due to country clustering.

MPs/population: natural log of no. of elected representatives in legislature per 100,000 population.

Age of democracy: number of years since current democratic regime established (or since 1900 if regime established before then).

perhaps, the more MPs there are per 100,000 citizens, the higher the level of reported contact. The second factor is how long a country has been democratic. Those living in the longest established democracies were also more likely to report contact. After taking these factors into account, however, the impression from Table 8.2 appears confirmed. Those who live in countries that only employ single member districts have a significantly higher level of contact than do those who live in the default category in our model, that is, those living in countries with multimember districts that provide no opportunity for voters to express a personal preference for a candidate.

Even so, Table 8.3 constitutes far from a clear endorsement of the claims of the advocates of single member districts. True, it shows that those living in countries that only employ single member districts are more likely to report contact, but it also shows that those living in mixed systems also report contact. Reported contact is also higher in countries that use multimember districts but allow voters to express a candidate preference, just indeed as advocates of open lists would anticipate. Moreover, the coefficient for those living in countries that use single member districts (either wholly or as part of a mixed system) is little different from that for those living in countries with multimember districts that allow voters to express a candidate preference. In short, it appears that using single member districts is not the only means of encouraging contact between voters and their representatives.

Meanwhile analysis of voters' ability to recall correctly the name of at least one candidate standing in the election does not fit any theoretical

Table 8.4. Electoral systems and recall of candidates (pseudo $R^2 = 0.13$)

	Coefficient	Standard error	z
Electoral system			
All single	0.34	0.19	1.81
Mixed	1.00	0.32	3.11
Multi—some choice	−3.69	1.00	−3.67
MPs/population ratio	0.12	0.08	1.44
Interaction of MPs ratio with multi—some choice	−1.01	0.22	−4.57
Age of democracy (×100)	0.74	0.20	3.76
Mexico (term limits)	−1.23	0.32	−4.57
Constant	−0.16	0.39	−0.41

Probit model, robust standard errors to take into account autocorrelation due to country clustering.

preconceptions at all. As Table 8.4 shows, our modeling suggests that once the significant controls have been taken into account, it is those who live in countries with mixed systems who are most likely to recall the name of a candidate, while paradoxically it is those who live in countries with multimember districts that allow voters to express some kind of candidate preference who are least likely to do so. Meanwhile residents of single member districts lie somewhere between, only just significantly more likely to recall the name of a candidate than citizens of countries with closed list systems. Central to this finding, which is not one that we would have immediately anticipated from results of the earlier informal analysis displayed in Table 8.2, is that those living in more mature democracies are more likely to recall the name of a candidate. It was in fact this pattern that accounted for the higher average recall of candidates among those living in countries that provided some degree of candidate choice in Table 8.2, rather than the character of their electoral system. Meanwhile we can note also that term limits as implemented in Mexico apparently make it more difficult for voters to remember for whom they might have voted.

Single member districts may then encourage contact between voters and their representatives, albeit that they share this characteristic in common with multimember systems that allow voters to express a candidate preference. Meanwhile neither seems to be particularly effective at ensuring that citizens are better informed about the candidates for which they are voting and thus neither seems to be particularly likely to encourage voters to take the personal characteristics of candidates into consideration in deciding how to vote. What, however, does this imply for voters' evaluations of their elected representatives and of democracy

Table 8.5. Modeling perceptions of elected representatives' knowledge of public opinion ($R^2 = 0.02$)

	Coefficient	Standard error	t
Contact with representative	0.25	0.04	6.82
Recall candidate name	0.11	0.05	2.29
Electoral system			
All single	−1.26	0.23	−5.56
Mixed	−0.27	0.12	−2.17
Multi—some choice	−0.10	0.11	−0.88
MPs/population ratio	0.14	0.05	2.50
Interaction of MPs ratio with All single	−0.25	0.05	−4.67
GDP	−0.02	0.01	−2.72
Constant	3.63	0.26	13.99

Linear regression model, robust standard errors to take into account autocorrelation due to country clustering.

GDP: gross domestic product per capita in US$2,000.

in general? Does the greater level of contact in systems other than on those with closed lists mean that voters living in countries that use such systems have a higher regard for their elected representatives and are more satisfied with the operation of democracy?

Table 8.5 examines what indicators of perceptions as to whether elected representatives are in touch with public opinion. Those who have recently had contact with an elected representative and, to a lesser degree, who can correctly remember the name of an election candidate are indeed more likely to think that elected representatives know what ordinary people think. The presumption of the advocates of single member districts that contact between voters and their representatives enhances the standing of the latter in the eyes of the former is upheld. Alas little else of their case does. Recall the earlier argument that if elected representatives act as citizen intermediaries then this should not only have a positive impact on the evaluations of those who have experienced such contact themselves but should also make a favorable impression on the remainder of the electorate. Yet there is no direct positive relationship between having a single member district and believing that elected representatives are in touch with public opinion. Rather, it appears that after taking into account respondents' level of contact and knowledge of candidates (together with the ratio of MPs to population in their country and the level of GDP per capita), those living in countries with single member districts or mixed systems are actually less likely than are those living in countries with closed systems to think that elected representatives are in touch with

Table 8.6. Electoral systems and perceptions of elected representatives' knowledge of public opinion ($R^2 = 0.01$)

	Coefficient	Standard error	t
Electoral system			
All single	−0.14	0.13	−1.09
Mixed	−0.29	0.12	−2.39
Multi—some choice	−0.08	0.09	−0.87
Constant	2.89	0.07	42.31

Linear regression model, robust standard errors to take into account autocorrelation due to country clustering.

public opinion. Table 8.6 confirms that they are not more likely to think that elected representatives are in touch with public opinion even if we do not control for contact and knowledge of candidates.

Meanwhile, our story is even more straightforward when it comes to satisfaction with democracy. Table 8.7 reveals that having direct experience of contact with an elected representative does not necessarily mean that voters are more satisfied with democracy; nor does ability to recall the name of a candidate. There is no evidence to support the argument that the level of contact engendered by single member districts helps increase satisfaction with democracy in general for citizens of countries with single member districts. Rather, once the length of experience with democracy has been taken into account—and anticipating that citizens of mature democracies are more likely to be satisfied with democracy—those living in countries with wholly single member districts together with those living in mixed systems are actually less likely to be satisfied with democracy. In fact the safest conclusion of all is that type of electoral system, at least as conceptualized in this chapter, has little or nothing to do

Table 8.7. Modeling satisfaction with democracy (pseudo $R^2 = 0.07$)

	Coefficient	Standard error	z
Contact with representative	0.02	0.05	0.51
Recall candidate name	0.05	0.08	0.66
Electoral system			
All single	−0.53	0.26	−2.06
Mixed	−0.47	0.24	−1.90
Multi—some choice	−0.07	0.22	−0.32
Age of democracy (×100)	0.92	0.26	3.57
Constant	0.16	0.21	0.78

Probit model, robust standard errors to take into account autocorrelation due to country clustering.

Table 8.8. Electoral systems and satisfaction with democracy (pseudo R^2 = 0.08)

	Coefficient	Standard error	z
Electoral system			
All single	−0.33	0.26	−1.27
Mixed	−0.37	0.26	−1.43
Multi—some choice	0.10	0.22	0.47
Age of democracy (×100)	0.92	0.23	3.91
Constant	−0.01	0.21	−0.03

Probit model, robust standard errors to take into account autocorrelation due to country clustering.

with satisfaction with democracy. As Table 8.8 shows, once we leave aside whether someone has had contact with a representative or can remember the name of a candidate (but does still take account of the impact of the maturity of a democracy), there is no significant relationship at all between satisfaction with democracy and type of electoral system.

Conclusion

We have been able to supply some support for the claim that single member districts encourage elected representatives to act as citizen intermediaries and that this role is appreciated by the citizens on whose behalf they act. We did find that those living in countries with single member districts were slightly more likely to report having had contact with an elected representative over the previous 12 months than those living in countries with closed list systems. Moreover those who had enjoyed such contact were rather more likely to think that elected representatives were in touch with public opinion. However, those living in countries with single member districts were not significantly more likely to report contact than were those living in multimember systems that give voters the chance to express a candidate preference. Those living in single member districts were only somewhat better able to remember the name of an election candidate (and far less so than those who live in a mixed system), were not more likely to think that elected representatives were in touch with public opinion, and were not more satisfied with democracy.

By way of contrast, there is also little evidence to suggest that living in a multimember district is any more desirable than living in a single member one. So far as the criteria that we have been considering and the indicators of those criteria that we have been able to deploy are concerned, we are simply forced to conclude that there is little difference between single and multimember districts with regard to the intimacy of representation. This goes against much intuition and the tenaciously held beliefs of advocates for individual representation, but our evidence suggests that neither side has much of a case. This particular debate about electoral systems simply appears to be a blind alley, and it certainly provides no grounds for preferring one electoral system over another.

Notes

1. Of course multimember systems are not necessarily proportional. Multimember plurality and the single non-transferable vote are two obvious examples.
2. The module was in fact administered after two different elections in Mexico, Russia, and Spain. In each case, the two sets of data were pooled and regarded as a single data set. The module was also administered twice in Hong Kong, after both the 1998 and 2000 elections. However, Hong Kong was excluded from the analysis entirely. The 1998 election was the territory's first ever under universal suffrage and thus the electoral system has had insufficient opportunity to shape the relationship between citizens and elected representatives.
3. In both cases, some of the countries included in our analyses use something other than the simple plurality rule to determine the outcome in the single member districts. There are however too few instances within each of the two groups to permit further subdivision along these lines.
4. Note that one key feature of our approach is that each of the four categories are treated as distinct categories and are not scored and ordered on a continuum from most to least "candidate centered" in the manner theorized by Carey and Shugart (1995) and Shugart (2001) or operationalized by Farrell and McAllister (2006). Our analysis makes no a priori assumptions about which is most or least "candidate centered," taking this to be an empirical question. This seems the only sensible approach given that our discussion has demonstrated that there is plenty of room for theoretical dispute about which systems are most likely to encourage representatives to act as citizen intermediaries.
5. We also allow for the possibility that this ratio may matter more under some systems than others by fitting interaction terms. It may be, for example, that the existence of a high ratio (and thus large districts) reduces the level of contact in single member districts more than it does in multimember ones because such contact is relatively rare in multimember districts under any circumstances.

6. Note in particular that in contrast to Norris (2001) and Farrell and McAllister (2006) we do not include any individual level sociodemographic controls in our modeling. Such controls can of course only affect our estimate of the impact of electoral systems if their distribution is correlated with the kind of electoral system that a country has. Of Norris's controls, age and gender differ little by country, while the income measure in the CSES dataset is a measure of relative income within country and thus cannot differ by country—in contrast to our country level GDP measure. As for Norris's final control, education, whose incidence does vary by country, we have found that including this variable makes no difference to our substantive conclusions.
7. To quote Greene (2000: 465), "The [robust] estimators are becoming ubiquitous in the econometrics literature and represent major advances in the set of available techniques." See also STATA (1985–99: 256–9) and Sribney (1998).
8. The sample size prior to the equalization of sample sizes between countries is 57,906. As in other chapters in this book, each country is weighted so that it represents 1,500 cases in total.
9. As indicated earlier, in this and subsequent tables we only include those control variables that were statistically significant. This means that the test statistic had to be relevant (on either a one or two-tailed test, as appropriate) at the 5 percent level.

9

Economic Voting: Do Institutions Affect the Way Voters Evaluate Incumbents?

Yoshitaka Nishizawa[1]

Introduction

A classic reward-punishment model of economic voting is a simple yet powerful tool to explain voting decisions (Goodhart and Bhansali 1970; Key 1966; Kramer 1971; Mueller 1970). It holds that when voters find that an incumbent government has done a good job in controlling the state of the economy during its term, they vote for the incumbent government parties or candidates on election day, and when voters are not happy about the way that incumbents have handled the economy, they vote for the opposition parties or their candidates.

Naturally, a large body of literature has developed under this topic since the model was first introduced. Many theories about the mechanism of economic voting, far more sophisticated than the original simple reward-punishment model, have been proposed and tested empirically. Lewis-Beck and Paldam (2000) concisely summarize the findings of some 30 years of research in the field.[2] According to them, we now know that economic changes are associated with both day-to-day popular support of the incumbent government (popularity function) and support of the government at polls on election day (vote function). We also know that unemployment and inflation, among other available macroeconomic indicators, most successfully exhibit associations with the vote and the popularity functions. Most researchers also agree that voters' memories about the economic variables that affect the voting decision are short term. We also know that voters react to past economic events (retrospective) more than to future ones (prospective). We also believe that voters evaluate their government's performance based both on the national economic well-being (sociotropic) and on personal economic situation (pocketbook). Past empirical studies, however, tend to support the former more often than the latter. It is also reported that voters' response to the economy is not symmetrical. They seem to react more when the economy fails than when it progresses. Little is known, however, about voters' cognitive processes when they make political decisions using macroeconomic information. Finally, Lewis-Beck and Paldam (2000) point out that the economic voting literature suffers from instability. Any particular proposition related to the aforementioned findings may be empirically supported with one type of data (e.g. aggregate data), but may not be so with other types of data (e.g. individual survey data). The same proposition tested and found to be valid in one country may not be applicable to other countries, or may not be sustained even in the same country at different times. Given the amount of energy and time devoted to these topics, such contradictory results are rather striking, and Lewis-Beck and Paldam conclude that this instability is "the main reason why this research has shown no tendency to die" (2000: 113).

The Comparative Study of Electoral Systems (CSES) data set (Module 1) is not designed to further investigate any of the particular topics set forth by Lewis-Beck and Paldam. It does, however, provide us with an important opportunity to test a set of propositions that may help us understand the reasons for the instability problem. It allows us to systematically investigate the effect of institutional factors that mediate and shape the mechanism between voters' evaluation of the economy and support for the incumbent government. Combining cross-sectional survey data from different countries with varying political institutions, we can now study the effect of the economy on voting while taking institutional factors into consideration. The data set is unique in that an identical set of survey questions was administered in the participating countries specifically designed to measure institutional effects.

In recent years, the role of political context received increased attention (Anderson 1995a, 2000; Kiewiet 2000; Lewis-Beck 1988; Leyden and Borrelli 1995; Lowry, Alt, and Ferree 1998; Pacek and Radcliff 1995; Paldam 1991; Powell and Whitten 1993; Rudolph and Grant 2002). This is a natural development. A basic logic of economic voting requires that voters be able to identify who is responsible for the current economic situation. If, for example, a voter observes economic growth but does not believe the president is responsible, the link between the economy and support for the president cannot logically exist. Similarly, even if a voter feels that his financial situation has recently worsened, if he cannot decide whether he should blame the president or members of the legislature, the link between the economy and support for particular actors in the government will be unclear. Importantly, it is political institutions that determine the clarity of responsibility.

Among possible institutional comparisons, this chapter showcases two sets of comparisons: one between parliamentary countries and presidential countries, and another between countries with plurality electoral systems and those with proportional representation (PR) electoral systems. First, it will be demonstrated that economic voting can be found more often in parliamentary countries than in presidential countries. As will be discussed in more detail below, there are competing hypotheses as to whether parliamentary systems or presidential systems facilitate economic voting. The empirical analysis here suggests that the former is stronger than the latter. Second, it will be shown that a stronger link between the economy and support for the government can be found among plurality electoral system countries than the PR countries.

Another unique aspect of the CSES data set is that it includes developing countries along with established OECD countries. Unlike most of the comparative studies conducted so far that only deal with OECD counties (e.g. Anderson 1995a, 1995b; Lewis-Beck 1988; Powell and Whitten 1993), the CSES data set provides us with an opportunity, for the first time, to test whether economic development is a prerequisite for economic voting to take place. It will be demonstrated that economic management is even more important for incumbent governments in developing countries than OECD countries.

The remainder of this chapter will proceed in the following manner. In the next section, competing hypotheses as to which system, parliamentary or presidential, exhibits better clarity of responsibility will be reviewed. Arguments about electoral systems will also be considered, again, in terms of clarity of responsibility. In the following section, the statistical model is introduced. Because the dependent variable is an incumbent vote that is a dichotomous choice, I will use logistic regression models. The models will include interaction terms between the institutional type and evaluation of the economy. The estimated coefficients for the interaction terms are the main interests of the study. The operational definitions of dependent variables and the main independent variables are then studied. Subsequently, the estimation results in a form of post-estimation simulation will be presented, highlighting the effects of interaction terms. The chapter will end with a summary and a discussion of the limitations the CSES data set inherits. I do not pretend to have solved the instability question, but I believe I can demonstrate significant implications for the future study of economic voting.

Clarity of Responsibility and Political Contexts

Parliamentarism Versus Presidentialism

Among possible classifications of democracies, the most fundamental distinction is between parliamentarism and presidentialism.[3] In parliamentary governments, the head of the government (often called the prime minister or premier) is elected by members of the legislature, and therefore is responsible to the legislature. And she herself and her cabinet are dependent on the confidence of the legislature. She will serve for a fixed term, but can be removed from office by the legislature with a no confidence vote. In presidential governments, the head of the government (mostly called president) is elected directly by citizens separately from the legislature. She serves for a fixed term and, except for the rare case of impeachment, she cannot be politically removed from her office by the legislature (Lijphart 1984).

The question here is which of the two institutional arrangements is more favorable to facilitating economic voting. Arguments can be made in support of both systems. The most distinctive nature of presidential government is the direct election of the chief executive. Lijphart considers this one of the most significant advantages of presidential systems (Lijphart 1992: 12). In terms of the level of direct accountability between voters and elected officials, Shugart and Carey (1992: 44), too, also claim that presidentialism is "clearly" superior to parliamentarism, "since voters vote directly for an executive that cannot be removed by shifting coalitions in the assembly." Because a president is elected by a direct popular vote, unlike his or her counterpart in a parliamentary government who is indirectly elected, voters regard the president as the most important and powerful figure in government. In addition, an incumbent candidate running for reelection frequently appears in newspapers and network news programs while in office. As such, voters may find it easier to associate policy responsibility with the president than with any other political figure in the government.

The same argument, however, can be made for a prime minister in most parliamentary countries. Particularly in parliamentary systems with a dominant two-party system, the head of the majority party usually becomes the prime minister. Thus, even if the selection process is indirect, voters, in effect "elect" a head of the government by selecting a majority party in the parliament. In everyday politics too, strong prime ministers can be a focus of mass media, perhaps as much as their counterparts in presidential countries. In such cases, voters find it almost as easy to assign responsibility to the prime minister as in presidential countries. In other words, due to the phenomenon of highly visible prime ministers, we cannot decide which of the two agents, presidents in pure presidential countries or prime ministers in pure parliamentary countries, is likely to attract more voter attention.

In terms of clarity of responsibility, the more important distinction between parliamentarism and presidentialism lies in the fact that there is only one agent of the electorate, a legislature, for parliamentary systems whereas in presidential systems there are two—a legislature and a president (Shugart and Carey 1992: 1). The separation of power for the presidential systems means division of responsibility, which in turn implies unclear responsibilities.[4] As a consequence, the voters cannot know whom to credit or blame for the policy outcomes.

The fact that there are two agents, both of which are supposed to be working for the interest of the electorate, makes it difficult for the voters to identify which of the two is responsible for the current state of the economy. Identifying responsibility becomes even more difficult when the two agents are controlled by different political parties, just like the recent situation in the United States where the presidency is controlled by the Democratic party and congress by the Republican party. When a seemingly effective economic package prepared by the congress was supported by the president, and the package, in fact, was successful, should voters credit the congress (the Republican party) or the president (the Democratic party)? Or, when the congress and the president cannot agree with each other on a certain set of economic programs, and the delay of action caused by this deadlock made the situation even worse, which of the two, the congress (the Republican party) or the president (the Democratic party) should voters blame for their inability to compromise in a timely fashion?

Provided that clarity of responsibility is the main mediating factor in the link between the economy and support for the government, and assuming all other things to be equal, I will have a better chance of finding supportive evidence of economic voting in parliamentary countries than in presidential countries.

Electoral Rules: Majoritarian Versus Proportional Democracy

Another important classification of democracy has to do with two distinctive types of electoral rules and two corresponding principles that each rule aims to realize. The two principles are, to use Huber and Powell's terms, the "majority control" vision of democracy and the "proportionate influence" vision of democracy (Huber and Powell 1994; Powell 2000). The former is mostly associated with single-member plurality electoral systems, and the latter is often realized in proportional representation systems.

Under the majority control vision of democracy, the political institutions and electoral rules are designed to produce a single majority party. The majority party is expected to take control of the policymaking process. The congruence between citizens and policymakers is observed in that the majority of citizens explicitly support the government. And a majority party is produced most likely by a single-member plurality electoral system. Under single-member plurality rules, voters whose first preference is a candidate of a third party or even weaker party have no chance of winning, and thus tend to vote for the better of the candidates offered by the top two parties. As a result, the rules tend to produce two-party systems (known as Duverger's Law).

Under the proportional influence vision of democracy, legislatures are expected to be made of all parties that represent all citizens. In such legislatures, any one party is unlikely to win a majority of seats, so governments are formed by coalitions of several parties. The congruence between citizens and policymakers, in other words, is expected to be obtained by the postelection bargaining among parties. This type of party system is most often realized by proportional representation rules.

Obviously, clarity of responsibility is greatest when the government is composed of a single party. Voters can easily identify which party to credit when the economy is in good condition, and which party to blame when the economy is poor. If, on the other hand, the responsibility is dispersed among several governing parties, especially if the governing parties are decided not directly by the vote at election time but by bargaining between parties after elections, voters have a hard time deciding which party to credit or blame for the economy. It is therefore more likely that one would find more evidence of economic voting among countries that employ single-member plurality rules than in countries with PR rules.

Does Economic Voting Assume Economic Development?

Given the large number of studies on economic voting, it is surprising to find that virtually all use economically developed countries (mostly OECD countries) as cases. The fact that most of the theories and hypotheses so far have only been tested in the OECD countries leaves us with an important question: Is economic development a prerequisite for economic voting to take place? Does what we know so far about economic voting remain valid in all democratic countries or will it hold only in highly developed countries? The CSES data set, with data from both OECD countries and non-OECD countries, provides us with a rare chance to confront this puzzle.

There are several possible reasons why non-OECD countries have not been studied to date. For one, it is not easy to collect comparable and reliable data on economic conditions and political behavior in developing countries. But, more importantly, it is likely that those who have studied the relationship between the economy and political support of incumbents, consciously or unconsciously, assume that there must be a certain degree of economic stability before economic voting can take place. Surely, governments must be able to control the economy, or at least the voters must have good reasons to believe that their government is in control of the economy, before governments are held responsible for economic management. And it takes years of "experiments" before governments learn to acquire effective economic policies to control their economy.

In his study of economy and voting behavior of four postcommunist countries (the Czech Republic, Hungary, Poland, and Slovakia), Fidrmuc (2000: 200) suggests that voters in postcommunist countries may behave differently from those in Western countries. He offers four reasons: voters' lack of experience with the political processes and institutions of democracy, uncertain effects of retrospective voting in times of extraordinary economic turbulence, unique economic circumstances that reflect more of the consequences of the collapse of communism than of poor economic policies of the postcommunist government, and much higher voter concern about economic well-being in these countries than in developed countries. In another study of economic voting in 17 OECD countries with special attention to differing levels of welfare spending, Pacek and Radcliff (1995) claim that the lack of a social "safety net" can increase voters' sensitivity to economic fluctuations. Both of the studies— although their data are from OECD countries—suggest a need for attention to the level of economic development. I will, therefore, test whether there are observable differences in the probability of economic voting between economically developed countries and developing countries.

Strategy to Identify Institutional Effects: A Basic Conceptual Model

The strategy in this chapter is to take full advantage of the unique nature of the CSES data set. Because it is a pooled cross-national data set, the CSES Module 1 permits direct measurement of the magnitude of institutional influence on the probability of economic voting. Unlike most studies in which model estimations are conducted at the country level and the coefficients for economic evaluations are then compared across countries (see Lewis-Beck 1988), this study does not subdivide the data set by country. Instead, the pooled cross-national data are used as one data set, while a set of dummy variables for institutional factors is also prepared. By including interaction terms between the economic evaluation variable and the institutional dummies in the model, the impact of institutional factors may be directly accessed and tested.[5]

A basic conceptual model is represented in the following equation:

$$\ln\left\{\frac{P_{ij}}{(1 - P_{ij})}\right\} = B_0 + B_1 X_{ij} + B_2 X_{ij} Z_j + B_3 D_1 + \cdots + B_m D_{J-1} + e_{ij}$$

In this equation, P_{ij} represents a probability of voter i voting for an incumbent candidate or an incumbent party in country j. Because the dependent variable is a dichotomous choice, a log ratio is assumed. The main independent variable (evaluation of economic performance) is denoted by X_{ij}. The parameter B_1, therefore, shows the magnitude of the main effect (X). The term Z_j indicates a dummy variable that identifies a specific institutional type. The interaction term is a simple multiplication of the main effect and the institutional dummy variable. It is the B_2 parameter, along with B_1 for the main effect that we are interested in.

The role of the main effects and that of the interaction terms are conceptually represented in Figure 9.1. Let us suppose that the effect

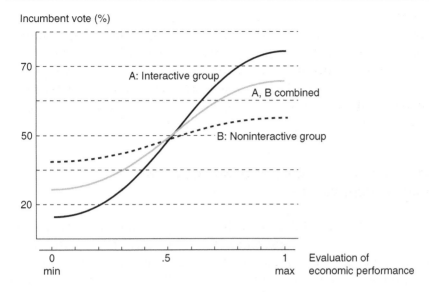

Figure 9.1. Conceptual representation of interaction effects

of the main independent variable is operating in countries in group A (denoted as "interactive group"), but not in the rest of the countries (group B) ("noninteractive group"). When a model is specified without an interaction term, it in effect attempts to reproduce a line in the middle (denoted by "A and B combined"). But, the middle line clearly is a misrepresentation of the reality. In that case, the effect of the main independent variable is underestimated for the interactive group, and it is overestimated for the noninteractive group. A model with an interaction term will enable us to identify the fact that the main independent variable is operating only in one of the groups.

The D terms in the equation are binary dummy variables representing the $J-1$ countries where J represents a total number of countries in the analysis. They are included in the model to depict variances in the dependent variable that are specific to each country but not explained in the model.

A careful reader might have noticed that the equation above lacks a term for the institutional main effect (Z). As most standard texts for regression methods suggest, a model normally should include both main effects that "compose the interaction" (X and Z, in this case) when it has an interaction term (XZ) (e.g. Fox 1997: 149). Omitting the institutional main effect in my equation appears as if it forces the same Y-intercept for different types of institutions. It does not, however, create such a constraint. Once again, please note that this model has country dummy variables. By including country dummy variables, I am, in effect, estimating Y-intercepts for each country individually. In other words, it is assumed that a country dummy is composed of the variance that is unique to its institutional category and a variance that is associated specifically to each country.[6]

Operational Definitions of Dependent and Independent Variables

The dependent variable here is the incumbent vote: in parliamentary elections, whether a respondent voted for or against the parties (or a candidate of the parties) that formed a cabinet during the term prior to the general election; and in presidential elections, whether a respondent voted for or against the candidate who held the presidential office during the term prior to the election.

In a comparative study of this kind, even a simple concept of an "incumbent vote" poses some complicated empirical issues. Of those, the most critical one is which vote among multiple votes that voters can cast in national level elections is most suitable for comparing across different political systems. The CSES data set has three different types of vote information: the presidential vote, the parliamentary party list vote, and the parliamentary candidate vote (Table 9.1). When parliamentary systems are compared with presidential systems in the analysis below, the parliamentary votes are used for the former countries and the presidential votes are used for the latter. Even for the presidential countries, however, when a particular election in the data set is for its parliament, the parliamentary votes naturally are evaluated. When I make other comparisons, one between single plurality electoral systems with PR systems and another between OECD countries with non-OECD countries, the parliamentary votes are used for both parliamentary and presidential countries. For more information, interested readers should refer to the notes at the bottom of Table 9.1.

Another issue is how to define "incumbents." For presidential elections, if the contest is a reelection of the incumbent president (e.g. Clinton at the US 1996 election), the "incumbent" is obvious. If, however, it is an open-seat election in which the past president decides not to run

Table 9.1. Macro classification of elections in the data set

Country/region	Election date	Vote choice (x: reported, X: used)			Institutional classification for analysis						Economic development		
		Presidential	Parliamentary		Presidential vs. parliamentary		Electoral system				OECD		Non-OECD
			Party list	Candidate	Presidential	Parliamentary	Plurality	MMM	MMP	PR	Old	New	
Canada, non-Quebec	97.06.02			X		x	x				x		
Canada, Quebec	97.06.02			X		x	x				x		
Czech Republic	96.05.31		X			x				x		x	
Denmark	98.03.11		X			x				x	x		
West Germany	98.09.28		x	X		x			x		x		
East Germany	98.09.28		X	X		x			x			x	
Hungary	98.05.10		X	x		x		x				x	
Israel	96.05.29	X	X			x				x			x
Japan	96.10.20		x	X		x		x			x		
Korea	00.04.13			X	x			x				x	
Mexico	97.07.06			X	x			x				x	
Mexico	00.07.02	X		X	x			x				x	
The Netherlands	98.05.06		X			x				x	x		
New Zealand	96.10.12		X	x		x			x		x		
Norway	97.09.15		X			x				x	x		
Poland	97.09.21	X	X		x					x		x	
Romania	96.11.03	X	X		x					x			x
Russia	99.12.19		X	x	x		—	x		—			x
Russia	00.03.26	X			x		—	—		—			x
Slovenia	96.11.10		X		x					x			x
Spain	96.03.11		X			x				x	x		
Spain	00.03.12		X			x				x	x		

(cont.)

Table 9.1. (Continued)

Country/region	Election date	Vote choice (x: reported, X: used)			Institutional classification for analysis						Economic development		
		Presidential	Parliamentary		Presidential vs. parliamentary		Electoral system				OECD		Non-OECD
			Party list	Candidate	Presidential	Parliamentary	Plurality	MMM	MMP	PR	Old	New	
Sweden	98.09.20		X			x				x	x		
Switzerland	99.10.24		X			x				x		x	
Taiwan	96.03.12	x		X	x			x					x
Thailand	01.01.06		X	X		x		x					x
Ukraine	98.03.29		X		x			x					x
Great Britain, without Scotland	97.05.01			X		x	x				x		
Great Britain, Scotland	97.05.01			X		x	x				x		
United States	96.11.05	X		X	x		x				x		

Israeli prime ministerial votes are treated as "presidential votes" in the analysis.

The vote choice to be used for parliamentary elections are determined by the following rules (x or X indicate that corresponding vote information is supplied in the data set, X represents the vote information used in the analyses):

1. For the pure PR elections, "Party List" votes are used;
2. For the pure plurality elections, "Candidate" votes are used; and
3. For the mixed-member electoral systems, when only one piece of the vote information is available, that information is used; when both "Party List" and "Candidate" votes are available, the vote information that exhibits higher positive correlation with the main independent variable (i.e. the evaluation of economic performance) is used.

In this table, "Russia (1999)" and "Russia (2000)" appear to be two different data sets. But, they are parts of the same panel survey. In order to avoid including the same respondents more than once in the analysis, I used only one of the appropriate data sets for the Russian sample.

"MMM" and "MMP" represent "mixed-member majoritarian" and "mixed-member proportional," respectively. They are subtypes of mixed-member electoral systems. In my analysis comparing plurality and PR electoral systems, I have treated MMM as "plurality" system and MMP as "PR" system. See Shugart and Wattenberg (2001a) for a definition and typology.

for reelection, identifying an incumbent is not so automatic. In such a case, the incumbents are determined individually. The Russian 2000 presidential election is one such example. Because Putin was considered to be a successor of the former president, a vote for Putin is coded as the incumbent vote.[7] For parliamentary systems, votes for any of the candidates (or party) of the government (or parties in the case of coalition government) are considered to be incumbent votes.[8]

The main independent variable is the evaluation of economic performance during the past government. It is measured as a response to the following question: "Would you say that over the past twelve months, the state of the economy in [country] has gotten better, stayed about the same, or gotten worse?" (For those who answered "gotten better"—"Would you say much better or somewhat better?") (For those who answered "gotten worse"—"Would you say much worse or somewhat worse?") Scores 0, 0.25, 0.5, 0.75, and 1 are assigned to these five response categories from "much worse" to "much better," respectively.[9]

Figure 9.2 summarizes the aggregate relationship between the percentages for incumbent votes and the mean scores of evaluation of economic performance for the 35 elections in the special release of the CSES Module 1.[10] An "eyeball" analysis of the scatterplot suggests that there is some association between the two indicators. In elections with high scores of evaluation of economic performance, the incumbent candidates or parties tend to receive higher vote percentages. And in elections with low scores, the incumbent candidates or parties tend to lose support.

Explaining Incumbent Vote: Models to be Tested

The models to be tested are summarized as following:
[Base model, Models 1, 2]

Incumbent vote = $b_1 \times$ satisfaction with democracy
$+b_2 \times$ state of economy
$+b_3 \times$ Evaluation of Economic Performance (EEP)
$+b_{10} \times$ close feeling to the government party
$+b_{11} \times$ Party Like/Dislike Scale $+ b_{12} \times$ income
$+b_{13} \times$ University education $+ b_{14-41} \times$ country
dummies + constant

Incumbent vote (%)

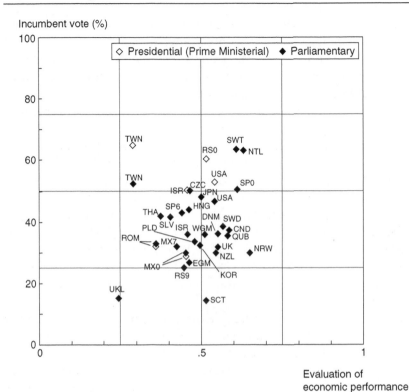

Figure 9.2. Evaluation of economic performance and incumbent vote in 35 CSES elections

Source: Country Keys—CND: Canada, CZC: Czech, DNM: Denmark, EGM: East-Germany, HNG: Hungary, ISR: Israel, JPN: Japan, KOR: Korea, MX7: Mexico 1997, MX0: Mexico 2000, NTL: Netherlands, NZL: New Zealand, NRW: Norway, PLD: Poland, QUB: Quebec, ROM: Romania, RS9: Russia 1999, RS0: Russia 2000, SCT: Scotland, SLV: Slovenia, SP6: Spain 1996, SP0: Spain 2000, SWD: Sweden, SWT: Switzerland, TWN: Taiwan, THA: Thailand, USA: USA, UKL: Ukraine, UK: Great Britain, WGM: West-Germany
Code — ◇: Presidential (Prime Ministerial), ◆: Parliamentry.

[Comparative models, Models 3–8]

Incumbent Vote = $b_1 \times$ satisfaction with democracy $+ b_2 \times$ state of economy
$+ b_3 \times$ Evaluation of Economic Performance (EEP)
$+ b_{4-9} \times$ EEP * institutional dummies
$+ b_{10} \times$ close feeling to the government party
$+ b_{11} \times$ Party Like/Dislike Scale $+ b_{12} \times$ Income
$+ b_{13} \times$ University Education $+ b_{14-41} \times$ country dummies $+$ constant

Evaluation of Economic Performance (EEP) is the main independent variable. As explained earlier, it runs 0 for the economy being "much worse" through 1 for it being "much better" during the past 12 months. The terms "Evaluation of Economic Performance × institutional dummies" are interaction terms. Take Models 3 and 4 (presidential vs. parliamentary) as an illustration. There are two institutional dummies for this comparison: A presidential system dummy has value 1 for the presidential countries and 0 for the rest, and a parliamentary system dummy has value 1 for the parliamentary countries and 0 for the rest of the countries. Interaction terms are created by simply multiplying the EEP and the institutional dummy variables. The EEP × presidential term, therefore, takes actual EEP values (EEP value × 1 = EEP value) for the presidential countries and 0 (EEP value × 0 = 0) otherwise. The EEP × parliamentary term has actual EEP values for the parliamentary countries and 0 otherwise.[11]

In addition to the economic evaluation variable, I included several other independent variables in the model. The evaluation of the current state of the economy is included to control for the fact that the economic evaluation of the past 12 months is always relative to the state of the current national economy. A respondent may find that the economy is getting better, but he may believe that the national economy is still in a poor shape. If this is the case, the respondent may not be satisfied with the economic policies of the current administration. Or another respondent may consider the state of the economy still to be good, though she thinks it is not as good as 12 months prior. She too may not be happy with the economic policies of the current government. I have adopted a 5-point scale running from 0 for "the economy is very bad" to 4 for "the economy is very good."

For some of the newly developed democracies, voters may be more concerned about the way the government is functioning than its economic performance. An indicator for satisfaction with democracy, therefore, is included in the model. It is a 4-point scale running from 0 for "not at all satisfied" to 3 for "satisfied" with the way democracy works in the country. I also include two variables in the model that measure general evaluation of the parties. One of them is the existence of a political party to which a respondent "feels close." The variable is coded 1, if a respondent feels close to any one of the incumbent parties and 0 otherwise. The second party evaluation measure is constructed from the "like/dislike" party indicators. In each country, up to six parties are evaluated on a 11-point scale running from 0 for "dislike" of a particular party to 10 for "liking that party." The variable here reflects a difference between the average liking of incumbent parties and the average liking of opposition parties. Table 9.2 lists parties in power for the closeness evaluation and opposition parties being evaluated on the like/dislike scale.

Two demographic variables—income and education—are added to the model. Clearly, change in the state of the economy affects poor voters differently from rich voters. Household income is a 5-point scale running from 0 for the lowest quintile to 4 for the highest quintile (with an increment of 0.25 points). Education is another control variable. A person needs some level of information to make an intelligent evaluation of the governmental performance on national economy. The education variable is also coded 1 for those who have some university education or higher and 0 otherwise.

Finally, the 28 country dummy variables are included to control for the difference of probability of the incumbent vote that is not explained by the independent variables included in the model. West Germany, whose mean value for the dependent variable was closest to the overall mean value for the entire data set, was used as a reference point.[12]

Estimation Results

Because the dependent variable is coded 0/1 (1 for an incumbent vote and 0 for an opposition vote), I used a logistic regression estimation method.[13] The results are summarized in Table 9.3. For each model, the left column lists estimated coefficients and the right column lists probabilities that the coefficients are not being 0 by chance (i.e. significance level).

Model 1 and Model 2 are the base models that do not have any institutional dummy variables. As the significance levels for "Evaluation of Economic Performance" (EEP) are 0.000 (i.e. smaller than 0.0005) for both Model 1 and Model 2, I can, statistically speaking, claim that economic voting is taking place in these 29 elections. Incumbent parties (or candidates of incumbent parties) are more likely to receive votes when voters consider the state of the economy on election day to be better than that of 12 months before, while opposition parties tend to collect votes when voters think the state of the economy fell behind during the past year.

Because the coefficients for the logistic regression estimation cannot be interpreted by their numeric magnitude, I have calculated the probability of incumbent vote for hypothetical values of the independent variable.[14] The results of these post-estimation simulations are summarized in

Table 9.2. Political parties in power and opposition at elections for the 24 countries

Country	Election date	Political parties	
		In power[a]	Oppositions considered for like/dislike
Canada	97.06.02	Liberal Party	Progressive Conservative, New Democratic Party, Reform Party, Bloc Quebecois
Czech Republic	96.05.31	Christian Democratic Union, Civic Democratic Alliance, Civic Democratic Party	Czech Social Democratic Party, Communist Party of Bohemia and Moravia, Association for the Republic
Denmark	98.03.11	Social Democrat, (Social Liberal)	Conservative, Centre Democrat, Socialist People, Danish People, Liberal
Germany	98.09.28	Christian Democratic Party, Christian Social Union in Bavaria	Social Democratic Party, Free Democratic Party, Alliance 90/Greens, Party of Democratic Socialism
Hungary	98.05.10	Hungarian Socialist Party, Alliance of Free Democrats	Alliance of Young Democrats, Independent Smallholder's Party, Hungarian Truth and Life Party, Hungarian Worker's Party
Israel	96.05.29	Avoda, Shas, Meretz	Likud, Mafdal
Japan	96.10.20	Liberal Democratic Party, Social Democratic Party, New Party Harbinger	New Frontier Party, Democratic Party of Japan, Japan Communist Party
Korea	00.04.13	Millennium Democratic Party	Grand National Party, United Liberal Democrats, Democratic People's Party, New Korean Party of the Hope, Democratic Liberal Party
Mexico	97.07.06	Institutional Revolutionary Party	National Action Party, Democratic Revolutionary Party, Labor Party, Mexican Ecological Party
Mexico	00.07.02	Institutional Revolutionary Party	Labor Party, Mexican Ecological Party, Authentic Party of the Mexican Revolution, Alliance for Change, Alliance for Mexico
The Netherlands	98.05.06	Labor Party, People's Party for Freedom and Democracy, Democrats 66	Christian Democratic Appeal, Green Left, Socialist Party
New Zealand	96.10.12	National	Labour, New Zealand First, Alliance, ACT, Christian Coalition
Norway	97.09.15	Labor	Socialist Left Party, Christian People's Party, Center Party, Conservative Party, Progress Party
Poland	97.09.21	Democratic Left Alliance, Polish Peasant Party	Union of Labor, Freedom Union, Solidarity Election Action, Movement for the Reconstruction of Poland
Romania	96.11.03	(Democratic Party), Romanian Party of Social Democracy, National Liberal Party, (National Peasant and Christian Democratic Party), Democratic Union of Hungarians in Romania (Romanian Social Democratic Party)	Romanian Party for National Unity, Greater Romania Party, Romanian Democratic Convention, Social Democratic Union

(cont.)

Table 9.2. (*Continued*)

Country	Election date	In power[a]	Political parties — Oppositions considered for like/dislike
Russia	99.12.19	Yedinstvo (Unity)	YABLOKO, Zhirinovskiy, Fatherland All Russia, Communist Party of the Russian Federation, Union of Right Forces
Russia	00.03.26	Yedinstvo (Unity)	YABLOKO, Zhirinovskiy, Fatherland All Russia, Communist Party of the Russian Federation, Union of Right Forces
Slovenia	96.11.10	Liberal Democratic Party, Slovenian Christian Democrats	Slovenian People's Party, Social Democratic Party, United List of Social Democrats, Democratic Party of Retired Persons
Spain	96.03.11	Partido Socialista Obrero	Partido Popular, Izquierda Unida, Convergencia i Unio, Partido Nacionalista Vasco, Coalicion Canaria
Spain	00.03.12	Partido Popular	Partido Socialista Obrero, Izquierda Unida, Convergencia i Unio, Partido Nacionalista Vasco
Sweden	98.09.20	Sweden's Social Democratic Worker's Party	Left Party, Center Party, People Party's Liberals, Moderate Rally Party, Christian Democrats
Switzerland	99.10.24	Christian Democrats, Social Democrats, Swiss People's Party	Freethinking Democrats, Liberal Party, Green Party
Taiwan	96.03.12	Nationalist Party	Democratic Progressive Party, Chinese New Party
Thailand	01.01.06	Thai National Party, Rassadorn Party Justice and Freedom Party, Democratic Party, National Development Party	New Aspiration Party, Thai Love Thai Party, Prachakornthai Party
Ukraine	98.03.29	(Agrarian Party of Ukraine), Rukh, People's Democratic Party	Party of Greens of Ukraine, Communist Party of Ukraine, Socialist Party of Ukraine, Peasant Party of Ukraine
Great Britain	97.05.01	Conservative	Labour, Liberal Democrats, Scottish National Party, Plaid Cymru
United States	96.11.05	Democratic Party	Republican Party, Reform Party

[a] "Political parties in power" includes party (or parties) that held at least one cabinet position in the incumbent administration.

Parties in parentheses, that is ( ), have no party codes assigned in the data set. They, therefore, are not included in the analysis.

Table 9.3. Incumbent vote-estimation results, logistic regression

Independent variables	Model 1		Model 2		Model 3		Model 4		Model 5		Model 6		Model 7		Model 8	
Satisfaction with democracy	0.328	0.000	0.251	0.001	0.319	0.000	0.319	0.000	0.251	0.001	0.251	0.001	0.254	0.001	0.254	0.001
State of economy	0.591	0.000	0.477	0.000	0.592	0.000	0.592	0.000	0.481	0.000	0.481	0.000	0.471	0.000	0.471	0.000
Evaluation of Economic Performance (EEP)	0.783	0.000	0.552	0.000	0.601	0.000	1.054	0.000	0.728	0.000	0.335	0.007	0.224	0.111	0.728	0.000
EEP × presidential					0.453	0.007	−0.453	0.007								
EEP × parliamentary									−0.393	0.015	0.393	0.015				
EEP × plurality vote																
EEP × PR vote																
EEP × OECDs													0.504	0.003	−0.504	0.003
EEP × non-OECDs																
Feel close to the government parties	1.064	0.000	1.022	0.000	1.064	0.000	1.064	0.000	1.021	0.000	1.021	0.000	1.021	0.000	1.021	0.000
Parties like/dislike (Government parties—opposition parties)	0.480	0.000	0.473	0.000	0.481	0.000	0.481	0.000	0.473	0.000	0.473	0.000	0.471	0.000	0.471	0.000
Income	0.057	0.293	0.059	0.281	0.058	0.290	0.058	0.256	0.058	0.287	0.058	0.287	0.052	0.339	0.052	0.339
University education	−0.222	0.000	−0.237	0.000	−0.218	0.000	−0.218	0.000	−0.237	0.000	−0.237	0.000	−0.242	0.000	−0.242	0.000
Country dummies (Base: West Germany)																
Canada	−0.689	0.000	−0.646	0.000	−0.675	0.000	−0.675	0.000	−0.417	0.040	−0.417	0.040	−0.657	0.000	−0.657	0.000
Quebec	−0.231	0.390	−0.207	0.436	−0.221	0.409	−0.221	0.409	0.017	0.951	0.017	0.951	−0.217	0.416	−0.217	0.416
Czech Republic	0.210	0.162	0.199	0.178	0.200	0.181	0.200	0.181	0.208	0.162	0.208	0.162	0.208	0.161	0.208	0.161
Denmark	−0.537	0.000	−0.485	0.001	−0.531	0.000	−0.531	0.000	−0.492	0.001	−0.492	0.001	−0.489	0.001	−0.489	0.001
East Germany	−0.120	0.502	−0.144	0.414	−0.133	0.456	−0.133	0.456	−0.132	0.456	−0.132	0.456	−0.133	0.453	−0.133	0.453
Hungary	0.102	0.524	0.085	0.591	0.096	0.549	0.096	0.549	0.292	0.105	0.292	0.105	0.090	0.571	0.090	0.571
Israel	1.649	0.000	0.384	0.015	1.637	0.000	1.637	0.000	0.393	0.014	0.393	0.014	0.640	0.000	0.640	0.000
Japan	1.088	0.000	1.048	0.000	1.085	0.000	1.085	0.000	1.255	0.000	1.255	0.000	1.050	0.000	1.050	0.000
Korea	0.085	0.581	0.050	0.742	−0.152	0.390	−0.152	0.390	0.254	0.144	0.254	0.144	0.055	0.715	0.055	0.715
Mexico (1997)	0.104	0.522	0.064	0.691	−0.123	0.500	−0.123	0.500	0.260	0.148	0.260	0.148	0.075	0.642	0.075	0.642
Mexico (2000)	−0.468	0.004	−0.268	0.092	−0.699	0.000	−0.699	0.000	−0.069	0.701	−0.069	0.701	−0.258	0.104	−0.258	0.104
The Netherlands	1.314	0.000	1.360	0.000	1.334	0.000	1.334	0.000	1.342	0.000	1.342	0.000	1.342	0.000	1.342	0.000

(cont.).

Table 9.3. (*Continued*)

Independent variables	Model 1		Model 2		Model 3		Model 4		Model 5		Model 6		Model 7		Model 8	
New Zealand	-0.674	0.000	-0.622	0.000	-0.664	0.000	-0.664	0.000	-0.633	0.000	-0.633	0.000	-0.630	0.000	-0.630	0.000
Norway	-0.950	0.000	-0.851	0.000	-0.927	0.000	-0.927	0.000	-0.875	0.000	-0.875	0.000	-0.870	0.000	-0.870	0.000
Poland	0.629	0.000	0.619	0.000	0.391	0.040	0.391	0.040	0.621	0.000	0.621	0.000	0.620	0.000	0.620	0.000
Romania	-0.435	0.004	-0.576	0.000	-0.634	0.000	-0.634	0.000	-0.543	0.000	-0.543	0.000	-0.365	0.027	-0.365	0.027
Russia (1999)	—		-1.109	0.000	—		—		-0.906	0.000	-0.906	0.000	-0.851	0.000	-0.851	0.000
Russia (2000)	1.757	0.000	—		1.517	0.000	1.517	0.000	—		—		—		—	
Slovenia	1.175	0.000	1.107	0.000	0.968	0.000	0.968	0.000	1.131	0.000	1.131	0.000	1.332	0.000	1.332	0.000
Spain (1996)	0.105	0.505	0.081	0.599	0.092	0.557	0.092	0.557	0.096	0.546	0.096	0.546	0.093	0.551	0.093	0.551
Spain (2000)	-0.111	0.476	-0.059	0.701	-0.095	0.540	-0.095	0.540	-0.074	0.632	-0.074	0.632	-0.073	0.636	-0.073	0.636
Sweden	-0.319	0.031	-0.294	0.044	-0.310	0.036	-0.310	0.036	-0.304	0.038	-0.304	0.038	-0.303	0.038	-0.303	0.038
Switzerland	1.792	0.000	1.818	0.000	1.524	0.000	1.524	0.000	1.800	0.000	1.800	0.000	1.798	0.000	1.798	0.000
Taiwan	1.417	0.000	0.822	0.000	1.250	0.000	1.250	0.000	0.977	0.000	0.977	0.000	1.005	0.000	1.005	0.000
United States	0.886	0.000	0.538	0.000	0.641	0.000	0.641	0.000	0.751	0.000	0.751	0.000	0.539	0.000	0.539	0.000
Ukraine	-0.699	0.000	-0.796	0.000	-0.889	0.000	-0.889	0.000	-0.631	0.001	-0.631	0.001	-0.597	0.002	-0.597	0.002
Great Britain	0.286	0.093	0.318	0.059	0.300	0.077	0.300	0.077	0.543	0.005	0.543	0.005	0.304	0.071	0.304	0.071
Scotland	-0.928	0.001	-0.881	0.002	-0.912	0.002	-0.912	0.002	-0.652	0.029	-0.652	0.029	-0.896	0.002	-0.896	0.002
Thailand	1.459	0.000	1.393	0.000	1.437	0.000	1.437	0.000	1.574	0.000	1.574	0.000	1.613	0.000	1.613	0.000
Constant	-2.324	0.000	-2.075	0.000	-2.225	0.000	-2.225	0.000	-2.171	0.000	-2.171	0.000	-2.162	0.000	-2.162	0.000
Percent predicted correctly	80.9		80.9		81.0		81.0		80.9		80.9		80.9		80.9	
N	27,692		27,647		27,692		27,692		20,947		20,947		20,947		20,947	

In each model, the left column lists logistic regression coefficients, and the right column lists their probability of being different from zero by chance.

Figure 9.3. As the solid line in Figure 9.3a shows, when all respondents judged the state of economy to be much worse, some 30 percent of the respondents would vote for incumbent parties, and when all considered the state of economy to be much better, 44 percent of the respondents would vote for incumbent parties. The variable, in other words, could theoretically produce a maximum increase of 14 percentage points in the support level for the incumbent party. Note, at the same time, that the line for Model 1 does not go across the 50 percent horizontal line which suggests that the EEP by itself would not make the incumbent parties a majority when other factors stay the same.

Models 3 and 4 compare presidential elections with parliamentary elections. The estimation results turn out to be exactly as anticipated. It does exhibit the same pattern in Figure 9.1. While the coefficients of the main effect show statistically strong effects (0.000, 0.000), the interaction terms, too, are statistically significant (0.007, 0.007). And as Figure 9.3a illustrates, the parliamentary interaction line (Model 4) runs steep in slope, and the presidential interaction line (Model 3) stays flat, while the base line (Model 1) runs in between. In theory, the EEP can raise incumbent support by 19 percent points in parliamentary elections, while it can only add 10 points in presidential elections. This is strong evidence to support the following proposition: parliamentary incumbents are more susceptible to the voters' evaluation of the economy than are presidential incumbents. Note, however, that the parliamentary interaction line still does not reach the 50 percent incumbent vote line, which suggests that even in the parliamentary countries the EEP by itself would not make the incumbent parties a majority when other factors stay the same.

Models 5 and 6 compare the plurality electoral systems with the PR electoral systems. For this comparison, the dependent variable is parliamentary incumbent votes for both presidential and parliamentary countries. The estimation results are, once again, exactly as anticipated. Although not as dramatic as the parliamentary versus presidential comparison (note that the chances of error are higher (0.015, 0.015, respectively) for this set of interaction terms), as in Figure 9.3b, the plurality interaction line (Model 5) runs steep in slope, and the PR interaction line (Model 6) stays flat, while the base line (Model 2) runs in between. In theory, the EEP can raise the chance of an incumbent vote by 13 percent points in plurality elections, but by only 5 percent points in PR elections. This supports my second proposition: incumbents in plurality elections are more vulnerable to the voters' evaluation of the economy than are the counterparts in PR elections.

Finally, Models 7 and 8 compare OECD countries with non-OECD countries. For this comparison, too, the dependent variable is parliamentary incumbent votes. The estimation results indicate that EEP influences the

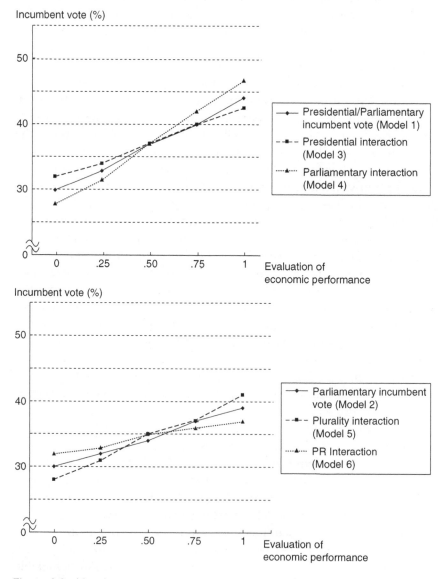

Figure 9.3. (*Cont.*)

Incumbent vote (%)

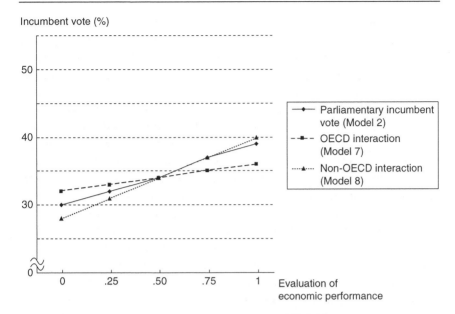

Figure 9.3. Summary effects of economic performance: (a) Presidential vs. parliamentary, (b) Plurality vs. PR, and (c) OECD vs. non-OECD countries

probability of an economic incumbent vote more in non-OECD countries than in OECD countries. The interaction terms are statistically significant (0.000, 0.000).[15] As in Figure 9.3c, the non-OECD interaction line (Model 8) runs steep in slope, and the OECD interaction line (Model 7) stays flat, while the base line (Model 2) runs in between. In theory, the EEP can raise the chance of an incumbent vote by 12 percentage points in non-OECD elections, but only by 4 percentage points in OECD countries. This suggests that voters in newly developing countries are not patient enough to wait for the economic infrastructure to be established before assigning responsibility to the government for its economic policy. The voters in such countries are even more sensitive to economic well-being in evaluating incumbent candidates and parties than those in economically developed countries.

Conclusion

Using the CSES Module 1, I have tested the possibility of economic voting in 29 elections included in the data set. The estimation results confirm that economic voting is taking place in these elections. The evaluation of economic performance during the 12 month period prior to the election does affect the probability of voting for the incumbent party or parties (and candidates of incumbent parties). If the incumbent government is successful in managing the economy, it is rewarded with more votes at the next election, and if it fails, it is punished by a loss of votes.

I also tested the effects of institutional setting by comparing two sets of factors: parliamentary versus presidential systems and plurality versus pure PR electoral systems. I anticipated that the more the political institutions facilitate the clarity of responsibility, the higher the likelihood of economic voting among the electorates. The results did confirm these propositions. Parliamentary incumbents are more susceptible to the voters' evaluation of the economy than are presidential incumbents. Also, incumbents in plurality elections are more vulnerable to voters' evaluation of the economy than are their counterparts in PR elections. It was also tested whether economic development is a prerequisite for economic voting to take place. The estimation results suggest otherwise. The economy seems to be the prime concern of voters, particularly in countries whose welfare safety-net is underdeveloped.

While the empirical results presented here are all supportive of the idea that political or institutional context is an important intervening factor in economic voting, and while the statistical results are robust, I do not claim to have solved the instability puzzle. The results nonetheless suggest that any future studies on economic voting must take the institutional factors into consideration.

There are at least two factors that make these statements modest: one is technical and the other is empirical. The statistical model used here is a hybrid of what Jones and Steenbergen call "dummy variable models" and "interactive models" (Jones and Steenbergen 1997; Steenbergen and Jones 2002). As they suggest, these traditional methods "fail to account for macro-level stochastic variation across contextual units." If a multilevel modeling technique had been used instead, the picture might have been different. The decision not to use the hierarchical multilevel modeling was simply because I did not feel comfortable with a small amount of level-two variance (i.e. the number of countries).

Second, the idiosyncrasy associated with each election in different countries is a source of concern. Each election is unique. The US presidential election in 1996, for example, was contested during a relatively stable economic period. Accordingly, the economy may not have been the central issue for many American voters at that time. Or consider the 1996 Taiwanese election when voters chose a president by popular vote for the first time. For them, establishing a democratic system must have been at least as important an input in voting behavior as economic performance. In New Zealand, the 1996 general election was contested for the first time under the new electoral system. Although the election was categorized as "PR" for the purpose of this analysis, New Zealanders' voting behavior must have been influenced by the customs carried over from the previous electoral system. If a different set of elections had been used for the analysis, estimation results might have been different.

This by no means discredits the power of the data set. Perhaps the real significance and power of the CSES project is that despite technical limitations and idiosyncratic factors, statistical analyses can illuminate some consistent and important patterns in voting behavior. The analyses here clearly suggest that institutional context matters.

Notes

1. An earlier version of this chapter was presented at the XVIII IPSA WORLD CONGRESS at the Quebec Hilton in Quebec City, August 1–5, 2000. I am thankful for comments offered by the commentator, Hans-Dieter Klingemann, and other participants, including Gary Cox, John Curtice, and W. Phillips Shively at the meeting. Advices from Ulises Beltran, Takashi Hashimoto, Mikitaka Masuyama, Tetsuya Matsubayashi, Takeshi Iida (Minakuchi), Etsuhiro Nakamura, and Ole Borre at different stages of the project were also helpful.
2. For reviews of the literature, see Paldam (1981), Kiewiet (1983), Kiewiet and Rivers (1984), Lewis-Beck (1988), Norpoth, Lewis-Beck, and Lafay (1991), and Nannestad and Paldam (1994). For a most recent discussion on this topic, refer to Lewis-Beck and Paldam's introduction to the special issue of *Electoral Studies* (Lewis-Beck and Paldam 2000).
3. Even within the category of presidential system, there are variations. For example, while there is a pure presidential system (Type 1), there are hybrid systems in which there are both a prime minister (as in a parliamentary system) and a directly elected president (Types 2 and 3). See Shugart and Carey (1992), Shugart (1993), and Shugart and Haggard (2001). Shugart (1993) considers Type 4 (parliamentary with "president") and Type 5 ("pure" parliamentary) as essentially identical in executive-legislative relations. For the purpose of this chapter, however, I will treat the countries as "presidential" as long as their head of the state is elected directly by the people.
4. For critics of presidentialism, this is a major drawback of the presidential system (e.g. Bagehot 1867).
5. For a supportive discussion of using multiplicative terms in regression equations, see Friedrich (1982).

6. I could include institutional dummies instead of country dummies. But, knowing the fact that a cross-country variance is larger than cross-institutional variances (see Figure 9.2), I chose to include country dummies instead.

7. *Asahi Daily Newspaper*, March 27, 2000.

8. Identifying "incumbent parties" for all countries included in the data set was not an easy task. I adopted the following rules. For countries whose macro pdf files are available on the CSES web site and whose documentation provides cabinet member information with party affiliation, I considered as "incumbent" any party that had at least one minister. For other countries, I searched for newspaper reports and articles about the elections in the *Asahi Daily Newspaper* (corresponding various years). When a party is quoted as "government party" in the reports and articles, I identified them as "incumbent." This method does not guarantee an exhaustive list of the incumbent parties.

9. The planning committee for Module 1 decided to adopt this ANES standard question for the evaluation of economic well-being of the past 12 months. This particular set of wordings measures: (1) retrospective, and not prospective; and (2) sociotropic and not pocketbook nature of economic voting. Numerous detailed studies on these topics exist. (See, for example, Kinder and Kiewiet 1981; Feldman 1982, 1988; Kiewiet 1983, 2000; Kramer 1983; Kiewit and Rivers 1984; Rosenstone, Hansen, and Kinder 1986; Abramowitz, Lanoue, and Ramesh 1988; Markus 1988; Kinder, Adams, and Gronke 1989; Erikson, MacKuen, and Stimson 2000.) They all imply one should be careful, theoretically and empirically, of selecting the measurement (i.e. the question wording).

10. The analysis in this chapter is based on the CSES_BERLIN.SAV (special release of CSES Module 1, prepared for this volume by Hans-Dieter Klingemann, Bernhard Weßels, and Hossein Shahla, Social Science Research Center Berlin, June 2002. I am thankful to them for their permission to use the data set. The original data set prepared by Klingemann, Wessels, and Shahla contains information from 35 elections in 31 countries (or regions). I excluded some of the elections from the analysis for different reasons, mostly when one or more variables were missing. In the end, I included 29 elections (counting Canada, Quebec, East Germany, West Germany, Great Britain, and Scotland as different elections, as defined in the original data set). Furthermore, they defined each "vote cast" as a unit of analysis, which means that respondents who cast two votes (presidential and parliamentary votes in the United States, or party list and candidate votes in Germany, for example) appear twice in the data set. While this design allows us to study fine distinctions between different votes even for the same individual, my unit of analysis is not the individual vote, but the individual voter. For this reason, I have altered the data structure back to the regular pooled cross-section format. For interested readers, I have made my SPSS command file available on my website at: http://www1.doshisha.ac.jp/~ynishiza/pleasedownload.html.

11. In a statistical sense, Models 3 and 4 are just mirror images of the same model because they differ from each other only by the institutional dummies that identify one of the two mutually exclusive, but exhaustive group categories. Presidential countries, for example, are coded 1 and non-presidential (i.e. parliamentary) countries are coded 0 for its institutional dummy in Model 3. In Model 4, however, presidential countries are coded 0 and non-presidential countries are coded 1 for the institutional dummy. In other words, Model 3 uses parliamentary countries as its base for dummy estimation while Model 4 uses presidential countries as its base. Nevertheless, they are estimating the same model. The same is true with Models 5 and 6, and Models 7 and 8, respectively. I will estimate both models in each set because I need estimates for both models to conduct a post-estimation simulation.

12. The West Germany dummy does not appear in the equation for that reason.

13. Sample sizes for different elections in the data set are different. All elections are weighted so that each becomes 1,500 respondents per election. I have treated Canada and Quebec as one country by assigning separate weights so that the two regions together become 1,500 respondents. I treated East Germany and West Germany in the same manner, as well as Great Britain and Scotland.

14. First, I assigned a hypothetical value of 0 (i.e. "much worse") for all respondents to the variable of interest (EEP) in the estimated equations, and calculated the probability of incumbent vote for that particular value. In other words, I estimated the probabilities of incumbent vote assuming all voters considered the economy as "much worse." Then, I repeated the same procedure for other values of the EEP up to 1.0 (i.e. "much better") with an increment of 0.25 points.

15. The main effect (EEP) for the OECD model is statistically not significant (0.111).

10

The Ease of Ideological Voting: Voter Sophistication and Party System Complexity

Martin Kroh

Introduction

In representative democracy, parliamentary elections are the primary instrument for citizens to communicate their political preferences to political parties and their politicians. To the extent that voters are aware of their own interests and the policy agendas of political competitors, they are in a position to choose the parties and candidates that represent their preferred politics. This communication of interests depends on social cognition, including liberal–conservative and left–right heuristics, which enable voters to orient themselves in a complex political environment (e.g. Fuchs and Klingemann 1990; Lupia, McCubbins, and Popkin 2000). Acting on their perception of certain political objects as being, for instance, on the "left" or the "right," they vote for parties and candidates that match their own views.

This vision of the democratic process embodying the basic assumption of all spatial models of voting (e.g. Downs 1957; Enelow and Hinich 1984; Stokes 1963) has been challenged repeatedly by empirical research which shows that many citizens have only limited levels of political sophistication.[1] Voters are frequently found to be unable to describe the substantive meaning of abstract ideologies such as the liberal–conservative semantic the same way as defined by experts. Moreover, citizens often lack cohesion in their political views across time and related concepts (Converse 1964; Jacoby 1986; Klingemann 1979; Luttberg and

Gant 1985). All this has led many scholars to conclude that a great number of citizens do not form meaningful political attitudes (for a review see Kinder 1983; Sniderman 1993). As a consequence, these citizens may also be unable to base their vote choice on abstract cognitions of politics such as the left–right or liberal–conservative framework.

The inability of voters to express their political interests by drawing on ideological concepts has been attributed by and large to the political demand side, that is, to voters themselves. However, this assessment neglects the political supply side, that is, the context of elections. This chapter aims to integrate both voters and contexts into a unified model of ideological voting. In contrast to previous research, this perspective emphasizes the importance of party system complexity in addition to voter sophistication. Thus, the normative ideal of "rational" voting is as much a function of party system complexity as it is of voter sophistication. In some contexts, the political supply side presents itself in such a way that ideological voting becomes exceedingly difficult and thus uncommon even among highly competent voters, while in other contexts ideological voting is fairly easy and for this reason widespread even among less sophisticated voters.

Voter Sophistication

Studies of voting behavior increasingly acknowledge that models of individual processes leading to vote choice do not uniformly apply to all voters in the electorate. That is, citizens systematically differ in the extent to which they consider things like economic performance, immigration policies, or charismatic leadership when deciding which party or candidate to support. A growing body of empirical studies offers evidence for this heterogeneity in voting behavior (Glasgow 2001; Kroh 2003; Rivers 1988).[2] This variation in the individual calculus of voting does not just reflect a random process but can be attributed systematically to certain characteristics of individuals.[3]

Models of ideological voting are considered relevant only to certain parts of the electorate (e.g. Converse 1964).[4] Most important for our problem, the individual level of political sophistication is expected to discriminate between voters who choose their party or candidate on ideological grounds, and voters who support a party or candidate for other reasons.[5] Several studies empirically support the validity of this hypothesis by demonstrating that the weight of ideological argument in voting decisions increases with levels of sophistication (Kroh 2003; Palfrey and Poole 1987; Pattie and Johnston 2001).

Converse (1975) describes political sophistication as the ability of respondents to link information to preexisting political beliefs. Sources of individuals' political sophistication include cognitive skills, that is, ability to process information related to generalized criteria, and willingness to collect political information (Converse 1975). In the literature, both individual cognitive skills and the willingness to collect political information are both linked to different levels of ideological voting. First, relating one's own political views to party positions on the basis of abstract cognitions of politics such as the left–right or the liberal–conservative framework is cognitively more complex than voting on the basis of figurative heuristics from everyday life like the personality of political candidates (Glass 1985; Rosenberg et al. 1986; Vetter and Gabriel 1998). Second, ideological voting is not only cognitively more demanding than other ways of making a voting choice but also requires more political information (Popkin 1991). It assumes sufficient knowledge of the ideological positions of parties and candidates and presupposes an ability to elaborate one's own political views accordingly.

Because of the complexity of politics, many voters will not be able or willing to spend limited resources on obtaining and processing extra information that would permit ideological voting. Rather, they tend to draw on less demanding heuristics of voting (Campbell et al. 1960; Downs 1957; Lazarsfeld, Berelson, and Gaudet 1944; Popkin 1991). So far, studies of ideological voting have treated the complexity of elections as being fixed and exogenous. But the decision situation clearly is not the same for all elections, countries, and points in time. On the contrary, there is a noticeable difference in the complexity of electoral choice situations which may ease or restrict voters in their consideration of ideological positions.

Party System Complexity

Turning from voters to contexts, this section aims to identify aspects of elections which ease ideological voting (van der Eijk, Franklin, and Oppenhuis 1996). Party system characteristics describing the competitive structure of the political supply are particularly relevant. In the following section, some characteristics of party systems are identified and included in a straightforward scenario of complexity of ideological supply in elections.

Ideological voting requires, in one form or another, that voters relate their own ideological preferences to those of the political parties. The ease of discriminating between parties in terms of ideological positions may first of all be a function of sheer quantity: the more parties compete on an ideological dimension, the more difficult it is for voters to be informed and/or process the information about each party's position. This condition makes it more difficult to vote ideologically. As the *absolute* number of parties competing for votes is to a large extent a function of legal access to the electoral competition, the *effective* number of parties is usually used to capture the number of viable vote options (Laakso and Taagepera 1979). The effective number of parties in parliament, with v_j, the share of votes obtained by party j, serves as our first indicator of the ideological complexity of party systems.

$$\text{Effective Number of Parliamentary Parties} = \frac{1}{\sum_{j=1}^{m} v_j^2} \qquad (1)$$

Independent of the number of parties in an election, one can imagine situations in which parties jointly occupy a position in the ideological space (while leaving other spaces unoccupied). This, again, makes it difficult for voters to come to a voting decision on ideological grounds. Put differently, if parties agree on certain policy positions (e.g. pro-immigration, antiabortion, etc.), the issue or ideological dimension does not lend itself easily to discrimination. This property of party systems is commonly captured by the concept of party system polarization. Among the various measures of polarization that have been proposed in the literature, the measure discussed by Klingemann (2005: 46) captures most closely the idea of ideological distance. In one of its versions, it is defined as the mean pairwise distance of all party positions p_j on an ideological dimension weighted by the share of votes obtained by these parties, v_j.

$$\text{Polarization} = \frac{\sum_{j=1}^{m-1} \sum_{j+1}^{m} v_j \cdot v_{i+1} \cdot |p_j - p_{j+1}|}{\sum_{j=1}^{m-1} \sum_{j+1}^{m} v_j \cdot v_{j+1}} \qquad (2)$$

Both low levels of fragmentation (i.e. few parties) as well as high levels of polarization (i.e. large distances) maximize the ideological space between parties, thus, making it easier for voters to discriminate between parties. Both measures treat parties' ideological positions as single points. However, the assumption that parties hold a clearly identifiable ideological position is quite unrealistic. Parties are not homogenous units. Rather, they comprise various political groups and interests. As such, parties do not occupy a single ideological point but cover a certain ideological range. The size of this ideological range is reflected in labels such as "catch-all" (Kirchheimer 1965) or "multi-policy parties" (Downs 1957). Clearly, voting on the basis of ideological considerations may be difficult for voters if several catch-all parties compete for their votes.[6] Van der Eijk (2001) proposes a measure of the level of consensus on party placements on ordered rating scales which serves in this chapter as a measure of the ideological concentration of parties. The lowest level of concentration exists if a party occupies both ends of an ideological scale in equal shares; perfect concentration of party placement is achieved if a party occupies a single scale position only. For simplicity, the equation reports the calculation of the concentration measure for uni-modal distributions on a k-point ideological scale only. For the extension of the measure to multimodal distributions, refer to van der Eijk (2001). The number of scale points occupied by party j is denoted by q_j. The concentration measure is weighted for the size of parties v_j and ranges between -1 and $+1$.

$$\text{Concentration} = \sum_{j=1}^{m} v_j \left(1 - \frac{q_j - 1}{k - 1} \right) \tag{3}$$

The previous paragraphs argue that ideological voting is facilitated by the presence of few effective parties with minimum interparty ideological overlap (i.e. high levels of polarization) and maximum intraparty ideological overlap (i.e. high levels of concentration). The discussion, particularly of the consequences of interparty overlap, implies that all parties compete independently of one another for government. In other words, the degree of competition between parties is the same for all pairs of parties. In many political systems, however, this assumption does not hold empirically as parties do not single-handedly govern the country but often (have to) form multiparty governments.

Not all theoretically possible constellations of multiparty governments are equally likely. Quite often parties join in coalitions if they occupy ideologically compatible policy platforms (Laver and Budge 1992). Put differently, parties with maximum ideological overlap form coalition governments. If this continues over time, it also creates stability in possible coalition constellations. Hence, multiparty constellations may be recognizable to the electorate due to experiences with past governments, or because parties act jointly during the election campaign. Possible coalition partners may also support only one government program or a single candidate for prime minister. At the least, possible coalition partners will in most cases refrain from aggressive campaigning against each other and, instead, try to emphasize their differences with parties out of reach for possible coalitions.

If potential coalition partners have a history of joint action, there is less need for voters to discriminate between their ideological platforms which are likely to be close in any case. If political systems are commonly governed by multiparty governments, the voter's task in ideological voting is reduced to discriminating between possible coalition constellations or political camps instead of each and every party within these camps. Thus, contexts with frequent multiparty governments may, *ceteris paribus*, ease ideological voting. That is, for a fixed number of parliamentary parties, coalition systems provide a smaller choice set of governmental options than systems run by single-party governments.[7]

The construction of the effective number of governmental parties' measure follows the same logic as the construction of the effective number of parliamentary parties described in the first equation. There are, however, two important differences. First, the measure is not based on the share of votes but on the share of seats obtained by each government party. This is because the relative weight of parties in government flows more directly from their strength in parliament. Second, governments represent an indirect element of the voter choice situation as their formation not only depends on election outcomes but also on negotiations between parties. In order to capture voters' anticipation of likely governmental formations, the measure takes advantage of longitudinal information. That is, governmental fragmentation is measured as the average number of parties in government weighted by their share of seats in parliament s_{tj} in T-years before the election.

$$\text{Effective Number of Governmental Parties} = \frac{1}{T} \sum_{t=1}^{T} \frac{1}{\sum_{j=1}^{m} v_j^2} \qquad (4)$$

This section has set forth a straightforward additive model of the complexity of elections in terms of the ideological competition between parties. The hypothesis is that low levels of complexity of political supply help voters link their own ideological views with those on offer by parties, and that this condition allows for testable expectations about the prevalence of ideological voting across contexts. Choosing the government that represents voters' ideological interests is thus facilitated by party systems with a concise set of alternative single- or multiparty governments that are ideologically distinct.

Ideological Voting

This section describes the measurement model of ideological voting employed in this chapter and alludes to the implications of the under-lying assumptions. Investigating ideological voting means that the choice people make in the voting booth is not of primary interest to the analy-sis. Rather, it is the process that gives rise to this outcome. As only the outcome of this decision-making process is observable, the question arises of how to analyze the process itself. Two solutions to this problem are usually suggested. First, analyzing the respondents' self-report about the considerations for his or her vote choice, and second, modeling the decision-making process from observable information about the outcome and about possible causes. The usefulness of the first approach is limited. The calculus of voting is likely to be complex and in any case difficult for respondents to report (Kaplan 1964). Rahn, Krosnick, and Breuning (1994: 582) show on the basis of US data that "voters' reports of the reasons for their preferences were principally rationalizations." Because of the limitations associated with basing analysis on voter self-reporting, this chapter estimates ideological voting by regressing observable information about respondents' ideological views on their reported voting choices. The estimated effect parameter of this regression is the key dependent variable in the analysis that follows. To obtain an unbiased estimate of the effect of ideological considerations on vote choice across individuals and contexts, the analysis must take into account two potential problems: a multilevel data structure and omitted variables.

First, in order to test the expectations about individuals' decision-making formulated above, we need data with sufficient variation in the relevant variables across voters and elections. As in many comparative survey data projects, such variation is insured by CSES by a two-stage sampling procedure which first draws a sample of contextual units and then a sample of individuals nested within these contexts. The unbiased estimation of the effect of ideological considerations on vote choice relying on this hierarchical data structure calls for disturbance terms for both samples, that is, for the sample of contexts and for the samples of individuals within contexts (Snijders and Bosker 1999). A multilevel regression model with random effects of ideological considerations on

vote choice across contexts permits such an unbiased estimation of ideological voting. Because of the discrete nature of vote choice, the data
are fitted to a conditional logit regression model (Ben-Akiva and Lerman
1985; McFadden 1974). A multilevel conditional logit model estimates
$P(Y_{ic} = j)$, that is the probability of voter i in context c to cast her ballot for
party j as the integral of the ordinary conditional logit model. It does so
over all values of the ideological voting effect β_c across contexts weighted
by the probability that they are observed and assuming that the random
effects follow a multivariate normal distribution.

$$P(Y_{ic} = j) = \int_{\beta_c} \frac{e^{x_{ijc}\beta_c}}{\sum_{j=0}^{m} e^{x_{ijc}\beta_c}} \tag{5}$$

Controlling for the second caveat of the unbiased estimation of ideological voting, that is, factors which impact both on ideological views
and on vote choice, necessitates the inclusion of rival considerations.
Among the various sets of determinants of vote choice identified by
electoral research, two alternative information short-cuts may be relevant strategies to avoid ideological voting. The voting short-cut which
is probably the most prominent in electoral research assumes an affective
and stable attachment to a particular party (Campbell et al. 1960). Party
identification of this nature is transmitted within the family during early
adulthood and includes all sorts of influences derived from social positions and political milieus (for a review, see Zuckerman 2005). Without
further consideration of the political supply side, voters support "their"
party in an election. A second voting short-cut is the use of like–dislike
evaluations (Sniderman, Richard, and Tetlock 1993). In particular, sympathy for political leaders may function as an effective short-cut for voting.
This, too, can be based on apolitical information such as the appearance
or private lives of politicians (Glass 1985; Rosenberg et al. 1986; Vetter
and Gabriel 1998). Both party identification and candidate sympathy
may affect voters' perceptions of ideological positions. Because of selective exposure to political information and the tendency to reinterpret
deviating information, voters may perceive parties and candidates they
prefer as being ideologically closer to their own positions than they really
are (e.g. Campbell et al. 1960; Lazarsfeld, Berelson, and Gaudet 1944).
The estimation of ideological voting will thus have to be controlled for
possible antecedent effects of attachments to parties and politicians.

In the literature on spatial models of voting, a debate has emerged
on the appropriate form of the ideological utility function. The classical
view is that maximum utility for voters is derived when choosing the

ideologically closest party (Downs 1957). That is, ideological proximity is the best approximation for party utility. Other authors assume that a directional model of ideological voting is empirically more suitable (Rabinowitz and MacDonald 1989). According to this view, maximum utility flows from choosing the party that occupies an extreme position on the same side of the ideological division that is preferred by the voter (MacDonald, Rabinowitz, and Listhaug 1995). Again others combine both views and propose a mixed ideological utility function (Iversen 1994; Merrill and Grofman 1999). This chapter follows the classical proximity model of ideological voting. Ideological voting thus refers to the effect on individual vote choice of the absolute distance between a voter and a party's ideological position. The choice of the proximity model is based on its direct link to a particular normative vision of voting, that is, on the notion that voters prefer parties which most closely represent their interests (as presented in the introductory section of this chapter).

The empirical analysis outlined so far requires both individual and contextual variation in ideological voting. Contextual variation may be achieved across different ideological dimensions, across different points in time, and across different countries. Using a sample of countries insures sufficient variation in the complexity of party systems. As the competitive structure of parties is more or less stable, the complexity of party systems varies little in a country across different points in time and across different ideological dimensions. The analysis will therefore apply the model of ideological voting developed above to cross-national comparative data from Module 1 of the Comparative Study of Electoral Systems collected between 1996 and 2002 (Sapiro and Shively 2002). At the time of writing, data were available for 38 elections in 34 political systems. Some of these could not be used because of the lack of variables of central importance, or because they pertained to presidential rather than parliamentary elections. A detailed report on the selection of surveys is included in Kroh (2003). Parliamentary elections from the following countries are analyzed: Australia, Canada, Britain, the Czech Republic, Denmark, Germany, Hong Kong, Hungary, Iceland, Israel, Japan, Korea, Mexico, the Netherlands, New Zealand, Norway, Peru, Poland, Portugal, Romania, Russia, Slovenia, Spain, Sweden, Switzerland, Taiwan, and the Ukraine.

The CSES survey data provide for each context analyzed in this paper an ideological dimension which is considered by the local collaborators of CSES to be the most important for the country. In most of the countries this is the left–right scale or its functional equivalent, the liberal–conservative scale, in countries such as Japan and the United States. In the literature on spatial models of voting, one can distinguish between studies based on "true"[8] and those based on "perceived" party placements. This chapter is primarily interested in the extent to which voters successfully link their own and the parties' ideological positions. Whether their perception of the ideological party competition is accurate is a related question but goes beyond the scope of this chapter. In calculating the ideological distance between parties and voters, I therefore use the respondent's perception of her or his self-placement and the parties' placements irrespective of whether these perceptions are invalidated by expert ratings based on party platforms.[9]

As control variables for ideological considerations, the analysis includes the traditional measure of party identification and an 11-point like–dislike rating scale for each party leader. Both cognitive skills and willingness to collect political information—sources of individuals' political sophistication as distinguished by Converse (1975) and discussed as determinants of ideological voting—can be measured by CSES survey data. Education is used as a proxy of individuals' cognitive skills and three political knowledge items are utilized as indicators of individuals' willingness to collect information. The extent to which the answers to these three items reflect a unidimensional trait in each political system, that is, reflect political knowledge, was tested by means of a stochastic cumulative scaling model (Mokken 1971; for a detailed report of the construction of additive knowledge scales country-by-country, see Kroh 2003). The contextual measure of party system fragmentation is based on CSES macro data. Information on governmental fragmentation comes from World Bank databases (Beck and Keefer 2001). Note that the fragmentation of governments was calculated as the average effective number of parties in government in the period of 20 years before the election analyzed here. In transitional democracies, the period since the first free election was used to calculate this index. Both ideological polarization and concentration of party systems are based on the CSES survey data of the perceived party placements on the left–right scale.

Findings

To what extent does ideological voting depend on voter sophistication? Table 10.1 indicates, first of all, that the smaller the distance between parties and voters on the left–right or liberal–conservative scale, the greater the probability of voting for parties even after controlling for

Table 10.1. Multilevel conditional logit estimates of voting choice with variation in the effect of ideological proximity across levels of voter sophistication and contextual units

	Coefficient	S.E.
Mean structure (β)		
Ideological proximity	−0.430	(0.020)***
Ideological proximity × education	−0.104	(0.012)***
Ideological proximity × political knowledge	−0.102	(0.013)***
Covariance structure ($\sigma\beta$)		
Ideological proximity	0.061	(0.006)***
Ideological proximity, party identification	0.005	(0.006)
Ideological proximity, leader sympathy	0.011	(0.003)***
Model fit		
Pseudo R^2		0.48
$N_{\text{Individuals}}$		33,968
N_{Context}		30

Notes: $^*p < 0.10$; $^{**}p < 0.05$; $^{***}p < 0.01$. The model also includes the fixed and random effects of party identification and leader sympathy and all interaction effects between them and indicators of voter sophistication.

Data source: CSES Module 1.

party identification and sympathy for party leaders. Second, both high levels of education and political knowledge increase the size of the effect parameter for ideological proximity. In line with previous research, the analysis suggests that sophistication positively affects ideological voting. Explanatory variables have been standardized to allow a straightforward interpretation of effect parameters. For instance, respondents ranging one standard deviation lower than the average respondent in terms of political knowledge display lower levels of ideological voting $\hat{\beta} = -0.430 + (-1)(-0.102) = -0.328$ than respondents with average levels of political knowledge $\hat{\beta} = -0.430 + 0(-0.102) = -0.430$. And lower levels of ideological voting are also found for respondents one standard deviation higher in terms of political knowledge $\hat{\beta} = -0.430 + 1(-0.102) = -0.532$. The effects of education and all other moderating variables can be interpreted accordingly.

Note that the model reported in Table 10.1 includes all main and interaction effects between education and political knowledge on the one hand, and party identification and leader sympathy on the other. Since this chapter is not substantively interested in the effects of these control variables, I refrain from reporting or commenting them. Details about the effects of party identification and leader evaluations can be obtained from Kroh (2003). In the second panel, Table 10.1 reports information about the variation of effect parameters across contextual units: 95 percent of all

Table 10.2. Multilevel conditional logit estimates of voting choice with variation in the effect of ideological proximity across levels of party system complexity and contextual units

	Coefficient	S.E.
Mean structure (β)		
Ideological proximity	−0.498	(0.021)***
Ideological proximity × parliamentary parties	0.056	(0.024)**
Ideological proximity × government parties	−0.079	(0.018)***
Ideological proximity × polarization	−0.114	(0.020)***
Ideological proximity × concentration	−0.096	(0.015)***
Covariance structure ($\sigma\beta$)		
Ideological proximity	0.047	(0.006)***
Ideological proximity, party identification	−0.005	(0.002)**
Ideological proximity, leader sympathy	−0.029	(0.006)***
Model fit		
Pseudo R^2		0.48
$N_{Individuals}$		33,968
$N_{Context}$		30

Notes: * $p < 0.10$; ** $p < 0.05$; *** $p < 0.01$. The model also includes the fixed and random effects of party identification and leader sympathy and all interaction effects between them and indicators of party system complexity.

Data source: CSES Module 1.

estimates of ideological voting vary between $-0.430 \pm 2 \times \sqrt{0.061}$, that is, between 0.064 and −0.924.

To what extent does ideological voting depend on party system complexity? Table 10.2 reports estimates of ideological voting across contexts with differing numbers of parties in parliaments and governments and levels of ideological overlap between and within parties. The findings suggest that an increase in the effective number of parties in parliament by one standard deviation decreases the effect of ideological proximity on vote choice by a factor of 0.056 points. The effective number of parties in government causes an effect in the opposite direction. If the viable parties in government are ideologically close, voters are more likely to consider ideology when casting their ballot.

The quantity of political supply affects the prevalence of ideological voting across contexts as does the degree of ideological overlap between and within parties. This is in line with the expectation that ideological polarization, that is, low interparty overlap in left–right positions, increases ideological voting. Similarly, high concentration, that is, high intraparty overlap in left–right positions, is positively associated with levels of ideological voting. As each of the four indicators of party system complexity were standardized for the analysis, the relative difference in magnitude

Table 10.3. Linear predictions of the effect of ideological proximity on voting choices for Romania, Hungary, and Iceland dependent on party system complexity

	Romania	Hungary	Iceland
Parliamentary parties	6.14	4.44	3.57
$\Delta(\hat{\beta}\|parliamentary\ parties)$	0.05	−0.00	−0.03
Governmental parties	1.52	1.67	1.91
$\Delta(\hat{\beta}\|governmental\ parties)$	0.00	−0.01	−0.04
Polarization	2.00	3.41	3.84
$\Delta(\hat{\beta}\|polarization)$	0.17	−0.05	−0.11
Concentration	0.29	0.45	0.64
$\Delta(\hat{\beta}\|concentration)$	0.09	0.00	−0.11
$\Delta(\hat{\beta})$	0.31	−0.06	−0.29
$\hat{\beta}$	−0.19	−0.56	−0.79
β	−0.16	−0.59	−0.96

Note: Estimates are based on the model of Table 10.2.
Data source: CSES Module 1.

suggests that the effects of ideological polarization and concentration are somewhat more relevant for ideological voting than differences of contexts in terms of the number of choice options (parliamentary and governmental fragmentation).

To illustrate the size of effects, consider the linear predictions of ideological voting for three different contexts: one country with a highly complex party system (e.g. Romania), one country with a party system of average complexity (e.g. Hungary), and one country with a moderately complex party system (e.g. Iceland).

Table 10.3 reports that Romania has 6.64 effective parties in parliament more than Hungary (4.44) and Iceland (3.57) and at the same time fewer effective parties in government (1.52 in Romania vs. 1.67 and 1.91 in Hungary and Iceland, respectively). This makes ideological voting more complex in Romania than in Hungary and particularly Iceland. The deviation in ideological voting, that is, the difference in the effect of ideological proximity on voter choice, due to the high number of parties in the Romanian parliament is 0.05 points relative to the average ideological proximity effect of −0.50 reported in Table 10.2. The low parliamentary fragmentation in Iceland increases the country-specific estimate of ideological voting by −0.03 points. Ideological voting is especially limited by the low polarization, that is, the high interparty overlap, of the Romanian parties (deviation from the average ideological voting estimate of 0.17) and facilitated by polarization and concentration of the Icelandic parties (deviation from the average ideological vote choice estimate of −0.11

each). Because of the different levels of party system complexity, the 1999 parliamentary election in Iceland differs in terms of ideological voting from the average context by −0.29 points and the 1996 parliamentary election in Romania by +0.31 points leading to a situation in which the predicted effect of ideological voting for Iceland is $\hat{\beta} = -0.79$ or four times higher than Romania ($\hat{\beta} = -0.19$).[10] The last row of Table 10.3 reports the observed estimates of ideological voting in each context. The linear prediction of ideological voting based on the four indicators of party system complexity provides a reasonably good approximation of the observed scores.[11]

Conclusions

The empirical analysis of this chapter supports the hypothesis that that citizens' vote for parties and candidates which best represent their ideological interests is not only a function of voter sophistication but also depends on the complexity of political supply. Some contexts ease ideological voting while others make ideological voting a more demanding exercise.[12]

This general conclusion about the nature of ideological voting depends, as always, on the appropriateness of assumptions underlying the analysis. I will briefly discuss two possible caveats. First, although it is shown that ideological proximity is a better predictor of vote choice if, for instance, the number of competing parties is small, this does not necessarily exclude the possibility that in situations of many competing parties other functional forms of ideological party utility, such as the directional model proposed by Rabinowitz and MacDonald (1989), might compensate for the weakness of the ideological proximity model. In other words, party system complexity just like voter sophistication may not affect ideological voting per se but voting based on ideological proximity only. However, the ideological proximity model represents in my view the appropriate functional form to capture the normative notion of representation. Even if the analysis presented cannot exclude the possibility that voters bypass ideological proximity by ideological direction if the choice situation is complex, the analysis does establish that their behavior is compatible with the proximity model.

Second, the analysis presented in this chapter is cross-sectional and thus cannot unanimously establish a causal relationship between voter sophistication and party system complexity on the one hand and ideological voting on the other hand. It may well be, for instance, that a high polarization of party systems is a consequence rather than a cause of ideological voting. Parties may wish to stress their ideological differences if the voters in a political system are for one reason or another ideologically oriented regarding their voting behavior. If voters in that political system were not ideologically oriented in their vote choices, parties may not care whether there is ideological overlap with other parties. In the absence of a well-specified theory of the causal direction of ideological voting with regard to voter sophistication and party system complexity, I treat ideological voting as the dependent variable. However, the reader should be aware of the potential problem of endogeneity. Only the continuation of data projects like CSES will provide the longitudinal information necessary to test the causal direction between voter characteristics and party system characteristics.

From the unified model of ideological voting presented in this chapter, one can infer certain expectations about future developments in voters' decision-making. As a consequence of rising levels of cognitive mobilization in many developed societies in recent decades, several scholars have predicted increasing levels of ideological voting (e.g. Dalton, Flanagan, and Beck 1984; Franklin, Mackie, and Valen 1992; Nie, Verba, and Petrocik 1976). Although this expectation is well founded in cross-sectional studies showing the close link between voter sophistication and ideological voting, the empirical evidence for rising levels of ideological voting in a longitudinal perspective is scarce. On the contrary, the hypothesis of the end of ideological politics has attracted extensive attention (Bell 1965). The integration of context into the study of ideological voting may provide a plausible account for the mixed empirical findings: While many developed societies are indeed characterized by increasing levels of cognitive mobilization, their party systems are at the same time affected by higher levels of fragmentation (Dalton and Wattenberg 2000) and lower levels of ideological concentration (Kirchheimer 1965; Sigelman and Yough 1978). Hence, the last decades have produced not only more sophisticated electorates but also ideologically more complex party systems.

Notes

1. Early election studies show that voters are highly stable in their voting decisions and seem not to deliberately consider all the political information

available (Lazarsfeld, Berelson, and Gaudet 1944). Irrespective of changes in their social position, changes in the political supply, or changes in the economic climate, many voters maintain their "standing" voting decision acquired in early adulthood (Campbell et al. 1960). Butler and Stokes (1963) show that only three consecutive elections suffice to immunize voters against any partisan change.

2. The notion that voters may differ in the extent to which they respond to certain political issues is already embodied in the concepts of issue saliency and issue publics. In survey research, respondents are often asked not only to place themselves on some issue dimension but also to rate the importance of the issue (RePass 1971).

3. Individual characteristics commonly associated with variation in voters' reasoning are age and generation. Converse (1969) stresses the importance of electoral experiences for the development of party identification. Their relevance for vote choice is therefore not equal over the entire life span (Kroh 2003). Moreover, stable loyalties are said to gradually lose relevance for vote choice in more recent cohorts (e.g. Crewe and Denver 1985; Dalton, Flanagan, and Beck 1984; Franklin, Mackie, and Valen 1992).

4. The discussion on the effects of voter sophistication for the reasoning of vote choice invokes at least three scholarly traditions. First, the literature on the formation of opinions and the stability of attitudes speaks in this respect of levels of conceptualization (Achen 1975; Converse 1964). Second, the debate on partisan de-alignment draws on the term of cognitive mobilization (Dalton and Wattenberg 2000). Third, within the rational choice paradigm, the role of political information for the calculus of voting is discussed under the condition of uncertainty of decision-making (Downs 1957; Simon 1957).

5. Similarly, models of economic voting may be stratified for levels of voter sophistication. Campbell et al. (1960) argue that voters with low levels of political sophistication lack sufficient information on the general economic performance and thus take their own economic position into consideration when deciding which party to support. Conversely, Gomez and Wilson (2001) claim that it is more difficult for voters to recognize the link between governmental actions and their own economic well-being than to blame the government for the general economic climate. That is, voter sophistication may increase egocentric but not sociotropic voting.

6. It has often been argued that the ideological positions of single parties are increasingly diverse in Western societies in recent decades since political demands (and as a result supplies) are becoming more pluralistic (e.g. Weßels 1991). Single parties' ideological stands may therefore be less homogenous than in earlier times. Likewise, many transition democracies are supposed to have less developed party systems and therefore low levels of concentration in parties' positions (e.g. White, Rose, and McAllister 1997). Irrespective of the cause for loose party positions, such lack of ideological concentration

presumably has consequences for voters' reasoning. In both cases, one may expect that respective party systems make it more difficult for voters to base their voting decision on ideological considerations.

7. Moreover, these camps are usually formed on the basis of joint ideological platforms, that is, the ideological distance between two parties is a good approximation of their compatibility in most political systems. Ideological orientations, due to their importance for coalition formation, may also be an important consideration of vote choice.

8. Some scholars use party manifesto data to approximate parties' true ideological positions, others use the mean of the perceived party placement obtained in mass or expert surveys.

9. Many respondents are unable to locate single parties on left–right scales. As this is an important piece of information with respect to ideological voting, these cases are not deleted from the analysis. Instead, a complete random imputation replaces missing ideological data. For a detailed description of the imputation technique see Kroh (2006) and for a discussion of the application of the technique in studies of voting behavior see Kroh (2003).

10. The models reported in Tables 10.1 and 10.2 imply that a sophisticated voter in Romania (one standard deviation above average in terms of education and political knowledge) has a notably lower propensity for ideological voting due to the complex party competition, $\hat{\beta} = -0.19 - 0.10 - 0.10 = -0.39$, than an unsophisticated voter in Iceland (one standard deviation below average in terms of education and political knowledge), $\hat{\beta} = -0.79 + 0.10 + 0.10 = -0.59$.

11. A cautionary remark is in order for the interpretation of findings across contexts. The result that, for instance, the context of the Romanian election analyzed does not imply that the Romanian political system is not suited per se for ideological voting but that Romanian parties in that specific election positioned themselves on the left–right scale in such a way that makes it difficult for voters to discriminate between parties on the basis of that particular dimension. It may be the case that in a different election or on different ideological dimensions, the Romanian party competition eases ideological voting. The present analysis treats countries only as one possible source of contextual variation in individual choice behavior (Przeworski and Teune 1970). The estimated levels of ideological voting in different countries cannot be interpreted as fixed properties of these political systems.

12. This means that one cannot necessarily conclude, as some do, that voters lack ideological sophistication if there is a low degree of ideological voting.

11

How Voters Cope with the Complexity of Their Political Environment: Differentiation of Political Supply, Effectiveness of Electoral Institutions, and the Calculus of Voting[1]

Hans-Dieter Klingemann and Bernhard Weßels

Theoretical Orientation

This analysis focuses on how individual-level vote choice is influenced by macro-contexts, which constitute the voters' political environment. Are major evaluative criteria for vote choice—such as parties, candidates, and issues—systematically affected by characteristics of political macro-contexts? For example, does it make a difference in the evaluative process if citizens cast their votes in small, single-member constituencies or in large, multimember districts? How do voters cope with the complexity of their political environment? There is growing evidence that voters' evaluative criteria for electoral behavior are conditioned by the nature of their political environment (Kroh 2003; Paldam 1991). *Thus, generally we expect that the political macro-context matters for vote choice.*

We propose that two characteristics of political macro-contexts are of particular importance for electoral behavior. The first characteristic relates to the number of alternatives citizens can choose from in an election. This choice set is primarily defined by the party system, that is, by the number and strength of political parties or candidates competing for votes. We call this dimension of the political macro-context *differentiation of political supply*. The second characteristic is linked to electoral institutions, especially to election law. Electoral institutions facilitate or restrict the translation of the voter's choice into the desired result. There is wide variation in the degree to which electoral institutions impact the realization of the voters' true political preferences. Considering the importance of an effective translation of political preferences for the voter, we call this dimension of the political macro-context *effectiveness of electoral institutions*.

We assume that these two characteristics of political macro-contexts condition how voters weigh the major evaluative criteria determining their vote choice. Our reasoning starts with two assumptions that relate the complexity of the choice-situation and the motivation of voters to deal with this complexity. These assumptions can be summarized as follows:

1. *Differentiation of political supply*: The greater the number of meaningful alternatives to choose from in an election, the greater the voter's motivation to invest and weigh strongly those criteria which are best suited to support the particular choice.

2. *Effectiveness of electoral institutions*: The more effective electoral institutions translate preferred voting intentions into seats, the greater the voter's motivation to invest and to weigh strongly those criteria which are best suited to support the particular choice.

If a party system, at election time, offers a highly differentiated political supply, voters are faced with a complex and thus difficult selection problem. They have to think about the relative importance of evaluative criteria which tell them why they should prefer one particular party or candidate instead of any other. If a political system offers electoral institutions that effectively translate votes into seats, it makes much sense for voters to weigh the alternatives and consider the pros and cons of their voting decision. Thus, both a differentiated political supply and effective electoral institutions provide incentives for voters to focus on their options and base their decision on the evaluative criteria which is best suited to reduce the complexity of the choice situation. This argument leads to the following general assumption:

> The more differentiated the political supply in an election and the more effective the electoral institutions translate vote preferences into seats, the stronger the impact of the evaluative criteria which are best suited to reduce the complexity of the choice situation.

This general expectation needs further specification regarding the particular object of choice. Generally, and in our study also empirically, the voter has three different types of vote choice. The vote can be cast for political parties (party-list vote), candidates (candidate vote), or for a president (president vote). It seems plausible that different evaluation criteria are of different importance to determine the optimal choice of a political party or candidate. If it comes to the election of political parties, it is highly likely that characteristics of the party as an organization (e.g. whether the party is perceived as being able to govern, as being united or divided, etc.) are among the most important evaluation criteria. For the election of candidates for parliament or for the presidency, a similar argument applies. In this case, public recognition, political experience, or honesty in public service is likely to be among the most important evaluative criteria for a candidate.

The scenario sketched out above is well in line with Schumpeter's view of procedural democracy, which he defines as a method based on "... institutional arrangements for arriving at political decisions in which individuals acquire the power to decide by means of a competitive struggle for the people's vote" (Schumpeter 1942: 269). This conception of democracy allows citizens to select between competing groups of political elites, no more but no less. This understanding of democracy—which is close to Downs's arguments in the *Economic Theory of Democracy* (1957)— regards politicians as power seeking, not as policy seeking. Dahl (1971), however, convincingly argues that a political process can only be called democratic if it is responsive to the interests and demands of citizens and recognizes the importance of their policy orientations. In this view, citizens are entitled to expect that their interests and demands be recognized and, in addition, weighed equally in the conduct of government (Dahl 1971: 2). Indeed, empirical research provides much evidence that political parties and politicians are not just power seekers but also responsive to the citizenry when offering and pursuing policies. As such, when it comes to vote choice we must consider issues and issue positions of parties and candidates.

This discussion of the vote function highlights two general aspects of vote choice.

First, it specifies type of vote choice, and three evaluative criteria for vote choice at the micro level. Type of vote choice distinguishes between party-list vote, candidate vote, and president vote. Above we have listed some specific examples of how parties or candidates can be evaluated. However, in our analysis we do not consider specific evaluation criteria.

Rather, we propose generalized criteria. We do this for two reasons, the first being substantive. Electoral research has demonstrated that in the long run specific experiences with or evaluations of political objects translate into generalized orientations that are almost always better predictors of vote choice than specific evaluations (Fuchs and Kühnel 1994; Weßels 2004). The second reason is pragmatic. Measures for specific evaluations are simply not available in our data set. Thus, our generalized evaluative criteria include party-liking, candidate-liking, and generalized issue-distance.

Second, our argument proposes two characteristics of the voters' political environment or macro-context. These macro-level characteristics have been labeled differentiation of political supply and effectiveness of electoral institutions. We assume that these characteristics condition the impact of the individual-level evaluative criteria on the various types of vote choice.

What are the reasons for the assumption of conditioning effects of the political environment? Our reasoning resembles the reasoning of the familiar "cost of voting" argument (Sanders 1980; Sigelman and Berry 1982). However, we do not focus on an explanation of turnout. Rather, we discuss information costs in relation to vote choice in political environments of varying degrees of complexity. Under which conditions are voters willing to invest in political information able to weigh the utility of different evaluative criteria to cope with a specific decision situation? We assume different optima depending on the object of vote choice: parties, candidates for parliament or for the presidency. When it comes to party choice, the probability that evaluation criteria related to party cues are applied should rise with the rising number of parties competing for election. This reaction seems to be the most adequate and economic to cope with the complexity of the choice situation. When it comes to candidate vote, a similar logic applies. With an increase in the number of candidates standing for office, candidate-related criteria should be the most adequate and economic ones to reach a decision. This general evaluation mechanism implies a loss of relevance of other potential evaluation criteria. The more differentiated the supply of political parties, the less relevant the importance of candidate evaluation for vote choice; the more differentiated the supply of candidates, the less relevant the importance of party evaluation for vote choice. Under conditions of complexity, we assume that there is a tendency to simplify decision-making by reducing the number of potential evaluation criteria. Those evaluation criteria should be selected that are most closely related to the object of choice because this is the most economic way to reach a reasoned decision.

What about the evaluative criteria of generalized issue-distance of parties and candidates? One argument would be that issue-distance is closely related to type of electoral system. Proportional systems facilitate close issue-distance between voters and parties, whereas issue-proximity seems to be more difficult to establish in majority systems. In addition, these two types of electoral systems are closely connected to two different visions of democracy. Whereas those advocating the principle of proportionality want to ensure comprehensive representation, those favoring the plurality principle want to create strong and responsible party government. Thus, proportional systems are designed to channel a broad range of preferences and interests to the political process while this is not a priority of majority systems. The proportionality formula fits Dahl's concept of democracy; effective government selection, on the other hand, is closer to the majority formula and the ideas of Schumpeter. In reality, however, the problem cannot so easily be reduced to these two normative visions. A black and white picture does not correspond to reality. There is no doubt that both political parties and candidates are policy seekers. For this reason, they can be evaluated in terms of the policies and issues they propose, and in terms of those policies and issues they have helped to enact in the past. After all, political parties are historical beings and citizens remember them for what they have done to solve their society's problems. In general, we assume that the greater the differentiation of political supply and the more effective the electoral institutions, the more consistent the issue position will appear as a complement to party-liking or candidate-liking as an evaluative criterion.

Countries, Elections, and Macro-Contexts Included in the Analysis

Before proceeding with the analysis, we want to briefly describe the countries and elections analyzed. Like the other chapters in this volume, we rely on Module 1 of the Comparative Study of Electoral Systems (CSES). Our criterion for a survey to enter our data set is availability of individual-level dependent and independent variables needed for the analyses. Surveys from 26 different countries meet this criterion. Mexico (1997, 2000), Peru (2000, 2001), and Spain (1996, 2000) enter with surveys from two different election years. In 15 countries, all parliamentary seats are allocated by a proportional formula; three countries distribute all seats by using a majoritarian formula. Nine countries combine proportionality and plurality principles for seat allocation in mixed-member electoral systems. However, of these nine countries, just three surveys cover both the direct party-list vote and the candidate district vote. For two elections, we miss the candidate tier while in four elections the party-list tier is not available. Defining a "case" by type of election, our study is based on 20 parliamentary elections governed by a proportional formula, and 10 parliamentary elections using a majoritarian formula. In addition, we analyze seven direct presidential elections. These 37 cases also define the number of political macro-contexts available for analysis.

Although we will not pursue this aspect further, we want to note that one aspect of the complexity of the choice situation is not covered by our study. This aspect relates to the number of national institutions requiring popular elections. Table 11.1 provides a rough indication and places the elections for which data are available in this wider context.

Measuring the Characteristics of Political Macro-Contexts

In the first step of our analysis, we want to establish empirical evidence that the two dimensions of political macro-contexts we have proposed indeed do exist. To this end we have selected three variables to describe degree of differentiation of political supply and a similar number of variables to indicate degree of effectiveness of electoral institutions.

Differentiation of Political Supply

Differentiation of political supply is measured by three indicators describing different properties of the choice situation. The first variable indicates the number of active parties ("launched parties" in Cox's terms; Cox 1997: 26). The information is taken from various volumes of the *Political Handbook of the World* (Arthur S. Banks et al. 1995–7, 1998–9; 2000–2). We consistently sought to consult the volume closest to the election under consideration. The respective *Handbook* sections on political parties normally include government parties, parliamentary opposition parties, and "other" parties. We have counted all parties mentioned with the exception of extremist or terrorist parties. Number of "other" parties may be a source of error. It seems as if the number of "other" parties varies a great deal between different yearly reports for the same country. Thus,

Country	Parliamentary pure majoritarian	Parliamentary mixed-member independent (C/P)	Parliamentary mixed-member combined (C/P)	Parliamentary pure proportional	Parliamentary bi-cameral (directly elected)	Presidential directly elected president	Number of national institutions requiring direct elections
TWN Taiwan (1995)		xx			x	x	4
MEX-97 Mexico (1997)			xx		x	x	4
MEX-00 Mexico (2000)			xx		x	x	4
RUS Russia (1999)		xx				x	3
UKR Ukraine (1998)		xx				x	3
KOR South Korea (2000)		xx				x	3
PER-01 Peru (2001)				x	x	x	3
POL Poland (1997)				x	x	x	3
ROU Romania (1996)				x	x	x	3
PER-00 Peru (2000)				x	x	x	3
AUS Australia (1996)	x				x		2
DEU Germany (1998)			xx				2
NZL New Zealand (1996)			xx				2
HUN Hungary (1998)			xx				2
CZE Czech Republic				x	x		2
ESP-96 Spain (1996)				x	x		2
ESP-00 Spain (2000)				x	x		2
CHE Switzerland (1999)				x	x		2
ISR Israel (1996)				x		x	2
LTU Lithuania (1997)				x		x	2
CAN Canada (1997)	x						1
GBR Great Britain (1997)	x						1
DNK Denmark (1998)				x			1
ISL Iceland (1999)				x			1
NLD The Netherlands (1998)				x			1
NOR Norway (1997)				x			1
PRT Portugal (2002)				x			1
SVN Slovenia (1996)				x			1
SWE Sweden (1998)				x			1
Number of elections	3 (3)	2/2 (8)	5/3 (10)	15 (17)	12	7 (11)	

Bold face: elections covered by the data set.

the *Handbook* figures leave much to be desired. However, they constitute our best guess for the number of parties active in the period of time under study. Numbers range from 68 in Spain (1996) to 10 in Iceland. On average we count 28 active parties across the 37 elections. High numbers of active parties reflect different regional interests in the first place. Spain and the United Kingdom are typical examples where the high number of parties is linked to regional divides. However, in Ukraine and Russia, the number of parties is also affected by strategic elite action. Birch and Wilson (1999: 278–9) describe elite strategies to increase the number of (pseudo) parties designed to diminish the electoral fortunes of their competitors. Related to the Ukrainian parliamentary election of 1998, they report that "spoiler parties" were "... created before the election, primarily to erode the support bases of existing parties." Similar elite strategies are employed in Russia. Analyzing the 1999 parliamentary election, Golosov (2005: 49) writes "And it was not unusual that independents ran not in order to win a seat but rather, to split the vote for those candidates who were perceived as a threat by their rivals or local executive elites." "Parties" such as these are neither anchored in social cleavages nor do they represent any other citizen interests. They clearly constitute pathologies of the political supply side.

In an election, citizens may not be confronted with all parties active in their country. This applies, for example, to regional parties that are not presenting party lists or field candidates nationwide. It also depends on the electoral system that may allow different constellations of parties and candidates in the various regional districts. To capture this feature of the political supply side, we have computed the average number of party lists per district and the average number of candidates per district. For parliamentary elections, figures range from 7.0 (Iceland) to 46.5 (Romania)[2] as far as party lists per district are concerned, and from 5.5 (Canada) to 11.5 (Taiwan) for the average number of candidates per district. On average, this index gives a much lower figure for choice options than number of political parties active in the election (11.8 vs. 28.0). The number of parties presenting "presidential" candidates ranges from 16 (Romania) to 2 (Israel).

Parties differ in terms of shares of votes. This is taken into account by calculating the effective number of active parties. We have taken these figures from Kroh (2003: 296). By considering shares of vote, the index provides more information about the importance and viability of parties. Taking vote shares into account, the average number of active parties is reduced by a factor of 6.2 (28.0: 4.5). Vote and seat shares are well-established indicators for the parties' political importance. We want to note, however, that small parties may enter parliament by either winning seats in single-member districts or by crawling under the wings of an electoral party bloc. The 1998 parliamentary election in Ukraine is a good example of this situation. And small parties may be powerful too, because often they make and break coalition governments.

Effectiveness of Electoral Institutions

Indicators selected to measure *effectiveness of electoral institutions* include weight of candidate district vote, thresholds, and (log) district magnitude. Weight of candidate district vote roughly indicates electoral formula (majoritarian; proportional). It is calculated as the proportion of candidate vote district seats based on the total number of seats in parliament. Values of this index range from 0 (no seats distributed in candidate vote districts) in pure proportional systems to 100 (all seats distributed in candidate vote districts) in pure majoritarian systems. Thresholds are introduced to bar small parties from seat allocation. Most countries in the majoritarian electoral tradition use plurality. In this case, there is no formal threshold. Among the majoritarian countries under study, Australia uses the alternative vote (AV) and Hungary a second ballot system (2nd ballot). For candidates to win a seat, these systems require an absolute majority of votes. While the Australian is a preferential system where voters rank their preferences among candidates, the Hungarian system requires a second round of elections when no candidate obtains an absolute majority in the first round. Although there is no formal threshold under plurality, the effective threshold may be quite high. In our analysis, we rely in these cases on Kroh's estimate (2003: 292) of effective threshold which is based on Lijphart's conceptualization (1994: 25) and defined as "the minimum percentage of the vote that can earn a party a seat under the most favorable circumstances." Effective threshold may deviate from formal thresholds in proportional systems because Kroh (2003: 291) is taking into account variations across different levels of electoral districts. The third indicator is district magnitude. In 9 out of the 10 elections which distribute seats by a majoritarian formula, the district magnitude is 1; Taiwan (4.41 seats) which uses single nontransferable vote (SNTV) is the exception. For presidential elections, we also assume a district magnitude of 1. The proportional formulae allow seat numbers per district to go up from 4.8 (Peru 2001) and 7.7 (Switzerland) to 225 for the nationwide districts in Ukraine and Russia. On average, 27 seats are allocated per district. There is widespread agreement that district magnitude is a critical institutional variable. "The importance of district magnitude derives, in part, from its influence on the vote quota a party must secure to ensure representation in parliament. Also, magnitude influences a system's proportionality, which also influences the incentives to form and maintain parties" (Ordeshook and Shevetsova 1994: 105). According to Sartori's rule of thumb (1986: 53), the smaller the district the lesser the proportionality. Because the indicator is highly skewed, we use a log-transformed variable in our analysis.

Dimensional Analysis

Factor analysis is used to test the dimensionality of the variables described above and to create the respective scores for the political macro-contexts. Factor analysis confirms that the expected two dimensions, "differentiation of political supply" and "effectiveness of electoral institutions," exist empirically. Table 11.2 summarizes the basic statistical parameters of the variables and presents correlations of these variables with the two dimensions extracted by factor analysis.

Table 11.2. A summary of characteristics of political macro-contexts ($N = 37$)

Indicators	Min.	Max.	Mean	Std. dev.	Correlation factor 1	Correlation factor 2
					Effectiveness of electoral institutions	Differentiation of political supply
Variance explained					52.5%	24.2%
Threshold	1.00	50.00	21.43	17.02	**0.911**	0.067
Weight of candidate vote	0.00	100.00	43.46	41.81	**0.947**	−0.158
Log district magnitude	1.00	225.00	25.66	57.44	**−0.825**	0.424
Number of active parties	10.00	68.00	28.00	12.57	0.182	**0.834**
Effective number of active parties	2.42	10.67	4.54	1.65	−0.253	**0.747**
Average number of party lists/candidates per district	2.00	46.52	11.81	8.40	−0.414	**0.687**

Bold face: Correlation of variables which define factors scores.

Spatial Location of Types of Elections

In this section, we locate the three types of elections (party list; candidate; president) in the two-dimensional space. Table 11.3 summarizes their respective location.

Figure 11.1 presents results in detail. Effectiveness of electoral institutions divides elections into two broad groups. The first group is clustered at the low end of the effectiveness dimension. In these elections, the translation of votes into seats is highly affected by electoral institutions. The group includes all presidential elections and all candidate elections. In general, the presidential elections show the lowest degree of effectiveness, with those presidential elections requiring a majority of the vote for winning the presidency (Peru 2000, 2001; Israel; Romania) marking the end of the continuum. It should be noted that we have classified the direct election of the prime minister in Israel as a "presidential" election. Its location on the effectiveness axis of the graph justifies this classification. Netanyahu (Likud) finally won this "presidential" race with 50.5 percent of the votes beating Simon Peres (Labor) (Arian 1996). Elections governed by proportional representation are found at the high end of the effectiveness dimension. Degree of effectiveness is most expressed in the Netherlands followed by Israel (parliamentary election). These are also the countries that pose the lowest percent hurdle for the elections under investigation (1 percent in the Netherlands; 2 percent in Israel). Thus, effectiveness of electoral institutions can safely be interpreted in terms of the degree to which votes are translated into seats proportionally.

Distribution of elections by "differentiation of political supply" shows a more complex picture. The broad contours, however, command

Table 11.3. Summary statistics of factor scores and location of type of elections in the two-dimensional space of the political macro-contexts

Dimension	Min.	Max.	Mean	Std. dev.	N
F1: Effectiveness of electoral institutions	−1.60	1.55	0.00	1.00	37
Party-list vote	0.12	1.55	0.83	0.31	20
Candidate vote	−1.38	−0.10	−0.68	0.42	10
President vote	−1.60	−1.04	−1.40	0.25	7
F2: Differentiation of political supply	−1.38	3.56	0.00	1.00	37
Party-list vote	−1.35	3.56	0.22	1.21	20
Candidate vote	−1.38	0.21	−0.52	0.42	10
President vote	−0.77	1.05	0.10	0.71	7

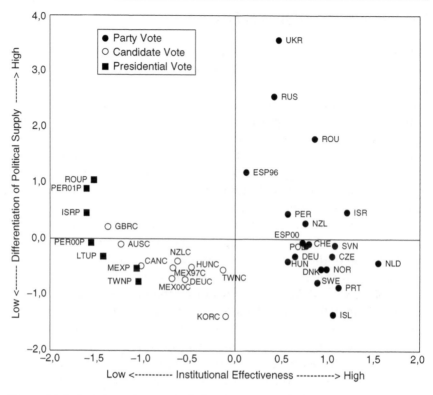

Figure 11.1. Location of type of elections in a space defined by effectiveness of electoral institutions and differentiation of political supply

plausibility. Ukraine, Russia, Romania, and Spain occupy the space in the upper right hand corner. This is where they should be because these elections are also located on the upper end of the effectiveness dimension. However, Ukraine (1998), Russia (1999), and Romania (1996), at that time were young and fledgling democracies. Their party systems were fluid and they experimented with their election laws to achieve more stability. In Ukraine, to give just one example, parliamentary seats were originally filled using the Soviet era, single-member, double-ballot system. Because the law required a candidate to gain an absolute majority of votes on an absolute majority turnout, nearly a quarter of the seats were left unfilled after the first set of elections in the spring of 1994. Furthermore, only half of the deputies elected were members of parties, the rest being independent political entrepreneurs and local bosses (Birch and Wilson 1999). To improve the situation, a new mixed electoral system was introduced in

September 1997. The new law stipulated that half of the seats would be filled in one round through a first-past-the-post formula (with no turnout requirements), and the other half through proportional representation with nationwide lists and a 4 percent threshold for representation. The two tiers were not linked. Candidates were allowed to run on both a party list and in a single-member constituency. This law encouraged party formation. Twenty-two parties were elected to parliament under pure single-member law and eight parties were elected from the proportional list ballot (Birch and Wilson 1999). The proliferation of old and the formation of new parties resulted in a total count of 57 active political parties in 1998. Similar accounts could be given for Russia in 1999, or Romania in 1996. Regional parties explain Spain's 1996 relatively high location on the political supply dimension.[3] To provide a convincing explanation of the variation within the two lower quadrants formed by the combination of effectiveness of electoral institutions and differentiation of political supply are beyond the goal of this analysis. What we know for sure is that the differences reflect the number of parties and candidates from which citizens are able to choose. The exact scores for effectiveness of electoral institutions and differentiation of political supply for each political macro-context are provided in Appendix 11.1.

The General Model and Method of Analysis

We need an appropriate model to test whether the conditioning effects of the two characteristics of political macro-context impact voters' evaluative criteria with regard to party-list voting, candidate voting, and president voting. We propose a model that takes into account the micro–macro interactions between the three evaluative criteria at the micro level (party-liking, candidate-liking, and generalized issue-distance), and the two macro characteristics described above (differentiation of political supply and effectiveness of electoral institutions).

Vote Choice as the Dependent Variable

Vote choice is the individual-level dependent variable. Three different types of voting are distinguished: voting for a political party (party-list vote), voting for a political candidate (leader; candidate vote), and voting for a presidential candidate (president vote).

— Party-list vote means that citizens have an option to vote directly for a party list at the district level;

— Candidate vote means that citizens have an option to directly vote for a candidate or candidates at the district level;

— President vote means that citizens have an option to directly vote for a presidential candidate. Party affiliation of the presidential candidate voted for is recorded.

As described earlier, our analysis comprises 20 elections which—at the district level—ask voters to choose a party list, 10 elections which request candidate voting, and seven direct elections for president.

Individual-Level Evaluative Criteria of Vote Choice

Voting for a political party, a candidate, or a president is explained at the individual level by three variables which are widely regarded as the most important (short-term) forces related to vote choice (the *locus classicus* is Campbell et al. 1960). The criteria are evaluation of political parties (party-liking) and candidates (candidate-liking), and generalized issue-distance.

Evaluation of political parties is measured by the following question:

> I'd like to know what you think about each of our political parties. After I read the name of a political party, please rate on a scale from 0 to 10, where 0 means you strongly dislike that party and 10 means that you strongly like that party. If I come to a party you haven't heard of or you feel you do not know enough about, just say so. The first party is . . . (up to six political parties could be offered for rating).

Evaluation of candidates is measured in a similar way:

> And now, using the same scale, I'd like to ask you how much you like or dislike some political leaders. Again, if I come to a leader you haven't heard of or you feel you do not know enough about, just say so. The first political leader is . . . (leaders from up to six different parties could be offered for rating).

Generalized issue-distance assumes that issue positions can be described in terms of left and right. The measure is operationalized by the following two questions:

1 *"In politics people sometimes talk of left and right. Where would you place yourself on a scale from 0 to 10 where 0 means the left and 10 means the right"?*

2 *"Now, using the same scale where would you place (party A)? (up to six political parties could be placed)"*

The absolute difference between the respondent's self-placement and her or his placement of the various political parties using the same scale is taken as a measure of generalized issue-distance.

Construction of the Data Set

The unit of analysis is "voting versus not voting" for a particular party (party-list vote, party of candidate vote, or party of president vote) rather than the individual respondent. The construction of the "stacked" data set is constraint by the number of political parties for which party evaluation, candidate evaluation, and left–right placements are separately available. The design of the questionnaire limits the maximum number of parties that can be included in the analysis to six. In order to overcome the massive missing data problems, we have applied multiple random imputation of incomplete data (Kroh 2003: 243–60; Kroh 2006). The resulting data set has as many cases per respondent as data for parties are recorded for the respective election's electoral tier. In this analysis, the total number of cases or observations ranges from 186,422 (party-list vote), 90,710 (candidate vote) to 35,400 (president vote). With a stacked data set such as this, one can estimate a logit model to explain the discrete ("dummy") dependent variable vote choice (party list; party of candidate; party of president) by party-liking, candidate-liking, and generalized issue-distance which are the independent variables at the individual level, as well as the conditional model which—in addition to the micro variables—also takes into account the properties of the two political macro-contexts.

The Micro-Part of the General Model and Micro-Level Results

We first test the unconditional individual-level model to show that our three criteria model makes sense for the explanation of vote choice. The results are presented in Table 11.4. They clearly indicate that the model includes central determinants of electoral behavior regarding all three types of vote (party-list vote; candidate vote; president vote). The effects for party-liking, candidate-liking, and generalized issue-distance on vote choice are all highly significant and have the expected signs. Signs are positive for party as well as candidate-liking, and negative for

Table 11.4. Basic regressions of party-list vote, candidate vote, and president vote on party-liking, candidate-liking, and generalized issue-distance between voters and parties

	Coefficient	Robust std. err.	z	$P > z$	[95% Confidence interval]	
P_{vote}						
Party-list vote						
1. Party-liking	0.457	0.005	92.950	0.000	0.447	0.467
2. Candidate-liking	0.184	0.004	45.890	0.000	0.176	0.192
3. General issue-distance	−0.235	0.005	−45.960	0.000	−0.245	−0.225
Constant	−5.347	0.036	−147.900	0.000	−5.418	−5.276
Logistic regression						
Number of observations	186422.000					
Wald $\chi^2(3)$	21272.480					
Prob > χ^2	0.000					
Log pseudolikelihood	−47532.284					
Pseudo R^2	0.322					
C_{vote}						
Candidate vote						
1. Party-liking	0.399	0.006	71.960	0.000	0.388	0.409
2. Candidate-liking	0.161	0.005	33.230	0.000	0.151	0.170
3. General issue-distance	−0.130	0.005	−24.460	0.000	−0.141	−0.120
Constant	−4.538	0.039	−117.790	0.000	−4.614	−4.463
Logistic regression						
Number of observations	90710.000					
Wald $\chi^2(3)$	12925.580					
Prob > χ^2	0.000					
Log pseudolikelihood	−30299.231					
Pseudo R^2	0.268					
Pr_{vote}						
President vote						
1. Party-liking	0.334	0.008	42.150	0.000	0.319	0.350
2. Candidate-liking	0.222	0.008	28.800	0.000	0.207	0.237
3. General issue-distance	−0.115	0.007	−15.640	0.000	−0.129	−0.100
Constant	−4.541	0.059	−76.430	0.000	−4.658	−4.425
Logistic regression						
Number of observations	35400.000					
Wald $\chi^2(3)$	5430.570					
Prob > χ^2	0.000					
Log pseudolikelihood	−11719.114					
Pseudo R^2	0.280					

generalized issue-distance. The negative sign means that an increasing distance reduces the likelihood of casting a vote for the respective party, candidate, or president. Variances explained are quite reasonable for a micro model. Pseudo R^2 of the pooled logistic regression amounts to 32 percent for party-list vote, 27 percent for candidate vote, and 28 percent for president vote.

The Micro–Macro Model

We do not want to explore these micro-level results any further because our hypotheses are conditional. Thus, we are neither interested in the effects of the micro-level nor the effects of the macro-level independent variables as such. A conditional hypothesis poses a multilevel question. It asks for the extent to which the strength of the coefficients of the individual-level explanatory variables is conditioned by the macro-level explanatory variables of the political context. This means that we are interested in the interaction of micro and macro effects (Franzese 2005: 434).

There are different ways to model the conditioning of micro effects by macro variables. Two-step modeling, as proposed by Long Jusko and Shively (2005) constitutes one possibility. A second option is hierarchical multilevel modeling, and a third is a pooled interactive regression analysis. Franzese (2005) has argued that the latter would be most suitable to study conditionality if two assumptions can be met: (1) the estimation must be effective, (2) heteroskedacity or clustered standard errors must be managed. Effective estimation is related to sample size. Since we base our analysis on very large, stacked representative surveys of 29 national elections, effective estimation does not cause any problem. Heteroskedacity is inherent in cross-section designs with independent samples such as ours. We take care of this by using robust, that is heteroskedacity-consistent, standard errors.

Our general micro–macro model takes into account the following five independent variables and their interactions:

— on the micro level: party-liking, candidate-liking, and generalized issue-distance;

— on the macro level: effectiveness of electoral institutions and differentiation of political supply;

— as interactions: the nine interactions of each of the three evaluative micro-level and the two macro-level independent variables plus an error term.

The resulting regression equation can be written as follows:

$$y = \beta_0 + \beta_1 p + \beta_2 c + \beta_3 d + \beta_4 S + \beta_5 E + \beta_6 SE + \beta_7 pS + \beta_8 cS + \beta_9 dS + \beta_{10} pE$$
$$+ \beta_{11} cE + \beta_{12} dE + \beta_{13} pSE + \beta_{14} cSE + \beta_{15} dSE + e$$

where *y* is the vote choice, *p* is the party-liking, *c* is the candidate-liking, *d* is the generalized issue-distance, *S* is the differentiation of political supply, and *E* is the effectiveness of electoral institutions.

We are interested in the variation of the effects of the micro-level predictor variables on vote choice as the dependent variable under varying conditions of effectiveness of electoral institutions and differentiation of political supply. Thus, the variation of the random effects under varying conditions of the political macro-context is our main concern. For this reason, we interpret the variation of the marginal effects on vote choice and not the parameters estimated by the regression. We choose this option because the coefficients resulting from the linear-additive model with interactions no longer represent the average effect of the independent variables. Brambor, Clark, and Golder (2006) have shown that the coefficient of the constitutive term *X should not* be interpreted as the average effect of a change in *X* on *Y*. The coefficient only captures the effect of *X* on *Y* under the condition that *Z* is zero. This would require that *Z* has a natural zero point. This cannot be assumed for effectiveness of electoral institutions or differentiation of political supply in democratic systems with competitive elections. As a consequence, the interpretation of single effect parameters does not help to answer our research question. It would make little sense, indeed, to talk about an unconditional average effect of *X* on *Y* when one wants to test a conditional hypothesis. Rather, our focus is on the marginal effects of individual-level independent variables on vote choice for substantively meaningful values of the two conditioning macro variables.

However, it is still interesting to observe whether the regressions with interactions yield significant effects. The ones that are of particular interest here are the ones which control for the interaction between the three individual-level independent variables and differentiation of political supply as well as effectiveness of electoral institutions, respectively. It should be kept in mind, however, that the regression model controls the interactions mentioned above also for all other interactions, including those which measure the conditioning effect of one set of micro–macro interactions by the other sets of micro–macro interactions (β_{12} to β_{15} in our regression equation). The interactions of particular interest are represented by β_7 to β_9 with regard to differentiation of political supply, and by β_{10} to β_{12} with respect to effectiveness of electoral institutions.

Table 11.5 shows that interactions are significant for party-list vote and candidate vote, although only weakly for the interaction of generalized

Table 11.5. Regression of vote choice on individual-level evaluations and their interactions with the macro-level characteristics differentiation of political supply (diff. pol. supply) and effectiveness of electoral institutions (eff. el. institutions)

	Coefficient	Robust std. err.	z	$P > z$	[95% Confidence interval]	
P_{vote}						
Party-list vote						
β_1: p (party-liking)	0.223	0.026	8.690	0.000	0.173	0.274
β_2: c (candidate-liking)	0.234	0.021	11.050	0.000	0.192	0.275
β_3: d (general issue-distance)	−0.040	0.026	−1.550	0.121	−0.091	0.011
β_4: S (diff. pol. supply)	−0.240	0.076	−3.140	0.002	−0.390	−0.090
β_5: E (eff. el. institutions)	−1.787	0.259	−6.910	0.000	−2.293	−1.280
β_6: $S * E$	0.317	0.154	2.060	0.040	0.015	0.619
β_7: $p * S$	0.082	0.010	7.970	0.000	0.062	0.102
β_8: $c * S$	−0.036	0.009	−4.210	0.000	−0.053	−0.019
β_9: $d * S$	−0.047	0.010	−4.860	0.000	−0.066	−0.028
β_{10}: $p * E$	0.467	0.036	12.870	0.000	0.396	0.538
β_{11}: $c * E$	−0.137	0.029	−4.670	0.000	−0.194	−0.079
β_{12}: $d * E$	−0.428	0.035	−12.200	0.000	−0.497	−0.360
β_{13}: $p * S * E$	−0.238	0.021	−11.170	0.000	−0.279	−0.196
β_{14}: $c * S * E$	0.114	0.018	6.240	0.000	0.078	0.149
β_{15}: $d * S * E$	0.191	0.019	10.030	0.000	0.154	0.229
Constant	−4.045	0.187	−21.660	0.000	−4.411	−3.679
Logistic regression						
Number of observations	186422.000					
Wald $\chi^2(15)$	22103.370					
Prob $> \chi^2$	0.000					
Log pseudolikelihood	−47001.176					
Pseudo R^2	0.330					
C_{vote}						
Candidate vote						
β_1: p (party-liking)	0.962	0.058	16.600	0.000	0.848	1.075
β_2: c (candidate-liking)	−0.166	0.053	−3.140	0.002	−0.270	−0.063
β_3: d (general issue-distance)	0.081	0.060	1.360	0.174	−0.036	0.198
β_4: S (diff. pol. supply)	0.500	0.308	1.620	0.104	−0.103	1.103
β_5: E (eff. el. institutions)	0.620	0.369	1.680	0.093	−0.104	1.345
β_6: $S * E$	0.275	0.241	1.140	0.254	−0.197	0.746
β_7: $p * S$	−0.347	0.041	−8.370	0.000	−0.428	−0.266
β_8: $c * S$	0.241	0.038	6.350	0.000	0.167	0.316
β_9: $d * S$	−0.156	0.042	−3.750	0.000	−0.238	−0.075
β_{10}: $p * E$	−0.467	0.052	−9.040	0.000	−0.569	−0.366
β_{11}: $c * E$	0.281	0.047	5.970	0.000	0.189	0.373
β_{12}: $d * E$	−0.103	0.052	−1.970	0.049	−0.205	0.000
β_{13}: $p * S * E$	0.108	0.035	3.120	0.002	0.040	0.176
β_{14}: $c * S * E$	−0.144	0.031	−4.660	0.000	−0.205	−0.084
β_{15}: $d * S * E$	−0.005	0.032	−0.150	0.884	−0.067	0.058
Constant	−5.550	0.428	−12.970	0.000	−6.388	−4.711
Logistic regression						
Number of observations	90710.000					
Wald $\chi^2(15)$	13075.410					
Prob $> \chi^2$	0.000					
Log pseudolikelihood	−30053.785					
Pseudo R^2	0.273					

(cont.)

Table 11.5. (*Continued*)

	Coefficient	Robust std. err.	z	P > z	[95% Confidence interval]	
Pr$_{vote}$						
President vote						
β_1: p (party-liking)	0.385	0.032	12.180	0.000	0.323	0.446
β_2: c (candidate-liking)	0.320	0.033	9.710	0.000	0.255	0.384
β_3: d (general Issue-distance)	−0.120	0.031	−3.860	0.000	−0.181	−0.059
β_4: S (diff. pol. supply)	0.706	0.195	3.630	0.000	0.325	1.088
β_5: E (eff. el. institutions)	4.028	0.579	6.960	0.000	2.893	5.162
β_6: S * E	1.398	1.137	1.230	0.219	−0.830	3.626
β_7: p * S	−0.126	0.023	−5.420	0.000	−0.171	−0.080
β_8: c * S	0.108	0.024	4.520	0.000	0.061	0.154
β_9: d * S	0.003	0.023	0.130	0.894	−0.042	0.048
β_{10}: p * E	−0.041	0.070	−0.590	0.556	−0.179	0.096
β_{11}: c * E	−0.146	0.067	−2.190	0.029	−0.276	−0.015
β_{12}: d * E	0.072	0.068	1.050	0.294	−0.062	0.205
β_{13}: p * S * E	0.592	0.155	3.810	0.000	0.287	0.896
β_{14}: c * S * E	−1.399	0.141	−9.950	0.000	−1.674	−1.123
β_{15}: d * S * E	−0.053	0.153	−0.340	0.731	−0.352	0.247
Constant	−6.500	0.288	−22.570	0.000	−7.065	−5.936
Logistic regression						
Number of observations	35400.000					
Wald $\chi^2(15)$	4757.590					
Prob > χ^2	0.000					
Log pseudolikelihood	−11220.588					
Pseudo R^2	0.311					

issue-distance and effectiveness of electoral institutions (β_{12}). For presidential vote, on the other hand, all interactions with effectiveness of electoral institutions and for generalized issue-distance and differentiation of political supply are insignificant. This does not imply, however, that differences in marginal effects should also be insignificant.

The Effect of Differentiation of Political Supply and of Effectiveness of Electoral Institutions on the Effect of Voters' Evaluation Criteria for Three Types of Vote Choice

In line with what has been presented in the theoretical orientation at the beginning of the chapter (see section "Theoretical Orientation"), we are now in a position to test the following three hypotheses:

H1 The impact of party-liking for party-list vote should increase the higher the differentiation of political supply and the more effective the electoral institutions. For candidate vote and for presidential vote, we expect a decreasing impact of party-liking under the same conditions.

H2 The impact of candidate-liking for candidate vote should increase the higher the differentiation of political supply and the more effective the electoral institutions. For party-list vote and for president vote, we expect a decreasing impact of candidate-liking under the same conditions.

H3 The impact of generalized issue-distance should increase the higher the differentiation of political supply and the more effective the electoral institutions. This tendency should be more expressed for party-list vote than for candidate or president vote.

To explore whether these hypotheses are supported by empirical evidence, we consider the marginal effects of the three individual-level evaluative criteria: party-liking, candidate-liking, and generalized issue-distance. We examine their effects on vote choice (party-list vote, candidate vote, president vote) under varying conditions of differentiation of political supply and effectiveness of electoral institutions. The marginal effects indicate the slopes of the respective variables under these different conditions, thus showing the strength of their absolute impact on vote choice.

The Conditioning Power of Differentiation of Political Supply

The marginal effects we have to inspect with respect to differentiation of political supply consist of the sum of the individual effects of each evaluative criteria plus the effect of the interaction of the evaluation with—in this case—the differentiation of political supply.

This can be written as:

$$\text{Marg. eff (party liking)} = \beta_1 + \beta_7$$
$$\text{Marg. eff (candidate-liking)} = \beta_2 + \beta_8$$
$$\text{Marg. eff (generalized issue-distance)} = \beta_3 + \beta_9$$

(for the definition of βs, see regression equation and Table 11.5).

Results of the analyses are presented in Panel A of Figure 11.2. Plots are limited to the range of differentiation of political supply that exists empirically. They do not show estimates for nonexisting variations of this dimension of the political macro-context.

Results reflect that the range for differentiation of political supply is much greater for party-list vote than for candidate vote or president vote. Much more important, however, is the finding that for party-list vote, marginal effects of party-liking become significantly larger when

A. Differentiation of political supply

A1. Party-Liking

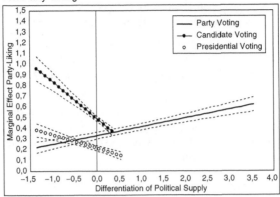

A2. Candidate-Liking

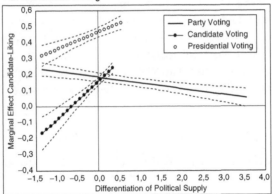

A3. Generalized Issue-Distance (left–right scale)

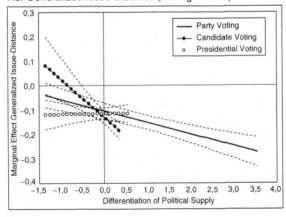

Figure 11.2. Marginal effects of party-liking, candidate-liking, and generalized issue-distance on three types of vote choice under varying conditions of differentiation of political supply and effectiveness of electoral institutions.

258

B. Institutional Effectiveness

B1. Party-Liking

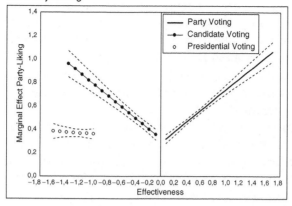

B2. Candidate-Liking

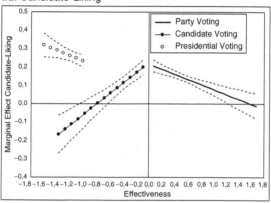

B3. Generalized Issue-Distance (left–right scale)

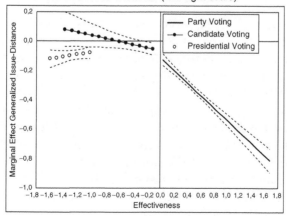

Figure 11.2. (*Continued*)

political supply is more differentiated (dotted lines represent confidence intervals at the 95 percent level). The opposite is the case for candidate and president vote. All this is in support of hypothesis 1. Hypothesis 2 assumes that results should have a similar structure for candidate vote and candidate-liking. This is, indeed, the case. Regarding generalized issue-distance, hypothesis 3 predicts that its impact should rise with an increasing level of differentiation of political supply. The sign is negative since an increase in proximity scores means an increasing distance between voters and parties. In this case, the likelihood of generalized issue-distance to contribute to vote choice decreases. In addition, we have assumed that generalized issue-distance should matter more for party-list vote than for candidate vote or president vote. This is, indeed, also the case empirically. For president vote, no significant differences between marginal effects could be observed at different levels of differentiation of political supply. Thus, results confirm hypothesis 3 for party and candidate voting but not for president voting.

The Conditioning Power of Effectiveness of Electoral Institutions

With respect to variations in effectiveness of electoral institutions, our hypotheses assume the same structure of the relations of marginal effects and the political macro-context as for differentiation of political supply (see above). This can be expressed as follows:

$$\text{Marg. eff (party-liking)} = \beta_1 + \beta_{10}$$
$$\text{Marg. eff (candidate-liking)} = \beta_2 + \beta_{11}$$
$$\text{Marg. eff (generalized issue-distance)} = \beta_3 + \beta_{12}$$

(for a definition of βs, see regression equation and Table 11.5).

We know from the exploration of the distribution of the macro variables (Figure 11.1) that ranges of effectiveness of electoral institutions do not overlap for systems based on a majority and on a proportional formula, that is, candidate and party voting. Furthermore, while the range for these two electoral systems is located in different areas, its size is very similar nevertheless. For party-list vote and for candidate vote, the variation of marginal effects across different levels of effectiveness of electoral institutions is in the expected direction. The more effective an electoral rule, the more important is the evaluation of parties for party vote. For candidate voting, the same is true for candidate-liking. For candidate voting, marginal effects of party-liking show a decrease with increasing effectiveness. The same is true for candidate-liking in the case of party voting. These results reflect that in general different types of voting reflect different complexities of choice which are moderated by institutional effectiveness (Panel B of Figure 11.2). The same is not true for the presidential vote. Here the range of institutional effectiveness is simply too narrow to produce significant moderating effects.

Trade-Off and Reinforcement

Results clearly indicate that the strength by which electoral choice is influenced by the evaluative criteria of parties, candidates, and issues varies by degree of differentiation of political supply and institutional effectiveness. Furthermore, patterns vary across different types of voting. Depending on the object of choice, there is a trade-off in the utility of criteria, which changes with degrees of differentiation of supply and effectiveness. The more complex a choice situation and the more effective electoral institutions are to translate choices into preferred outcomes, the more voters focus on the criteria that are most useful. This results in party-liking in the case of party voting, and candidate-liking in the case of candidate voting and—with some qualifications—presidential voting. Parallel to the increase of the impact of the respective core criteria for vote choice, the strength of the other criteria diminishes. Thus, voters reduce complexity by emphasizing one evaluation criterion and deemphasizing all others.

In addition, results suggest an interaction of the macro variables differentiation of political supply and effectiveness of electoral institutions. Theoretically, it seems plausible to assume that higher effectiveness increases the effects of the evaluative criteria. That is, when the system offers real chances to get one's vote choice translated into the preferred outcome, the effect of supply characteristics should matter more than under less favorable conditions. This lends itself to easy demonstration. If we fix political supply at the cross-country mean of the distribution, that is, at -0.52 for supply in case of candidate voting and 0.22 in case of party voting (Table 11.3) and estimate the marginal effects under varying conditions of effectiveness of electoral institutions, results confirm expectations. The range for effectiveness of electoral institutions in the case of candidate vote stretches from -1.4 to -0.1. At the minimum of institutional effectiveness, the marginal effect of candidate-liking at the average differentiation of political supply is close to zero, at -0.9 it is 0.9, at -0.4 it is 1.7, and at the maximum it is 1.9 (Figure 11.3). For party vote, linearity comes out in an even stronger way. Effectiveness of

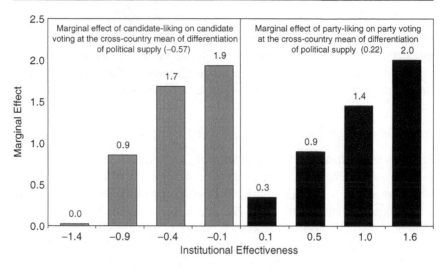

Figure 11.3. Marginal effects of candidate-liking and party-liking at the mean of political supply and variation in effectiveness of electoral institutions.

electoral institutions ranges from 0.1 to 1.6. From the minimum to the maximum, the marginal effect of party-liking at the average of political supply increases in a linear fashion from 0.3 to 2.0. Thus, voters clearly accord different utility to different evaluative criteria when making a choice, depending on the variation of differentiation of political supply, effectiveness of electoral institutions, *and* their interaction.

Conclusions

What do these results mean? Our hypotheses assume that when considering their vote choice, voters not only take into account the type of vote but also the three classic evaluative criteria: party, candidate, and issues. They also adapt the decision criteria to the broader characteristics of their political environment. In this view the act of voting is not, indeed, so simple (Dalton and Wattenberg 1993; Kelley and Mirer 1974). Our findings show that the more complex the situation for vote choice becomes, the more voters try to reduce this complexity. They do this by focusing on the criteria which are most closely related to the object of choice. The relative importance of the evaluative criteria differs across different types of vote choice such as party-list vote, candidate vote, and president vote. Furthermore, within one type of choice, the effects vary according to the degree of differentiation of political supply or the degree of effectiveness of electoral institutions. Thus, citizens are able to adapt to their electoral environment, its richness of choice, and the effectiveness of the electoral institutions that translate their preferences into the desired outcomes. Even more, the strength with which the respective evaluation criterion is applied, does not only vary separately by differentiation of political supply and degree of institutional effectiveness, but also by their interaction. Voters obviously reflect the choice situation not only with respect to what is on offer but also how they can make best use of their means to choose by taking jointly into consideration the range of choice and the effectiveness of the electoral institutions.

In a rational choice perspective, this can be interpreted as just one more example that voters want to reduce the costs of voting. However, we think there is more to it. The focus on specific evaluative criteria in the calculus of voting may also be driven by a need to reduce complexity in order to arrive at a more meaningful and viable choice. We see it as a most reasonable response of citizens, when contemplating vote choice to adapt their calculus of voting to the differentiation of political supply and the way electoral institutions constrain or facilitate the translation of their preferences into the desired outcome.

Appendix

Table 11.A1. Location of political macro-contexts (elections) on the dimension "differentiation of political supply" (factor scores)

Election		F2: Differentiation of political supply
		Low
KORC	Republic of Korea (2000)	−1.382
ISL	Iceland (1999)	−1.352
PRT	Portugal (2002)	−0.865
SWE	Sweden (1998)	−0.780
TWNP	Taiwan (1996)	−0.766
DEUC	Germany (1998)	−0.725
MEX00C	Mexico (2000)	−0.708
TWNC	Taiwan (1996)	−0.552
DNK	Denmark (1998)	−0.537
NOR	Norway (1997)	−0.535
MEXP	Mexico (2000)	−0.527
MEX97C	Mexico (1997)	−0.515
HUNC	Hungary (1998)	−0.504
CANC	Canada (1997)	−0.485

(cont.)

Table 11.A1. (*Continued*)

Election		F2: Differentiation of political supply
		Low
NLD	The Netherlands (1998)	−0.424
HUN	Hungary (1998)	−0.401
NZLC	New Zealand (1996)	−0.397
LTUP	Lithuania (1997)	−0.317
DEU	Germany (1998)	−0.308
CZE	Czech Republic (1996)	−0.306
POL	Poland (1997)	−0.118
SVN	Slovenia (1996)	−0.116
AUSC	Australia (1996)	−0.100
CHE	Switzerland (1999)	−0.087
PER00P	Peru (2000)	−0.072
ESP00	Spain (2000)	−0.063
GBRC	United Kingdom (1997)	0.215
NZL	New Zealand (1996)	0.283
PER01	Peru (2001)	0.451
ISRP	Israel (1996)	0.462
ISR	Israel (1996)	0.480
PER01P	Peru (2001)	0.895
ROUP	Romania (1996)	1.051
ESP96	Spain (1996)	1.195
ROU	Romania (1996)	1.797
RUS	Russia (1999)	2.551
UKR	Ukraine (1998)	3.563
		High

Table 11.A2. Location of political macro-contexts (elections) on the dimension "effectiveness of electoral institutions" (factor scores)

Election		F1: Effectiveness of electoral institutions
		Low
ISRP	Israel (1996)	−1.602
PER01P	Peru (2001)	−1.598
PER00P	Peru (2000)	−1.547
ROUP	Romania (1996)	−1.518
LTUP	Lithuania (1997)	−1.417
GBRC	United Kingdom (1997)	−1.371
AUSC	Australia (1996)	−1.231
MEXP	Mexico (2000)	−1.060
TWNP	Taiwan (1996)	−1.037
CANC	Canada (1997)	−1.010
MEX00C	Mexico (2000)	−0.683
MEX97C	Mexico (1997)	−0.674
NZLC	New Zealand (1996)	−0.624
DEUC	Germany (1998)	−0.539
HUNC	Hungary (1998)	−0.470

Table 11.A2.

Election		F1: Effectiveness of electoral institutions
		Low
TWNC	Taiwan (1996)	−0.128
KORC	Republic of Korea (2000)	−0.100
ESP96	Spain (1996)	0.118
RUS	Russia (1999)	0.425
UKR	Ukraine (1998)	0.469
HUN	Hungary (1998)	0.567
PER01	Peru (2001)	0.568
DEU	Germany (1998)	0.653
ESP00	Spain (2000)	0.735
NZL	New Zealand (1996)	0.759
POL	Poland (1997)	0.768
CHE	Switzerland (1999)	0.804
ROU	Romania (1996)	0.861
SWE	Sweden (1998)	0.890
DNK	Denmark (1998)	0.933
NOR	Norway (1997)	0.991
CZE	Czech Republic (1996)	1.054
ISL	Iceland (1999)	1.063
SVN	Slovenia (1996)	1.077
PRT	Portugal (2002)	1.120
ISR	Israel (1996)	1.205
NLD	The Netherlands (1998)	1.547
		High

Notes

1. The authors want to express their gratitude to Martin Kroh who provided the imputation of incomplete data.
2. The very high number of party lists in Romania is mainly caused by lists presented by national minority parties. Of the 65 party lists nationwide, 33 belonged to the national minorities (communication by Silviu Matei).
3. There is a great discrepancy between the number of "other" parties listed in Banks et al. (1995–7, 1998–9, 2000–2) for the entries of Spain in 1996 and 2000 which—partly—explains the different locations of the two Spanish elections.

Part V

Expressive and Instrumental Voting

12

Expressive Versus Instrumental Motivation of Turnout, Partisanship, and Political Learning

Gábor Tóka

Introduction

An exciting recent development in theories of voting is the increasing formalization of the difference between electoral outcomes under instrumental and expressive models of voting. Although the relevant literature concentrates on the problem of turnout, the choice between these models has to be confronted with respect to every aspect of voting behavior, including party choice (Brennan and Buchanan 1984) and the information-processing activities that shape choices (cf. Downs 1957; Popkin 1991).

In instrumental models of electoral politics, commonly associated with Downs's legacy, voters are interested in the political consequences of election outcomes and especially in government policies and performance. In the expressive model, the benefit of voting for the individual citizen derives solely from the intrinsic rewards of casting a vote. The two models lead to different predictions about turnout and thus imply different equilibria in terms of the optimal location for vote-maximizing parties in the policy space (cf. Brennan and Hamlin 1998).[1] Moreover, intriguing—even troubling—questions arise about the kind of political representation that can emerge in the electoral arena if vote choice itself were to be affected by expressive motives (Brennan and Buchanan 1984; Brennan and Lomasky 1994).

More or less widespread agreement seems to have emerged in the scholarly literature about three points. First, probably no advocate of the importance of instrumental rationality for voting behavior would debate that nonzero turnout is explained partly or entirely by expressive factors like a sense of civic duty or of belonging to a political community (e.g., Riker and Ordeshook 1968). Second, it remains a widely held view that even if electoral participation follows a purely expressive logic, the making of a choice between parties nonetheless follows the instrumental model (cf. Enelow and Hinich 1984; for challenges to this position, see Brennan and Buchanan 1984; Fischer 1996; Kan and Yang 2001; Schuessler 2000). Even advocates of expressive models of vote choice like Brennan and Hamlin (1998) and Schuessler (2000) assume that instrumental political rationality plays some role in these choices, in contrast to the purely expressive motivation of turnout.

Third, apparently many scholars see it as an alarming possibility that expressive rationality may dominate vote choices. Unlike instrumental rationality, expressive rationality does not necessarily connect voting behavior to the politically relevant collective consequences of individual vote choices. Hence, expressive voting raises the spectre of mindless voters supporting causes that they came to like for some essentially nonpolitical reason, and in spite of disagreement with their political substance, as in Brennan and Lomasky's analyses (1994) of popular support for wars. The same intuition about the dangers of expressive behavior brings Brennan and Hamlin (1999) to conclude that the more impact expressive motives have on vote choice, the stronger the justification for representative democracy over direct democracy.

This chapter concurs with and builds on the first point, but provides empirical evidence that contradicts the second and qualifies the third. I start the analysis with discussing the concepts of expressive and instrumental voting behavior. The conceptual analysis generates expectations about how the relative weight of these motivations varies across different institutional settings and three forms of electorally relevant political involvement: turnout, the development of a party preference, and political information processing. The empirical analysis uses data from over 30 postelection surveys conducted on five continents as part of the Comparative Study of Electoral Systems (CSES) project, and follows the lead of Guttman, Hilger, and Schachmurove (1994) with respect to the operationalization of the difference between expressive and instrumental behavior. The conclusions discuss how the results suggest practically and theoretically relevant insights regarding the role of expressive behavior in the electoral arena and its functionality for democratic representation.

Instrumental and Expressive Voting

Theories of both "instrumental" and "expressive" voting assume that voting behavior is, procedurally speaking, rational. That is, voters act in a goal-oriented fashion, and their preferences inform their political choices. They weigh benefits against costs. They consistently and transitively rank the political objects in their choice set, always selecting the one that ranks highest in their ordering of the alternatives (Downs 1957: 6). Their responses to stimuli are not some kind of unconditional, automatic reaction, but are mediated by reasoning and intuition about the link between those stimuli and their relationship to the voters' preferences. Though political cognition may be influenced by unconscious reactions that the voters cannot control (e.g., Baldwin and Masters 1996; Forgas and Moylan 1987), these involuntary responses do not fully determine voting behavior.

The hallmark of expressive actions is that the reward of bearing the costs of a particular action is intrinsic to the activity itself. For instance, participation in an election may be gratifying for the thrill of it, or the opportunity that it offers for self-expression, or the feeling of fulfilling a civic duty. For an instrumentally rational action, in contrast, gratification is not immediate as in the case of consumption, but delayed like returns to investments. These delayed benefits are uncertain public goods—policies or symbolic rewards—that, in retrospect, may appear to have been brought about by the election outcome.

Hence we run into the paradox of voting. No matter how much value the individual citizen attaches to the political consequences of an election going one way rather than another, the weight of a single vote in determining the outcome is infinitesimally small in a large electorate. Thus, the collective benefits of the outcome occur to individual citizens essentially independently of whether they themselves voted. As long as voting is costly, that is, it takes time, effort, and involves risks like being run over by a car on the way to the polling station, instrumentally rational voters will not turn out unless they are coerced.

Limits of space prohibit here a review of the enormous intellectual efforts invested in eliminating the paradox in the last few decades. Suffice to say that the proposed solutions either fail in large electorates, lack logical consistency, or invoke what are essentially intrinsic individual rewards of turnout—side payments, social signalling, alienation, and so forth—to explain why some vote and others do not (see Mueller 1989: 348–69). Some evidence exists that the closeness of elections and the perceived political stakes involved show the expected correlations with turnout both at the individual and at the aggregate level (e.g., Blais 2000; Franklin 2004). Yet, it would be a mistake to read this as evidence of instrumental voting: the same correlations can obtain if the intrinsic rewards of voting were changing in response to the stakes and the closeness of the election. This can happen if citizens' sense of duty and entertainment *ceteris paribus* increases in close and consequential elections, or if strategic politicians make bigger efforts to reduce the costs—and increase the intrinsic rewards—of voting in such situations (Aldrich 1993; Cox 1999).

Indeed, direct and indirect empirical evidence abound that expressive factors like a sense of civic duty bring about turnout (Blais 2000; Campbell et al. 1960). Disturbing implications emerge, however, if intrinsic rewards motivate not just turnout but voters' choice as well, since the intrinsic benefits of voting for a party may be totally disconnected from whether the party's victory is expected to bring about the collective outcomes desired by the same voters. Knowingly or not, expressive actors may end up voting for a rather different party than the one they would if their choices followed an instrumentally rational logic with collective political outcomes in their mind (Brennan and Lomasky 1994; Schuessler 2000). This can happen either if the development of a party preference itself directly follows an expressive logic, or if the information basis of individual vote choice has been acquired due to expressive motivation, and therefore its composition does not reflect the concerns of an instrumental voter strictly focused on collective political outcomes.

The Motivation of Information Processing and Choice

The key question is thus whether the development of party preference and the processing of political information are also subject to a similar paradox as turnout, and thus driven by expressive motives alike. For formulating expectations about this question, it is useful to synthesize the conventional algebraic formulae for instrumental and expressive models of voting in a single equation.

$$U = P * B - C + D \tag{1}$$

In Eq. (1), U is the individual citizen's utility of electorally relevant political involvement like turnout or information processing. Rational actors only do things that seem to have a positive utility U. The P term stands for the probability that the vote cast by this individual can break or create a tie in the election outcome, and as such is inevitably close to zero in a large electorate (cf. Brennan and Lomasky 1994). The benefit of voting, B, is the voter's utility difference between the conceivable outcomes of the election. C is the total cost of action, including the time and the effort that it takes. Turnout is expressively motivated because in a large electorate P times B is so small that the utility of turnout can only be positive if D, the intrinsic rewards of the action, is higher than C.[2]

One could argue, however, that the size of C and D become rather different when the political involvement in question is the psychological process by which party preference is developed, or acquiring the knowledge necessary for making the best possible individual choice. It is indeed a widely held view among followers of both Downs (1957) and Key (1966) that even if turning out to vote is an expressive act, the choice among the parties is determined by instrumental political considerations. The implicit reasoning behind this view seems to be that choice is basically costless, and its intrinsic rewards are zero—that is, this is how it must be if vote choice is instrumental, since the P times B part of the equation remains exactly the same negligible quantity for choosing between the parties as it was in the case of turnout.

Yet anyone who has ever hesitated between several equally (un)appealing choice options knows that the psychological burden of choosing can be sizeable. Only expressive motivation can explain if someone spends long days thinking about the otherwise inconsequential matter of choosing for which party—if any—to vote. Indeed, given how small the P times B term is, even fairly small efforts to reach a choice should be explained by such motives. The intrinsic rewards of choosing, in their turn, are likely to be substantial even in the absence of a strong sense of citizen duty to choose. Having a partisan preference is a possible avenue for self-expression, group membership, and self-affirmation in front of other people. It gives subjective meaning to our voting rights and the political world as a whole, suppresses uncomfortable doubts about whether we can control our political environment, and permits us to follow politics as if it were a thrilling spectator sport. It is perfectly conceivable that these intrinsic rewards of partisan choice are, for most people, much larger than the negligible P times B term. If so, then expressive motives surely dominate voter choices.

Contradictory expectations obtain regarding political information processing. Making electoral choices that faithfully express the true underlying preferences of the individual tend to require considerable political knowledge. Information shortcuts and cues may abound, but their effective use requires a great deal of knowledge to begin with (Lau and Redlawsk 2001). Even the relatively modest bites that most of us actually take from this constantly changing body of knowledge require much time, attention, and cognitive effort to process. Thus, these costs easily exceed the negligible value of P times B, undermining the potential of instrumental motives to shape voters' stock of political knowledge.[3] This does not mean that all citizens remain rationally ignorant. The excitement of partisan voters about being part of their team's effort appears to make quite a few people follow news stories regularly, attentively, and quite closely. Indulgence in infotainment and involuntary exposure to news also create ample space for expressively motivated political learning (Fiorina 1990). The downside of this possibility is that expressively motivated information processing may make citizens well equipped with a large stock of entertaining information, but still unaware of those things that they would need to know in order to vote in line with their instrumental political preferences.

Yet, in the case of information processing, a whole range of truly instrumental considerations influence the utility of the action that have no parallel in the case of turnout and developing a party preference, and do not easily fit into Eq. (1) above. The reason is that citizens are not only makers but, above all, recipients of political outcomes. In order to adjust their economic, protest (and so forth) behavior to politically induced changes in their environment, they need to monitor political events all the time. For instance, they may need to fill in tax forms and hence learn about rates and exemptions, discover legislation that opens new opportunities for their disabled children, be forced to visit abortion clinics abroad due to recent legislation back home, or see their real estate change market value because commuter train schedules and fares changed as a result of privatization. Rational citizens will therefore invest some effort into a continuous processing of information conducive to successful adaptation to government policies. The more uncertainty they sense about the direction of public policy and other real world events, the bigger their investments into political information processing will be.

Thus, the same party differential B that appears in the P times B term in Eq. (1) can appear among the factors motivating political information-processing. By coincidence, the rational investments of public policy recipients into political learning may well make them pick up much the same information that instrumentally rational voters focused on collective political outcomes would attend to in order to arrive at their best electoral choice.

The key expectations that we can formulate based on the above discussion relate to the relative importance of B and D in motivating electoral activities. Turnout, as it was suggested above, has clearly expressive roots, and should be positively influenced by D, whatever residual impact B may register. Political knowledge, in contrast, may well be detached from expressive motivations and be influenced by B—though not by P—instead. However, this expectation is not as firm as the one concerning turnout. The expectations are even less clear about the development of a party preference since the empirical values of C and D may or may not be so high that this process would be driven by expressive motives instead of instrumental ones. For choice, C and D are both psychological in nature, and are thus likely to vary across individuals. Therefore, mixed expressive-instrumental models can conceivably be appropriate. All in all, here we have yet another question that needs empirical exploration.

Of course, the above reasoning about the likely importance of B depends on assumptions about P, the value of which may greatly vary across political contexts. This brings in another family of hypotheses. Pappi (1996), for one, argued that expressive voting, when it occurs at all, is largely a product of multiparty systems, which reduce the voters' capacity for truly rational behavior. The idea behind the proposition is that a multiparty system encourages sincere voting among citizens for the party that best matches their feelings, values, and so forth, as the consequences of the vote for government formation and government policies are hard to predict in these settings and thus get unduly discarded by the voters. By the same token, two party systems focus citizens' attention on the policy consequences of their vote, and thus instil an instrumental logic to party choice.

Although Pappi did not discuss this possibility, the same proposition can apply to turnout and political information processing too. The argument can be further generalized to say that the more consensual and less majoritarian the political system is in Lijphart's terms (1999), the more expressive voting becomes the rule rather than the exception. This is because the consequences of citizens' votes for government formation and policies become less predictable in consensus than in Westminster-type democracies. Several testable hypotheses obtain along those lines, but I will concentrate here only on the three that seem to be closest to Pappi's reasoning. The first is that the number of parties is a determinant of how expressive citizens' behavior is. The second follows the second-order elections model (Reif and Schmitt 1980): voting is less instrumental and more expressive in elections in which national executive office is not at stakes. The third hypothesis focuses on electoral systems and the incentives they create for strategic behavior. The proposition here is that the bigger the mismatch between vote and seat distributions is, the more motivated citizens are to think carefully about wasted votes rather than just supporting whatever party seems most sympathetic to them for some expressive reasons. The three propositions seem to capture neatly how the party system, constitutional design, and the electoral system might impact the incidence of expressive voting.

Of course, all these three hypotheses were plain wrong if, as suggested, the empirical values of C and especially D are sufficiently high compared to a tiny value of P times B. In that case, turnout and the development of party preferences remain expressively motivated in any electoral context, and that this picture obtains irrespective of the institutional context. Likewise, the motivation of information processing would be invariably instrumental if the cost of knowledge nearly always exceeded its D value but lagged behind the B value of behavioral adjustment to policy outcomes in everyday life.

An Empirical Test of Expressive versus Instrumental Behavior

Empirically distinguishing between instrumental and expressive motivation is proverbially difficult (Fischer 1996: 172). For example, the impact of subjectively perceived closeness of an electoral contest on turnout is often treated as evidence of instrumental rationality (see Blais 2000: 72–7), but it is plausible that expressive voters are also thrilled by, and thus become more likely to vote in close races. Many see strategic voting as another *par excellence* instrumental behavior, but expressive voters may also vote strategically to avoid the uncomfortable feeling that they did not make the best possible use of their vote. Another common belief is that apparent altruistic behavior is more likely to stem from expressive than instrumental motivation (Fischer 1996; Tullock 1971). Yet, there is no hard evidence that actors derive less pleasure from egoistic and more from altruistic behavior when they act expressively rather than instrumentally. It may thus seem that with a little imagination any seemingly mindless—and hence, as some would hasten to presume, expressive—behavior can be explained in instrumental terms too, and any apparently outcome-oriented act could be seen as if it aimed merely at intrinsic rewards.

The one operational distinction that seems to escape this fate was offered by Guttman, Hilger, and Schachmurove (1994). They argue that if voting were an instrumental investment in uncertain collective outcomes, then participation must be influenced solely by its costs, the closeness of the election, and the voters' utility differential between alternative election outcomes. If, however, voting is expressive—that is, an act of consumption—then the attractiveness of the alternatives, in an absolute sense, should also matter. If the relatively most preferred outcome is still appalling in absolute terms, then even a very big utility differential can fail to justify effort. Conversely, as long as the choice options are sufficiently attractive, people will still turn out to vote even if their utility differential between the worst and best outcome approaches zero.

There are two remaining problems with this distinction. First, the intrinsic rewards of voting may be sensitive to the utility differential between the alternative outcomes. Thus, purely expressive motivation may be consistent with a positive effect of the perceived utility differential between parties on electorally relevant acts like turnout, the development of a party preference, and political information processing. Second, the absolute value of the most preferred outcome may not capture more than just a fraction of the cross-individual variation in the intrinsic rewards of voting. For instance, it probably has little to do with a sense of citizen duty. Yet a partial empirical test of expressive versus instrumental motivation remains possible. If the absolute value of a party for the voter has an effect on voting behavior, voting has to be, at least in part, an expressive act, driven by intrinsic rewards.[4] Furthermore, in the case of turnout we know a priori that the motivation cannot be instrumental at all, but has to be fully expressive. Thus, the estimates regarding turnout provide a benchmark that will help assessing the relative weight of expressive and instrumental motives in the case of the two cognitive processes in the analysis.

The extension of the Guttman–Hilger–Schachmurove test is straightforward for these processes. The development of a party preference is more likely driven by expressive than instrumental motives if the utility differential has less impact on it than the absolute utility of the most preferred outcome. Similarly, if the processing of political information is driven by the instrumental rationality of public policy recipients, then it will be related to their utility differential between the parties; but if knowledge is driven by the consumption value of learning, then it is more likely to be related to the absolute evaluation of the most liked alternative. This is so because rationally ignorant voters should process political information only for its entertainment value or as a by-product of other activities than trying to make a well-informed vote choice. The more one likes at least one party, the more partisan excitement can be generated by the political world, and hence the higher the consumption value of information processing will be. Conversely, citizens' interest in monitoring political outcomes in order to adjust to them in their everyday life in a timely and effective manner may prompt instrumentally rational political learning and at the same time is likely to reflect, among other things, perceptions about possible variation in likely political outcomes—and thus the utility difference between the least and most liked party.

Therefore, in the tests below, the highest score attached to any one of the parties by a citizen on a feeling thermometer (variable *CONSUME*) will stand for that component of the consumption value of electoral activities for the individual in question that can be clearly distinguished from the utility differential. The difference between the thermometer evaluations of the most and least liked party (variable *INVEST*), in its turn, will show the investment value of electorally relevant activities. Both indicators may vary across national political contexts. For instance, they may be higher in multiparty than two-party systems where fewer voters find a party really close to them and greatly different from the only alternative. However, this has no impact on the analysis below because their impact is estimated separately for each individual election, and only then will the estimated impact be correlated with features of institutional design.

Data, Models, Variables

The tests below were carried out with data from Module 1 of the CSES, administered to national samples between 1996 and 2001. Demographic weights, if available, are used to correct for unequal rates of nonresponse across population groups. Thailand was dropped from the analysis because more than one dependent variable was completely missing for that country. Chile, Lithuania, and Russia 2000 were dropped because their data referred to presidential elections only, for which the respondents' evaluations of the main contenders on feeling thermometers were not available. A few more elections covered by CSES Module 1 are excluded from one part of the analysis or another due to missing data regarding political knowledge or partisanship.

The research question at hand may seem to call for a conventional multilevel analysis. Yet, the two-stage analytical strategy proposed by Long Jusko and Shively (2005) seems preferable instead. The first reason is that the number of respondents per election is sufficiently high to support separate individual level analyses of each election. The second reason is that the number of elections covered is relatively small, and form a nonrandom sample of the theoretical universe of elections from which they are taken. Hence, it would not be appropriate to use a conventional multilevel analysis.

In the first stage of the analysis, a total of 96 regression equations were estimated with three different dependent variables for individual legislative elections covered by CSES Module 1 surveys. The TURNOUT variable shows whether the respondent voted in the last election. Voters' political information level (INFO) is measured on an additive scale summing up correct responses from each respondent to three country-specific knowledge questions. Whether citizens paid whatever psychological costs it took to make up their mind between the contending parties is shown by the CHOICE variable, which is based on a binary (yes or no) party identification variable in the CSES data set.

The independent variables in the first stage of the analysis are all measured at the individual level. A set of sociodemographic variables enter the analysis as proxies for differences in the costs of voting across individuals within the same country. Variables INVEST and CONSUME, in their turn, were derived from feeling thermometers showing the respondents' rating of the major parties in their country. CONSUME shows the highest rating given by each respondent to any one of the evaluated parties. INVEST shows the difference between the highest and lowest rating given by each respondent to any one of the parties.[5] Some respondents only evaluated one party or none at all. Since the instrumental model cannot be assessed in their case, they are excluded from the statistical analyses reported in this chapter.[6] The appendix to this chapter gives further details about the variables in the analysis.

Following the research design suggested by Long Jusko and Shively (2005), the second stage of the analysis assesses the relationships between relevant macro variables and the regression coefficients estimated in the first stage regarding the impact of *CONSUME* and *INVEST* on the three dependent variables. The macro variables in this analysis refer to three aspects of institutional design (see above) that may influence whether expressive or instrumental rationality dictates political involvement in a particular context.

Results

Table 12.1 shows summary statistics about the relevant regression coefficients in the 96 equations estimated in the first stage. The findings regarding the impact of the sociodemographic variables are neither shown in the tables nor discussed in the text since they are irrelevant for the purposes of the present analysis. Expressive motivation must be present if *CONSUME* registers significant positive effects on any of the three dependent variables, but would not be contradicted if *INVEST* has some effects too. If, however, instrumental political rationality motivates political involvement, then the party differential of the respondents—that is, the *INVEST* variable—must have a significant positive effect on the dependent variables, and *CONSUME* must have no effect whatsoever.

A brief look at Table 12.1 suffices to see that for turnout and choice the expressive account receives stronger support than the instrumental explanation. *CONSUME* shows a statistically significant and positive effect on turnout in 22 of the 35 elections in the analysis, and *INVEST* has

Table 12.1. Summary statistics about the impact of CONSUME and INVEST on three indicators of political involvement in national samples

Dependent variable	Independent variable	Number of surveys	Average value of regression coefficients	Standard deviation of regression coefficients	Number of positive effects significant at $p \leq 0.05$	Number of negative effects significant at $p \leq 0.05$
INFO	CONSUME	27	−0.019	0.038	2	7
INFO	INVEST	27	0.050	0.036	22	0
CHOICE	CONSUME	34	0.334	0.126	32	0
CHOICE	INVEST	34	0.113	0.069	17	0
TURNOUT	CONSUME	35	0.196	0.165	22	0
TURNOUT	INVEST	35	0.081	0.091	15	0

Note: Table entries summarize the key results of within-country logistic regression analyses of the determinants of TURNOUT and CHOICE and OLS-regression analyses of the determinants of INFO. All dependent variables were regressed on variables CONSUME, INVEST, and the sociodemographic proxies for the cost of voting described in the appendix to this chapter.

a similar effect only 15 times. Note again that the significant effects of *INVEST* do not contradict a fully expressive account, while any significant effect of *CONSUME* is clearly anomalous for the instrumental model.[7]

Given the paradox of voting it is, of course, only to be expected that the expressive account of turnout would receive support from the data. The truly interesting finding is that the development of a party preference as indicated by *CHOICE* seems even more clearly expressively driven than turnout itself. *CONSUME* records a significant positive effect on *CHOICE* in 32 out of 34 electoral contexts, while *INVEST* has a similar effect on *CHOICE* only 17 times.[8] Hence, party preferences appear to develop on an even more clearly expressive ground than turnout.

The results in Table 12.1 show no support for an expressive account of political information processing. Where *CONSUME* shows a significant effect on knowledge level, the effect is more often negative than positive, which contradicts the expectations drawn from the expressive model. It is hardly conceivable that these negative effects occur because the consumption value of information is lower for those citizens who have the highest sympathy for their most favored party. Rather, the explanation should be that the investment value of new political information is lower for these people because they are anyway less likely to change their mind.

In contrast, *INVEST* records a significant positive effect on *INFO* in 22 out of the 27 CSES Module 1 samples for which all the necessary data are available. This suggests that citizens become more attentive to political information when they think that the stakes in the electoral process, namely, the utility differences between the parties, are higher. In other words, although the high opportunity costs of learning can hardly justify investments into improving the information basis of one's electoral choices, something else nevertheless appears to create a link between instrumental motivation to learn and the act of learning. The theoretical discussion above suggested that this linking factor is the interest of citizens in learning as recipients—rather than as makers—of political outcomes.[9] The result seems to be that political learning among citizens is actually rooted in instrumental motivation, and thus may be undertaken the same way as citizens would learn about politics if their electoral choices had a far bigger impact on actual outcomes than they really do.

The final hypotheses suggest that expressive choices among parties occur not because of the general characteristics of the electoral arena that create the paradox of voting, but because of particular institutional settings, like a multiparty system. Table 12.2 checks whether this is the

Table 12.2. Correlation of the first-stage regression coefficient estimates with macro characteristics of the electoral context

First stage regression estimates	Second stage statistics	Macro characteristics of electoral context		
		STAKES	ELECTORAL SYSTEM	PARTY SYSTEM
Effect of CONSUME on INFO	Pearson correlation	−0.067	−0.326	−0.052
	Sig. (two-tailed) with $N = 25$	0.751	0.112	0.807
Effect of INVEST on INFO	Pearson correlation	0.186	0.244	0.045
	Sig. (two-tailed) with $N = 25$	0.372	0.241	0.830
Effect of CONSUME on CHOICE	Pearson correlation	0.245	−0.094	0.132
	Sig. (two-tailed) with $N = 30$	0.193	0.622	0.488
Effect of INVEST on CHOICE	Pearson correlation	0.009	0.118	−0.047
	Sig. (two-tailed) with $N = 30$	0.963	0.534	0.804
Effect of CONSUME on TURNOUT	Pearson correlation	0.305	−0.035	−0.073
	Sig. (two-tailed) with $N = 31$	0.095	0.850	0.697
Effect of INVEST on TURNOUT	Pearson correlation	0.009	0.067	−0.149
	Sig. (two-tailed) with $N = 31$	0.963	0.721	0.425

case by correlating three macro variables that seem relevant here with the parameter estimates summarized in Table 12.1 and discussed above.[10] The theory would be supported if evidence for expressive motivation were more likely to come from elections with little significance for the composition of the executive, where the electoral system is "feeble" in that it faithfully reproduces the distribution of popular votes in the composition of the legislature, and where the party system is fragmented.

With 18 correlation coefficients displayed in the table, we would expect that one may reach statistical significance at the 0.05 level even by chance alone. None does if we use two-tailed significance tests, and the one that would be significant at the 5 percent level if we used one-tailed tests has the wrong sign, suggesting that the more dependent the composition of the executive is on the election, the stronger the impact of expressive motivation on turnout may be. Hence, the pairwise correlations are so discouraging for the presented extension of Pappi's theory that there is little point in presenting multivariate analyses of the problem. Indeed, exploratory regression analyses did not identify any significant effects of the three macro characteristics on the regression coefficients obtained at the individual-level within countries (data not shown). Thus, the analysis does not lend support to the idea that institutional design could alter the relative weight of expressive versus instrumental motives in voting behavior.

Conclusion

Explaining political involvement by its intrinsic rewards has several attractive features. Unlike models based on instrumental rationality, it is not prima facie incapable of explaining the observed range of electoral turnout in the world's democracies. It can account for why exactly the most sophisticated citizens are the most likely to behave seemingly irrationally and vote: their longer schooling years and exposure to other forms of informal civic education instil an above average sense of civic duty (Mueller 1989: 365), and their higher information level helps them better appreciate the relatively subtle entertainment of voting.

Expressive voting can explain not only why people vote but also makes a convincing case for turnout being sensitive to the costs of voting and its possible political benefits. The intrinsic rewards of electorally relevant political involvement provide sufficient motivation of information processing, decision-making, and turnout only if the expected costs of the latter are lower than the reward.

What the present analysis added to these theoretical arguments is above all a novel empirical demonstration that if turnout is expressively motivated, then the development of a preference among parties is even more so. Somewhat surprisingly, the same cannot be said about the potentially most demanding activities that citizens need to perform to become voters. The processing of political information seems less likely to be rooted in expressive, and probably more likely to be rooted in genuine instrumentally rational motives than either turnout or developing a party preference. I argued that this is possible for two reasons. First, monitoring political developments is so costly that its consumption value may be insufficient to motivate the act. Second, citizens are not just makers, but also recipients of collective political outcomes. Since they need to adjust their everyday activities to these outcomes, they may well attend to them exactly as instrumental voters would if simple calculus would not reveal to them that rational ignorance is their best choice.

Last but not least, the analysis suggests that expressive voting is probably an inevitable feature of mass democracy, rather than linked to certain institutional contexts. There is thus little point in trying to reduce its role through institutional engineering. What may be more promising is to exploit the fact that political information processing follows such motives that can embed the knowledge basis of even the most expressive electoral choices in those real-life circumstances that matter most to citizens in their everyday life. Although we cannot tell whether expressive voters are more or less altruistic, more or less engaged in strategic games, more or less materialistic, and so forth than instrumental voters are, it is quite conceivable that they are not making the same choices, and this should reduce the quality of political representation. However, electoral democracy seems to be dependent for citizen input on expressive motivation, and at least the information basis of expressive choices can probably approximate the information basis that those instrumental voters would rely on whose choices we will never see, but who will nevertheless remain the inevitable reference point for normative assessments of democratic representation.

Acknowledgments

Josep Colomer, Gary Cox, Tamas Meszerics, and the editor provided insightful comments on previous drafts that helped to improve this paper. Work on this paper was completed while the author held a Marie Curie Intra-European Fellowship under the Training and Mobility of Researchers Program of the European Union, contract no. 025384. The views expressed and all remaining errors are those of the author only.

Appendix

1. Data source

The micro-data analyzed in this chapter come from the August 2003 release of the Integrated Micro-Data Set of the Comparative Study of Electoral Systems. After each election covered by the study, national probability samples of the adult population were interviewed. The data sets and study documentation can be downloaded from the website of the project at http:/www.umich.edu/~nes/cses/. The collaborators in the project are not responsible for my interpretations and errors.

2. Number of cases and weighting procedures in the analyses

Only legislative elections are covered. Those respondents who gave sympathy ratings for only one party or no party at all are excluded from the analysis. In all analyses reported here the data were weighted with the demographic weight variables distributed together with the Integrated Micro-Data Set. The values of the weight variables were adjusted so that the weighted and unweighted number of cases are identical in each national sample. A total of 35 surveys are used in the analysis, including two studies from Belgium (separate surveys for Walloonia and

Flanders in 1999), Hong Kong (the 1998 and 2000 elections); Mexico (1997 and 2000), and Spain (1996 and 2000).

3. The dependent variables in the regression analyses

INFO: The collaborators in the CSES project were asked to include three neutral, factual, and unequally demanding country-specific political knowledge questions in the questionnaire module. The INFO variable is a simple count of the number of correct responses given by each respondent. Note that the INFO variable is entirely missing for the following elections: Belarus 2001; Denmark 1998; Iceland 1999; South Korea 2000; Peru 2000 and 2001; Russia 1999; and Slovenia 1996.

CHOICE: party identification, based on A3004 of the CSES data set. The respective question to the respondents read: "Do you usually think of yourself as close to any particular political party?" "Yes" responses were coded 1 and "nays" 0. Note that the CHOICE variable is entirely missing for the French-speaking part of Belgium in the 1999 federal elections.

TURNOUT: electoral participation, based on A2028 of the CSES data set. The variable was coded 1 if the respondent claimed to have voted in the last election and 0 if he or she reported abstention from the polls.

4. The party utility variables

CONSUME: the "consumption value of the vote," that is, the highest rating given by the respondent to any one of the major parties on 11-point like/dislike scales (A3020_A to A3020_I in the integrated CSES data set), which asked respondents to evaluate each of the major parties (up to six) in the given country. See question 7 of the CSES Module 1 questionnaire.

INVEST: the party differential of the respondent or "investment value of the vote," that is, the difference between the highest and the lowest rating given by the respondent to any one of the parties on the like/dislike scales.

5. Sociodemographic control variables employed in all stage 1 models

AGE: age of respondent in years (missing values substituted with sample mean).

AGE SQUARED: the squared value of AGE.

FEMALE: coded 1 for women and 0 for men.

INCOME: personal income, divided into quintiles by country (missing values substituted with the median).

HEDUC: coded 1 for university education or more and 0 otherwise.

LEDUC: coded 1 for primary education or less and 0 otherwise.

6. Macro variables

STAKES: a scale rating the legislative elections included in the analysis in terms of their possible de facto impact on the composition of the executive. All legislative elections in pure parliamentary systems—including Poland and Romania, which are often considered semi-presidential, but the government is only responsible to parliament—were rated 5; legislative elections in Hong Kong, Korea, Mexico, and Peru were rated 1 because the executive is not at all responsible to the legislature; those in Russia, Ukraine, and the United States were rated 2 because appointments to the executive were to be confirmed in at least one house of the legislature. The 1996 legislative election in Taiwan was rated 3 because of the dual answerability of the executive to legislature and the directly elected president.

ELECTORAL SYSTEM: the degree of deviation between the percentage distribution of votes and seats, as measured by the Loosemore-Hanby index calculated for the given legislative election. These data were kindly provided by Hans-Dieter Klingemann and Bernhard Weßels of the Wissenschaftszentrum Berlin in 2002. Data for Iceland and Portugal were added by the author.

PARTY SYSTEM: the effective number of electoral parties. These data were kindly provided by Hans-Dieter Klingemann and Bernhard Weßels of the Wissenschaftszentrum Berlin in 2002. Data for Iceland and Portugal were added by the author.

Note that some elections were excluded from the analysis reported in Table 12.2 because of missing information about one or more macro variables. These were the following elections: Belarus 2001; Hong Kong 2000; Mexico 2000; and Peru 2001.

Notes

1. Under instrumental probabilistic voting, turnout is predicted to increase modestly by the party differential, thus leading to a higher turnout among the more extreme voters. Under expressive probabilistic voting, alienation must be the chief determinant of nonvoting, thus leading to a higher turnout among voters who are ideologically close to a large number of parties. Under realistic assumptions about the location of parties, these voters should be predominantly centrist in terms of ideology.

2. I understand the D term broadly to include not just the utility of gratifying one's sense of civic duty but also the entertainment value of the action in question, its value to send signals about the actor, and any other benefits that are not conditional on the outcome of the election.

3. Strictly speaking, the P times B term borrowed from the turnout equation shows the benefit of voting (for one's ideal choice) rather than not voting. In a similar equation for information processing, B may double if the information gain moves one's vote from the worst to the best possible choice. Yet, the bottom line is that P times B will still be negligible.

4. Downs (1957: 19) speculated that in a world characterized by uncertainty regarding party positions, abstention can be rational for some extremist voters who would like to force their most preferred party to move closer to their own position in the future. Hence alienation can drive turnout not only among expressive but among instrumentally rational actors too. However, Downs did not offer any support for his implausible proposition that the clear and immediate loss that the abstaining extremist voters accept in this way could be counterbalanced by a highly uncertain future gain. This gain would presumably be a move towards a more extreme position by the median legislator as a result of party repositioning aimed at preventing abstention among extremist voters. It seems that for Downs to be correct on this point, extremist voters would have to attach much greater utility either to a future gain than to an equally large present gain, or to a unit change in the position of their favorite party than to an equally big change in the position of the median legislator. Both preference schedules are possible—but only if voters are motivated by the intrinsic rewards of the vote, rather than its policy impact.

5. Calculated separately for each respondent, the range and the standard deviation of the ratings had a Pearson-correlation over .9 with each other in all national samples. Thus, they could not enter the regression analyses simultaneously. Of the two measures, the range was selected for the greater ease of interpretation it allows.

6. One could even argue that those respondents who have no comparative assessments of the parties use the absolute value of the only party they evaluate as a handy information shortcut helping to judge the investment (i.e., political) value of the vote. Thus, the predictions of the Downsian theory and that of its alternative may be indistinguishable in this part of the electorate.

7. One might want to argue that CONSUME can record significant effects among instrumental voters if they use the absolute value of the best alternative as a cue regarding the utility difference between the best and worst alternative. But all the respondents included in the analysis could evaluate on the same thermometer scales at least two, and usually all the relevant parties running in the election. Thus, it is not clear why they would rely on a cue when the real thing itself is also available for leading their judgment.

8. It could be objected that the causal connection behind the recurrent significant relationship between CHOICE and CONSUME runs in the opposite direction: people with a clear preference among the parties give inflated estimates of their liking of the most favored party as a mere rationalization of their standing preference. However, if such a rationalization effect is present in the data, then it should also inflate the correlation between INVEST and CHOICE too, and thus cannot explain why CONSUME appears to be more readily related to CHOICE than INVEST.

9. One might want to speculate that the causal arrow between INFO and INVEST goes the other way round: the more one knows about politics, the bigger

differences are perceived between the utilities of the competing parties. Unfortunately, no panel data are available for the CSES surveys that would allow one to test this proposition for all the countries covered by the study. However, the 1998 Hungarian election survey that provided postelection data for CSES Module 1 also had a preelection wave featuring both feeling thermometers and political knowledge questions, thus allowing a dynamic analysis of causal linkages between INFO, INVEST, and CONSUME. The findings indicated that INVEST is significantly more likely to have a significant positive effect on INFO than the other way round (data not shown).

10. Note that due to missing macro data some elections had to be omitted from this analysis (see appendix to this chapter for details).

13

District Magnitude and the Comparative Study of Strategic Voting

Thomas Gschwend

Introduction[1]

Do electoral systems matter? The political consequences of electoral laws fall in two distinct categories. They encompass direct as well as indirect effects. The particular rules which determine how votes are generated into legislative seats have a direct impact on the number and the type of parties in a given polity. This has profound and well-known consequences for the type of government and the nature of representation in general. It is well known that the same distribution of votes can be translated in totally different distributions of seats in parliament using different electoral rules. If the outcome of an election is not just a foregone conclusion then the differences in the way votes are translated into seats may be a crucial determinant deciding who will govern and who has to stay put.

What is the impact of electoral rules, though, on the way people make decisions in the voting booth? Do voters actually care about electoral rules? Do such rules in some sense shape their electoral choice because they anticipate the outcome of an election and include these expectations in their decision calculus? If voters are systematically drawn away from their most preferred party, just because they realize that supporting a marginal party might be equivalent to wasting their vote given a particular electoral institution, then we speak of an indirect effect. Duverger's (1954) "psychological effects" are the prime example for these types of effects. In order to avoid wasting their votes, voters cast a *strategic* vote for a viable party (or candidate)[2] although they most prefer another one.

Duverger suggested that this logic should not apply to PR systems, since even marginal parties can expect to gain seats in such a system.

Contrary to Duverger's propositions, Leys (1959) and Sartori (1968) expect significant amounts of strategic voting even in PR systems—the more the smaller the district magnitude, that is, the less seats are awarded per electoral district. The Leys–Sartori conjecture posits that the various electoral institutions can be arrayed along a single dimension defined by the district magnitude and predicts that the smaller the district magnitude the more strategic voting we should expect at the primary district level, that is, at the level of the smallest geographic unit in which seats are allocated. The consequences of the frequency of strategic voting given varying district magnitudes, to my knowledge, have never been tested comparatively. Does the frequency of strategic voting at the electoral district depend on the number of seats that are awarded? In order to answer this question this chapter considers first the individual level and then aggregate voting decisions with regard to electoral district in order to be able to estimate the impact of district magnitude on the frequency of strategic voting.

The contributions of this chapter are threefold. First, based on a theory of how voters form expectations about the election outcome in their electoral district I propose a measure to operationalize strategic voting across more than 30 election studies using the Comparative Study of Electoral Systems (CSES) data Module 1. Second, I will test hypotheses about the relationship between the frequency of strategic voting and institutional incentives that are channeled cross-nationally through district magnitude. Third, I further provide some evidence that speaks directly to the controversy in the literature surrounding the question of how district magnitude effects should be modeled. Results yield support for the claim that district magnitude and frequency of strategic voting at the district level are negatively correlated.

A Comparative Look at Strategic Voting—Some Micro-Foundations

No matter whether you believe in the Columbia, Michigan, or Rochester school of thought, traditional theories of voting behavior have in common the prediction that voters should end up casting a vote for their most preferred party (or candidate). This is called a *sincere vote*. Students of strategic voting point out that we nevertheless observe systematic deviations from these traditional vote-choice predictions. In an attempt to model these deviations they suggest that voters do not merely take into account the utility that a voter derives from voting for her most preferred party (U_{pref}) but also the expectation about the outcome of the election, for instance whether the most preferred party is actually a viable alternative to win a seat in her primary electoral district (Blais 2002; Blais et al. 2001; Cox 1997; Fisher 2004). It is far from clear how voters actually form and weigh their expectations against their preferences. It is quite likely that different voters employ different decision rules.

The particular approach followed here is to assume that a voter's decision rule is to vote for a party that maximizes her expected utility from voting for viable parties. Thus, a *strategic voter* is someone who votes for a less-preferred party if the expected utility that this party is likely to gain a seat in their district is higher than the expected utility derived from a sincere vote, namely that their most preferred party has a viable shot at a seat in that district.

The probability that a voter expects her most preferred party to be viable to win a seat is denoted by p_{pref}. The expected utility, EU(pref), that her most preferred party is competitive as a viable alternative to gain a seat combines the traditional utility component weighted by the voter's expectation. Thus EU(pref) = $p_{pref} \cdot U_{pref}$. This also implies that with probability $1 - p_{pref}$ no gain will be realized from voting for her most preferred party. If the voter does not expect his or her most preferred party to be viable then he or she might cast a strategic vote for a less-preferred party that is expected to be viable (i.e., $p_{pref} < p_{strat}$) in order to avoid wasting his or her vote. Given that a strategic choice cannot be the voter's most preferred option, the utility from voting strategically has to be lower, that is, $U_{strat} \leq U_{pref}$.

Moreover, *not* voting for someone's most preferred party might induce cognitive dissonances (Festinger 1957), although voters, of course, are motivated to avoid that. In general perceived cognitive dissonance does not need to have behavioral consequences per se. For instance, from public opinion polls we know that people value public spending and hate paying taxes. People appear too easily to square with facts that stay in logical contrast. What is needed for a cognitive dissonance to arouse and to yield behavioral consequences? There has to be an "aversive event" (Cooper and Fazio 1984: 232) that the voter expects to happen when casting a strategic vote. Arousal of cognitive dissonance might actually prevent such a behavior at the polls if despite being important to the voter, the perceived consequences of such a vote-choice are deemed to be rather unfavorable. Such an "aversive event" could be that *not* voting for the voter's most preferred party is perceived as a threat to the voter's self-esteem or is expected to lead to an outcome that is counter to the voter's self-interest. Voters, however, might be able to a priori reduce the costs of a strategic vote. They could justify their voting behavior by attributing the responsibility—not voting for their most preferred party—to the specific decision-making situation. Clearly, some voters are likely to perceive the decision-making situation, which is prestructured by the electoral rules, as being in some way coercive (Cooper and Fazio 1984: 236–7).

Therefore it appears safe to assume that voting for a party other than the most preferred party imposes additional costs (c) to the voter independent of the expected outcome of the election. The expected utility of a strategic vote depends, consequently, on the expected gain and the costs of a strategic vote. Thus $EU(strat) = p_{strat} \cdot U_{strat} - c$.

When can we expect a voter to deviate from their most preferred party? Following the expectation maximization decision logic, a voter casts a strategic vote if and only if $EU(strat) > EU(pref)$, that is, if:

$$p_{strat} \cdot U_{strat} - c > p_{pref} \cdot U_{pref} \tag{1}$$

or equivalently, if

$$(p_{strat} \cdot U_{strat} - c)/p_{pref} > U_{pref} \tag{2}$$

The left hand side of this inequality can be interpreted as the *risk* of casting a strategic vote. Voters, then, are predicted to cast a strategic vote if these risks outweigh the potential gains from a sincere vote. Given the utility and the costs that are expected to come with a strategic vote as opposed to a sincere vote, the crucial factor for voters in deciding whether to desert or to stick with their most preferred party is the expected probability of their most preferred party's chances for winning a seat in their electoral district relative to the expected probability that a strategic vote is not wasted. Assuming that voters consider only viable parties as potential beneficiaries of a strategic choice, that is, they expect $p_{strat} = 1$, and holding utilities as well as costs constant, the key result from Eq. (2) is as follows: the more uncertain voters are whether their most preferred party is likely to win, that is, the lower the expected probability p_{pref}, the greater the left hand side of this inequality and, consequently, the more likely strategic a vote becomes.

What factors determine these expectations? Voting behavior is no different from any other behavior in that it can be explained by institutional as well as dispositional factors. I am going to distinguish between dispositional and institutional criteria of how voters generate expect-ations about the probability that their preferred party is likely to gain a seat. Dispositional criteria have on the one hand to do with intrap-ersonal psychological motivations, with the ability to understand various institutional factors and employ them in the decision-making process. On the other hand, voting decisions have to do with the use of appropriate decision heuristics. Party elites or the media are likely to provide voters with cues, and as "cognitive misers" (Fiske and Taylor 1991) voters can simply rely on various heuristics to simplify the decision-making process (Gschwend 2004: 22–4). Dispositional factors are necessary in order to explain the variance of how voters generate their preferences and costs, as well as estimate the expected probabilities.

Here, however, individual-level determinants are taken as a starting point and aggregate the respondents' vote choices to the electoral district level. In doing so omitted dispositional effects are implicitly averaged over in order to try to predict the causal effect of institutional criteria. The purpose is to see if incentives of a given institutional design make the use of the wasted vote strategy at the electoral district level more or less likely.

Institutional Criteria and the Duvergerian Logic

Can we predict the level of strategic voting that should occur in a given decision context? Contrary to the approach taken here, the literature on institutional effects on elections typically does not focus on voters them-selves but merely on the predictive implications of their hypothetical strategic behavior on the number of parties (e.g., Amorim Neto and Cox 1997; Clark and Golder 2006; Mozaffar, Scarritt, and Galaich 2003). The first reference point in the literature is Duverger (1954) who discusses the impact of institutional factors. In particular, he focuses upon the reduc-tive effect of electoral systems on party systems due to the mechanism whereby voters try to avoid wasting their vote and cast a strategic vote for a less-preferred party which they believe has a chance of gaining representation. Given the workings of Duverger's proposed dichotomy—plurality systems produce strategic voting while PR systems do not—the "psychological" effects anticipating the "mechanical" effects of a given institutional decision context should operate at least on two levels: party elites and voters. Parties have to decide whether to compete in a given election, form a preelectoral coalition (Golder 2006; Gschwend and Hooghe 2008) or endorse yet another party or coalition that is effectively competing for seats. Depending on how party elites coordinate their entry into the electoral market the menu or choice-set (Ben-Akiva and Boccara 1995) may differ even within the same institutional context. For voters the expected probability p_{pref} that their most preferred party is viable therefore depends on the choices offered to them on the ballot.

Duverger would nevertheless predict that the expected probability p_{pref} is constant within an electoral system while in terms of disposition there should be variance of how voters generate their preferences, costs and how they estimate expected probabilities. Implicitly averaging those dispositional factors, Duverger's theory would predict that the expected probability p_{pref} that a given party is viable is higher in PR systems than in plurality systems.

Contrary to Duverger, Leys (1959: 13.3) suggests that the effect of institutional factors varies across districts because a vote for a nationally small party might not be automatically wasted in every electoral district. Electoral support for a given party is often not uniformly distributed across all electoral districts. There are electoral strongholds where even a nationally small party is likely to gain seats. Consequently Leys would predict that the expected probability p_{pref} that an average voter's most preferred party in dispositional terms is viable should vary across electoral districts even within the same electoral system. Sartori (1968: 278) similarly argues that "... the influence of PR merely represents an enfeeblement of the same influence that is exerted by the plurality systems." He thus expects significant amounts of strategic voting even in PR systems.

The Leys–Sartori conjecture becomes relevant for the discussion of institutional factors that influence voters' expectations of the probability that their vote is not wasted on their preferred party. It posits that various electoral institutions can be arrayed along a single dimension defined by the district magnitude (i.e., by the number of seats awarded in each electoral district). The prediction is that the higher the district magnitude, the less likely voters are to avoid wasting their vote for smaller parties and, hence, the less strategic voting is expected to occur in that district. To put it differently, the larger the district magnitude the higher the expected probability p_{pref} that an average voter (in terms of potential dispositional criteria) believes their most preferred party is viable. According to Eq. (2), the higher the expected probability p_{pref} the less likely such an average voter will be to deviate from their most preferred party in order to cast a strategic vote.

Finally, it is thought that forming expectations as to whether a particular party is viable is a difficult task for voters. Some scholars argue that strategic voting should fade out when district magnitude is greater than 5 because it becomes too complicated to generate expectations about which party is able to gain representation (Cox 1997: 100; Cox and Shugart 1996: 311). Evidence to support this claim comes from empirical regularities based on Japanese and Colombian district level results (Cox 1997; Cox and Shugart 1996) as well as electoral returns in Spanish districts (Cox 1997: 115–7; Gunther 1989). Despite the evidence it remains somewhat unclear, however, why voters in larger districts suddenly systematically overestimated the expected probability p_{pref} of their preferred party's electoral viability in order to vote sincerely for their preferred party rather than strategically. To sum up, the literature agrees that there is a hypothetical negative relationship between district magnitude as the institutional criterion and the frequency of strategic voting in determining voters' behavior.

Besides this general trend with regard to district magnitude and strategic voting, the literature elaborates on two different functional forms of this relationship. Some scholars assume a simple linear relationship (e.g., Cox 1997; Cox and Shugart 1996) while others argue (e.g., Benoit 2001; Ferrara, Herron, and Nishikawa 2005; Monroe and Rose 2002; Taagepera and Shugart 1989) that the marginal effect of district magnitude on the frequency of strategic voting will diminish as the magnitude increases. This is consistent with the idea that the expected difference in the frequency of strategic voting between a single-member district (as for districts in the United States, UK, or Canada) and a district with magnitude of 11 (as in some districts of Slovenia, Belgium, Sweden, or Spain) is more consequential and not at all negligible than in large districts. In districts with a magnitude of, say 30 or 40, voters should expect their most preferred party to gain representation anyway. No strong reduction in the frequency of strategic voting is expected.

Data and Measurement

The Leys–Sartori conjecture has never been tested with individual-level data. Most studies in the literature on institutional effects on elections employ cross-national data in order to pin down the relationship between district magnitude and the size of the party system (e.g., Amorim Neto and Cox 1997; Clark and Golder 2006; Mozaffar, Scarritt, and Galaich 2003). Scholars who look more closely at strategic voting use district level rather than national level data (e.g., Cox 1997; Cox and Shugart 1996;

Gschwend 2007; Herron and Nishikawa 2001). Nevertheless, employing district level data is only an indirect way to assess an individual level phenomenon like strategic voting. Heroic assumptions about voters' preferences as well as the well-known problems of ecological fallacy plague the process of making inferences based on such a research design. Moreover, different strategic voting patterns might even cancel out in the aggregate and are therefore lost from any analysis geared at this level of observation. Thus, on theoretical grounds, if one is interested in investigating effects of electoral institutions on voting behavior, the individual level is the preferred level of observation to carry out analyses of strategic voting. With survey data it is possible to measure (sincere) preferences of a given respondent directly and compare it to their stated voting behavior. This is a great advantage compared to all studies that look only at aggregated election results because one does not need to make any additional assumption about voters' preferences in order to distinguish strategic from other voting behavior.

The CSES project is an ideal data set for this approach. It is a cross-national project with election studies across countries with great variance in their electoral institutions, variance which also provides comparable individual level data. Moreover, systematic information about characteristics of the primary electoral districts as well as the electoral system at large is merged to the individual data. Thus, the CSES data (Module 1) is especially suitable for study of the effects of electoral institutions on citizens' attitudes and behavior.

The comparative literature on strategic voting and electoral systems traditionally speaks to the (primary electoral) district level because this is the level where the institutional effects should operate. I will choose the same level of observation in order to assess the consequences of varying district magnitude on the frequency of strategic voting.

The dependent variable is the fraction of all voters per electoral district who cast a strategic vote. In order to construct this variable it is necessary to derive voters' preference rankings of parties which actually field lists or candidates in a particular electoral district, that is, *after* elite coordination took place that might have reduced the number of available options on the ballot.[3] This accounts for the complications that even within the same country voters do not necessarily have the same choice-set and that their vote choices might be menu dependent. Party preferences are measured by standard 10-point party like–dislike scales and ranked accordingly for each respondent.[4]

According to my conceptualization, a strategic vote following the Duvergerian logic is a vote for a less-preferred party if the expected utility that this party is electorally viable is higher than the expected utility of the preferred party gaining a seat in the district. Unfortunately, it cannot be directly assessed how individuals form their expectations about the viability of a party, no matter how they weigh their preferences against those expectations. This holds in most CSES countries where the common module was administered as part of a postelection study. Thus I have to employ some simplifying assumptions.

In a single-member district the two parties expected to be first and second are considered viable to gain this seat (Cox 1997).The larger the district magnitude the more parties will be viable. Conceptually, voters have to calculate the expected probabilities for their most preferred party to get the last seat in a multimember district in order to decide whether their vote might be wasted. Particularly in large districts with many parties this will be quite difficult. Given the complexity it might be more reasonable to assume that "viability" of a given party is perceived differently in such districts. It is assumed that voters simply form expectations, whether or not parties gain a seat in a particular electoral district. As such, parties that are expected to win a seat are perceived as viable parties in that electoral district. Employing this heuristic is easier than calculating expected probabilities for parties winning the last district seat and, moreover, it is easily available since voters can infer this from previous election results.

There is also a methodological warning associated with attempts to operationalize the concept of "viability" for parties in multimember districts using CSES data. These data cover vote shares of up to six parties at the district level. There is no information in the CSES data, however, as to whether those parties in fact actually came first, second, third, and so forth. The parties covered by CSES are not automatically the most successful parties in every electoral district. There is always the possibility that independent candidates or parties not covered by the CSES could have been more successful in a particular district than parties that are covered by the CSES. Thus from ranking district-level results of the available parties one cannot reliably asses the "viability" of a given party.

In order to get a measure for voters' expectations about a party's electoral viability the concept was defined as "coming in first or second" in single-member districts and as "gaining at least a seat" in multimember districts. Consistent with prior research (e.g., Cain 1978; Gschwend 2004; Karp et al. 2002: 8), it is assumed that on average voters' expectations are correct, that is, they expect a party to be viable (or to gain a seat) if the party actually ends up first or second (or winning a seat) in that district.

Consequently, the dependent variable is coded as the proportion of respondents per electoral district who cast their vote for a less-preferred party if that party comes in first or second (in single-member districts), or wins a seat in their electoral district (in multimember districts) when the preferred party does not. This group of strategic voters is most likely to follow the Duvergerian logic to avoid wasting their vote.[5] The advantage of such strategic voting is that it disentangles strategic voters following a wasted-vote strategy from voting behavior that can be interpreted as a result of other strategies (Blais et al. 2001). Thus the frequencies of strategic voting are not falsely magnified as if we would take, for instance, simply every deviation from someone's most preferred party as a strategic vote. In order to construct a measure of which party gained seats in a given electoral district this information was compiled separately from country-specific data sources and merged with the CSES data. The group of nonstrategic voters is comprised of all other voters, for example, sincere voters or voters of a party that is on the ballot in a respective electoral district but not being evaluated on the corresponding party like–dislike scale.

Some Descriptive Results

The empirical section of this chapter begins by providing an overview of the independent and the dependent variables. In the following analysis, all CSES election studies are included which passed a data consistency test and provided the relevant variables. Thus, countries without any parliamentary vote-choice variable were not included in the analysis (Belarus, Chile, Lithuania, Peru 2000); nor were countries where district level information is not available (Taiwan, Korea, Russia, Ukraine, and Thailand).

There are 1,949 electoral districts in the CSES election studies where seats are distributed at least partly on the local district level. The district magnitude varies between 1 and 48. The distribution of this variable is extremely skewed. About 80 percent of the observations have a district magnitude of 1. However, the respective seat allocation rules that determine the winner in such districts vary to some extent. Besides the single-member plurality districts of Canada, the UK, and the United States, there are also Australian alternative vote districts as well as the SMD-tier

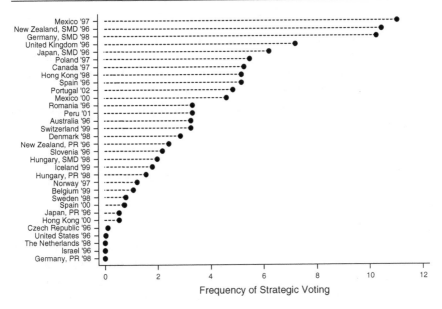

Figure 13.1. Frequency of strategic voting by election study—CSES Module 1

districts of all mixed-electoral systems (including the single ballot system of Mexico). If the Netherlands and Israel are also included—two countries where the primary electoral district is at the national level, and the available PR-tier districts of the two-ballot mixed electoral systems that are covered by CSES Module 1 (Germany, Hungary, Japan, and New Zealand)—the number of observations increases by 35 to 1,984. Those PR-tier districts have district magnitudes that range from 4 (Hungarians' PR-tier is composed of regional multimember districts) to 656 (Germany).

The dependent variable is the proportion of respondents per electoral district who cast their vote for a less-preferred party if that party comes in first or second (in single-member districts), or a party which wins a seat in their electoral district (in multimember districts) when the preferred party does not. In order to capture the distribution Figure 13.1 provides summary statistics while summing up the observed levels of strategic voting at the electoral districts within every election study.

Figure 13.1 shows that there is considerable variation in the frequency of strategic voting even on a more aggregate level. It is reassuring that based on my measurement strategy one does not find any strategic voting where votes are essentially never wasted. In neither of two PR systems with very low thresholds—Israel and the Netherlands—is strategic voting discernable. At most 10–12 percent of the voters follow the wasted-vote logic. These high rates are observed in the SMD-tier of some mixed-electoral systems. The variation is even stronger at the electoral district level. In the following section electoral districts are chosen as the level of analysis because the hypothesized institutional effects should be present at this level.

District Magnitude and the Frequency of Strategic Voting

What is the relationship between district magnitude and the frequency of strategic voting? Theory suggests that it should be a negative relationship: the lower the district magnitude the higher a voter's expectation that their vote will be wasted because parties find it more difficult to win seats. So far, there is no agreement reached about the functional form. Moreover we should expect a sudden decline of strategic voting in electoral districts with a district magnitude greater than 5 if the "fading-out" argument is correct. The CSES provides an opportunity to examine these issues empirically.

The fraction of strategic voting per district is calculated over a different number of grouped individuals and bounded between 0 and 1. I follow the advice of the econometric literature on how to deal with this type of response data (e.g., Papke and Wooldridge 1996) and will later employ a generalized linear model (GLM) with a logit link. This particular estimation strategy makes it possible to appropriately model the binomial data generation process at the electoral district level, while at the same time accounting for the fact that the precision of those fractions depends on the number of respondents within each electoral district. The logit link finally makes sure that the model predictions are bounded between 0 and 1.

When modeling the fraction of strategic voting per district the current theory does not offer any clear guidance as to which functional form for the district magnitude should be used. Therefore, I start by fitting a slightly more flexible model, a generalized additive model (GAM) (Beck and Jackman 1998), to the data to avoid any parametric restrictions for district magnitude as the sole predictor of the expected frequency of strategic voting at the district level.

Figure 13.2 displays the fractions of strategic voting as predicted by a smooth function (estimated through a cubic smoothing spline; based

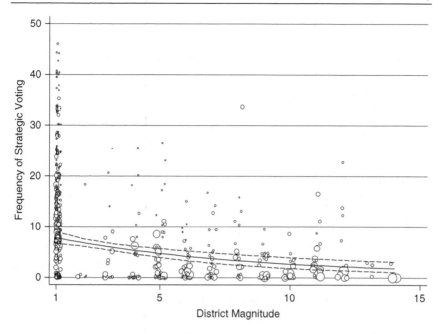

Figure 13.2. Smooth function of district magnitude and the frequency of strategic voting

on 5 df) of the district magnitude together with pointwise 95 percent confidence intervals as solid and dashed lines, respectively. While the circles represent the actual district level fractions of strategic voting, the size of the circles is proportional to the number of respondents that were interviewed in that district. To maximize readability outlying districts (about 6 percent) are excluded from Figure 13.2.

The analysis reveals that it is very difficult to obtain a precise prediction of the level of strategic voting in the districts based on the district magnitude as sole predictor. The variability of the observed fraction of strategic voting is quite high even for electoral districts of the same district magnitude. Nevertheless, electoral districts that have unexpectedly high fractions of strategic voting are mostly displayed with small circles indicating that these fractions are based on small numbers of respondents only.

In general though, the figure supports the expectation that there is a negative relationship between district magnitude and the number of strategic voters in a given electoral district. This is consistent with the theory that the larger the district magnitude the higher voters' expectations

p_{pref} that their most preferred party is viable in that district and, consequently, the less likely they are to cast a strategic vote. Moreover, the expected decrease of strategic voting seems to be rather smooth. There is no evidence, at least in these data, for the argument advanced by Cox and Shugart (1996) and Cox (1997) of a sudden decline of strategic voting in electoral districts with a district magnitude greater than 5. Instead, there is some strategic voting even in electoral districts of large district magnitude. The analysis thus far has moved beyond the dominant case study design logic that characterizes the literature on strategic voting, establishing that there is a negative relationship between district magnitude and the frequency of strategic voting even if one looks at electoral districts cross-nationally.

What can be said about the functional form of the relationship between district magnitude and the frequency of strategic voting? The literature does not offer clear guidance. Comparing the model fit of a GLM with a GAM using the same dependent and independent variables allows one to assess how reasonable the linearity constraint is for the predictors DISTRICT MAGNITUDE or log(DISTRICT MAGNITUDE) in a GLM. If all predictors in a GAM are modeled linearly (i.e., df = 1) then such a model is equivalent to a GLM. Now, if the deviance increases (significantly) when a linear predictor is used instead of a smooth function (i.e., df > 1), that is, the model fit gets worse, then the smooth functions of the predictors show significant signs of nonlinearity. Appropriate significance tests show that there are neither significant nonlinearities when one uses DISTRICT MAGNITUDE nor log(DISTRICT MAGNITUDE) for electoral districts where seats are distributed at least partly on the local district level and the district magnitude varies between 1 and 48. Consequently for such electoral districts the linearity constraint of the predictors is not really consequential substantively. Scholars can employ either functional form, DISTRICT MAGNITUDE or log(DISTRICT MAGNITUDE). No gain can be made by going nonparametric. However, if the PR-tier districts are included, and, consequently, the district magnitude ranges between 1 and 656, DISTRICT MAGNITUDE shows signs of nonlinearity while log(DISTRICT MAGNITUDE) does not. This implies that when adding those 35 PR-tier districts to the sample—some of which have very large district magnitudes (New Zealand: 120; Israel: 120; the Netherlands: 150; Germany: 656)—scholars should rather use log(DISTRICT MAGNITUDE) instead of DISTRICT MAGNITUDE as a predictor when modeling such effects.

All told, the assessment of the controversy in the literature about the appropriate functional form when modeling district magnitude yields

Table 13.1. Generalized linear models predicting the frequency of strategic voting as a function of district magnitude

	Dependent variable: fraction of strategic voting			
	Excluding PR	All districts	Excluding PR	All districts
DISTRICT MAGNITUDE	−0.104 (0.032)**	−0.015 (0.010)		
log(DISTRICT MAGNITUDE)			−0.583** (0.071)	−0.492 (0.115)**
Constant	−2.622 (0.097)**	−3.036 (0.081)**	−2.631 (0.046)**	−2.671 (0.062)**
AIC	2.20	2.45	2.16	2.24
BIC	−11,996	−11,740	−12,074	−12,157
N	1949	1984	1949	1984

Robust standard errors in parentheses; * Significant at 5%; ** Significant at 1%.

a Solomonic sentence at least in light of the dependent variable used here. As long as the district magnitudes of the electoral districts are not greater than 50, that is, for almost all electoral districts that are covered by the CSES module, it does not make a huge difference whether DISTRICT MAGNITUDE or log(DISTRICT MAGNITUDE) is used. This is true as long as there is an appropriate link function that permits out-of-bound predictions.

Finally it is worthwhile to look at the estimation results from a GLM predicting the level of strategic voting conditional on institutional effects that get channeled through the district magnitude. To facilitate a comparison across functional forms—either DISTRICT MAGNITUDE or log(DISTRICT MAGNITUDE) as predictor, as well as samples which either exclude ($n = 1,949$) or include ($n = 1,984$) the PR-tier districts—Table 13.1 presents the estimation results across all four models.

Three out of four models yield essentially the same result. The incentives that get channeled through the district magnitude are in fact systematically related to the frequency of strategic voting at the electoral district level. No matter which functional form is used for the predictor variable, the relationship is negative: lower district magnitudes yield more strategic voting. Merely the inclusion of the large PR-tier districts of New Zealand, Israel, the Netherlands, and Germany cause problems when one attempts to model DISTRICT MAGNITUDE without transforming it. Moreover, the smaller samples excluding all PR-tier districts always yield better predictions given the presented fit indices even when the same functional form is used. Smaller values for the Akaike (AIC) as well as the Bayesian (BIC) information criterion, indicate better fitting models. Finally, the model fit

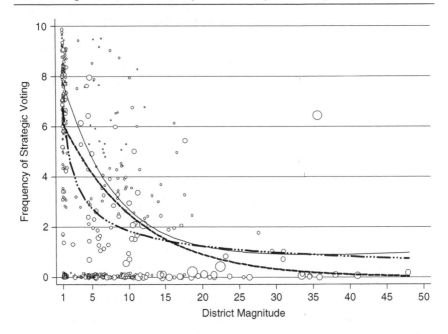

Figure 13.3. Comparison of model predictions across three estimated relationships between district magnitude and the frequency of strategic voting

is consistently slightly better when one uses *log*(DISTRICT MAGNITUDE) as the independent variable.

How large are the predicted differences in strategic voting across different models? In Figure 13.3, three functions are plotted to predict the frequency of strategic voting across a wide range of district magnitude. The range of the independent variable, which is shown on the horizontal axes, comprises more than 99 percent of the electoral districts in the CSES Module 1 data. There are two thick lines. The dashed line represents the GLM predictions based on the model where DISTRICT MAGNITUDE is untransformed while the dashed line separated by dots represents the respective predictions where *log*(DISTRICT MAGNITUDE) is the independent variable. The solid thin line corresponds to the GAM predictions from before.

Almost consistently the GAM predictions yield the highest district-level estimates for strategic voting across all three models. The GLM predictions with DISTRICT MAGNITUDE as untransformed predictor suggest the lowest levels of strategic voting across all three models when the district magnitude is larger than 15 and, consequently, the model with *log*(DISTRICT MAGNITUDE) as independent variable predicts comparatively the lowest levels of strategic voting for districts with smaller district magnitudes. The predicted differences across those models are largest in small districts with a district magnitude between 2 and 4 and differ not more than by about 2.5 percentage points. For more than 90 percent of the districts in the sample the model predictions differ by less than 1 percentage point from one another. Thus in most situations the differences across the three models have little substantive relevance. Depending on how the relationship between district magnitude and the frequency of strategic voting is modeled one can expect on average around 6–8 percent of strategic voting in single member districts, while for electoral districts with a district magnitude of greater than 10 we should not expect to find more than about 2 percent strategic voters.

Conclusion

The workings of electoral laws have profound and well-known consequences for the party system, the type of government, and the nature of representation in general. It also has an impact on the way people make decisions in the voting booth. Some voters anticipate the outcome of an election because they form expectations about it and act accordingly. The ways these expectations play out seem to be systematically related to institutional factors that prestructure a voter's choice situation. Since voting behavior is not only determined by institutions I conceptually distinguished institutional and dispositional criteria of how voters generate expectations about the probability of a vote cast for their preferred party going to waste. For this study I focused on the institutional criteria that operate at the primary district level, possibly moderating voters' expectations and thus causing them to deviate from supporting their preferred party. These individual-level mechanisms have predictable implications for the frequency of strategic voting at the electoral district level.

The results of this study provide evidence that the level of strategic voting at the district level is related to district magnitude. Leys (1959) and Sartori (1968) suggested this long ago: The higher the district magnitude the less strategic voting we should expect. For the first time this study provides evidence for this relationship that holds across various electoral systems. Depending on how this relationship is modeled one can expect on average around 6–8 percent strategic voters in single-member districts. Nevertheless even in districts with a large district magnitude, contrary to what Duverger would have predicted, one can still systematically observe strategic voting although at a very low level.

Although this negative relationship seems to be quite robust, there is still a great deal of variance that is not accounted for even when comparing the levels of strategic voting in electoral districts of the same district magnitude. It might be that the institutional incentives that are channeled through the district magnitude and supposedly moderate a voter's expectation formation process differ across types of electoral systems. For instance, are the incentives to cast a strategic vote in a single-member district in Australia (employing an alternative vote system) systematically different from the ones in Canada, the UK, or the United States or even from the SMD-tier districts in mixed electoral systems? Further research should seek to identify the mechanism by which other institutional effects potentially moderate the incentives that are channeled through the district magnitude.

The controversy in the literature surrounding the functional form of those district magnitude effects appears to be somewhat suspect. At least based on the analysis of the Module 1 CSES data the basis of disagreement is lost. It simply does not make a significant difference whether the district magnitude is logistically transformed or not. My sense is that the controversy should be rather around how we model the dependent variable on which the district magnitude should have an impact. A typical dependent variable in this controversy is certainly the "effective number of parties" (Laakso and Taagepera 1979). It may be more useful to theorize about the data generating mechanism behind such a concept rather than arguing about transformations of independent variables. This would also seem to be a more promising approach with regard to policy applications of the research.

Notes

1. I thank Kerstin Hönig for valuable research assistance and Martin Elff for helpful comments.
2. To simplify language I will just refer to political parties, even if voters can explicitly vote for candidates. Since I am looking at parliamentary elections, candidates are typically affiliated with a party list.
3. If the mechanism behind the Leys–Sartori conjecture were merely driven by elite coordination instead of strategic behavior of voters, marginal parties would not even contest an election. The implication for voters would be that they have no opportunity to waste their votes in the first place. Thus, the observed level

of strategic voting is driven by strategic behavior of voters in anticipation of the decision context and cannot be attributed to elite coordination.

4. In mixed systems I take the SMD vote as relevant vote choice since only in the majoritarian tier one expects an impact of the district magnitude. In order to do that I assume that party and candidate preferences coincide for voters who do not vote for the candidate of their most preferred party but for a more viable candidate.

5. If respondents simultaneously prefer two parties when one party is expected to be viable and the other party is not such a vote is counted as having been cast for the viable party as a strategic vote since not including expectations in voters' decision calculus could have resulted in a vote for a party with a lower expected utility.

Part VI

Political Support

14

Institutional Variation and Political Support: An Analysis of CSES Data from 29 Countries[1]

Ola Listhaug, Bernt Aardal, and Ingunn Opheim Ellis

Introduction and Review of Previous Research

The institutionalist turn in political science has become so strong that it is unlikely that many scholars would question that institutions matter. At the same time it is quite obvious that there is an imbalance between theory and empirical research. It is easier to find arguments in favor of institutional effects than to observe systematic evidence in support of such effects. The lack of appropriate empirical research is especially striking in the field of mass politics (Wenzel, Bowler, and Lanoue 2000), where there is scarce data that combine measurement of relevant attitudes and behavior for representative samples of the population, and institutional characteristics for a significant number of countries.

Within the field of mass politics, the study of the linkage between democratic attitudes and other forms of political support and political institutions constitutes an intriguing question for study. Moreover, the current wave of democratization has put the focus on the issue of constitutional design: Which institutional solutions are best suited to develop democracy in a country? (Lijphart and Waisman 1996) There are many ways to answer this question, depending on with which aspects of democracy one is concerned. We believe that one way to judge institutions is by their consequences for the link between mass and elite. The linkage between elite and mass is indeed multifaceted as we are reminded by recent contributions to the comparative study of political representation

(Esaiasson and Heidar 2000; Miller et al. 1999; Schmitt and Thomassen 1999). Our task here is limited to an investigation of one small part of linkage: how various institutional arrangements influence the level of political support.

Political support is used as a label for attitudes that citizens have towards various parts of the political system. Political support includes attitudes ranging from the most general and fundamental aspects of the political system such as political community and regime principles, to more specific characteristics like political institutions and political actors (Norris 1999b). Discounting that a dose of skepticism might be healthy, we see a preponderance of positive attitudes over negative attitudes as a good thing for the political system. It is widely accepted that political support is a multidimensional concept, and that variation in political support can be explained by a multitude of causes: the evolvement of policy distance between government and the governed, the economic performance of the political system, the impact of scandals and specific events, the popularity of leaders, the impact of mass media—just to mention a few of the most common explanations employed in empirical research. Most studies have been limited to single countries, although the pioneering *Civic Culture* by Almond and Verba (1963) laid an early groundwork for the comparative study of democratic culture. With the accumulation of surveys, both over time and across nations, recent research has seen the emergence of important comparative studies. These include the *Beliefs of Government* project of the European Science Foundation, where especially the volumes by Klingemann and Fuchs (1995) and Kaase and Newton (1995) contain material of interest. Also notable is the edited volume by Norris (1999a), which is even broader in scope than *Beliefs in Government* (Klingemann and Fuchs (1995); Kaase and Newton (1995). Both these projects rely mainly on reanalysis of existing survey data. These data sets vary considerably in their coverage of political support variables, and measurement of institutional variables was not part of the original data collection.

To overcome some of the limitations of previous data, the International Committee for Research into Elections and Representative Democracy (ICORE), which is a cooperative initiative between national election studies in a large number of countries, has launched a major new data collection on *The Comparative Study of Electoral Systems*. This study incorporates a comprehensive set of variables about political institutions, and it includes a set of measures of mass behavior and attitudes, including a battery of political support questions. The CSES design is suited to our research question and should hold the potential to add to existing research. Before we develop a model based on the data from CSES we review some of the relevant empirical studies of political support and institutions.

Building on the idea that political representation is important for political support, Miller and Listhaug (1990) reason that the more flexible multiparty systems are preferable to two party systems and more rigid multiparty systems. They compare trust in government in Norway, Sweden, and the United States from the 1960s to the 1980s and observe a long time decline in the United States and Sweden—which they contrast to the more cyclical pattern in Norway. Norway and Sweden are both multiparty systems, but Sweden has a higher threshold for representation of small parties than Norway. For most of the period new parties did not achieve representation in the Swedish parliament, in contrast to Norway where at least two significant new parties emerged in the 1960s and 1970s. Moreover, Listhaug (1995) demonstrates that the dominance of the Social Democratic party in Sweden, and the failure of the nonsocialist governments in 1976–82, weakened the beliefs among nonsocialist voters that their side could govern effectively. These beliefs were in turn linked to distrust of government. The empirical evidence is gathered from only three countries which strongly limits the conclusions that can be drawn from the study. Moreover, trust has continued its decline in Sweden after a break up of the party system in 1988–91, in which three new parties were represented in parliament: the Greens, the Christian Democrats, and, the short-lived, right wing New Democracy (Holmberg 1999; Miller and Listhaug 1998).

Weil (1989) analyzes a considerably larger number of nations. Based on the work of Sartori, Powell, and others he argues that party system polarization and fragmentation and government structure will influence political support levels in democracies. He sees the following factors as contributing to a decrease in political support: a high degree of party fragmentation, a high level of ideological polarization, oversized coalitions or minority governments, and low levels of government stability. These hypotheses are tested with time series of aggregate survey data of political support variables as well as aggregate data on economic and political performance for the United States, Britain, France, West Germany, Italy, and Spain for the period 1946–87. For most of the countries the time series is considerably shorter due to lack of data. The empirical evidence in general supports the hypotheses, although not quite consistent across all countries. This leads him to conclude: "Citizens judge democracy less by what it 'gives' them but by whether it presents them with real (but not polarized) alternatives and responds to their choices" (Weil 1989: 699). In other words, how institutions develop accountability is important for political confidence in representative institutions and for the legitimacy of the political system. An important contribution of the study is the demonstration that it allows for the study of institutional variation within a country. Although major changes in electoral institutions of established institutions are rare, change in government and in party system structure can occur over a time span of a few decades, thus making it worthwhile to study the impact of institutional variation on trust within countries.

Karp and Bowler (2001) study the effects of New Zealand's change to proportional reform. This was a reform that was designed to increase support for democracy in a country that had one of the clearest majoritarian systems in the world. The change from a Westminster model to a proportional system did not produce the desired effects. The data show that support for the electoral system declined, and that satisfaction with how democracy works fell markedly from 1996 to 1998. The authors demonstrate that support for the two forms of the electoral system is explained by partisan self-interest with voters of the dominant National Party showing the strongest support for the old system. Despite the fact that confidence in democracy declined after the reform, they are not unequivocally pessimistic, and speculate that it will take time to see the positive effects, primarily due to resistance from major party supporters (Karp and Bowler 2001: 74).

Listhaug and Wiberg (1995) report a limited study that follows up of some of the ideas from Weil, but now with cross-section data from 13 Western European democracies in 1981 and 1990. They correlate confidence in parliament and confidence in government institutions (the average sum of confidence in armed forces, education system, police, parliament, and civil service). Three institutional measures are used: number of governments, duration of governments relative to maximum (reversed), and number of parties in government. They hypothesize that government instability, measured by number and duration, and multiparty governments, would lead to a decline in confidence. The time period used was the last 10 years before the survey. Ten of 12 correlation coefficients had the predicted negative sign. The small number of observations virtually precludes the performance of a statistical analysis. However, the tentative findings suggest that institutional factors are related to political support.

Anderson and Guillory (1997) use data from Eurobarometer 34 in 1990 to analyze the impact of type of democracy in 11 EU countries on satisfaction with how democracy works in each country. They make a distinction between winners and losers, operationalized by who supports the parties in government or not. They hypothesize that winners will be more satisfied than losers, and that this differential will be greater in majoritarian systems than in consensual systems. Majoritarian systems with one party government and few alternate channels for the losing political interests to make their voice heard in the actual making of policy after the election, make it tough on the losers. The chance is that winners will see many of their policies enforced in actual politics. The difference between winning and losing is big in such polities. In consensual systems governments are normally coalitional or nonmajority single party governments. These systems also have an elaborate system for consultation with the interests not represented in cabinet. Losing as well as winning will mean less in such systems. The authors employ Lijphart's consensus/majority index as a measure of type of democracy and apply statistical controls for economic performance evaluations, political interest, and demographic variables. The results of the statistical analysis are supportive of their claims: the difference between winners and losers are larger in majoritarian countries than in countries with consensual political institutions.

With Eurobarometer data from the period 1975–94 Huseby (1999: 148) demonstrates that winners are more satisfied with the way democracy works than are losers if the country has a single party government compared to the case with coalition governments. Interestingly, she finds that the gap is explained by the fact that winners are more satisfied with the way democracy works in single party government systems than in systems with coalitions; losers show no difference by system. This calculation is based on 68 single party governments and 252 coalition governments. One problem with the data is that most of the single party governments are from Britain. We know that British single party governments also are majoritarian, while single party governments in other countries normally are of the minority variety. It is therefore of interest to see if the relationship holds for countries that have both types of governments. She examines three such countries, Denmark, Italy, and Ireland, and finds the expected relationship for Denmark and Italy but not for Ireland. Besides her considerable extension of the research by Anderson and Guillory, Huseby pursues a more ambitious research agenda to link institutional arrangements and the impact of economic variables on satisfaction with democracy. Her findings in this area are, however, more ambiguous. She finds that negative perceptions of the economy (those who say the economy is worse than before) is dependent on institutional structure, with the gap between winners and losers much larger in systems with one party governments than in coalitional systems. The difference is 28.8 percentage points versus 12.4 percentage points, respectively (Huseby 1999: 148). The smaller gap in countries with two or more parties in government is explained partly by the fact that losers in such systems hold less negative perceptions and winners hold more negative perceptions than similar groups in one party government systems. Correlations between perceptions of the economy, as well as changes in the real economy—tapped by common indicators of inflation and unemployment, and satisfaction with democracy is strongly negative for countries with coalition governments, but not significant, and partly with wrong signs for one party governments (Huseby 1999: 147).

Klingemann (1999) has presented the most extensive global mapping of political support. His study includes 63 countries in the mid-1990s, which represent nearly half of the world population. For subsets of these countries he performs a limited analysis of the impact of institutions. He classifies the countries by their level of political rights and civil liberties according to the Freedom House index. He then divides the countries into two groups, low democracy (below 2 on the index) and high democracy (2 and higher on the index). He further divides the systems into two groups based on age of democracy. For systems over 40 years old he can compare support levels between low and high democracy countries. The average support for democracy as an ideal form of government as well as support for regime performance is higher in high democracy countries than in low democracy countries (Klingemann 1999: 46, 49). Lijphart, in his influential book *Patterns of Democracy* which advocates consensual democracy, uses the Klingemann and Anderson and Guillory data to demonstrate that citizens in proportional countries show higher levels of satisfaction with democracy than citizens in majoritarian systems (Lijphart 1999).

Using much of the same data as Klingemann, Norris (1999c) delivers the most ambitious measurement and multivariate analysis of the impact of institutions on support. Her dependent variable is confidence in institutions, which is the average for the following institutions: parliament, the civil service, the legal system, the police, and the armed forces. Five of her hypotheses are related to the impact of institutions.

Like Klingemann, Norris sees widespread political rights and liberties as positive for political support. This factor is measured by the seven-point Freedom House index. Second, she argues that parliamentary systems where all parties are involved in the policymaking process will show higher confidence levels than the less inclusive presidential systems. This variable is measured by a single dichotomy between parliamentary and presidential systems based on Lijphart's classification. Third, she hypothesizes that two party systems and moderate multiparty systems will have higher confidence levels than systems with a predominant party or polarized pluralism. Fourth, she sees federal states as more flexible and able to integrate diverse interests into the policy process and create fewer losers than unitary states. This argument leads to the hypothesis that confidence levels will be higher in federal states than in unitary systems. Fifth, Norris argues that proportional electoral systems will produce more institutional support than majoritarian systems. She classifies this variable in three groups (1 for proportional, 0.5 for mixed, and 0 for majoritarian systems).

In addition to the institutional variables her model includes variables for winning/losing, indicators for cultural and economic development, and demographic controls. The multivariate model is tested on pooled data for 25 major democracies ($N = 38,828$). Two of the variables—level of democratization and party system—have relatively strong effects in the expected direction, both with betas of 0.10. Parliamentary systems barely beat presidential systems; the beta is 0.02, which is statistically significant with a very large N, but otherwise not impressive. The two remaining institutional variables have wrong signs and are both statistically significant. The beta for the federal-unitary state dichotomy is $-.06$, giving unitary states an edge on confidence. The beta for electoral system is $-.15$, showing that majority systems have an advantage. Besides the impact of institutions Norris finds that economic development as well as postmaterialism are positively associated with confidence. Two of the demographic variables, age and education, are also positively associated with confidence in institutions.

In summing up these contributions we would like to emphasize four points. First, in developing the hypotheses we observe that the theoretical arguments are often indecisive for identifying which type of institution is most likely to develop higher support among citizens. The case can be made both for majoritarian and consensual systems, for presidentialism as well as for parliamentarism, for federalism as compared to unitary states, as well as for competing alternate political institutions. This theoretical indeterminacy is to a large extent created by the fact that institutional alternatives do not combine accountability and representation (CSES 1994: 7; Powell 2000). If we argue that a consensual system is better for support than a majoritarian system, we are using the representation argument because consensual systems are more inclusive in power sharing than majoritarian systems. If we stress the accountability argument we would be more likely to argue that majoritarian systems would be better since such systems allow us to know whom we can reward or punish for performance in office (Appendix 1, pp. 353–4). Much the same will hold if we compare parliamentarism and presidentialism. The arguments that Norris (1999c) musters in favor of federalism are related to the advantage that federal structures may have for maximizing representation in divided or fragmented societies. On the other hand it is plausible to argue that a federal structure will obscure accountability, often in the form of divided government—and that this might contribute to political alienation and distrust among citizens.

Second, in thinking about institutions we observe that this is a very wide concept. In a narrow meaning, institutions are the rules of the game as defined by constitutions and electoral laws. In a wider meaning institutions include the broader sets of arrangements or patterns of behavior that have evolved around main functions of political systems. The actual structuring of political alternatives will depend on rules, but this correlation is far from perfect (Blais and Massicotte 1996; Powell 2000). We would thus be wise to include operationalizations based on both rules and on actual configurations.

Third, we should investigate if the impact of institutions varies across the dimensions of political support. It is widely accepted that political support is multidimensional. But most of the studies have examined only one measure of support, typically a measure for support of regime performance or confidence in regime institutions. To find out if institutions have a different impact on different aspects of support we need to include two or more such measures in the same study.

Fourth, any decisive test of the impact of institutions on political support must also test for competing explanations. Most of the studies, and especially those which are based on aggregate percentages, do not control for competing independent variables measured both at the level of the nation or the individual. An exception is Norris (1999c) who includes postmaterialism, economic development, and some standard demographics in her pooled model.

Data, Model, and Measurement

The purpose of the CSES study is to strengthen comparative electoral research. This is achieved through two data collection efforts. First, a module with questions is included in a large number of national election surveys of representative samples of citizens. The micro-data include questions about parties, political participation, political support, and a standardized battery of demographic variables. Second, the project collects a set of macro-data for each country, including a detailed registration of information about electoral institutions.

In Table 14.1 we present an overview of the institutional classifications. An extensive documentation is available from CSES, and will not be presented here. Information and documentation about political rights and liberties are coded from Freedom House (1999), and the Gallagher disproportionality index is used as presented in Lijphart (1994: 60–1).

Political support is a multidimensional concept. Following Easton (1965) most scholars make the distinction between diffuse and specific support. The most recent version of this conceptualization (Norris 1999*b*: 10) sees the hierarchy as divided into five main classes (ordered from diffuse to specific): political community, regime principles, regime performance, regime institutions, and political actors. A second but less frequently cited distinction is the one between output and input support (Easton 1965). Political support may be related to feelings that individuals think that they can influence the political process (input support) or to individuals' assessments of the outcomes of the political process (output support) (House and Mason 1975). Measures of input support can be divided into two groups: internal efficacy and external efficacy. Internal efficacy is tapped by questions that ask if individuals feel that politics is too complex to understand, or of little relevance as exemplified by not seeing differences between parties, or lack of participation beyond voting. In short, internal efficacy is concerned with citizens' political competence to influence the political process. External efficacy, on the other hand, is related to citizens' assessments of how responsive the political system is to their policy positions and interests. One aspect of output support is measured by responses to questions about the ability of the system to produce different policies depending on who is in government.

Based on a dimensional analysis of political support items in the CSES module we have selected variables that tap distinct dimensions of political support (unfortunately, CSES does not ask questions that measure internal efficacy). The first is a question of regime performance based on a question

Table 14.1. Classification of political institutions

	Constitutional system	Years since last regime transition	Electoral system Type	Electoral system Gallaghers disprop. index	Freedom House (mean)	Gross domestic product	Gini	Intensity of ethnic conflict
Belgium	Parliamentary	98	PR: list	4.18	44.8	22.75	25.0	70
Denmark	Parliamentary	83	PR: list	0.56	49.0	23.69	24.7	10
Germany	Parliamentary	49	PR: mixed member, MMP	4.19	42.0	21.26	28.1	20
The Netherlands	Parliamentary	81	PR: list	1.87	49.0	21.11	31.5	15
Norway	Parliamentary	98	PR: list	3.80	49.0	24.45	25.2	10
Spain 1996	Parliamentary	20	PR: list	5.98	44.8	15.93	32.5	40
Spain 2000	Parliamentary	20	PR: list	4.82	42.0	15.93	32.5	40
Sweden	Parliamentary	81	PR: list	2.08	49.0	19.79	25.0	15
Switzerland	Presidential	98	PR: list	5.61	49.0	25.24	36.1	45
United Kingdom	Parliamentary	98	Plurality, SMD	16.80	42.0	20.73	32.6	30
Belarus	Presidential	2	Majority[a]	N.A	4.0	4.85	21.6	5
Czech Republic	Parliamentary	5	PR: list	9.02	39.6	10.51	26.6	15
Hungary	Parliamentary	8	Mixed: MMM	8.31	42.0	7.20	27.9	10
Lithuania	Premier-presidential	7	Majority[a]	14.90[a]	39.2	4.22	33.6	30
Poland	Premier-presidential	7	PR: list	13.12	38.4	6.52	27.2	5
Romania	Premier-presidential	2	PR: list	6.48	6.0	4.31	25.5	30
Russia 1999	Premier-presidential	7	Mixed, MMM	9.63	19.2	4.37	31.0	60
Russia 2000	Premier-presidential	7	Majority[a]	9.63[a]	17.5	4.37	31.0	60
Slovenia	Parliamentary with president	7	PR: list	8.06	40.8	11.80	29.2	10
Ukraine	President-parliamentary	7	Mixed, MMM	16.97	19.2	2.19	25.7	30
Canada	Parliamentary	98	Plurality, SMD	13.26	49.0	22.48	25.6	50
United States	Presidential	98	Plurality, SMD	3.85	49.0	29.01	40.1	40
Mexico 1997	Presidential	4	Mixed	6.63	17.6	8.37	50.3	50
Mexico 2000	Presidential	4	Mixed	4.44	19.3	8.37	50.3	50

Chile	Presidential	8	Majority[a]	8.90[a]	34.8	12.73	56.5	10
Peru	President-parliamentary	4	Majority[a]	9.37[a]	13.4	4.68	44.9	80
Australia	Parliamentary	97	Majority preference, SMD	11.62	49.0	20.21	33.7	10
New Zealand	Parliamentary	98	PR: mixed member, MMM	5.09	49.0	17.41	35.9	23
Israel	Parliamentary	49	PR: list	2.33	35.6	18.15	35.5	120
Japan	Parliamentary	46	Mixed	13.22	39.6	24.07	35.0	5
Korea	Presidential	50	Mixed	8.85	36.0	13.59	33.4	0
Thailand	Parliamentary	6	Mixed, MMM	N.A.	28.0	6.69	46.2	15

Note: [a]Presidential election, Gallaghers index is calculated on the basis of the nearest parliamentary election. *Constitutional system:* the variable has five values, ranging from "pure" presidential systems (value 1) to "pure" parliamentary systems (5). *Regime transition:* the longer since last regime transformation. *Gallaghers disprop. index:* Gallagher's least square disproportionality index: the higher the value, the more disproportional the system. *Freedom House:* the index represents the product of Freedom House political rights and civil liberty for a five-year average before and including the election year. Freedom House ranges from 1 (lowest) to 49 (highest). *Gross domestic product:* gross domestic product per capita in US $ (purchasing parity power). *Gini:* is measuring economic inequality. Gini ranges from 0 (perfectly egalitarian) to 100 (perfectly unequal). *Intensity of ethnic conflict:* the higher the value, the higher the intensity of ethnic conflict.

of satisfaction with the way democracy works. The second measure is an external efficacy index based on two questions that ask if political parties and members of parliament (or similar institutions) care what ordinary people think. The third is a statement if it makes a difference who is in power. Note that we have reversed the scales (where appropriate) so that high numbers always indicate high support. The questions are listed in the appendix to this chapter.

Previous empirical research has investigated if political support is linked to institutions but has not considered if the impact varies across dimensions of support. In our review of the literature we noted a major ambiguity about the impact of accountability and representation. Some scholars argue that citizens would be better served by political institutions that maximize accountability, while others contend that institutions that are strong on representation would yield more favorable support ratings from citizens. One problem of testing the contradictory predictions is, as noted above, that variables of representation and accountability are negatively correlated.

Three of the institutional variables tap directly into the distinction between representation and accountability: type of executive, type of electoral system, and degree of disproportionality. Basically we argue that it is an open question whether institutions that are high on accountability or high on representation will lead to a greater satisfaction with the political process. If concerns for the representation of group interests and policy positions across the political spectrum weigh heavily in the minds of citizens, democratic satisfaction should be stronger in parliamentary systems than in presidential systems and in proportional systems as compared to majoritarian systems. If accountability is the most important criterion in the minds of voters, the opposite should be true.

For external efficacy the expectation is that the representational qualities of the system will be more important than accountability since external efficacy is a measure of how responsive the system is to input from citizens. For this dimension we expect that support levels should be higher in institutions that maximize representation (parliamentarism, PR, high proportionality). For output support we expect that accountability is more critical than representation, and we expect that support on this dimension should be higher in presidential systems, systems with majoritarian voting, and in systems with strong disproportionality.

For the level of political rights and civil liberties in society, the relationship to the three support variables poses some intriguing problems. We could see level of rights as an indicator of how strongly democracy is rooted in society. In this case we expect that deep democracy (strong rights and liberties) would contribute to satisfaction with democracy, stimulate beliefs in the responsiveness of the system (external efficacy), and possibly also make citizens aware of differences in considering alternatives. The effect of institutionalization of democracy on political support attitudes may, however, not be this straightforward when we take into account that new democracies, which often have less than perfect scores on political rights, will be quite distinct from nondemocratic systems that preceded democracy in these countries (Listhaug and Ringdal 2004). If citizens' evaluations of the new, imperfect democratic system, draw strongly on experiences with the past system, evaluations of the current system measured by efficacy and how much it matters who is in power might be more positive than if we considered the present only.

A test for institutional effects should be estimated in a model that includes a broad range of factors that influence political support levels. The CSES data allow us to include a number of the most important explanatory factors. In line with the research review above we expect that those who vote for the winning parties will show higher support than those who vote for the losers. This mechanism is one example of many possible operationalizations of the partisan- or policy-distance hypotheses (Listhaug 1995; Miller and Listhaug 1990, 1998).

The data include two performance measures, evaluation of the current state of the economy and assessment of whether the economy has improved over the last months. We expect that positive evaluations will have a positive impact on support. The statistical control for economy is important as we expect that the state of the economy will vary across institutions. This might especially be the case for age of democracy and for political rights. Many of the new democracies in Eastern Europe have suffered economic hardships in the process of implementing market reforms in their economies, and it is important to control for economic variables before we conclude anything about the impact of institutions.

Political parties provide citizens with linkages to the political system in the way of supplying information, stimulating political interest, and opening up pathways of political participation. We expect that those who identify with a political party will be more likely to express high support. The exception would be for those who identify with protest or anti-system parties (Miller and Listhaug 1990), but these are most likely to be a small minority in most countries. Recently, Paskeviciute and Anderson (2003) have demonstrated that supporters with different goals vary in levels of support for the political system. More specifically they demonstrate that supporters of office-seeking parties have the highest levels of political support.

We include a set of demographic variables in the model: gender, age, and education. We expect that the effects of demographic variables on political support in general will be weak. The theoretical justification for including such variables in the model rests on the argument that membership in demographic groups will be a weak indicator of political system distance. If the political interests of a group, that is, women or the elderly, are not adequately represented, we might expect such groups to have lower support levels than those whose interests are better taken care of by the political system. The resource aspect of group membership is especially relevant for education as we see this as an important cognitive resource that could have a positive impact on efficacy. In contrast to this it is not obvious how education could impact on support for regime processes and assessment of who is in power (Listhaug 1995; Listhaug and Wiberg 1995).

Finally, we add three macro-variables: gross domestic product (GDP), level of inequality measured by the Gini coefficient, and the degree of ethnic conflict within the country. The expectations for these variables are straightforward. We expect rich countries to have higher political support than poor countries while inequality and ethnic conflicts will weaken political support levels.

Empirical Results: An Overview

Table 14.2 gives a first overview of the results for the three support measures. There is considerable variation among the countries. Satisfaction with the democratic process is high in Norway (90 percent), Denmark (89 percent), and the Netherlands (88 percent), and low in Ukraine (9 percent), Russia (16 and 20 percent), and Lithuania (35 percent). External efficacy is high in Denmark (52 percent), Norway (45 percent), Romania (44 percent) and the Netherlands and Switzerland (43 percent) and low in Korea (16 percent), Lithuania and Australia (22 percent), and Japan (23 percent). Assessments that it makes a difference who is in power show high support in the Czech Republic (87 percent), Ukraine (86 percent), and Russia (85 percent), and low in Japan (44 percent), Chile (51 percent), and Canada (56 percent). These numbers, and a review of the complete distributions, show quite irregular and inconsistent patterns across the

Table 14.2. Percent indicating high level of political support by country

	Satisfied with democratic process, percent "satisfied"	Efficacy, percent "high efficacy"	Who's in power can make a difference, percent "can make a difference"
Belgium	62	31	58[a]
Denmark	89	52	69
Germany	68	24	65
The Netherlands	88	43	83
Norway	90	45	78
Spain 1996	63	36	76
Spain 2000	86	36	74
Sweden	71	26	76
Switzerland	75	43	72
United Kingdom	76	31	62
Belarus	47	31	84
Czech Republic	61	30	87
Hungary	42	37	70
Lithuania	35	22	77
Poland	63	24	77
Romania	44	44	81
Russia 1999	20	29	85
Russia 2000	16	NA	NA
Slovenia	32	35	85
Ukraine	9	41	86
Canada	73	25	56
United States	81	36	65
Mexico 1997	42	NA	70
Mexico 2000	64	30	70
Chile	NA	33	51
Peru	NA	31	76
Australia	78	22	68
New Zealand	69	27	75
Israel	53	33	83
Japan	64	23	44
Korea	41	16	59
Thailand	77	37	62

Note: *Satisfied with democratic process*: combining "very satisfied" and "fairly satisfied." *Efficacy*: additive index of "political parties care what ordinary people think" and "members of Parliament know what ordinary people think," but reversed so that high values indicate high support. The four highest values of the resulting index are coded high efficacy. *Who's in power*: values 1 and 2 are coded "who's in power can make a difference."
[a]The index is in the opposite direction in the Wallonian data set, and has been reversed.

dimensions. The distribution also suggests that explanations might have different weight for the three support variables.

Multivariate Analysis

When combining individual and aggregate level data we need to address the question of appropriate sample size. Although the number of individual cases is relatively large (N = ca. 50,000), the number of countries is much smaller (N = ca. 30). However, information about a specific country's electoral system is assigned to each and every respondent from that country. This means that the number of cases for the aggregate data is greatly inflated. Thus, standard errors for electoral system variables are deflated, making standard tests of statistical significance of estimates unreliable. In order to remedy the problem, we use robust OLS-estimation, adjusting for country clustering. This procedure does not affect the estimates of the regression coefficients, but the significance tests are more reliable (Moulton 1986, 1987, 1990).

We have excluded some of the countries from the models due to missing data and we have estimated missing data for other units to save cases for analysis (see footnotes to tables for detailed information).

For satisfaction with the way democracy works the results in Table 14.3 show that institutional variables have no significant effects. In some contrast to the meager findings for institutions we observe support for the hypotheses about the effect of two macro-variables. Satisfaction with how democracy works is higher in richer societies and lower in countries with ethnic conflicts. The effects of voting for the winning party, party identification, and economic evaluations are all in the expected direction. The impact of satisfaction with the current state of the economy is especially strong with a beta of 0.31. The demographic control variables have no impact on satisfaction with the democratic process.

Table 14.4 sums up the multivariate analysis for efficacy. None of the coefficients for institutions are statistically significant. For some of the other variables we find the same effects as in the model for satisfaction with the democratic process. Positive economic evaluations of the economy produce high efficacy, and voting for the winners and identifying with a party have positive effects on efficacy. In addition, education is positively related to efficacy.

In contrast to efficacy, where we expected that concerns for the representative function of the system should be dominant, we expect that accountability moves to the forefront in voters' considerations about whether it makes a difference who is in power. This leads us to expect that voters see clearer differences in power between competing alternatives in presidential and mixed systems than in parliamentary system. Likewise, disproportional systems would be more likely to produce majority governments that can implement distinct policies, and we would expect that voters who live in disproportional systems will have a stronger inclination

Table 14.3. Satisfaction with democratic process

	B	Beta
Constitutional system	.02	.05
Gallaghers disprop. Index	−.00	−.02
Freedom House, mean	−.00	−.02
GDP	.01*	.13*
Gini	.01	.08
Degree of ethnic conflict	−.00*	−.08*
Voted for "the winning party"	.09*	.05*
State of the economy	.25*	.31*
Economy improved	.08*	.10*
Party identification	.11*	.07*
Sex	.00	.00
Age 30 and under	.03	.01
Age over 50	−.02	−.01
Education	.01	.01
Constant	1.06	
Adjusted R^2	.21	

Entries are OLS-coefficients with robust standard errors (N = 49,199, number of country observations = 28)

Note: * $p < 0.05$. Chile, Peru, Ukraine, and Thailand are excluded from the regression analysis due to missing data. Belarus, Lithuania, and Russia (2000) lack information on Gallagher since data are from a presidential election. For Lithuania and Russia values on Gallagher are estimated from the nearest parliamentary election, and for Belarus we have used the value for majoritarian systems (13.26). Australia lacks data on "the state of the economy." Australian respondents are given the average value for old democracies (3.36) on this variable.

The dependent variable has four values: 1–4, where 4 is high satisfaction (see appendix to this chapter for questionnaire).

Coding of independent variables: *Constitutional system*: the variable has five values, ranging from "pure" presidential systems (value 1) to "pure" parliamentary systems (5). *Regime transition*: the higher the value, the longer since last regime transition. *Gallagher*: the higher the value, the more disproportional the system. *Freedom House*: Freedom House combined index, five-year average before and including the election year. *GDP*: the higher the value, the higher the gross domestic product. *Gini*: ranges from 0 (perfectly egalitarian) to 100 (perfectly unequal). *Degree of ethnic conflict*: the higher the value, the higher the degree of conflict. *"Winning party"*: voted for the winning party 1, else 0. *State of the economy*: high values—the economy is good. *Economy improved*: high values: the economy has improved the last 12 months. *Party identification*: identifies with a party 1, no identification 0. *Sex*: men 1, women 0. *Age 30 and under* 1, other 0. *Age over 50*: 1, other 0. *Education*: nine categories ranging from no education (=0) to completed university level (=8).

to say that who is in power makes a difference. The regression coefficient for the executive is not significant, while the impact of proportionality goes in the opposite direction of the hypothesis (Table 14.5). There is a relatively strong negative effect of economic level measured by GDP (beta −.20)—voters in poorer countries are more likely to agree that who is in power can make a difference. The effects of economic evaluations are positive, but much weaker than in the models for democratic support

Table 14.4. Political system efficacy

	B	Beta
Constitutional system	−.01	−.01
Gallaghers disprop. index	−.02	−.05
Freedom House, mean	−.01	−.06
GDP	.00	.01
Gini	−.01	−.04
Degree of ethnic conflict	−.00	−.01
Voted for "the winning party"	.23	.05*
State of the economy	.36	.18*
Economy improved	.20	.09*
Party identification	.46	.11*
Sex	.01	.00
Age 30 and under	.06	.01
Age over 50	−.06	−.02
Education	.05	.04*
Constant	3.57	
Adjusted R^2	.08	

Entries are OLS-coefficients with robust standard errors (N = 47,850, number of country observations = 28).

Note: *p < 0.05. Mexico (1997), Peru, Russia (2000), Ukraine and Thailand are excluded from the regression analysis due to missing data. For Lithuania and Russia values on Gallagher are estimated from the nearest parliamentary election, and for Belarus we have used the value for majoritarian systems (13.26). Australia lacks data on "the state of the economy." Australian respondents are given the average value for old democracies (3.36) on this variable. The dependent variable is the efficacy index where high value is high efficacy (see appendix to this chapter for questionnaire). Coding of independent variables: *Constitutional system*: the variable has five values, ranging from "pure" presidential systems (value 1) to "pure" parliamentary systems (5). *Regime transition*: the higher the value, the longer since last regime transition. *Gallagher*: the higher the value, the more disproportional the system. *Freedom House*: Freedom House combined index, five-year average before and including the election year. *GDP*: the higher the value, the higher the gross domestic product. *Gini*: ranges from 0 (perfectly egalitarian) to 100 (perfectly unequal). *Degree of ethnic conflict*: the higher the value, the higher the degree of conflict. *"Winning party"*: voted for the winning party 1, else 0. *State of the economy*: high values—the economy is good. *Economy improved*: high values—the economy has improved in the last 12 months. *Party identification*: identifies with a party 1, no identification 0. *Sex*: men 1, women 0. *Age 30 and under* 1, other 0. *Age over 50*: 1, other 0. *Education*: nine categories ranging from no education (= 0) to completed university level (= 8).

and efficacy—which makes sense, as it is not obvious that performance evaluations would be equally relevant for evaluations of differences by who is in power.

The strong impact of party identification (beta = 0.15) is quite interesting as we expect that those who identify with a party are more likely to see important differences between government alternatives than are those who are not involved with parties. The demographic variables have weak effects—the most important is that education leads to a somewhat clearer emphasis on differences.

Table 14.5. Who is in power can make a difference

	B	Beta
Constitutional system	−.02	−.03
Gallaghers disprop. index	−.02	−.07*
Freedom House, mean	.00	.02
GDP	−.03	−.20*
Gini	−.01	−.07
Degree of ethnic conflict	.00	.02
Voted for "the winning party"	.22	.09*
State of the economy	.09	.07*
Economy improved	.06	.05*
Party identification	.39	.15*
Sex	.05	.02*
Age 30 and under	.08	.03
Age over 50	.00	.00
Education	.02	.04*
Constant	4.03	
Adjusted R^2	.07	

Entries are OLS-coefficients with robust standard errors. ($N = 50,731$, number of country observations = 29).

Note: $^* p < 0.05$. Russia (2000), Ukraine and Thailand are excluded from the regression analysis due to missing data. Belarus, Lithuania, and Chile lack data on Gallagher since data were collected in a presidential election. For Lithuania and Chile values on Gallagher are estimated from the nearest parliamentary election, and for Belarus we have used the value for majoritarian systems (13.26). Australia lacks data on "the state of the economy." Australian respondents are given the average value for old democracies (3.36) on this variable. The dependent variable is the efficacy index where high value is high efficacy (see appendix to this chapter for questionnaire). Coding of independent variables: *Constitutional system*: the variable has five values, ranging from "pure" presidential systems (value 1) to "pure" parliamentary systems (5). *Regime transition*: the higher the value, the longer since last regime transition. *Gallagher*: the higher the value, the more disproportional the system. *Freedom House*: Freedom House combined index, five-year average before and including the election year. *GDP*: the higher the value, the higher the gross domestic product. *Gini*: ranges from 0 (perfectly egalitarian) to 100 (perfectly unequal). *Degree of ethnic conflict*: the higher the value, the higher the degree of conflict. *"Winning party"*: voted for the winning party 1, else 0. *State of the economy*: high values—the economy is good. *Economy improved*: high values—the economy has improved in the last 12 months. *Party identification*: identifies with a party 1, no identification 0. *Sex*: men 1, women 0. *Age 30 and under* 1, other 0. *Age over 50*: 1, other 0. *Education*: nine categories ranging from no education (= 0) to completed university level (= 8).

Conclusion

Recent scholarship in political science has attempted to demonstrate how political institutions influence citizens' beliefs in government. The review of these studies shows that there is considerable ambiguity in the hypotheses that are used to guide empirical research. Much of the problem is created by the fact that accountability and representation are properties that should be maximized simultaneously if systems want to have high political support. Since institutions that score high on one of these variables are low on the other, it is impossible to predict how familiar types of institutions (classified by executive structure and proportionality of the electoral system) will affect support. While this may be the case for assessments of how democracy works, we propose that some forms of political support might be more dependent on either accountability or representation. We hypothesize that efficacy, which denotes voters' evaluations of the system's ability to respond to policy concerns, would be more positive in systems that maximize representation, while agreement with a statement which says that it matters who is in power, would be higher in systems that maximize accountability.

The tests of these expectations produce meager empirical results. We are not able to demonstrate clear effects of institutional choices on political support. Norris (2001) is slightly more positive as she gives majoritarian systems the edge, although her conclusion may be located in the same ballpark as ours when we consider that she uses an early version of CSES data, and a somewhat different statistical model.

For two of the macro-variables, the GDP of a country and the intensity of ethnic conflict, we find the expected relationship with support for how democracy works positive for GDP and negative for ethnic conflict. Ethnic conflict is often linked to conflicts between regions in a country. We have pursued this question of analysis by aggregating the data with regions as units, but without finding strong relationships between the variables in the model and the support variables.

The lack of empirical effects of conventional electoral institutions on attitudes stands in some contrast to recent scholarship that shows that direct democracy has a positive effect on citizen attitudes in similar or related areas. Bowler and Donovan (2002) find that citizens who are most frequently exposed to initiatives in US states have higher levels of internal and external efficacy than citizens who are less frequently exposed to direct democracy. In a cross-regional analysis of Swiss cantons, Frey and Stutzer (2000) find that happiness is positively affected by the prevalence of initiatives and referendums as well as local autonomy of the cantons. They attribute these effects to political outcomes closer to voters' preferences, and to procedural utility of possibilities for political participation.

The findings that the institution of the referendum, as well as the possibility that we have not chosen the appropriate model specifications linking institutional variables and political support, ensure that the pursuit of research which seeks to establish links between macro-institutions and mass political behavior is still worthwhile.

Appendix

Political support items

Values are reversed (if necessary) in the empirical analysis. High values indicate support.

Q1. On the whole, are you very satisfied, fairly satisfied, not very satisfied, or not at all satisfied with the way democracy works in [country]?

1 Very satisfied
2 Fairly satisfied
3 Not very satisfied
4 Not at all satisfied
8 Don't know

Q4. Some people say that political parties in [country] care what ordinary people think. Others say that political parties in [country] don't care what ordinary people think. Using the scale on this card (where ONE means that political parties care about what ordinary people think, and FIVE means that they don't care what ordinary people think), where would you place yourself?

1 Political parties in [country] care what ordinary people think.
2
3
4
5 Political parties in [country] don't care what ordinary people think.
8 Don't know

Q11. Some people say that members of [Congress/Parliament] know what ordinary people think. Others say that members of [Congress/Parliament] don't know much about what ordinary people think. Using the scale on this card (where ONE means that the members of [Congress/Parliament] know what ordinary people think, and FIVE means that the members of [Congress/Parliament] don't know much about what ordinary people think), where would you place yourself?

1 Members of [Congress/Parliament] KNOW what ordinary people think.
2
3
4
5 Members of [Congress/Parliament] DON'T KNOW what ordinary people think.
8 Don't know

Q13. Some people say it makes a difference who is in power. Others say that it doesn't make a difference who is in power. Using the scale on this card (where ONE means that it makes a difference who is in power and FIVE means that is doesn't make a difference who is in power), where would you place yourself?

1 It makes a difference who is in power.
2
3
4
5 It doesn't make a difference who is in power.
8 Don't know

Note

1. Earlier versions of this chapter were presented at the conference on The Comparative Study of Electoral Systems, WZB, Berlin, February 21–14, 2002, and at the XVIII International Political Science Association World Congress, Quebec City, August 1–5, 2000. CSES data from ICORE are made available from the CSES secretariat at the University of Michigan. We appreciate helpful comments from Jacques Thomassen, Hans-Dieter Klingemann, Kristen Ringdal, and participants at the two meetings.

15

Effectiveness and Political Support in Old and New Democracies

Jacques Thomassen and Henk van der Kolk

The Vulnerability of New Democracies

Establishing a democracy is one thing, maintaining a stable democratic regime is another. In the current "third wave of democratization," many new democratic regimes have succeeded nondemocratic regimes (Doorenspleet 2001; Huntington 1991). Most of the old regimes could only prolong their life by suppressing people and relying on violence as an instrument to enforce compliance with the rules and policies of the government. The new democratic regimes almost by definition cannot rely on force, but depend on political support for their survival. Political support, therefore, is a necessary condition for the stability and survival of new democracies.

As we will argue in more detail in later sections of this chapter, a major source of political support is the extent to which a regime matches the norms and values of citizens (the moral dimension of support), and the extent to which it is able to provide the essential outputs as they are seen by important groups in society (the instrumental dimension of support). Since people in nondemocratic states were not socialized into democratic norms and values, the moral dimension of support is probably not well established in new democracies. Also, since new democracies are likely to have inherited a bankrupt economic system, the ineffectiveness of which more often than not will be the very cause of the breakdown of the former regime, their ability to provide the essential outputs will be severely limited. As a consequence, the *level* of political support will probably be lower in new than in old democracies (Tóka 1995: 356).

But, as will be argued in this chapter, it is not only the *level* of political support which may differ between old and newly established democracies. We also expect that political support in newly established democracies will depend on people's satisfaction with the day-to-day output of the political system—more so than in old democracies. In old democracies, both the moral and the instrumental dimension of political support become more or less generalized. The moral dimension will be deeply rooted in the political culture, whereas instrumental support will have cumulated over the years. Even when the output of the system is temporally failing, people will realize either from their own observation or from socialization, that *in the long run* the performance of the political system will be satisfactory. This buffer of generalized instrumental support, or *trust*, means that citizens' support for the democratic regime will hardly be shaken by a temporary output failure.

New democracies, however, are troubled by the fact that their citizens by definition do not have long-term experience with the regime. Therefore, they have not been able to develop generalized instrumental support or trust in the democratic regime. Moreover, socialization of trust in the new democratic regime is absent. The absence of trust means that it cannot serve as a buffer, smoothing the possible effect of satisfaction with day-to-day outputs on satisfaction with the democratic regime. Therefore, we expect that the effect of people's perception of the effectiveness of the political system to provide day-to-day outputs on satisfaction with democracy will be stronger in new than in old democracies.

It is the purpose of this chapter to test this hypothesis regarding the relationship between specific support for government policy and satisfaction with the democratic system. Before we can test this hypothesis, however, we should refine our argument and clarify the main concepts.

Legitimacy and Effectiveness

A classic contribution to the relevant literature is Lipset's (1959; 1966) exposé on the significance of "effectiveness" and "legitimacy" for the stability of democracy. Lipset defines legitimacy as "the capacity of the system to engender and maintain the belief that the existing political institutions are the most appropriate ones for the society" (1966: 64). In this sense it is a characteristic of the "system," but based upon the beliefs of citizens. According to Lipset groups regard a political system as legitimate or illegitimate according to the extent to which the values

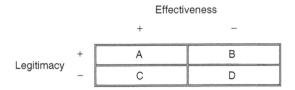

Effectiveness

Figure 15.1. Effectiveness and legitimacy (Lipset 1966: 81)

of the political system fit with their own. This is very similar to Easton's concept of legitimacy. He defines it as

> the conviction on the part of the member that it is right to and proper for him to accept and obey the authorities and to abide by the requirements of the regime. It reflects the fact that in some vague or explicit way he sees these objects as conforming to his own moral principles, his own sense of what is right and proper in the political sphere. (Easton 1965: 278)

Effectiveness in Lipset's vocabulary refers to "actual performance, the extent to which the system satisfies the basic functions of government as most of the population and such powerful groups within it as big business or the armed forces see them" (Lipset 1966: 77). Thus, effectiveness is not related to values or moral principles, but to instrumental orientations.

Both legitimacy and effectiveness are supposed to have an impact on stability, but independently of each other (see Figure 15.1). A system that is both effective and legitimate will be highly stable, whereas systems that are neither are by definition unstable and break down, unless they are dictatorships maintaining themselves by force.

Lipset uses this scheme to explain why during the economic crisis of the 1920s and 1930s some countries like Austria, Germany, and Spain gave in to a totalitarian or authoritarian regime whereas other West European democracies that were hit equally hard by the crisis did not. Lipset's explanation is that the democratic system in the first group of countries at first was effective, satisfying the basic functions of government, but not legitimate (cell C). When these systems lost their effectiveness as well (and moved to cell D), there was nothing that could prevent their breakdown. At the same time, the legitimacy of the other democracies in Western Europe formed a strong enough buffer to prevent their breakdown. As long as people tend to see the system as legitimate, a temporary breakdown of effectiveness will not cause a decline in support for the regime and regime stability. However, if the system is seen as illegitimate,

335

Types of support	Sources of support	Objects of support	
		Regime	Authorities
Diffuse	Norms and values	Legitimacy of regime	Legitimacy of authorities
	Generalized utility	Trust in regime	Trust in authorities
Specific	Short-term utility		Satisfaction with day-to-day output

Figure 15.2. Objects, types, and sources of support

a breakdown of the effectiveness of the system will cause a breakdown in support, and indirectly a breakdown of the political system.

Sources of Political Support

In Lipset's theoretical framework the distinction between moral and instrumental orientations, legitimacy versus effectiveness, is essential for our understanding of the stability of democratic systems. The less a system is sustained by people's moral orientations, the more sensitive its stability is for fluctuations in its effectiveness. This analysis is an important first step in the development of our argument why the effect of effectiveness of the political system in newly established democracies should be stronger than in older democracies.

However, in order to develop our argument further, we should make a distinction within the concept of instrumental orientations. The conceptual framework as originally developed by Easton and expanded and clarified by others (a.o. Dalton 1999; Fuchs 1989) enables us to do so. Essential for Easton's conceptual framework is the distinction between *objects* and *types* of support (Easton 1965, 1975). Both these distinctions, inasmuch as they are relevant, are presented in Figure 15.2.[1] At least as important for our purposes is a third distinction, between two different sources of support, *moral orientations*, which refer to norms and values, and *instrumental orientations*, which refer to perceived utility.

In the previous section we have argued why this distinction is important for our understanding of the relationship between effectiveness and support for the democratic system in new and old democracies. Equally important is the distinction between the two sorts of instrumental orientations.

Satisfaction with day-to-day output refers to the short-term responses of citizens to the policy performance of the government. Of course, policy dissatisfaction in itself is not a threat to democracy. One of the essential characteristics of democracy is that people have the opportunity to express and enforce their dissatisfaction with specific policies by voting the responsible politicians and the government out of office. Dahl (1966: xvii) once called "The system of managing the major political conflicts of a society by allowing one or more opposition parties to compete with the governing parties for votes in elections and in parliament one of the greatest and most unexpected social discoveries that man has ever stumbled upon." It is such an important discovery because it enables the people to replace a government they no longer support within the framework of the existing political institutions. The regular alternation of government and opposition only confirms the working of the democratic system. In established democracies this interplay of government and opposition has become a self-evident aspect of political life. Therefore, in established democracies there is no reason to expect that the poor performance of an incumbent government would affect the support for the political regime. A temporarily poor policy performance will not jeopardize the continuity of established democracies because they can rely on a reservoir of *diffuse support*, that is, support that by definition does not depend on people's judgment of day-to-day politics. Diffuse support forms a reservoir of favorable attitudes or good will that helps members to accept or tolerate outputs to which they are opposed or the effect of which they see as damaging to their wants. It consists of a reserve of support that enables a system to weather the many storms when outputs cannot be balanced off against inputs of demands (Easton 1965: 273).

In addition to legitimacy we are interested in the kind of diffuse support that (in contrast to legitimacy) is based on an assessment of the utility of political authorities and the political regime, on instrumental orientations. The peculiar characteristic of this assessment is that it is not conditional upon specific returns at any moment. It still depends on output satisfaction, but in contrast to specific support these assessments do not depend on the day-to-day performance of the authorities and the regime but on the assessment of their effectiveness over a longer period of time. Just like legitimacy it helps the political system to survive periods of poor policy performance because the knowledge that the system can do better and has done better in the past is stored in the collective memory of the people. Easton calls this form of diffuse support *trust in the authorities* and *trust in the regime,* respectively. A spillover from dissatisfaction with day-to-day policy output to trust in authorities might occur because of a persistent output failure. In that case people might not just blame the politicians and party or coalition of parties in power but lose their trust in politicians as a species. This will almost certainly infect the trust in political institutions as well. But in the short run trust will serve as a buffer preventing dissatisfaction with day-to-day output from having much of a direct effect on people's evaluation of the democratic system.

The consequence of this argument is that we can expect that in established democracies trust—just like legitimacy—will have a moderating effect on the relationship between satisfaction with day-to-day output and people's evaluation of the democratic system.

Diffuse Support in Old and New Democracies

In the previous section we have argued that the two forms of diffuse support, legitimacy and trust, will have a moderating effect on the relationship between satisfaction with day-to-day output and satisfaction with the democratic regime. If we can assume that either legitimacy or trust, or both, are structurally lower in new than in old democracies, the relationship between satisfaction with day-to-day output on the one hand and satisfaction with democracy on the other will be stronger in new than in old democracies. How plausible is this assumption?

With respect to generalized utility or trust, it is true by definition that compared to established democracies new democracies have hardly had the opportunity to build up this reservoir of goodwill as a result of a continuous high performance in the past.

With regard to legitimacy the evidence seems to be mixed. Following Easton and Lipset, legitimacy is also determined by the extent to which the political system conforms to people's norms and values. According to one school of thought it is very unlikely that in new democracies, in particular in the emerging democracies in East and Central Europe, the norms and values of citizens can serve as a source of support for the democratic regime. People's norms and values are developed and internalized as part of the socialization process in their youth. In established democracies citizens almost automatically are socialized in democratic norms and values. But in countries where a democratic regime recently replaced a nondemocratic system, most people were socialized in the nondemocratic norms and values of the old regime. Therefore, it is highly unlikely that legitimacy will be high shortly after the transition to the new regime (Fuchs and Roller 1998; Tóka 1995).

However, the validity of the traditional argument that democratic norms and values will only gradually become part of people's belief systems has become a matter of dispute. It was shown before that people in new democracies start out with a high level of support for democratic norms and values (Klingemann 1999; Mishler and Rose 1994, 1999; Weil 1989). This is probably due to two factors. First, in the global village that the world has gradually become the development of people's value orientations no longer exclusively depend on processes of socialization within their own country. More and more the whole world has become a relevant frame of reference. In that sense it is related to a possible second factor. Even if it might be somewhat exaggerated to claim the end of history, Fukuyama (1989, 1992) might have a point in arguing that after the breakdown of most communist regimes the ideology of liberal democracy as a principle of government has no serious rival anymore. As a consequence the principles of democracy as an ideal form of government are hardly contested even when people have their doubts about the effectiveness of the democratic regime in their own country.

Despite the reservation regarding legitimacy, we expect diffuse support to be lower in new democracies than in old established democracies. However, we will not test this assumption, but rather focus on its consequences.

The Effect of Effectiveness

The remaining part of this chapter is built on the assumption that diffuse support is lower in new democracies than in old democracies. What consequences will this have? Turning back to Lipset's scheme, if legitimacy is high, a short-term decline of effectiveness will not cause instability. However, if legitimacy is low, a decline of effectiveness may cause a decline in stability.

Our analysis differs somewhat from Lipset's. First, in the previous sections we have refined Lipset's argument by adding trust to legitimacy as a second dimension of diffuse support. We expect that the relationship

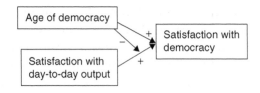

Figure 15.3. Central hypotheses

between effectiveness and instability will differ between countries according to their level of diffuse support. Second, our research focuses not primarily on stability as a dependent variable, but on the intervening processes at the micro-level which might explain a possible relationship between effectiveness and stability. It is hard to see how a lack of effectiveness might lead to instability unless this lack of effectiveness is perceived by the people and translated into dissatisfaction with the democratic system. Therefore, in our analysis satisfaction with democracy will be the main dependent variable.

We expect satisfaction with the democratic regime in new democracies to be lower than in old democracies (*hypothesis 1*). More importantly, however, we also expect the *relationship* between people's perception of effectiveness, that is, their evaluation of day-to-day output, and satisfaction with the democratic system to be stronger in new than in old democracies (*hypothesis 2*). In statistical terms, we expect the regression line, representing the effect of output satisfaction on satisfaction with democracy to be steeper and the constant to be smaller in new than in old democracies (see Figure 15.3).

Data

To test these hypotheses we use data collected in the context of the CSES project (Module 1). In order to correct for different sampling probabilities (household size, sometimes region or size of the municipality), we use some of the weights available.[2] In the overall analysis, size of samples is standardized while in the separate country analyses it is not. Because we are interested in the difference between new and old democracies, we split the German sample into two separate samples, the first one containing voters from West Germany and the second one voters from the former GDR.

The extensive literature on the conceptual status of the different aspects of support has led to an equally voluminous literature on how these aspects should be operationalized. For the purpose of this chapter it is not very useful to dwell upon this literature extensively. The following question in the CSES survey is used as an indicator of political support at the level we need: "On the whole, are you very satisfied, fairly satisfied, not very satisfied, or not at all satisfied with the way democracy works in [country]?" This question clearly asks for a general evaluation of the performance of democratic institutions.

Now that we have operationalized our dependent variable as satisfaction with the way democracy works, we still need to come to a better understanding and operationalization of our independent variable, the *perception of the effectiveness of government*. According to Lipset (1966: 77) "Effectiveness means actual performance, the extent to which the system satisfies the basic functions of government as most of the population and such powerful groups within it as big business or the armed forces see them." That effectiveness in the context of our research question should refer to what people consider as "basic functions of government" is almost self-evident. Therefore, a comprehensive analysis of the relationship between effectiveness and satisfaction with democracy ideally should start with an assessment of what people consider as "the basic functions of government."

However, none of the studies on the relationship between effectiveness and legitimacy of which we are aware of starts with this logical first step. In most studies the researchers themselves fill in what these functions are. Lipset is only one of a great many scholars who implicitly or explicitly tends to see economic well-being as the most relevant basic function of government: "In the modern world, such effectiveness means primarily constant economic development" (1966: 70). We will follow this tradition by operationalizing performance as economic performance. Economic performance as such can best be measured with objective indicators. However, if we want to understand the relationship between economic performance and satisfaction with democracy we will have to rely on people's perception of economic performance. Without a perceptual translation at the individual level it would be hard to understand how a relationship between economic performance and satisfaction with democracy could come about. Therefore, we will restrict ourselves to perceived economic performance.

A final relevant decision is whether it is the level of economic performance or the change in economic performance which matters most.

Both aspects may be ascribed to performance of a new government. However, as we explained before, the low level of economic development in new democracies is often inherited from the old regime. The new regime can hardly be blamed for it. Therefore we expect short-term changes in economic performance to be more relevant. We will rely mainly on perceived economic growth as an indicator of economic performance. The measure of subjective economic performance used as an operationalization of the perception of economic growth, or at least of the dynamics of the economy is: "Would you say that over the past twelve months, the state of the economy in [country] has gotten better, stayed about the same, or gotten worse? (if 'gotten better'): Would you say much better or somewhat better? (if 'gotten worse'): Would you say much worse or somewhat worse?"[3]

The age of a democracy was measured using the operationalization developed by Doorenspleet (2001) based on both universal suffrage and competitiveness of the political system. We reduced this measure to two broad categories: old (before 1950) and new democracies (democratized after 1989). One country in the CSES data set was given an intermediary position (Spain).[4]

Analysis

Table 15.1 presents some basic facts of the countries in our study. The countries are ranked according to the age of their democracy. This ranking makes it immediately clear that the level of satisfaction with democracy indeed varies with the age of democracy (hypothesis 1). In the older democracies the average satisfaction is substantially higher than in new democracies.

If we look at the percentage of the electorate satisfied with democracy, the differences are even more pronounced. In old democracies, without a single exception, a majority of the electorate is satisfied. In only four of the 12 new democracies can such a majority be found. This is not to say that in each and every case satisfaction in old democracies is higher than in new ones. The Polish electorate, for example, seems to be equally satisfied with Polish democracy as the Japanese electorate is satisfied with theirs. But the general pattern is that satisfaction with democracy in new democracies is lower than it is in old democracies.

However, the most important question from the perspective of this chapter is to what extent the effect of people's perception of the state

Table 15.1. Basic figures per country (26 countries)

Country	Democracy		Economy	Support		
	Introd.	Age	Percent positive	Mean[a]	Percent positive	Rank order
Australia	<1945	Old	16	3.0	77	4
Belgium	<1945	Old	31	2.6	57	15
Canada	<1945	Old	21	2.9	74	8
Denmark	<1945	Old	40	3.1	88	2
The Netherlands	<1945	Old	40	3.0	75	6
New Zealand	<1945	Old	31	2.7	62	13
Norway	<1945	Old	47	3.2	90	1
Sweden	<1945	Old	38	2.8	62	12
Switzerland	<1945	Old	51	2.8	75	5
United Kingdom	<1945	Old	38	2.9	74	7
United States	<1945	Old	26	3.1	79	3
Japan	1947	Old	21	2.6	55	17
Israel	1948	Old	25	2.7	52	19
Germany (West)	1949	Old	27	2.7	69	11
Spain	1978	Med	29	2.9	73	10
Czech Republic	1990	New	21	2.6	58	14
Germany (East)	1990	New	15	2.6	56	16
Hungary	1990	New	28	2.3	42	22
Korea (South)	1988	New	24	2.4	37	23
Lithuania	1992	New	25	2.4	32	24
Poland	1990	New	16	2.6	54	18
Romania	1990	New	12	2.5	43	21
Russia	1991	New	31	2.0	14	26
Slovenia	1991	New	54	2.2	30	25
Taiwan	1991	New	13	2.8	47	20
Thailand	1988	New	15	3.0	73	9
Ukraine	1991	New	4	1.6	8	27

Note: *Democracy introduced in:* based upon the measurement of minimal democracy (Doorenspleet 2001). Of the CSES countries we left Belarus out because it cannot be classified as a democracy (classified as not free by Freedom House). Mexico was left out because of its restricted democratic practice (Doorenspleet 2001; Vanhanen 1997). Peru was left out because of the *autogolpe* by Fujimori in 1992. Hong Kong was left out because it is not an independent state and has never been a democracy. Chile was left out because of missing data. *Age of democracy:* a threefold classification of democracies based on the previous variable. *Economy improved?* Mean score on a CSES question having five categories (see text). *Satisfied:* Mean score on a CSES question with four categories (see text), the higher the score, the higher the level of satisfaction. *% satisfied:* Percentage answering affirmative to a CSES question about satisfaction with democracy (see text).
[a] The mean on a 4-point scale, running from 1 (not at all satisfied) to 4 (very satisfied).

of the economy on their satisfaction with democracy is stronger in new than in established democracies. In Table 15.2 this effect at the individual level is presented for each country separately. The main hypothesis seems to be supported by these data. In general, the effect of the perception of economic performance on satisfaction with democracy is stronger in new democracies than in the other two groups of countries.

Table 15.2. The effect of perceived improvement of the economy on satisfaction with the democratic process in one's own country (26 countries)

Country	Age	Const.	Improve			Rank order effect
			B	S.E.	Beta	
Australia	Old	2.86	0.07	0.02	0.09	3
Belgium	Old	2.20	0.11	0.02	0.12	9
Canada	Old	1.95	0.27	0.02	0.31	23
Denmark	Old	2.94	0.06	0.02	0.06	2
Germany (West)	Old	2.21	0.17	0.03	0.21	13
Israel	Old	2.41	0.09	0.03	0.11	8
Japan	Old	2.31	0.10	0.03	0.10	5
The Netherlands	Old	2.71	0.08	0.02	0.11	7
New Zealand	Old	2.05	0.23	0.03	0.28	19
Norway	Old	2.91	0.07	0.02	0.10	4
Sweden	Old	2.47	0.09	0.02	0.14	10
Switzerland	Old	2.48	0.09	0.01	0.15	11
United Kingdom	Old	2.09	0.25	0.02	0.29	20
United States	Old	2.47	0.18	0.03	0.19	12
Spain	Med	2.06	0.27	0.02	0.32	25
Czech Republic	New	1.60	0.34	0.02	0.50	27
Germany (East)	New	1.97	0.21	0.03	0.23	17
Hungary	New	1.39	0.31	0.02	0.41	26
Korea (South)	New	1.87	0.17	0.02	0.23	15
Lithuania	New	1.41	0.31	0.03	0.30	22
Poland	New	2.04	0.20	0.02	0.22	14
Romania	New	1.89	0.24	0.03	0.23	16
Russia	New	1.40	0.19	0.02	0.26	18
Slovenia	New	1.22	0.38	0.03	0.31	24
Taiwan	New	2.56	0.09	0.03	0.10	6
Thailand	New	2.94	0.00	0.02	0.01 n.s.	1
Ukraine	New	1.15	0.21	0.02	0.29	21

Note: n.s. Not significant at the 0.01 level.

Finally, we performed a regression analysis on the combined dataset in order to assess the effect of subjective economic performance on satisfaction with democracy. The results of this analysis (all 26 countries excluding Spain) are summarized in Table 15.3 and graphically presented in Figure 15.4. Figure 15.4 nicely shows that both our hypotheses are corroborated. First, the regression line for old democracies starts and remains above the line for new democracies, meaning that the level of satisfaction with democracy is higher in old than in new democracies (*hypothesis 1*). Second, the regression line for new democracies is steeper than for old democracies, showing the predicted stronger effect in the first group of countries (*hypothesis 2*). However, we should not overinterpret our findings with respect to the second hypothesis. First, although statistically significant, the difference in effect between the two groups of countries is quite small. Second, as it turns out, satisfaction with the state of the

Table 15.3. Satisfaction in new, medium aged, and old democracies[a]

	B	S.E.	Beta
Constant	2.60	0.02	
Age (new)	−0.54	0.02	−0.33
Economy improved	0.12	0.01	0.15
Interaction effect	0.08	0.01	0.10
Adjusted R^2	0.12		
N (weighted)	47,552		

[a]Linear regression model, estimated by OLS survey data from 25 countries, all countries weighted as having the same number of respondents.

economy does have an effect on satisfaction with democracy, not only in new democracies but in old democracies as well. Although our argument does not necessarily exclude this, it at least would suggest that in old democracies satisfaction with democracy is more or less immune from short-term fluctuations in economic performance. Obviously, it is not.

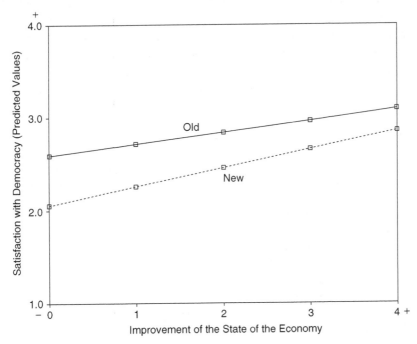

Figure 15.4. The effect of satisfaction with democracy and the state of the economy in old and new democracies on a 4-point scale, where "Improvement of the state of economy" is 0 = gotten much worse; 4 = gotten much better, and "Satisfaction with democracy" is 1 = not at all satisfied; 4 = very satisfied.

Conclusion

In this chapter we tested the classic notion that the support for the democratic system in newly established democracies is more sensitive to fluctuations in the effectiveness of the system than in old and well-established democracies. The argument behind this notion is that young democracies have not yet been able to build up a reservoir of goodwill that might help them to survive shorter periods of time in which they cannot meet the expectations of their citizens.

We found some evidence supporting this notion. The effect of people's perception of the state of the economy on their satisfaction with democracy is indeed stronger in new than in old democracies. Therefore, support for democracy in new democracies seems to be somewhat more vulnerable to economic performance than in established democracies.

However, the differences we found between old and new democracies in this respect are quite small. This is partly due to the fact that dissatisfaction with the effectiveness of the political system seems to affect old democracies more than we expected. Moreover, we had to restrict our analysis to economic performance whereas it is self-evident but often overlooked that satisfaction with democracy will most likely also depend on the overall democratic performance of the regime. CSES Module 1, however, does not allow us to follow up these considerations empirically.

Notes

1. This figure is based on the conceptual analysis by Fuchs (1989: 18, 26). The political community as a third object of support was left out here, because it is not relevant for this analysis.
2. Canada (CA97WT1), the Netherlands (DTCHWT2), Japan (Japanwt), New Zealand (NZWT), Russia (RU00_WGT), and Switzerland (SWISSWT). For the other countries either no weight variables were available, or the weight variables were not (only) based on different sampling probabilities.
3. According to the CSES codebook, the questions have been combined in the Japanese questionnaire.
4. See also Przeworski et al. (2000) for a somewhat different classification of regime transitions.

APPENDIX 1

Final Report of the 1995–6 Planning Committee

The Comparative Study of Electoral Systems: Final Report of the 1995–6 Planning Committee

February 3, 1996

Members of the Planning Committee

Rita Bajarunieni (Lithuania)
John Curtice (Great Britain)
Juan Diez Nicolas (Spain)
Oscar Hernandez (Costa Rica)
Sören Holmberg (Sweden)
Hans-Dieter Klingemann (Germany)

Marta Lagos (Chile)
Felipe B. Miranda (Philippines)
Yoshitaka Nishizawa (Japan)
Steven J. Rosenstone (United States)
Jacques Thomassen (The Netherlands)
Gábor Tóka (Hungary)

Consultants to the Planning Committee

Gary Cox (University of California, San Diego)
Ekkehard Mochmann (Zentralarchiv für empirische Sozialforschung)
Richard Rockwell (Interuniversity Consortium for Political and Social Research)
Herman Schmitt (European Election Study)
W. Phillips Shively (University of Minnesota)

CSES Secretariat

Center for Political Studies, Institute for Social Research, Ann Arbor, Michigan, 48106-1248, USA
Fax: 313-764-3341
Telephone: 313-764-5494
E-mail: cses@umich.edu
WWW: http://www.umich.edu/~cses
FTP: ftp.nes.isr.umich.edu

The Comparative Study of Electoral Systems (CSES) is a collaborative program of cross-national research among election studies conducted in over 50 consolidated and emerging democracies. The goal of this collaboration is to illuminate how the institutions that govern the conduct of elections constrain the beliefs and behaviors of citizens to condition the nature and quality of democratic choice as expressed through popular elections. By coordinating the collection of electoral data across polities, the Comparative Study of Electoral Systems strives to advance the understanding of enduring and fundamental debates about electoral behavior in a way not possible through the secondary analysis of existing data. Social scientists from around the world have collaborated to specify the research agenda, the study design, and the micro- and macro-level data that indigenous teams of researchers will collect within each polity.

Organizational Structure of the Comparative Study of Electoral Systems

Study design: The Comparative Study of Electoral Systems focuses on the nature of electoral choice in democratic polities (consolidated democracies, those undergoing democratic transitions, and those recovering from democratic breakdown). Beginning in 1996, collaborators will include in their national election studies a module of common questionnaire content. The module contains 16 questions (running about 10 minutes in length) and will be asked in its entirety in a postelection survey. Collaborators will also provide macro-level data as well as data on the background (demographic) characteristics of respondents, coded to be agreed upon standards. Collaborators shall aspire to a set of scientific standards concerning sample quality, study administration, and data quality.

Study planning: Collaborators have participated broadly in setting the study's substantive agenda, in specifying the questionnaire module, and in specifying the demographic and macro-level data to be collected (see section "The Study Planning Process" below). The Planning Committee has drawn upon the advice offered by colleagues at every stage of the planning process.

Data collection: In each democracy, between 1996 and 1999, indigenous teams of researchers conducted a national election survey that included a common module of questions and demographic variables. Each team was responsible for securing funding to finance its national data collection, though the Planning Committee made efforts to identify sources of support that subvented the costs of individual or multiple data collections. Teams of researchers collected macro-level data, and additional macro-data were collected by collaborators within each country.

Data archiving and dissemination: Each collaborator shall deposit his data and accompanying documentation in a central archive in a timely fashion. Micro- and macro-level data from all polities will be merged into a single, cross-national data set. Data will be placed in the public domain as quickly as possible.

The future: We envision that the CSES will be an ongoing program of research. This report summarizes agreements reached concerning this initial collaboration. Planning for the next round of collaboration will begin in 1997 (see section "Future Rounds of Collaboration" below). The second and subsequent rounds may focus on a subset of the themes covered in the first collaboration, or may turn to a new set of themes.

The Study Planning Process

Initial stimulus paper: In March 1994, the International Committee for Research into Elections and Representative Democracy (ICORE) circulated to directors of election studies around the world a stimulus paper (The Comparative Study of Electoral Systems) that identified several themes around which collaborative data collection might be organized, sketched a study design, and suggested how the planning process might unfold.[1] A Steering Committee (composed of Thomassen, Rosenstone, Klingemann, and Curtice) invited colleagues to comment on the paper and to participate in an initial planning conference scheduled for August 20–21, 1994, in Berlin at the Wissenschaftszentrum Berlin für Sozialforschung. Eighty-five social scientists responded with comments and suggestions that were summarized in a second document, "Comments on The Comparative Study of Electoral Systems."

1994 Berlin Planning Conference: Social scientists representing 31 democracies, participated in the Berlin Planning Conference where discussion focused on the need for comparative electoral data, the intellectual agenda, strategies for coordinating micro- and macro-level data collections, the lessons that should be learned from previous cross-national efforts, and how the project's planning activities should unfold. Collaborators in Berlin charged an International Planning Committee composed of social scientists from Eastern and Western Europe, Asia, and the Americas with several tasks: formulate recommendations on the content of a questionnaire module, identify background data to be collected, specify macro-level data to be gathered, draft aspired to standards of data quality, and establish norms and standards for archiving and disseminating the data. Following the Berlin Conference, the Planning Committee communicated with collaborators around the world to solicit their advice on these topics.

January 1995 Meeting of the Planning Committee: The American National Election Study (which was asked to serve a two-year term as Secretariat for the project) organized the January 1995 meeting of the Planning Committee with financial support from the US National Science Foundation. Two weeks before the meeting, the Secretariat distributed to members of the Planning Committee 200 pages of written materials relevant to the Committee's deliberations. The documents studied by each committee member included: correspondence to the Planning Committee, a detailed summary of the suggestions that social scientists had made

349

concerning the project, a listing of background and attitude measures currently employed in various cross-national opinion surveys, a collection of the alternative wordings employed in various national election study questionnaires for the items being considered for inclusion in the CSES survey module, and detailed summaries of the advice that prospective collaborators had offered concerning the project.

The Planning Committee met on January 26–28, 1995, in Ann Arbor, Michigan, at the Institute for Social Research. Every member of the Planning Committee participated in discussion and debated over the merits of the various organizing themes around which the data collaboration might focus. Everyone strove to understand the different points of view that colleagues from the diverse political cultures brought to the table. Every member of the Planning Committee contributed to each aspect of this report. The Committee worked to formulate a set of recommendations that would significantly advance our substantive and theoretical understanding of electoral politics, that would be feasible to implement, and that would win the endorsement of collaborators around the world.

By the end of the first day of discussion, the Committee reached consensus on the priorities and concepts that should be at the heart of the collaboration (these are spelled out in more detail below). On the second day, the Committee divided itself into subcommittees to work on the various planning tasks. Bajarunieni, Curtice, Holmberg, Lagos, and Nishizawa were responsible for crafting the initial draft of the questionnaire module. Responsibility for formulating the initial recommendations on the background (demographic) data were taken up by Cox, Diez Nicolas, Hernandez, Klingemann, Miranda, Mochmann, Schmitt, and Tóka. Cox, Hernandez, Klingemann, Miranda, Schmitt, Thomassen, and Shively worked as a subcommittee to delineate the initial recommendations on the macrolevel data that should be collected while Diez Nicholas, Mochmann, Rockwell, and Rosenstone drafted recommendations on the archiving and dissemination of the data. Cox, Klingemann, Rockwell, Rosenstone, Thomassen, Shively, and Tóka formulated the initial recommendations on aspired to standards for data quality and comparability. On the third day, the entire Planning Committee reconvened to discuss in detail each subcommittee report. Following that discussion, each report was rewritten to reflect the consensus. The Secretariat assembled an initial draft of the current document which the Planning Committee reviewed. Proposed changes were discussed through an email conference and by fax.

March 1995 Preliminary Recommendations of the Planning Committee: The CSES Secretariat circulated the Planning Committee's Preliminary Recommendations to nearly 200 social scientists in 63 polities. Collaborators provided comments and suggestions which led to revisions to the proposed questionnaire module.

Pilot work: During the summer and fall of 1995, collaborators in seven polities (Belarus, Costa Rica, Hungary, The Netherlands, Romania, Spain, and the United States) conducted pilot studies to test the questionnaire module. Several items were also piloted in the Philippines, Japan, and South Africa. In November 1995, these collaborators prepared pilot study reports that evaluated the performance of the questionnaire module. The Secretariat circulated these reports to members of the CSES Planning Committee and to collaborators who attended the Budapest Planning Conference in December 1995. The Secretariat also prepared a compilation of the Pilot Studies Reports Prepared to the Comparative Study of Electoral Systems which integrated into a single document the pilot analysis carried out in five of the polities. The Secretariat circulated this compilation to all collaborators.

December 1995 Budapest Planning Conference: All collaborators were invited to participate in the Second Planning Conference that was held at the Central European University in Budapest, Hungary, on December 8–9, 1995. Forty colleagues from 29 polities attended the Conference. Colleagues participating in the Conference engaged in a detailed review of every aspect of the study plan: the questionnaire module, the measurement of voter turnout and vote choice, the background data to be collected, the aspired to standards for data quality, the norms regarding the archiving and disseminating of the data, and the macro-level data to be collected.

Preparation of final report: In the weeks following the Budapest meeting, the Planning Committee codified the consensus reached in Budapest. The Secretariat prepared the Final Report of the Planning Committee and accompanying study materials which the Planning Committee reviewed before the materials were sent to all collaborators.

Theoretical and Substantive Focus

Guiding Principles

1. The power of the study design rests on its ability to make theoretical and substantive advances in our understanding of how variation in the institutional arrangements that govern the conduct of elections affect the nature and quality of democratic choice. Through comparative analysis, where citizens are observed in different settings, the impact of institutions can be established. We have given priority to concepts that help us understand the impact that macro-level properties of the political system have on political evaluations, turnout, and electoral choice.

2. The timing of the data collection (in the weeks following national elections) provides a unique opportunity to study the nature and quality of electoral choice in ways not possible through existing data or through other cross-national projects that collect their data outside of the context of national elections. Our recommendations try to exploit this opportunity.

3. The power of this project lies not only in its ability to tackle new questions, but in its capacity to shed new light on longstanding and important debates about electoral behavior.

4. We acknowledge that other projects are also collecting cross-national survey data (such as the ISSP and the World Values Survey) and see little reason to spend the scarce 10 minutes of questionnaire time replicating those efforts.

5. The questionnaire module should cover a small number of themes well rather than many topics thinly. We selected items that will serve multiple research purposes. We recognize the inherent tension here, but have tried to strike a delicate balance between items that will help test specific theoretical propositions and those that will support a variety of inquiries.

6. We have given priority to substantive and theoretical questions that can be addressed within the constraints of a cross-sectional study design.

7. We have tried to formulate recommendations that are feasible for collaborators to implement.

With these principles in mind, we recommend that the initial round of collaboration in the Comparative Study of Electoral Systems focus on three general themes: the impact of electoral institutions on citizens' political cognition and behavior (parliamentary versus presidential systems of government, the electoral rules that govern the casting and counting of ballots, and political parties), the nature of political and social cleavages and alignments, and the evaluation of democratic institutions and processes.

The Impact of Electoral Institutions

If elections are central to democracy, then how should a society organize the institutions that govern the processes by which government leaders are selected? The possibilities are legion. Should there be a parliament or a president and a legislature? Should legislative seats be allocated in proportion to the popular vote, or should the winner in each district take all? Should there be two or three or a dozen political parties? Should the parties be strong or weak, centralized or decentralized, ideologically unified or diverse?

These are not merely abstract considerations that busy social scientists as they ponder the meaning of democracy. They are the pragmatic issues that policymakers, constitutional experts, and the founders of democratic systems have debated, increasingly so over the last two decades, as new democracies have emerged in southern and eastern Europe, in Latin America, East Asia, and Africa. Such debates are heated because the political stakes could not be higher: institutional arrangements influence the distribution of power, shape the ways that politicians pursue their goals, and constrain the ability of citizens to control their government.

How the institutional arrangements that govern elections affect voters in a particular polity can only be appreciated through comparative research. Without variation in institutional arrangements, it is impossible to learn how any particular configuration of institutions structures votes, public opinion, and political participation. We need to examine how otherwise comparable citizens behave when operating under different institutional constraints—and this requires that we move beyond a single nation's borders.

Parliamentarism vs. Presidentialism

Parliamentary and presidential governments are the two principal models by which democracies are organized. And although the debate between parliamentarism and presidentialism is a familiar one (see, e.g., Lijphart 1992; Linz 1990; Mainwaring 1990; Powell 1989; Shugart and Carey 1992), many of the arguments central to this debate entail assumptions about voters: about the information that they possess, the beliefs they hold, and the considerations they bring to bear on the electoral choices they make. Such assumptions are rarely tested.

For example, if accountability makes retrospective sanctions of the executive more available in presidential than in parliamentary systems, then one should find that voters in presidential systems have greater clarity about the performance of the incumbent government and are more willing to rely on retrospective evaluations in their vote choice.

Or, to take another example, consider the charge that divided control of government obscures accountability in presidential systems. Nowhere has this claim been confronted with evidence. Do citizens living under divided government have more difficulty figuring out who is to blame than citizens living under united presidential government or parliamentary rule? Under divided control are voters less likely to rely on retrospective evaluations of the performance of the executive when casting their ballots? We simply don't know.

Do coalition governments obscure accountability and reduce the ability of the electorate to assign blame (Austen-Smith and Banks 1988, 1990; Laver and Shepsle 1990; Strom 1990)? How does a party's participation in a coalition government affect the public's evaluation of the party? Do all parties in the coalition get held equally accountable or does the size of the party or its role (share of portfolios) affect the extent of blame or credit? And, does a change in the composition of a parliamentary government during the period between elections make it more difficult for voters to know whom to blame on election day? We do not know.

Nor do we know whether accountability is undermined in presidential systems because voters give too much weight to the personal attributes of presidential candidates and too little weight to issues. Does the evidence sustain this familiar critique of presidential elections? Do the personal characteristics of party leaders play a less dominant role in parliamentary systems or do some parliamentary systems like a German type of "Kanzlerdemokratie" display effects similar to those found in presidential systems (Lijphart 1992)?

The Political Consequences of Electoral Laws

Electoral laws determine how citizens cast votes, how votes are aggregated, and how aggregated votes are converted into positions of governmental authority.

Electoral systems differ in the formula used to decide how votes are translated into legislative seats, in district magnitude and threshold, in ballot structure, and in the timing of elections. Such laws constitute a second set of institutional arrangements for cross-national study (Lijphart and Grofman 1984).

Although we know that electoral laws have profound effects on the number, size, and ideological diversity of parties, on the way in which votes get converted into legislative seats, and on the strategies that political parties pursue,[2] we do not possess, as Michael Steed (1985) has argued, knowledge of the ways in which electoral laws ultimately affect voters and their representation in government.

For example, which electoral arrangements facilitate the close connection between individuals and their representatives and which do not (Bogdanor 1985)? Just what are the circumstances under which personal ties between citizens and candidates matter to voters? How do variations in district magnitude, for instance, affect the nature of the interaction between constituents and their representatives? When electoral laws permit representatives in a multimember district to free ride on constituent services performed by their colleagues, does the propensity to engage in constituency service and develop personal relationships with constituents go down (Cain, Ferejohn, and Fiorina 1987)?

Do high district thresholds not only discourage parties from contesting seats, but do they also discourage voters from casting their ballots for small parties that hover perilously close to the threshold? How powerful are Duverger's "psychological effects" (1954) in reducing the tendency for voters to waste their vote on smaller parties that have no chance of winning seats? Is the effect really a psychological one, as Duverger posited, or does it stem from the unwillingness of parties to invest scarce resources in those districts where things seem hopeless? Although it is well understood that different voting rules offer different opportunities and incentives for strategic voting (Black 1978; Cain 1978; Johnston et al. 1992; Niemi, Whitten, and Franklin 1992), it is not at all clear whether the propensity of citizens to engage in strategic behavior varies with the occasions that electoral rules present.

These questions, which are fundamental to our understanding of the political consequences of electoral laws, deal with the impact of these laws on individual citizens: on the ways they make choices and on the relationship they establish with their representatives. They are questions that as yet have no firm answers.

Political Parties

Democracy, E.E. Schattschneider argued, is "unthinkable save in terms of the parties" (1942). Modern democratic theorists of all stripes embrace parties as institutions that organize electoral competition, aggregate disparate social interests, mediate social conflict, increase voter rationality, enlarge the electorate through mobilization, link people to their government, and constrain those in positions of power.[3] In emerging democracies, it is the political parties that play an instrumental role in consolidating the new regimes (Dix 1992; Mainwaring 1988).

But how well do political parties actually perform these functions? Electoral systems differ in conspicuous ways with respect to parties: in their number, ideological distinctiveness, and their organizational strength. Our concern is with understanding how such differences affect electoral choice and party performance.

We know much about how electoral arrangements affect the electoral styles of political parties (e.g. Katz 1980), but very little about the impact of different party systems on beliefs and behavior of ordinary people. For example, whether two-party or multiparty systems best facilitate democracy depends on how citizens think, what they know, and how they choose. Do citizens in fact have more trouble assigning blame under a multiparty than a two-party system, making accountability lower?

How does voter choice differ between two-party and multiparty systems? Do two parties really simplify the voter's task, and do many parties make things more confusing? In multiparty systems, is a citizen better able to find a party that approximates her ideal point (Huber 1993; Strom 1990)? When parties stake out ideologically distinct positions on salient issues, do citizens have an easier time perceiving where the parties stand than when party positions are muddled? As the ideological distinctiveness of parties grows, is there a parallel increase in the intensity with which mass publics hold their opinions, in the ideological coherence that underlies those opinions, or in the impact of issues on vote choice?

Does strategic voting mitigate the representational benefits claimed for multiparty systems? Under what circumstances will voters decide to throw their support to a larger party that has a chance of winning a seat? What is the impact on ordinary citizens of the parties acting strategically by entering into alliances with other parties through joint lists, list alliances, or through legislative or portfolio coalition? Do voters get confused about the position of the various parties in the coalition? Does party attachment and loyalty go down?

Parties can also be thought of as organizations, and as such, they differ enormously in structure and strength (Dix 1992; Janda 1993; Katz 1980; Mainwaring 1988; Mayhew 1986; McDonald and Ruhl 1989). In some systems, parties are strong: they control resources and nominations; there are local, regional, and national organizations; there is formal party membership; local party organizations play an important role in the social life of citizens (Banfield and Wilson 1963; Duverger 1954; Gosnell 1968; Michels 1962; Wilson 1962, 1973). In other systems, political parties are relatively weak (Mayhew 1986).

In recent decades, parties have declined as other institutions have taken over many of their traditional functions (Flanagan and Dalton 1984; Ware 1985). Interest groups press citizen concerns outside of party channels; the mass media inform and mobilize (Ranney 1983; Semetko et al. 1991; Zaller 1992); party leaders have lost their grip over the slating of candidates (Katz 1986); centralized, capital

355

intensive, professional campaign organizations have replaced decentralized, labor intensive, grassroots political organizations.

Does it matter whether parties are weak or strong? Do strong parties do a better job of educating the electorate and structuring their political outlooks than do weak parties (Kleppner 1982; McGerr 1986)? Are citizens more attached or more loyal to strong parties than to weak ones? What types of party organizations are most effective at mobilizing citizens to action and what impact does party mobilization have on citizens' political beliefs, information about politics, stands on issues, party loyalty, and likelihood of participating in politics? Does mobilization have an equalizing effect because it incorporates into electoral coalitions citizens (often the havenots) who otherwise would not take part in politics (Dahl 1966; Key 1949; Schattschneider 1942; Valen 1994)?

The Nature of Political and Social Cleavages and Alignments

Lipset and Rokkan's claim that "the party systems of the 1960s reflect, with few but significant exceptions, the cleavage structures of the 1920s" set in motion a torrent of research. The class, religious, ethnic, linguistic, and regional foundations of party alignments have all been documented, and in the beginning it appeared that in Western democracies, at least, electoral stability prevailed as Lipset and Rokkan (1967) had predicted (Alford 1967; Dix 1989; Lijphart 1979, 1980; Rose 1974; Rose and Urwin 1969, 1970).

Over the last three decades, however, electoral alignments have weakened, party strength has grown increasingly volatile, and party systems have become increasingly fragmented.[4] In Belgium, Switzerland, Canada, and Britain, for example, voters have thrown new electoral support to parties based upon linguistic and ethnic cleavages long thought to have been depoliticized. Elsewhere new parties have championed causes that cut across existing party lines: constitutional reform for Dutch Democrats, traditional morality for new Christian Democratic parties in some Scandinavian countries, tax reductions for Glistrup's party in Denmark, and civil liberties for the Italian Radicals. Electoral support for parties of the left has declined across Europe. Ecological or "green" parties have placed environmental issues on the political agenda, slowly increasing year to year their share of the popular vote (Franklin, Mackie, and Valen 1992; Kinder and Kiewiet 1989; Rose and Urwin 1990; Rudig and Franklin 1992; Kitschelt 1989; Rudig 1991). These developments have not only transformed the nature of their party systems, they have called into question the relevance of the social cleavages that had once prevailed. What is needed, is a genuinely comparative cross-national study that assesses the current state of alignments and cleavages in the face of all this social change (see Franklin et al. 1992).

What is also needed is an assessment of the impact that institutional differences across political systems have on cleavages and alignments. How do institutional structures affect the nature and intensity of social and political cleavages? Do federal systems suppress social cleavages as Chhibber and Petrocik (1989) have suggested? How well do different party systems "encapsulate conflict" by constraining social divisions (Bartolini and Mair 1990)? Do plurality systems produce more broadly based parties that discourage the kind of sectional and ideological parties (and hence intense political cleavages) that can more easily survive under proportional representation? While much is known about the relationship between short-term economic changes and electoral choice within individual countries, we know little if anything about how different electoral systems condition the likelihood that political parties will exploit or ameliorate the political conflict that emerges from moments of profound economic change.[5] The Comparative Study of Electoral Systems is uniquely poised to shed light on all of these issues.

The Evaluation of Democratic Institutions and Processes

The Comparative Study of Electoral Systems is also well positioned to advance our understanding of the ways in which citizens assess their polity's democratic institutions and processes. Given the project's general concern with electoral choice and participation, it makes sense to focus on evaluations of the electoral process and on perceptions of the performance of political parties and representatives as institutions that link citizens to government. There are several opportunities here.

First is the opportunity to monitor and understand the nature and evolution of citizen evaluation of democratic institutions. The CSES study design provides several powerful analytical strategies. Evaluations found in consolidated democracies can be compared to those that exist in regimes undergoing democratic transition. Regimes at various stages along the road to democratization consolidation can also be compared. And to the extent that our initial collaboration represents the first round of an ongoing collaborative effort, changes in the evaluations of democratic institutions and processes can be monitored over time. In doing so, we will also be able to assess whether support for democratic institutions is maintained through periods of intense political or economic conflict, economic reform, economic disruption, political scandal, and crisis.

We are also in a position to assess how differences in the institutional arrangements that govern the electoral process affect the way that citizens' evaluate democracy. What impact, if any, do institutional differences—in electoral laws, in the nature of political parties, or in the structure and longevity of the political regime—have on the way that citizens assess the performance of the electoral process, political parties, and democracy as a whole? Do some kinds of institutional arrangements produce more positive evaluations than others? For example, does citizen satisfaction with the performance of political parties increase with the number and ideological diversity of the political choices that citizens are offered?

Another line of inquiry focuses on the widely held belief that democracies are sustained by political cultures in which there is widespread approval of the fundamental institutions and process of democratic government. By aggregating citizens' evaluations of democracy and monitoring those evaluations over time, we will be in a position to assess whether democratic institutions do indeed crumble following the withdrawal of public support (Almond and Verba 1963; Easton 1965; Inglehart 1988, 1990; Muller and Seligson 1994). Just how vital is support of democratic institutions to the survival of democracy?

We are also concerned about how the opinions that citizens hold about the performance of democratic institutions and processes may influence behavior under a given set of electoral arrangements. For example, compared with the single-member district plurality system, a national party-list system offers citizens the opportunity to vote for the party rather than on the basis of local issues or the characteristics of individual candidates. Whether citizens do so or not, however, may depend on their perceptions of the effectiveness of political parties, or of the extent to which parties are willing and able to service the needs of their constituents.

Finally, evaluations of the functioning of the political system are also thought to affect both the willingness of citizens to participate in the electoral process and the kinds of parties and candidates they are willing to endorse. The core hypothesis is that disaffected citizens either abstain (or invalidate their vote where voting is compulsory) or vote for "anti-system" parties or candidates. The cross-national data that will be collected in the Comparative Study of Electoral Systems will enhance our ability to address these claims.

Questionnaire Module

Introduction

The constraint of a 10-minute module presented a formidable challenge. The Planning Committee spent a great deal of time discussing the concepts that should be given highest priority in the questionnaire. Each concept regarded as central to the study is represented by at least one question. When it made sense to do so, we adopted question formats employed in existing election studies. But, we did not feel bound to old questions, particularly questions that were developed in one context but do not travel well to other political cultures or settings. We regarded the Comparative Study of Electoral Systems as an opportunity to make a fresh start—to write questions de novo and to modify old questions as needed.

The performance and efficacy of each item across a variety of political settings was established through a series of pilot studies conducted in seven polities (described in section "The Study Planning Process" above). The results of this pilot work led to the modification of some items and the deletion of others.

The variety of institutional arrangements for voting in different countries makes it impracticable to ascertain turnout and vote choice by means of common questions in each polity. Instead, collaborators shall gather data on turnout and vote choice with questions that are most relevant to their countries' institutional setting and that these data be coded to a common set of standards (described in section "Voter Turnout and Vote Choice" below).

The questions below are organized by concept. The question number refers to the order in which the question should be asked. A mockup of the CSES questionnaire module is also provided to facilitate implementation of the questionnaire. The document, "Instructions for the Administration of each Question in the CSES Module," describes the detailed instruction concerning the implementation of each question.

Party Identification and Leader Evaluation

The Comparative Study of Electoral Systems provides a powerful opportunity for advancing our understanding of the ways in which differences in the number, ideological distinctiveness, and organizational strength of parties affects the nature of the relationship that develops between citizens and political parties.

A central theme in the literature on electoral politics has been the contrast between voting for the person versus voting on the basis of issues or party. It is often charged that in presidential systems, voters give excessive weight to the personal attributes of candidates. To assess this claim requires measures of voters' perceptions of party leaders and candidates. How do citizens evaluate the personal character of leaders and candidates and under what circumstances do these assessments affect vote choice?

Q3. Do you usually think of yourself as close to any particular political party?

- a. [if yes] Which party is that?
- b. [if more than one party mentioned or party block mentioned] Which party [in the name of block] do you feel closest to?
- c. [if no to DK or No to Q3] Do you feel yourself a little closer to one of the political parties than the others? Which party is that?
- d. Do you feel very close to this [party/party block], somewhat close, or not very close?

Q7. I'd like to know what you think about each of our political parties. After I read the name of a political party, please rate it on a scale from 0 to 10, where 0 means you strongly dislike that party and 10 means that you strongly like that party. If I come to a party you haven't heard of or you feel you do not know enough about, just say so. The first party is PARTY A.

Where would you place party A on this scale? PARTY B? PARTY C? PARTY D? PARTY E? PARTY F?

NOTE: Where possible, collaborators should ask about all parties represented or likely to be represented in the parliament (or running in the presidential contest). In circumstances where there are more than six such parties, collaborators should ask at least about the six most relevant parties. In assessing relevance, collaborators should consider likely size, likely importance in coalition formation. If parties only contest elections in part of the country, those parties need only be asked about in those parts of the country where they contest seats.

Q8. And now, using the same scale, I'd like to ask you how much you like or dislike some political leaders. Again, if I come to a leader you haven't heard of or you feel you do not know enough about, just say so. The first political leader is LEADER A.

Where would you place LEADER A on this scale? LEADER B? LEADER C? LEADER D? LEADER E? LEADER F?

NOTE: Collaborators need only ask about a minimum of one leader per party. That person should be the person who would have been expected to be the prime minister (or equivalent) should that party have gained control of the government. In circumstances where there are important candidates who are not members of a party, they should be added. In addition, collaborators shall provide information on the gender and party of the leaders.

Spatial Issue Voting: Left–Right Scale

To understand how electoral arrangements, the number of political parties, and their ideological distinctiveness affect the ease with which voters can identify the positions of parties and locate a choice close to their ideal point, requires that we measure both the voters' issue positions and their perceptions of the parties' positions as well. Such information will also make it possible to identify the political circumstances that prompt voters to act sincerely, to act strategically, to act out of ignorance, or to ignore policy and ideology altogether.

Q16. In politics people sometimes talk of left and right. Where would you place yourself on a scale from 0 to 10 where 0 means the left and 10 means the right?

Using the same scale, where would you place PARTY A? PARTY B? PARTY C? PARTY D? PARTY E? PARTY F?

NOTE: Q16 should be asked of all political parties asked about in Q7. In polities where investigators think that the left–right scale is not interpretable by respondents or does not adequately capture the principle political cleavage in the polity, collaborators should ask a supplemental question that taps the central political division (e.g. liberal/conservative). The left–right placement of self and parties appears as the last question in the CSES module. This supplemental question should be asked in addition to Q16. The supplemental question should appear elsewhere in the questionnaire and should be asked using a 0–10 scale.

Candidate Recognition and Interaction with Representatives

Q6. Do you happen to remember the name of any candidates who [ran/stood] in your [lower house primary electoral district, for example, constituency, district, riding] in the last [parliamentary/congressional] election? [IF YES: If name not volunteered) What were their names?]

NOTE: Collaborators will need to code whether the respondent correctly identified none, one, or more than one candidate. In addition, collaborations shall code the gender and party of the candidates recalled.

Election studies are motivated, in part, by an interest in the degree of communication and control that citizens exert over the leaders they elect. One line of research has examined the nature of the personal relationship that gets established between citizens and their representatives in the national legislature/parliament. The following question (along with Q6 on candidate recognition) should help us sort out how the electoral arrangements that govern the conduct of legislative/parliamentary elections affect the nature of the interaction between citizens and their representatives.

Q12. During the past 12 months, have you had any contact with [a Member of Parliament/a Member of Congress] in any way?

Retrospective Evaluation of Performance of National Economy

Elections are opportunities for citizens to endorse or repudiate the performance of the incumbent government. Measures of citizens' retrospective evaluations of the government performance will enable us to assess how electoral institutions, divided control of government, and minority governments affect the capacity of citizens to sort out who is to blame and to translate that blame into sanctions at election time. Retrospective evaluations of economic conditions also clearly affect electoral outcomes. The Comparative Study of Electoral Systems will provide an opportunity for social scientists to assess the political circumstances under which these retrospective evaluations matter most.

Q9. What do you think about the state of the economy these days in [country]? Would you say that the state of the economy is very good, good, neither good nor bad, bad, or very bad?

Q10. Would you say that over the past 12 months the state of the economy in [country] has gotten better, stayed about the same, or gotten worse? [IF BETTER: Would you say much better or somewhat better?] [IF WORSE: Would you say much worse or somewhat worse?]

Evaluation of Democratic Institutions and Process

The CSES questionnaire module will also focus on how citizens evaluate democratic institutions and processes. The concern here is twofold: First, provide data that will illuminate the impact of institutional arrangements, regime type, and the nature of political and economic conflict on the ways in which citizens evaluate democracy. Second, identify what impact, if any, those evaluations have on electoral participation, vote choice, and regime stability. These concerns, alone, could sustain an ambitious program of research. Given the constraints, the questionnaire module will focus on two sets of evaluations.

Evaluations of the electoral process: whether it is open, fair, and whether voting and election outcomes matter.

Q15. When people are asked to express an opinion, do you believe most people in [country] usually say what they think about politics or do you believe most people usually hide what they really think about politics? Using the scale on the card (where ONE means that most people in [country] usually say what they think about politics, and FIVE means that most people usually hide what they really think), where would you place yourself?

Q2. In some countries, people believe their elections are conducted fairly. In other countries, people believe that their elections are conducted unfairly. Thinking of the last election in [country] where would you place it on this scale of one to five where ONE means that the last election was conducted fairly and FIVE means that the last election was conducted unfairly?

Q14. Some say that no matter who people vote for, it won't make any difference to what happens. Others say that who people vote for can make a difference to what happens. Using the scale on this card (where ONE means that voting won't make any difference to what happens and FIVE means that voting can make a difference), where would you place yourself?

Evaluations of the responsiveness of representatives, the performance of political parties, and of democracy in general.

Q13. Some people say it makes a difference who is in power. Others say that it doesn't make a difference who is in power. Using the scale on the card (where ONE means that makes a difference who is in power and FIVE means that it doesn't make a difference who is in power), where would you place yourself?

Q11. Some people say that members of [Congress/Parliament] know what ordinary people think. Others say that members of [Congress/Parliament] don't know much about what ordinary people think. Using the scale on the card (where ONE means that the members of [Congress/Parliament] know what ordinary people think, and FIVE means that the members of [Congress/Parliament] don't know much about what ordinary people think), where would you place yourself?

Q4. Some people say that political parties in [country] care what ordinary people think. Others say that political parties in [country] don't care what ordinary people think. Using the scale on the card (where ONE means that political parties care about what ordinary people think, and FIVE means that they don't care what ordinary people think), where would you place yourself?

Q5. Some people say that political parties are necessary to make our political system work in [country]. Others think that political parties are not needed in [country]. Using the scale on the card (where ONE means that political parties are necessary to make our political system work, and FIVE means that political parties are not needed in [country]), where would you place yourself?

Q1. On the whole, are you very satisfied, fairly satisfied, not very satisfied, or not at all satisfied with the way democracy works in [country]?

Voter Turnout and Vote Choice

The variety of institutional arrangements for voting in different polities makes it impracticable that vote choice and turnout can be ascertained by means of a common question in each country. For example, in Great Britain or Canada, one can ask which party a respondent voted for. But this makes no sense in countries such as the United States, Russia, Germany, or Luxembourg where respondents can vote for more than one party at the same election. In countries that make use of runoff elections, collaborators should provide data on turnout and vote choice for the first ballot. In addition to the first ballot data, individual collaborators may chose to collect survey data for turnout and vote choice for the runoff election. Collaborators are thus requested to derive the following standardized information using questions which are most relevant to their country's institutional circumstances.

1. Whether or not respondent cast a ballot (regardless of whether or not the ballot was valid)

1. Respondent cast a ballot
2. Respondent did not cast a ballot
3. Don't know
9. No answer

In formulating the question used to ascertain this information, collaborators should try to ask the question in a way that minimizes the overreporting of voter turnout where this is known to be a problem.

2. Which party the respondent voted for (or the party affiliation of the candidate for whom he/she voted in all relevant national elections [e.g. President, Senate, and House in the United States, or first and second vote in Germany]).

Coding conventions to be established. This will include a provision to record separately those voters who disclose that they cast an invalid ballot (null/blank/discarded vote).

The following should be noted:

(a) In those countries where voters are required to express an ordinal preference (e.g. Ireland and Malta), collaborators should record the first preference. (b) In those countries where voters can distribute their votes across parties in an individual election (e.g. Finland and Luxembourg), collaborators should record the party for whom the voter casts the majority of his/her votes.

3. In those countries where voters have the option of voting for individual candidates, but are not obliged to do so, collaborators should code whether the

voter exercised that option. [Examples: (1) In the old Italian system, voters cast votes for party lists first; they then had the option to cast "preference votes" for individual candidates on that list. Here we would want to know whether the respondent cast preference votes or not. (2) In Brazil, voters can either cast a vote for a party list of candidates, or a vote for an individual candidate. Here we would want to know whether the respondent cast a candidate vote or a list vote.]

1. Voter exercised candidate preference
2. Voter did not exercise candidate preference
3. Voter did not vote
4. Voter did not have opportunity to exercise candidate preference
8. Don t know
9. No answer

4. Recall of vote choice and vote turnout in the national election prior to the one just conducted.

Coding conventions should follow (1), (2), and (3) above.

Background (Demographic) Variables

Collaborators shall also provide data on background (demographic) characteristics of respondents, coded to be agreed upon set of standards.

Principles: 1. There is great international variation in the ways that collaborators will go about soliciting information on the background characteristics of their respondents. The objective here is not standardization of the way collaborators ask these background questions, but instead, standardization to a common, cross-national scheme for coding each variable. This standardization should avoid unnecessarily fine distinctions that will be difficult for collaborators to implement.

2. Where feasible, we have followed the standardized coding that other cross-national surveys (such as the Eurobarometers, the ISSP, and the World Values Survey) have employed.

3. Each collaborator shall ask respondents the questions needed to elicit the data required to construct the background variable. The questions needed to elicit the background information may be asked either before or after the questionnaire module and may be asked in any order. The only circumstance under which a question does not need to be asked is when there is no variation among respondents in the population (e.g. a collaborator would not need to ask about language spoken if everyone in the polity speaks the same one). If a collaborator does not ask a question because there is no variation in the response, the variable should nevertheless be appropriately coded in the data set delivered.

The document, "Coding Conventions for Background (Demographic) Variables," provides the detailed standards to which the background variables should be coded. Examples of questions that might be used to elicit the background information are provided in the document, "Sample Questions for Eliciting Background Data."

Background (demographic) variables to be collected and coded:

1. Age
2. Sex
3. Education
4. Marital status
5. Respondent member of a union
6. Someone else in household other than respondent is a member of a union
7. Current employment status
8. Main occupation of respondent
9. Private or public employment of respondent
10. Industrial sector of respondent
11. Occupation of chief wage earner or spouse
12. Household income (coded into quintiles)
13. Number of people in household
14. Number of people in household under the age of 18
15. Attendance of religious services
16. Religiosity
17. Religious denomination
18. Language usually spoken at home
19. Region of residence
20. Race of respondent
21. Ethnicity of respondent
22. Rural/urban residence
23. Political information
24. Month of interview
25. Day of interview
26. Year of interview
27. Number of days interview conducted after the election
28. Respondent's primary electoral district

Macro-Level Data

Principles Concerning the Gathering of Macro-Level Data

The analytical power of the Comparative Study of Electoral Systems depends heavily upon the availability of macro-level data on electoral laws, political parties, and other institutional arrangements.

1. We recognize that collaborators in the Comparative Study of Electoral Systems have limited resources that must be utilized judiciously, and that the quality of the macro-level data collected may vary across polities. Where possible, these macro-data should be collected and coded through a centralized process.

2. When the centralized collection of macro-level data is infeasible, each collaborator in the Comparative Study of Electoral Systems should provide macro-level data. The limited number of variables for which collaborators are being asked to provide data is identified below.

3. We do not think it is feasible to collect, at this time, data at the level of the electoral (parliamentary or congressional) district. Each collaborator, however, should identify the primary electoral district for each survey respondent. This will permit social scientists in the future to merge survey data for each polity with district-level variables not currently being collected. Where possible, a

national map of all districts should be provided to the Archives, to facilitate district identification.

4. To the extent possible, macro-level data should be those which apply at the time of the survey. However, additional data may be necessary in certain cases, particularly for nations undergoing institutional change.

5. A centralized coordinating function must also be provided, as discussed below.

Macro-Data that Collaborators Shall Provide

Macro-data shall be provided on the form entitled "CSES Macro-Level Data." These data include:

1. The names and party affiliations of all cabinet-level ministers serving at the time of the dissolution of the most recent government.

2. The collaborator's own expert judgment on which of nine ideological families each party is closest to.

3. Whether each party has formal membership in an international organization (e.g. Socialist International).

4. The collaborator's own, expert judgment of where each party should be placed on a left–right scale.

5. Age of each political party.

6. The collaborator's assessment of the five most salient factors that would help scholars unfamiliar with the polity to understand the outcome of the election (e.g. major scandals or economic events, the presence of an "independent" political actor).

7. Whether electoral alliances are permitted and if so, which ones formed in the election.

8. Where applicable, the full name and party affiliation of all presidential candidates.

9. Information on the type of political regime.

10. Information on the nature of electoral districts and the method by which votes are cast and counted.

11. Collaborators shall provide a copy of the current electoral statute governing elections to the lower house of the national legislature. (An annotated version of the statute is preferable.) Also, if the constitution contains sections relevant to the conduct of elections, collaborators shall include these as well. Complete bibliographic information on the source of the material sent is essential. If the material is available in a number of different languages, materials should be sent in the most internationally accessible language available.

12. Collaborators shall provide a copy of the party manifesto for each party.

Macro-Data That will be Gathered Centrally

Every effort is being made to gather, centrally, the remaining macro-data:

1. Institutional arrangements: A number of questions regarding the operationalization of certain measures, particularly regarding the nature of presidential versus parliamentary systems, remain unresolved at this point. We have identified several resources for assistance, including East European Constitutional Review and Professors Matthew Shugart (University of California, San Diego) and John Carey (University of Rochester). Specific variables to be collected include:

- degree of centralization vs. decentralization of the political system (i.e. federalism)
- fiscal structures of local and central budgets (as an indicator of de facto federalism)
- degree of bicameralism
- partisan control and composition of legislature (including composition of upper house)
- relative power of the two houses of the legislature (if bicameral)
- selection of the chief executive (parliamentary or presidential; type of presidential system)
- extent of presidential powers (i.e. appointment of ministers)
- term limits and qualifications for president

2. Electoral laws: Collaborators in the Comparative Study of Electoral Systems should participate in an effort led by Professor Gary Cox (University of California, San Diego) to collect annotated electoral codes for each nation. Although the collection of the codes will be undertaken by collaborators within each polity, Cox will coordinate the coding of the laws which would include the following variables:

- district magnitude
- electoral formula
- single vs. dual constituencies
- number of candidates per district
- thresholds
- number of constituencies
- closed or open list; ease with which the voter can revise or create a voter list
- possibility of electoral alliances (apparentements)
- inclusiveness of the franchise
- other provisions (such as the bonus for winners in Greece)

3. Electoral results shall be gathered at the national level for the first and subsequent rounds of voting. Data should include:

○ vote for president (where applicable)
○ vote for lower house of parliament (first and second rounds, and primary electoral district, where applicable)
○ national turnout

4. Political parties: Hans-Dieter Klingemann (Wissenschaftszentrum Berlin für Sozialforschung), whose Manifestos Research Group has devised a protocol for coding party platforms, will coordinate and lead manifesto analyses for collaborators who choose to join the manifesto studies.

5. Economic data

○ unemployment data (average for the six months before election)
○ inflation data (average for the six months before election)
○ trade/exposure to international capital
○ measures of GNP/GDP and GNP/GDP per capita (particularly change over time)
○ life expectancy
○ literacy
○ education levels

6. Other data, such as Cingranelli's data on civil rights and repression of opposition, that can be easily obtained should be coded. Other possible sources include data that Przeworski and Vanhanen have gathered.

The CSES Secretariat will try to facilitate collaborations among social scientists interested in gathering and coding the macro-economic data and macro-political data on institutional arrangements and electoral results. Because the macro-level data do not need to be in hand for several years, there is a reasonable period of time in which to carry out this data collection.

Aspired to Standards for Data Quality and Comparability

Collaborators in the Comparative Study of Electoral Systems shall adhere to the following standards of data quality:

1. Mode of interviewing: Interviews should be conducted face-to-face, unless local circumstances dictate that telephone or mail surveys will produce higher quality data.

2. Timing of interviewing: We strongly recommend that collaborators in the Comparative Study of Electoral Systems conduct their interviews in the weeks following their national election. Out of concern for data quality, data collection should be completed in as timely a fashion as possible. In the event of a runoff election, interviewing shall be conducted after the first round election. The date of interview shall be provided for each respondent.

3. Placement of module in postelection questionnaire: The questionnaire module should be asked as a single, uninterrupted block of questions. We leave it to each collaborator to select an appropriate location for the module in his national survey instrument. Collaborators should take steps to ensure that questions asked immediately prior to the questionnaire module do not contaminate the initial questions in the module. Collaborators are also free to select an appropriate place in their survey instrument to ask the turnout, vote choice, and demographic questions.

4. Population to be sampled: National samples should be drawn from all age-eligible citizens. When noncitizens (or other non-eligible respondents) are included in the samples, a variable should be provided to permit the identification of those non-eligible respondents. When a collaborator samples from those persons who appear on voter registration lists, he should quantify the estimated degree of discrepancy between this population and the population of all age-eligible citizens.

5. Sampling procedures: We strongly encourage the use of random samples, with random sampling procedures used at all stages of the sampling process. Collaborators should provide detailed documentation of their sampling practices, as described in section "Archiving and Disseminating the Data" below.

6. Sample size: We strongly recommend that no fewer than 1,000 age-eligible respondents be interviewed.

7. Interviewer training: Collaborators should pretest their survey instrument and should train interviewers in the administration of the questionnaire. The Planning Committee will provide each collaborator with documentation that clarifies the purposes and objectives of each item and with rules with respect to probing don't-know responses.

8. Field practices: Collaborators should make every effort to ensure a high response rate. Investigators should be diligent in their effort to reach respondents not interviewed on the initial contact with the household and should be diligent in their effort to convert respondents who initially refuse to participate in the study. Data on the number of contact attempts, the number of contacts with sample persons, and special persuasion or conversion efforts undertaken should be coded for each respondent.

9. Strategies for translation (and back-translation): Each collaborator should translate the questionnaire module into his or her native language(s). To ensure the equivalence of the translation, collaborators shall perform an independent retranslation of the questionnaire back into English. Collaborators engaged in translation of the questionnaire module into the same language (e.g. Spanish, French, English, German, and Portuguese) should collaborate on the translation.

Archiving and Disseminating the Data

Institutional Structure

The Comparative Study of Electoral Systems is a data collection project that includes an international team of principal investigators and international data archives. The CSES is joining forces with the Interuniversity Consortium for Political and Social Research (ICPSR) and the Zentralarchiv für empirische Sozial-forschung (ZA) to make the data produced from this project widely available to the social science community.

Institutions responsible for archiving and disseminating the data:

- ICPSR and ZA (hereafter jointly referred to as the Archives) offer to be the institutions responsible for the archiving and dissemination of the data, and they will support this activity to the extent that they have/can obtain available funding.

- The Archives will undertake this effort in cooperation with the Council of European Social Science Data Archives (CESSDA) and the International Federation of Data Organizations for the Social Sciences (IFDO).

- The Archives should participate in all planning activities of CSES, in order to coordinate the archiving and dissemination of the data. Also, the assembling of the macro-level data in a comparable fashion should involve consultation with Archives early in the planning stage.

- The Archives will strive to provide the most efficient ways to disseminate data to interested users, under the rules of IFDO and CESSDA.

Funding Strategies

Collaborators in the Comparative Study of Electoral Systems and the Archives should act in concert to pursue, simultaneously, several funding strategies:

- Investigators collaborating in the Comparative Study of Electoral Systems that obtain funding through a grant mechanism should request specific budgetary support to cover the cost of the documentation, archiving, and dissemination of data. A portion of those funds would be transmitted to the Archives for the purpose of carrying out their responsibilities, and a portion will be used by the investigator to prepare data and documentation according to agreed standards.

- The Archives and the Secretariat of the Comparative Study of Electoral Systems will provide central coordination to raise funds for collaborators who are unable to obtain the resources to cover the cost of documentation, archiving, and dissemination of data. One source might be the Intergovernmental Group of Funding Agencies (Oakley Caucus).

Depositing Data

Each collaborator shall deposit in the Archives their micro-level data (responses to the questionnaire module, data on voter turnout and vote choice, and the background variables) as well as macro-level data that were collected.

Conventions for coding the data: The CSES, in consultation with the Archives, will develop standard conventions by which each collaborator will code the data. The CSES Secretariat shall make available to each collaborator a codebook as well as SPSS and SAS control cards.

How data and documentation should be deposited: Standards will be established to guide the media, format, and method by which the data will be transmitted to the Archives.

Data quality: Collaborators are responsible for ensuring that the data provided to the Archives are in accordance with the codebook. (For example, collaborators need to clean the data to remove any wild codes.)

Deadline for deposit and dissemination of data: Data must be deposited in a timely fashion, not to exceed one year after the election date, and in accordance with a set of standards specified by the CSES. The Archives cannot guarantee that data deposited after that date will be included in the integrated data file. The Archives will make the data for a particular country available in a timely fashion, not to exceed two years after the date of the election.

Depositing Documentation

Each investigator will provide documentation for the data following archival standards as well as documentation about the sampling process, response rate, and study implementation. This documentation should be written using the Oxford English language. The CSES, in collaboration with the Archives, will develop a checklist of materials to be included with documentation, including the following information:

- investigators responsible for data collection
- fieldwork dates
- sample size
- mode of interview
- complete details of sampling procedures, including precise specification of the population from which the sample was chosen, the stages of the sampling process, method of randomization used at each stage of sampling, and replacement methods
- if the data are drawn from a panel study, description of panel attrition from previous waves

371

- response rate, with detail on efforts made to obtain a response
- information about nonresponse
- known systematic properties of sample (including bias, attrition, design effects, and percentage of the population excluded from the sampling frame)
- description of field methods, including information on the interviewers and their training
- a hard copy of the entire survey instrument and show cards, both in Oxford English and in the native language of the participating country
- language(s) of interview
- precise details on how the sample weight was constructed
- benchmark frequencies (weighted and unweighted)
- statistical data that compares the sample to the national population

Archival Functions

- The Archives will merge micro- and macro-level data from all polities into a series of cross-national data sets as elections are added. That is, the data set will be continuously updated with each new election. The Archives will organize the data sets in a way that will permit micro-level analysis, macro-level analysis, and macro–micro linkages within single countries and across countries.
- The Archives will ascertain whether the documentation provided by each collaborator is complete and whether the documentation matches the data. The Archive will consult collaborators to resolve discrepancies between the documentation and the data.
- The Archives will provide a unified set of documentation based on the Oxford English language materials provided by the investigators.
- The Archives will consult with the CSES to resolve questions that arise concerning data comparability.

Data Dissemination

- The Archives will place the data in the public domain and will make it available without restrictions to all social scientists.
- Collaborators will not have privileged access to the integrated data.
- The Archives will employ a wide range of current media, including computer network service, will be used to disseminate the data and documentation.
- The Archives will distribute the data and documentation according to agreements specified by IFDO and CESSDA.

Future Rounds of Collaboration

Although the Planning Committee's efforts have been directed to working out all the details needed to launch the CSES and this first round of collaboration that will be in place for national elections held between 1996 and 1999, the next step is to begin to think about the long-term intellectual agenda and structure of the project. Our sense is that soon after the field work for this initial cooperative effort is underway, discussion should begin on the second and subsequent rounds of collaboration. As discussed in the 1994 Berlin Planning Conference, the next round might focus on a subset of the themes covered in the first collaboration, or might well focus on an entirely different set of themes. We anticipate that a Planning Conference will be held in Seoul, Korea, in August 1997, in conjunction with the International Political Science Association (IPSA) meetings. Members of the Planning Committee will circulate a stimulus paper prior to that meeting to initiate conversation on a variety of themes that might be the focus of future rounds of collaboration. Colleagues with suggestions for themes for discussion or who would like to participate in the drafting of this stimulus paper should contact the CSES Secretariat.

Notes

1. All CSES documents are available on the CSES World Wide Web site (http://www.umich.edu/~cses) and by FTP from the American National Election Studies (NES) fileserver, or by contacting the Secretariat for the Comparative Study of Electoral Systems, Center for Political Studies, Institute for Social Research, Ann Arbor, Michigan, 48106-1248, USA. The NES server is "ftp.nes.isr.umich.edu."
2. For example, see Duverger (1954), Katz (1980), Lijphart (1984, 1990, 1994), Powell (1982, 1989), Rae (1971), Riker (1986), and Taagepera and Shugart (1989).
3. See Dahl (1966), Downs (1957), Epstein (1967), Huntington (1968), Key (1949), Lawson (1980), Sartori (1976), Schattschneider (1942), Sorauf (1976), and Eldersveld (1982).
4. Borre (1984), Clarke et al. (1980), Crewe and Denver (1985), Czudnowski (1976), Dalton (1988), Dalton, Flanagan, and Beck (1984), Dix (1984, 1989), Franklin et al. (1992), Holmberg (1994), Inglehart (1977), Klingemann and Wattenberg (1992), Maguire (1983), Mair (1983), Pedersen (1979), Percheron and Jennings (1981), Rose (1982), Sarlvik and Crewe (1983), and Wolinetz (1979, 1988).
5. Clarke and Whitely (1990), Eulau and Lewis-Beck (1985), Fiorina (1981), Hibbs (1987), Kinder and Kiewiet (1981), Lewis-Beck (1988), Norpoth, Lewis-Beck, and Lafay (1991), and Powell and Whitten (1993).

References

Alford, Robert R. (1967). "Class Voting in the Anglo-American Political Systems". In Seymour M. Lipset and Stein Rokkan (eds.). *Party Systems and Voter Alignments: Cross National Perspectives*. New York: The Free Press.

Almond, Gabriel A. and Sydney Verba (1963). *The Civic Culture: Political Attitudes and Democracy in Five Nations*. Princeton, NJ: Princeton University Press.

Austen-Smith, David and Jeffrey S. Banks (1988). "Elections, Coalitions, and Legislative Outcomes", *American Political Science Review* 82: 405–22.

——— (1990). "Stable Governments and the Allocation of Policy Portfolios", *American Political Science Review* 84: 891–906.

Banfield, Edward C. and James Q. Wilson (1963). *City Politics*. Cambridge, MA: Harvard University Press.

Bartolini, Stephano and Peter Mair (1990). *Identity, Competition, and Electoral Availability: The Stabilization of European Electorates, 1885–1985*. Cambridge: Cambridge University Press.

Black, Jerome H. (1978). "The Multicandidate Calculus of Voting: Application to Canadian Federal Elections", *American Journal of Political Science* 22: 609–38.

Bogdanor, Vernon (ed.) (1985). *Representatives of the People? Parliamentarians and Constituents in Western Democracies*. Aldershot, Hants, England: Gower Publishing Company.

Borre, Ole (1984). "Critical Electoral Change in Scandinavia". In Russell J. Dalton, Scott C. Flanigan and Paul Allen Beck (eds.). *Electoral Change in Advanced Industrial Democracies: Realignment or Dealignment?* Princeton: Princeton University Press.

Cain, Bruce E. (1978). "Strategic Voting in Britain", *American Journal of Political Science* 22: 639–55.

——— John A. Ferejohn and Morris P. Fiorina (1987). *The Personal Vote: Constituency Service and Electoral Independence*. Cambridge: Harvard University Press.

Chhibber, Pradeep K. and John R. Petrocik (1989). "The Puzzle of Indian Politics: Social Cleavages and the Indian Party System", *British Journal of Political Science* 19: 191–210.

Clarke, Harold and Paul Whitely (1990). "Perceptions of Macroeconomic Performance, Government Support and Conservative Party Strength in Britain", *European Journal of Political Research* 18: 97–120.

Clark, Harold D., Jane Jenson, Lawrence LeDuc and John Pammett (1980). *Political Choice in Canada*. Toronto: McGraw-Hill Ryerson.

Crewe, Ivor and David Denver (eds.) (1985). *Electoral Change in Western Democracies: Patterns and Sources of Electoral Volatility*. New York: St. Martin's Press.

Czudnowski, Moshe M. (1976). *Comparing Political Behavior*. Beverly Hills: Sage Publications.

Dahl, Robert A. (1966). *Political Oppositions in Western Democracies*. New Haven: Yale University Press.

Dalton, Russell J. (1988). *Citizen Politics in Western Democracies: Public Opinion and Political Parties in the United States, Great Britain, West Germany, and France.* Chatham, NJ: Chatham House Publishers.

—— Scott Flanagan and Paul Allen Beck (eds.) (1984). *Electoral Change in Advanced Industrial Democracies: Realignment or Dealignment?* Princeton: Princeton University Press.

Dix, Robert H. (1984). "Incumbency and Electoral Turnover in Latin America", *Journal of InterAmerican Studies and World Affairs* 26: 435–48.

—— (1989). "Cleavage Structures and Party Systems in Latin America", *Comparative Politics* 22: 23–38.

—— (1992). "Democratization and the Institutionalization of Latin American Political Parties", *Comparative Political Studies* 24: 488–511.

Downs, Anthony (1957). *An Economic Theory of Democracy.* New York: Harper.

Duverger, Maurice (1954). *Political Parties, Their Organization and Activity in the Modern State.* New York: Wiley.

Easton, David (1965). *A Systems Analysis of Political Life.* New York: Wiley.

Eldersveld, Samuel James (1982). *Political Parties in American Society.* New York: Basic Books.

Epstein, Leon D. (1967). *Political Parties in Western Democracies.* New York: Praeger.

Eulau, Heinz and Michael S. Lewis-Beck (eds.) (1985). *Economic Conditions and Electoral Outcomes: The United State and Western Europe.* New York: Agathon Press, Inc.

Fiorina, Morris P. (1981). *Retrospective Voting in American National Elections.* New Haven: Yale University Press.

Flanagan, Scott C. and Russell J. Dalton (1984). "Parties Under Stress: Realignment and Dealignment in Advanced Industrial Societies", *West European Politics* 7: 7–23.

Franklin, Mark, Tom Mackie, Henry Valen, et al. (1992). *Electoral Change: Responses to Evolving Social and Attitudinal Structures in Western Countries.* Cambridge: Cambridge University Press.

Gosnell, Harold F. (1968). *Machine Politics: Chicago Model*, 2nd edn. Chicago: University of Chicago Press.

Hibbs, Douglas A., Jr. (1987). *The Political Economy of Industrial Democracies.* Cambridge: Harvard University Press.

Holmberg, Soren (1994). "Party Identification Compared Across the Atlantic". In M. Kent Jennings and Thomas E. Mann (eds.). *Elections at Home and Abroad.* Ann Arbor: University of Michigan Press, 93–121.

Huber, John (1993). "Restrictive Legislative Procedures in France and the United States", *American Political Science Review* 86: 675–87.

Huntington, Samuel P. (1968). *Political Order in Changing Societies.* New Haven: Yale University Press.

Inglehart, Ronald (1977). *The Silent Revolution: Changing Values and Political Styles Among Western Publics.* Princeton: Princeton University Press.

Inglehart, Ronald (1988). "The Renaissance of Political Culture", *American Political Science Review* 82: 1203–30.

——(1990). *Culture Shift in Advanced Industrial Society*. Princeton: Princeton University Press.

Janda, Kenneth (1993). "Comparative Political Parties: Research and Theories". In Ada W. Finifter (ed.). *Political Science: The State of the Discipline II*. Washington: American Political Science Association.

Johnston, Richard, et al. (1992). *Letting the People Decide: Dynamics of a Canadian Election*. Montreal: McGill-Queens University Press.

Katz, Richard S. (1980). *A Theory of Parties and Electoral Systems*. Baltimore: John Hopkins University Press.

——(1986). "IntraParty Preference Voting". In Bernard Grofman and Arend Lijphart (eds.). *Electoral Laws and Their Political Consequences*. New York: Agathon.

Key, V. O., Jr. (1949). *Southern Politics in State and Nation*. New York: Vintage.

Kinder, Donald R. and Roderick D. Kiewiet (1981). "Sociotropic Politics: The American Case", *British Journal of Political Science* 11: 129–61.

Kitschelt, Herbert (1989). *The Logics of Party Formation: Ecological Politics in Belgium and West Germany*. Ithaca, NY: Cornell University Press.

Kleppner, Paul (1982). *Who Voted?: The Dynamics of Electoral Turnout, 1870–1980*. New York: Praeger Publishers.

Klingemann, Hans-Dieter and Martin Wattenberg (1992). "Decaying Versus Developing Party Systems: A Comparison of Party Images in the United States and West Germany", *British Journal of Political Science* 22: 131–49.

Laver, Michael and Kenneth A. Shepsle (1990). "Coalitions and Cabinet Government", *American Political Science Review* 84: 873–90.

Lawson, Kay (1980). *Political Parties and Linkage: A Comparative Perspective*. New Haven: Yale University Press.

Lewis-Beck, Michael S. (1988). *Economics and Elections: The Major Western Democracies*. Ann Arbor: University of Michigan Press.

Lijphart, Arend (1979). "Religion vs. Linguistic vs. Class Voting", *American Political Science Review* 65: 686.

——(1980). "Language, Religion, Class, and Party Choice: Belgium, Canada, Switzerland and South Africa Compared". In Richard Rose (ed.). *Electoral Participation: A Comparative Analysis*. Beverly Hills: Sage.

——(1984). *Democracies: Patterns of Majoritarian and Consensus Government in Twenty-One Countries*. New Haven: Yale University Press.

——(1990). "The Political Consequences of Electoral Laws, 1945–85", *American Political Science Review* 84: 481–96.

——(ed.) (1992). *Parliamentary versus Presidential Government*. Oxford: Oxford University Press.

——(ed.) (1994). *Electoral Systems and Party Systems: A Study of Twenty-Seven Democracies, 1945–1990*. New York. Oxford University Press.

——and Bernard Grofman (eds.) (1984). *Choosing an Electoral System: Issues and Alternatives*. New York: Praeger.

Linz, Juan J. (1990). "The Perils of Presidentialism", *Journal of Democracy* 1: 51–69.

Lipset, Seymour M. and Stein Rokkan (eds.) (1967). *Party Systems and Voter Alignments: Cross-National Perspectives*. New York: The Free Press.

McDonald, Ronald H. and J. Mark Ruh (1989). *Party Politics and Elections in Latin America*. Boulder, CO: Westview.

McGerr, Michael E. (1986). *The Decline of Popular Politics: The American North, 1865–1928*. New York: Oxford University Press.

Maguire, Maria (1983). "Is There Still Persistence? Electoral Change in Western Europe, 1948–1979". In Hans Daalder and Peter Mair (eds.). *Western European Party Systems: Continuity and Change*. Beverly Hills: Sage Publications.

Mainwaring, Scott (1988). "Political Parties and Democratization in Brazil and the Southern Cone", *Comparative Politics* 21: 91–120.

——(1990). "Presidentialism in Latin America", *Latin American Research Review* 25: 157–79.

Mair, Peter (1983). "Adaptation and Control: Towards an Understanding of Party and Party System Change". In Hans Daalder and Peter Mair (eds.). *Western European Party Systems: Continuity and Change*. Beverly Hills: Sage Publications.

Mayhew, David (1986). *Placing Parties in American Politics: Organization, Electoral Settings, and Government Activity in the Twentieth Century*. Princeton: Princeton University Press.

Michels, Robert [1911] (1962). *Political Parties: A Sociological Study of the Oligarchical Tendencies of Modern Democracy*. New York: Free Press.

Muller, Edward N. and Mitchell A. Seligson (1994). "Civic Culture and Democracy: The Question of Causal Relationships", *American Political Science Review* 88: 635–52.

Niemi, Richard G., Guy Whitten and Mark Franklin (1992). "Constituency Characteristics, Individual Characteristics and Tactical Voting in the 1987 British General Election", *British Journal of Political Science* 22: 229–54.

Norpoth, Helmut, Michael S. Lewis-Beck and Jean-Dominique Lafay (eds.) (1991). *Economics and Politics: The Calculus of Support*. Ann Arbor: University of Michigan Press.

Pedersen, Mogens N. (1979). "The Dynamics of European Party Systems: Changing Patterns of Electoral Volatility", *European Journal of Political Research* 7: 1–26.

Percheron, Annick and Jennings Kent M. (1981). "Political Continuities in French Families: A New Perspective on an Old Controversy", *Comparative Politics* 13: 421–36.

Powell, G. Bingham, Jr. (1982). *Contemporary Democracies: Participation, Stability, and Violence*. Cambridge: Harvard University Press.

——(1989). "Constitutional Design and Citizen Electoral Control", *Journal of Theoretical Politics* 1: 107–30.

Powell, G. and Guy D. Whitten (1993). "A Cross-National Analysis of Economic Voting: Taking Account of the Political Context", *American Journal of Political Science*. Forthcoming.

Przeworski, Adam and Henry Teune (1970). *The Logic of Comparative Social Inquiry*. New York: Wiley-Interscience.

Rae, Douglas (1971). *The Political Consequences of Electoral Law*. New Haven: Yale University Press.

Ranney, Austin (1983). *Channels of Power: The Impact of Television on American Politics*. New York: Basic Books.

Riker, William H. (1986). "Duverger's Law Revisited". In Bernard Grofman and Arend Lijphart (eds.). *Electoral Laws and Their Political Consequences*. New York: Agathon Press, Inc.

Rose, Richard (ed.) (1974). *Electoral Behavior: A Comparative Handbook*. New York: The Free Press.

—— (1982). *The Territorial Dimension in Politics*. Chatham, NJ: Chatham House.

—— and Derek W. Urwin (1969). "Social Cohesion, Political Parties and Strains in Regime", *Comparative Political Studies* 2: 7–67.

—— (1970). "Persistence and Change in Western Party Systems Since 1945", *Political Studies* 18: 287–319.

—— (ed.) (1990). *Green Politics One, 1990*. Edinburgh: Edinburgh University Press.

Rudig, Wolfgang (1991). "Green Party Politics Around the World". *Environment* 33: 7–9, 25–31.

—— and Mark N. Franklin (1992). "Green Prospects: The Future of Green Politics in Germany, France, and Britain". In Wolfgang Rudig (ed.). *Green Politics Two, 1991*. Edinburgh: Edinburgh University Press.

Sarlvik, Bo and Ivor Crewe (1983). *Decade of Dealignment: The Conservative Victory of 1979 and Electoral Trends in the 1970s*. Cambridge: Cambridge University Press.

Sartori, Giovanni (1976). *Parties and Party Systems: A Framework for Analysis*. New York: Cambridge University Press.

Schattschneider, E. E. (1942). *Party Government*. New York: Farrar and Rinehart.

Semetko, Holli A., Jay G. Blumer, Michael Gurevitch and David H. Weaver (1991). *The Formation of Campaign Agendas: A Comparative Analysis of Party and Media Roles in Recent American and British Elections*. Hillsdale: Lawrence Erlbaum Associates.

Shugart, Matthew Soberg and John M. Carey (1992). *Presidents and Assemblies: Constitutional Design and Electoral Dynamics*. Cambridge: Cambridge University Press.

Sorauf, Frank J. (1976). *Party Politics in America*, 3rd edn. Boston: Little, Brown.

Steed, Michael (1985). "The Constituency". In Vernon Bogdanor (ed.). *Representatives of the People: Parliamentarians and Constituents in Western Democracies*. Aldershot, Hants, England: Gower Publishing Company.

Strom, Kaare (1990). *Minority Government and Majority Rule*. New York: Cambridge University Press.

Taagepera, Rein and Matthew Soberg Shugart (1989). *Seats and Votes: The Effects and Determinants of Electoral Systems*. New Haven: Yale University Press.

Valen, Henry (1994). "List alliances: An Experiment in Political Representation". In M. Kent Jennings and Thomas E. Mann (eds.). *Elections at Home and Abroad*. Ann Arbor: University of Michigan Press, 289–321.

Ware, Alan (1985). *The Breakdown of Democratic Party Organization, 1940–1960*. New York: Oxford University Press.

Wilson, James Q. (1962). *The Amateur Democrat; Club Politics in Three Cities*. Chicago: University of Chicago Press.

—— (1973). *Political Organizations*. New York: Basic Books.

Wolinetz, Steven B. (1979). "The Transformation of Western European Party Systems Revisited", *West European Politics* 2: 7–8.

—— (1988). *Parties and Party Systems in Liberal Democracies*. London: Routledge.

Zaller, John (1992). *The Nature and Origins of Mass Opinion*. New York: Cambridge University Press.

The Micro-Level Questionnaire of Module 1

CSES Questionnaire Module 1

Module 1 is current until March 2000.
If no skip is indicated, follow with the next question.

Q1. On the whole, are you very satisfied, fairly satisfied, not very satisfied, or not at all satisfied with the way democracy works in [country]?

    1 Very satisfied
    2 Fairly satisfied
    4 Not very satisfied
    5 Not at all satisfied
    8 Don't know

Q2. (PLEASE SEE CARD 1) In some countries, people believe their elections are conducted fairly. In other countries, people believe that their elections are conducted unfairly. Thinking of the last election in [country], where would you place it on this scale of one to five where ONE means that the last election was conducted fairly and FIVE means that the last election was conducted unfairly?

    1 Last election was conducted FAIRLY.
    2
    3
    4
    5 Last election was conducted UNFAIRLY.
    8 Don't know

Q3 USED Check Point, Which version of Q3 are you administering (long or short)?

SHORT VERSION OF Q3: TO BE USED IN POLITIES WHERE NO PARTY
BLOCKS (OR ELECTION ALLIANCES) FORMED

SQ3. Do you usually think of yourself as close to any particular political party?

    1 YES
    5 NO → Skip to SQ3C
    8 Don't know → Skip to SQ3C

SQ3a. Which PARTY is that? (RECORD ALL PARTIES, response categories range from 0 to 96)

First PARTY mentioned: _____
IF ONLY ONE PARTY IS MENTIONED → SKIP TO SQ3e
Second PARTY (if volunteered): _____
IF MORE THAN ONE PARTY IS MENTIONED → SKIP TO SQ3b
Third PARTY (if volunteered): _____
IF MORE THAN ONE PARTY IS MENTIONED → SKIP TO SQ3b
98 Don't know → Skip to SQ3c

SQ3b. Which party do you feel closest to?

Party identified: _____ → Skip to SQ3e
97 No party identified → Skip to SQ4

SQ3c. Do you feel yourself a little closer to one of the political parties than the others?

1 YES
5 NO → Skip to Q4
8 Don't know → Skip to Q4

SQ3d. Which party is that?

Party identified:_____

SQ3e. Do you feel very close to this party, somewhat close, or not very close?

1 VERY CLOSE → Skip to Q4
2 SOMEWHAT CLOSE → Skip to Q4
3 NOT VERY CLOSE → Skip to Q4
8 Don't know → Skip to Q4

LONG VERSION OF Q3: TO BE USED IN POLITIES WHERE AT LEAST ONE
PARTY BLOCK (OR ELECTORAL ALLIANCE) FORMED

LQ3. Do you usually think of yourself as close to any particular political party?

1 YES
5 NO → Skip to LQ3c
8 Don't know → Skip to LQ3c

LQ3a. Which PARTY is that? (RECORD ALL PARTIES, response categories range from 0 to 96)

First PARTY mentioned: _____
IF ONLY ONE PARTY BLOCK IS MENTIONED → SKIP TO LQ3a1
IF ONLY ONE PARTY (WITHIN A BLOCK) IS MENTIONED → SKIP TO LQ3e
Second PARTY (if volunteered): _____
IF MORE THAN ONE PARTY IS MENTIONED → SKIP TO LQ3b
Third PARTY (if volunteered): _____
IF MORE THAN ONE PARTY IS MENTIONED → SKIP TO LQ3b
98 Don't know, no party mentioned → Skip to LQ3c

LQ3a(1). Which party in [NAME OF BLOCK] do you feel closest to?

First PARTY mentioned: _____

IF ONLY ONE PARTY BLOCK IS MENTIONED → SKIP TO LQ3e

Second PARTY (if volunteered): _____

IF MORE THAN ONE PARTY IS MENTIONED → SKIP TO LQ3b

Third PARTY (if volunteered): _____

IF MORE THAN ONE PARTY IS MENTIONED → SKIP TO LQ3b

98 Don't know → Skip to LQ3c

LQ3b. Which party do you feel closest to?

Party identified: _____ → Skip to LQ3e

No party identified

LQ3c. Do you feel yourself a little closer to one of the political parties than the others?

1 YES

5 No → Skip to Q4

8 Don't know → Skip to Q4

LQ3d. Which party is that?

Party identified: _____

LQ3e. Do you feel very close to this (party/party block), somewhat close, or not very close?

1 Very close

2 Somewhat close

3 Not very close

8 Don't know

Q4. (PLEASE SEE CARD 2) Some people say that political parties in [country] care what ordinary people think. Others say that political parties in [country] don't care what ordinary people think. Using the scale on this card, (where ONE means that political parties care about what ordinary people think, and FIVE means that they don't care what ordinary people think), where would you place yourself?

1 Political parties in [country] care what ordinary people think

2

3

4

5 Political parties in [country] don't care what ordinary people think

8 Don't know

Q5. (PLEASE SEE CARD 3) Some people say that political parties are necessary to make our political system work in [country]. Others think that political parties are not needed in [country]. Using the scale on this card, (where ONE means that political parties are necessary to make our political system work, and FIVE means that political parties are not needed in [country]), where would you place yourself?

    1 Political parties ARE NECESSARY to make our political system work

    2

    3

    4

    5 Political parties ARE NOT NEEDED in [country]

    8 Don't know

Q6. Do you happen to remember the name of any candidates who [ran/stood] in your [Lower house primary electoral district, e.g., constituency, district, riding] in the last [parliamentary/congressional] election?

    1 YES

    5 No → Skip to Q7

    8 Don't know → Skip to Q7

(if name not volunteered) What were their names?

    Q6a. CANDIDATE 1 NAME: _____
           GENDER: _____, PARTY: _____
    Q6b. CANDIDATE 2 NAME: _____
           GENDER: _____, PARTY: _____
    Q6c. CANDIDATE 3 NAME: _____
           GENDER: _____, PARTY: _____

Q7. (PLEASE SEE CARD 4) I'd like to know what you think about each of our political parties. After I read the name of a political party, please rate it on a scale from 0 to 10, where 0 means you strongly dislike that party and 10 means that you strongly like that party. If I come to a party you haven't heard of or you feel you do not know enough about, just say so. The first party is [PARTY A].

	Strongly dislike		Strongly like	DK	Haven't heard of
a PARTY A	0	1 2 3 4 5 6 7 8 9	10	98	96
b PARTY B	0	1 2 3 4 5 6 7 8 9	10	98	96
c PARTY C	0	1 2 3 4 5 6 7 8 9	10	98	96
d PARTY D	0	1 2 3 4 5 6 7 8 9	10	98	96
e PARTY E	0	1 2 3 4 5 6 7 8 9	10	98	96
f PARTY F	0	1 2 3 4 5 6 7 8 9	10	98	96

Q8. (PLEASE SEE CARD 4) And now, using the same scale, I'd like to ask you how much you like or dislike some political leaders. Again, if I come to a leader you haven't heard of or you feel you do not know enough about, just say so. The first political leader is [LEADER A].

		Strongly dislike											Strongly like	DK	Haven't heard of
a	LEADER A	0	1	2	3	4	5	6	7	8	9		10	98	96
b	LEADER B	0	1	2	3	4	5	6	7	8	9		10	98	96
c	LEADER C	0	1	2	3	4	5	6	7	8	9		10	98	96
d	LEADER D	0	1	2	3	4	5	6	7	8	9		10	98	96
e	LEADER E	0	1	2	3	4	5	6	7	8	9		10	98	96
f	LEADER F	0	1	2	3	4	5	6	7	8	9		10	98	96

Q9. What do you think about the state of the economy these days in [country]? Would you say that the state of the economy is very good, good, neither good nor bad, bad or very bad?

1 Very good
2 Good
3 Neither good nor bad
4 Bad
5 Very bad
8 Don't know

Q10. Would you say that over the past twelve months, the state of the economy in [country] has gotten better, stayed about the same or gotten worse?

1 Gotten better
3 Stayed the same → Skip to Q11
5 Gotten worse → Skip to Q10b
8 Don't know

Q10a. Would you say much better or somewhat better?

1 MUCH BETTER
2 Somewhat better
8 Don't know

Q10b. Would you say much worse or somewhat worse?

5 MUCH WORSE
4 Somewhat worse
8 Don't know

Q11. (PLEASE SEE CARD 5) Some people say that members of [Congress/ Parliament] know what ordinary people think. Others say that members of [Congress/Parliament] don't know much about what ordinary people think. Using the scale on this card, (where ONE means that the members of [Congress/Parliament] know what ordinary people think, and FIVE means that the members of [Congress/Parliament] don't know much about what ordinary people think), where would you place yourself?

1 Members of [Congress/Parliament] KNOW what ordinary people think.

2

3

4

5 Members of [Congress/Parliament] DON'T KNOW what ordinary people think.

8 Don't know

Q12. During the past twelve months, have you had any contact with [a Member of parliament/a Member of Congress] in any way?

1 Yes

5 No; No contact at all

8 Don't know

Q13. (PLEASE SEE CARD 6) Some people say it makes a difference who is in power. Others say that it doesn't make a difference who is in power. Using the scale on this card, (where ONE means that it makes a difference who is in power and FIVE means that is doesn't make a difference who is in power), where would you place yourself?

1 It MAKES A DIFFERENCE who is in power.

2

3

4

5 It DOESN'T MAKE A DIFFERENCE who is in power.

8 DON'T KNOW

Q14. (PLEASE SEE CARD 7) Some people say that no matter who people vote for, it won't make any difference to what happens. Others say that who people vote for can make a difference to what happens. Using the scale on this card, (where ONE means that voting won't make a difference to what happens and FIVE means that voting can make a difference), where would you place yourself?

1 Who people vote for WON'T MAKE A DIFFERENCE.

2

3

4

5 Who people vote for CAN MAKE A DIFFERENCE.

8 Don't know

Q15. (PLEASE SEE CARD 8) When people are asked to express an opinion, do you believe most people in [country] usually say what they think about politics or do you believe most people usually hide what they really think about politics? Using the scale on this card, (where ONE means that most people in [country] usually say what they think about politics, and FIVE means that most people usually hide what they really think), where would you place yourself?

1 Most people in [country] usually SAY WHAT THEY THINK about politics.

2

3

4

5 Most people usually HIDE WHAT THEY REALLY THINK about politics.

8 Don't know

Q16. (PLEASE USE CARD 9) In politics people sometimes talk of left and right. Where would you place yourself on a scale from 0 to 10 where 0 means the left and 10 means the right?

Now, using the same scale where would you place [Party A–F]?

And again, using the same scale where would you place [Leader A–F]

		LEFT		RIGHT	DK	Haven't heard of
a	YOURSELF	0	1 2 3 4 5 6 7 8 9	10	98	96
b	PARTY A	0	1 2 3 4 5 6 7 8 9	10	98	96
c	PARTY B	0	1 2 3 4 5 6 7 8 9	10	98	96
d	PARTY C	0	1 2 3 4 5 6 7 8 9	10	98	96
e	PARTY D	0	1 2 3 4 5 6 7 8 9	10	98	96
f	PARTY E	0	1 2 3 4 5 6 7 8 9	10	98	96
g	PARTY F	0	1 2 3 4 5 6 7 8 9	10	98	96
h	LEADER A	0	1 2 3 4 5 6 7 8 9	10	98	96
i	LEADER B	0	1 2 3 4 5 6 7 8 9	10	98	96
j	LEADER C	0	1 2 3 4 5 6 7 8 9	10	98	96
k	LEADER D	0	1 2 3 4 5 6 7 8 9	10	98	96
l	LEADER E	0	1 2 3 4 5 6 7 8 9	10	98	96
m	LEADER F	0	1 2 3 4 5 6 7 8 9	10	98	96

The Macro-Level Questionnaire of Module 1

Macro-Level Data Questionnaire

Part I: Data Pertinent to the Election at which the Module was Administered

1. Variable number/name in the dataset that identifies the primary electoral district for each respondent.

   ----

2. Names and party affiliation of cabinet-level ministers serving at the time of the dissolution of the most recent government.

Name of Cabinet Member	Name of the Office Held	Political Party
-------------------------	-------------------------	---------------

3. Political Parties (active during the election at which the module was administered).

Name of Political family	Year founded	Ideological family. Party is closest to	International Organization. Party belongs to (if any)
---------------	---------	--------------------	-----------------------------

   Ideological Party Families:

Ecology Parties	Liberal Parties	Agrarian Parties
Communist Parties	Right Liberal Parties	Ethnic Parties
Socialist Parties	Christian Democratic Parties	Regional Parties
Social Democratic Parties	Conservative Parties	Other Parties
Left Liberal Parties	National Parties	Independents

International Party Organizations:

Socialist International
Confederation of Socialist Parties of
the European Community
Asia-Pacific Socialist Organization
Socialist Inter-African

Christian Democratic International
European Christian Democratic Union
European People's Party

Liberal International
Federation of European Liberal,
Democrat, and Reform Parties

International Democrat Union
Caribbean Democrat Union
European Democrat Union
Pacific Democrat Union

The Greens

4. (a) Parties position on left–right scale (in the expert judgment of the CSES Collaborator):

Party Name	LEFT		RIGHT
1.	0	1 2 3 4 5 6 7 8 9	10
2.	0	1 2 3 4 5 6 7 8 9	10
3.	0	1 2 3 4 5 6 7 8 9	10
4.	0	1 2 3 4 5 6 7 8 9	10
5.	0	1 2 3 4 5 6 7 8 9	10
6.	0	1 2 3 4 5 6 7 8 9	10

4. (b) If you have asked respondents to rank political parties on a dimension other than the left–right dimension, please also provide your own rankings on this other dimension.

Name of dimension:

Label for left position: _____

Label for right position: _____

Party Name	LEFT		RIGHT
1.	0	1 2 3 4 5 6 7 8 9	10
2.	0	1 2 3 4 5 6 7 8 9	10
3.	0	1 2 3 4 5 6 7 8 9	10
4.	0	1 2 3 4 5 6 7 8 9	10
5.	0	1 2 3 4 5 6 7 8 9	10
6.	0	1 2 3 4 5 6 7 8 9	10

5. In your view, what are the five most salient factors that affected the outcome of the election (e.g. major scandals; economic events; the presence of an independent actor; specific issues)?

1. _____

2. _____

3. _____

4. _____

5. _____

6. Electoral Alliances

   Sometimes, electoral alliances are made at the constituency level as, for example, in Finland. Documenting who is allied with whom, and how, in each constituency is a large task and we do not expect you to do more than make some general reference to the existence of constituency-level alliances. Sometimes, electoral alliances are made at the national level—these are the alliances that we would like you will identify.

   Information is sought on who is allied with whom and on the nature of the electoral alliance.

   a) Were electoral alliances permitted during the election campaign?
      Yes _____ No _____

   b) (If yes) Did any electoral alliances form?
      Yes _____ No _____

   c) (If yes to b) List the party alliances that formed:

Name of Alliance	Parties in the Alliance
Alliance 1: _____	_____
Alliance 2: _____	_____
Alliance 3: _____	_____
Alliance 4: _____	_____
Alliance 5: _____	_____

7. (If a presidential election was held concurrently with the legislative elections) List presidential candidates

Name of Presidential Candidate	Party of Candidate*
--------------------------------	--------------------

   *or parties, if multiple endorsements are allowed.

8. If the national team plans to collect aggregate election returns (or constituency-level returns) please include these returns with the study materials provided when the data are archived.

Part II: Data on Electoral Institutions

A central theme in the Comparative Study of Electoral Systems concerns the impact of electoral institutions on voting behavior and election outcomes. In order to assess the impact of institutions properly, a necessary preliminary step is to obtain accurate information on those institutional arrangements. The purpose of this document is to describe the kind of information we are asking you to provide.

Overview of Information Needed

In most countries, the best source of the needed information is the electoral statute or code that currently governs lower house elections. If the text of the law is available in a variety of different languages, please send a version in the most accessible language available. In any event, please also provide full bibliographic information on the source of the information sent.

In a few countries, such as the UK, there may not be a single statute that governs elections. In such cases, our hope is that you will do your best to provide an accurate description of the electoral system in response to the detailed questions described below.

For those countries in which there is an electoral statute, there may also be other sources of information on the electoral procedure that you know of: perhaps the constitution specifies part of the electoral system, or perhaps a local scholar has written a description of the electoral system, or perhaps there is a map of the electoral districts available. It would be helpful if these materials could be sent as well.

Details of Information Needed

The kind of details that are needed are indicated by the following list of questions. If you are sending a copy of the electoral code, then there is no need to answer these questions separately. If you are not sending the electoral code, then these questions may help in deciding what to send.

I. QUESTIONS ABOUT ELECTORAL DISTRICTS.

Definitions: An electoral district is defined as a geographic area within which votes are counted and seats allocated. If a district cannot be partitioned into smaller districts within which votes are counted and seats allocated, it is called primary. If it can be partitioned into primary districts, and there is some transfer of votes and/or seats from the primary districts to the larger district, then the larger district is called secondary. If a district can be partitioned into secondary districts (again with some transfer of votes and/or seats), it is called tertiary.

In some electoral systems, there are electoral districts that are geographically nested but not otherwise related for purposes of seat allocation. In Lithuania, for example, there are 71 single-member districts that operate under a majority runoff system, and also a single nationwide district that operates under proportional representation (the largest remainders method with the Hare quota). Neither votes nor seats from the single-member districts transfer to the nationwide district, however. The two processes are entirely independent (with voters having one vote in each district). In this case, the nationwide district, although it contains the 71 single-member districts, is not considered to be secondary. It is primary. One might say that there are two segments to the electoral system in such cases.

1) How many segments (as just defined) are there in the electoral system?

    1 segment _____

    2 segments _____

For the first segment, please answer the following questions (questions 2 through 11):

2) How many primary electoral districts are there? _____

3) For each primary electoral district, how many members are elected from in that district? _____

4) How many secondary electoral districts are there? _____

5) How many tertiary electoral districts are there? _____

II. QUESTIONS ABOUT VOTING.

6) Exactly how are votes cast by voters? _____

    6a) How many votes do they or can they cast? _____

    6b) Do they vote for candidates, for lists, or for both? (Explain) _____

7) Are the votes transferable? _____

8) If more than one vote can be cast, can they be cumulated? _____

9) Are there any other features of voting that should be noted?

III. QUESTIONS ABOUT CONVERTING VOTES INTO SEATS.

10) Exactly how are votes converted into seats?

    10a) Are there legally mandated thresholds that a party must exceed before it is eligible to receive seats? _____ If so, what is the threshold?

10b) What electoral formula or formulas are used?

_____

_____

11) If there are lists, are they closed, open, or flexible?

closed   _____

flexible, but in practice virtually closed   _____

flexible   _____

flexible, but in practice virtually open   _____

open   _____

Definitions: A list is closed if the seats that are awarded to that list are always occupied by the candidates in order of their appearance on the list (i.e. if the list gets x seats then necessarily the top x names on the list get the seats). A list is open if the question of which candidates on the list get the seats that are awarded to the list is determined solely by the votes that each candidate receives. A list is flexible if it is neither closed nor open.

IV. QUESTIONS ABOUT THE POSSIBILITIES OF ELECTORAL ALLIANCE.

12) What are the possibilities of alliance in the system?

_____

_____

_____

12a) Can parties run joint lists? _____

12b) Is there apparentement or linking of lists? _____

12c) Can candidates run with the endorsement of more than one party?
_____

12d) Do parties withdraw their lists or candidates in some constituencies, urging their supporters there to vote for an ally's list or candidate?

12e) Other? _____

Definitions: A joint list refers to one on which candidates of different parties run together. Apparentement refers to a legal agreement between two or more lists to pool their votes for the purposes of an initial seat allocation, with seats initially allocated to the alliance then reallocated to the lists in the alliance.

13) If joint lists are possible, are they subject to different regulations than single-party lists? For example, higher thresholds, different numbers of candidates that may appear on the list, etc.

_____

14) If apparentement is possible, what lists can participate in such agreements lists of the same party in the same constituency?

lists of the same party from different constituencies? _____

lists of different parties in the same constituency? _____

15) If candidates can run with the endorsement of more than one party, is this reflected on the ballot?

Yes, candidate's name appears once, together with the names of all supporting parties _____

Yes, candidate's name appears as many times as there are different parties endorsing him or her, each time with the name of the endorsing party _____

Yes, other (please explain) _____

No party endorsements are indicated on the ballot paper _____

Part III: Data on Regime Type

Below are various questions about the type of regime—presidential, parliamentary, semi-presidential—in your country. There are two potential problems with these questions that should be noted at the outset. First, in some countries there may be a discrepancy between the de jure (or legal) situation and the de facto (or practical) situation. For example, in Great Britain the Queen still possesses a legal right to veto legislation, but this right has not been exercised since 1707. In the case of such obviously obsolete powers, please answer according to the de facto situation. Otherwise, describe the de jure situation. A second potential problem is that the questions may not be phrased optimally for the situation in your particular country. In such cases, please answer as best you can, providing some indication of the difficulties as you see them.

I.) Questions regarding the Head of State.

1) Who is the Head of State?

_____ President

_____ Monarch

_____ Prime Minister serves as ceremonial head of state

_____ Other (please specify) _____

2) How is the head of state selected?

_____ Direct election

_____ Indirect election

_____ Birth right

_____ Divine right

_____ Other (Explain) _____

a) If by direct election, by what process?

_____ Plurality election

_____ Run-off or two-ballot system

_____ Other (Explain) _____

    (i) If by run-off system, what is the

        threshold for first-round victory? ____
        threshold to advance to second round? ____
        threshold for victory in second round? ____

b) If by indirect election, by what process?
  ____ Electoral college
  ____ Selection by the legislature
  ____ Other (Explain)

    (i) If by electoral college,
    How are electors chosen?
    Does the electoral college deliberate? ____ Yes   ____ No
    What is the voting procedure used by the electoral college?
    (ii) If by the legislature,
    By which chamber(s) of the legislature?
    What is the voting procedure used?

3) If there is a Head of State, does the Head of State have the following powers? [Check all that apply.]

a) Introduce legislation? ____ Yes   ____ No

b) Require expedited action on specific legislation? ____ Yes   ____ No
If yes, what is the default if the legislature takes no action?

Definitions: A Head of State possesses a partial veto when he or she can target specific clauses of a piece of legislation for veto, while promulgating the rest. In the U.S., such vetoes are sometimes called line item vetoes. A Head of State possesses a package veto when he or she can veto the entire piece of legislation submitted by the legislature, but cannot veto some parts and accept others.

c) Package veto? ____ Yes   ____ No
If yes, what is the requirement to override the veto?

d) Partial veto? ____ Yes   ____ No
If yes, what is the requirement to override the partial veto?

e) Legislate by decree? ____ Yes   ____ No
If yes, does this require that the legislature must first specifically delegate decree authority to the head of state by statute? ____ Yes   ____ No
If yes, are there restrictions on the policy areas in which the head of state can legislate by decree? ____ Yes   ____ No
If yes, are there other restrictions on the head of state's authority to legislate by decree? ____ Yes   ____ No

f) Emergency powers? _____ Yes _____ No

If yes, what actions can the head of state take under emergency authority? If yes, under what conditions can the head of state invoke emergency authority?

If yes, what restrictions are there on the head of state's authority to invoke and exercise emergency authority?

g) Negotiate treaties and international agreements? _____ Yes _____ No
If yes, what other requirements are there for approval of treaties and international agreements negotiated by the head of state?

h) Commander of the armed forces? _____ Yes _____ No

If yes, does the head of state control promotions of high-ranking officers? _____ Yes _____ No

If yes, can the head of state dismiss or demote high-ranking officers? _____ Yes _____ No

If yes, can the head of state mobilize and demobilize troops? _____ Yes _____ No

j) Introduce referenda? _____ Yes _____ No

If yes, under what conditions?

k) Refer legislation to the judicial branch for review of constitutionality? _____ Yes _____ No

m) Convene special legislative sessions? _____ Yes _____ No

If yes, is this the head of state's power exclusively, or can any other (s) do this as well? _____ Yes, other power _____ No other powers

(If yes, explain): _____

II.) Questions about the Head of Government.

1) Who is the Head of Government?

_____ President
_____ Prime Minister (or equivalent)
_____ Other (please specify) _____

2) If the Head of Government is a prime minister, how is the prime minister selected?

_____ Appointed by the head of state alone
_____ Appointed by the legislature alone
_____ Nominated by the head of state, and approved by the legislature
_____ Nominated by the legislature, and approved by the head of state
_____ Other (Explain):

3) If there is a prime minister, what authorities does the prime minister have over the composition of the cabinet? [Check all that apply.]

_____ Names ministers and assigns portfolios alone

_____ Nominates ministers for approval by the president

_____ Reviews and approves ministerial nominations made by the president

_____ Dismisses ministers and reassigns portfolios at own discretion

_____ Other (Explain):

4) If there is a prime minister, what authorities does the prime minister have over the policy making process? [Check all that apply.]

_____ Chairs cabinet meetings

_____ Determines schedule of issues to be considered by the legislature

_____ Determines which alternatives will be voted on by the legislature, and in which order

_____ Refers legislative proposals to party or legislative committees

_____ Calls votes of confidence in government

_____ Other (Explain)

III.) By what method(s) can cabinet members, or the entire cabinet, be dismissed?

[Check all that apply.]

_____ By the head of state alone

_____ By the prime minister alone

_____ By majority vote of the legislature where a majority of all legislators is required

_____ By majority vote of the legislature where a majority of those legislators voting is required

_____ By some combination of the above, acting in concert (Explain)

_____ Other (Explain)

IV.) Can the legislature be dissolved prior to regularly scheduled elections? _____ Yes _____ No

1) If yes, by what method?

_____ By the head of state alone

_____ By the prime minister alone

_____ By majority vote of the legislature

_____ By some combination of the above, acting in concert (Explain)

_____ Other (Explain)

2) If yes, are there restrictions on when and how the legislature can be dissolved? [Check all that apply.]

_____ On the timing of dissolution (e.g. not within one year after a legislative election) (Explain)

_____ As a response to action/inaction by the legislature (e.g. only when the legislature has censured the cabinet; e.g. only if the legislature fails to pass the budget) (Explain)

_____ Other (Explain)

References

Abramowitz, Alan I., David J. Lanoue and Subha Ramesh (1988). 'Economic conditions, causal attributions, and political evaluations in the 1984 presidential election', *Journal of Politics* 50: 848–63.

Achen, Christopher H. (1975). 'Mass political attitudes and the survey response', *American Political Science Review* 69: 1218–31.

Ackaert, Johan, Lieven de Winter, and Marc Swyngedouw (1996). 'Belgium: An electorate on the eve of destruction'. In Cees van der Eijk and Mark N. Franklin (eds.). *Choosing Europe?* Ann Arbor: University of Michigan Press.

Aldrich, John (1993). 'Rational choice and turnout', *American Journal of Political Science* 37: 246–78.

Almond, Gabriel A. and Sidney Verba (1963). *The Civic Culture*. Princeton NJ: Princeton University Press.

Amorim Neto, Octavio and Gary Cox (1997). 'Electoral institutions, cleavage structures and the number of parties', *American Journal of Political Science* 41: 149–74.

Amy, Douglas (1993). *Real Choices/New Voices: The Case for PR Elections in the United States*. New York: Columbia University Press.

Anckar, Carsten (2002). *Effekter av Valsystem. En Studie av 80 Stater*. Åbo: Åbo Akademi.

Anderson, Christopher J. (1995a). *Blaming the Government: Citizens and the Economy in Five European Democracies*. Armonk, NY: M.E. Sharpe.

——(1995b). 'The dynamics of public support for coalition governments', *Comparative Political Studies* 28: 350–83.

——and Christine A. Guillory (1997). 'Political institutions and satisfaction with democracy: A cross-national analysis of consensus and majoritarian systems', *American Political Science Review* 91: 66–81.

——(2000). 'Economic voting and political context: A comparative perspective', *Electoral Studies* 19: 151–70.

Arian, Asher (1996). 'The Israeli election for prime minister and the Knesset, 1996', *Electoral Studies* 15: 570–5.

Bagehot, Walter (1867). *The English Constitution*. London: Oxford University Press.

Baldwin, M. Way, and Roger D. Masters (1996). 'Emotion and Cognition in political information-processing', *Journal of Communication* 46: 48–65.

Banducci, Susan A., Todd Donovan, and Jeffrey A. Karp (1999). 'Proportional representation and attitudes about politics: Evidence from New Zealand', *Electoral Studies* 18: 533–55.

Banks, Arthur S. et al. (1995–1997; 1998–1999; 2000–2002). *Political Handbook of the World*. Binghamton, NY: CSA Publications.

Beck, Nathaniel and Simon Jackman (1998). 'Beyond linearity by default: Generalized additive models', *American Journal of Political Science* 42: 569–627.

Beck, Thorsten and Philip Keefer (2001). 'New tools in comparative political economy: The database of political institutions', *The World Bank Economic Review* 15: 165–76.

Bell, Daniel (1965). *The End of Ideology: On the Exhaustion of Political Ideas in the Fifties*. New York: The Free Press.

Belli, Robert F., Michael W. Traugott, Margaret Young, and Katherine A. McGonagle (1999). 'Reducing vote over-reporting in surveys: Social desirability, memory failure and source monitoring', *Public Opinion Quarterly* 63: 90–108.

Ben-Akiva, Moshe and Bruno Boccara (1995). 'Discrete choice models with latent choice sets', *International Journal of Research in Marketing* 12: 9–24.

—— and Steven R. Lerman (1985). *Discrete Choice Analysis: Theory and Application to Travel Demand*. Cambridge, MA: MIT Press.

Benoit, Kenneth (2001). 'District magnitude, electoral formula, and the number of parties', *European Journal of Political Research* 39: 203–24.

Birch, Sarah and Andrew Wilson (1999). 'The Ukrainian parliamentary elections of 1998', *Electoral Studies* 18: 276–82.

Blais, André (2000). *To Vote or Not to Vote: the Merits and Limits of Rational Choice Theory*. Pittsburgh: University of Pittsburgh Press.

—— (2002). 'Why is there so little strategic voting in Canadian plurality rule elections?', *Political Studies* 50: 445–54.

—— and Agnieszka Dobrzynska (1998). 'Turnout in electoral democracies', *European Journal of Political Research* 33: 239–61.

—— and R. Ken Carty (1990). 'Does proportional representation foster voter-turnout?', *European Journal of Political Research* 18: 167–81.

—— and Louis Massicotte (1996). 'Electoral systems'. In Laurence LeDuc, Richard G. Niemi, and Pippa Norris (eds.). *Comparing Democracies: Elections and Voting in Global Perspective*. Thousand Oaks, CA: Sage.

—— —— (1997). 'Electoral formulas: A macroscopic perspective', *European Journal of Political Research* 32: 107–29.

—— Richard Nadeau, Elisabeth Gidengil, and Neil Nevitte (2001). 'Measuring strategic voting in multiparty plurality elections', *Electoral Studies* 20: 343–52.

Bogdanor, Vernon (ed.) (1985). *Representatives of the People?* Aldershot: Gower.

Bowler, Shaun and Todd Donovan (2002). 'Democracy, institutions and attitudes about citizen influence on government', *British Journal of Political Science* 32: 371–90.

Bowler, Shaun, David Lanoue, and Paul Savoie (1994). 'Electoral systems, party competition, and strength of partisan attachment: Evidence from three countries', *Journal of Politics* 56: 991–1007.

Bradburn, Norman M. and Seymour Sudman (1991). 'The current status of questionnaire design'. In P. P. Biemer, R. M. Groves, L. E. Lyberg, N. A. Mathiowetz, and S. Sudman (eds.). *Measurement Errors in Surveys*. New York: John Wiley.

Brady, Henry E., Sydney Verba, and Kay Lehman Schlozman (1995). 'Beyond SES: A resource model of political participation', *American Political Science Review* 89: 271–95.

Brambor, Thomas, William Roberts Clark, and Matt Golder (2006). 'Understanding interaction models: Improving empirical analyses', *Political Analysis* 14: 63–82.

Brehm, John (1993). *The Phantom Respondent: Opinions, Surveys and Political Representation*. Ann Arbor, MI: University of Michigan Press.

Brennan, Geoffrey and Alan Hamlin (1998). 'Expressive voting and electoral equilibrium', *Public Choice* 95: 149–75.

——— (1999). 'On political representation', *British Journal of Political Science* 29: 109–28.

—— and James Buchanan (1984). 'Voter choice and the evaluation of political alternatives', *American Behavioral Scientist* 28: 185–201.

—— and Loren Lomasky (1994). *Democracy and Decision: the Pure Theory of Electoral Preferences*. Cambridge: Cambridge University Press.

Butler, David and Donald E. Stokes (1963). *Political Change in Britain*. London: Macmillan.

Cain, Bruce E. (1978). 'Strategic voting in Britain', *American Journal of Political Science* 22: 639–55.

—— John Ferejohn, and Morris Fiorina (1987). *The Personal Vote: Constituency Service and Electoral Independence*. Cambridge, MA: Harvard University Press.

Campbell, Angus, Philip E. Converse, Warren E. Miller, and Donald E. Stokes (1960). *The American Voter*. New York: Wiley.

Carey, John and Matthew Sobert Shugart (1995). 'Incentives to cultivate A personal vote: A rank ordering of electoral formulas', *Electoral Studies* 14: 417–39.

Cassel, Carol A. (1999). 'Testing the Converse party support model in Britain', *Comparative Political Studies* 32: 626–44.

Castillo, Pilar del (1996). 'Spain: A dress rehearsal for the national elections'. In Cees van der Eijck and Mark N. Franklin (eds.). *Choosing Europe? The European Electorate and National Politics in the Face of Union*. Ann Arbor, MI: University of Michigan Press.

—— and Erik Oppenhius (1990). 'Turnout and second order effects in the European elections of June 1989—evidence from the Netherlands', *Acta Politica* 25: 67–94.

Caul Kittilson, Miki C. (2007). 'Research resources in comparative political behavior'. In Russell J. Dalton and Hans-Dieter Klingemann (eds.). *Handbook of Political Behavior*. Oxford: Oxford University Press, 865–95.

Clark, William R. and Matt Golder (2006). 'Rehabilitating Duverger's theory. Testing the mechanical and strategic modifying effects of electoral laws', *Comparative Political Studies* 39: 679–708.

Converse, Philip E. (1964). 'The nature of belief systems in mass publics'. In David E. Apter (ed.). *Ideology and Discontent.* New York: Free Press, 206–61.

——(1969). 'Of time and partisan stability', *Comparative Political Studies* 2: 139–71.

——(1975). 'Public opinion and voting behavior'. In Fred. I. Greenstein and Nelson W. Polsby (eds.). *Handbook of Political Science*, vol. 4. Reading, MA: Addison-Wesley, 75–169.

——(1976). *The Dynamics of Party Support.* Beverly Hills, CA: Sage.

Cooper, Joel and Russell H. Fazio (1984). 'A new look at dissonance theory', *Advances in Experimental Social Psychology* 17: 229–66.

Cox, Gary W. (1997). *Making Votes Count. Strategic Coordination in the World's Electoral Systems.* Cambridge: Cambridge University Press.

——(1999). 'Electoral rules and the calculus of mobilization', *Legislative Studies Quarterly* 24: 387–420.

——and Matthew Soberg Shugart (1996). 'Strategic voting under proportional representation', *Journal of Law, Economics, & Organization* 12: 299–324.

Crewe, Ivor (1981). 'Electoral participation'. In David Butler, Howard R. Penniman and Austin Ranney (eds.). *Democracy at the Polls: A Comparative Study of Competitive National Elections.* Washington, DC: American Enterprise Institute for Policy Research, 216–62.

——and David Denver (eds.) (1985). *Electoral Change in Western Democracies. Patterns and Sources of Electoral Volatility.* London: Croom Helm.

Dahl, Robert A. (ed.) (1966). *Political Oppositions in Western Democracies.* New Haven, NJ: Yale University Press.

——(1971). *Polyarchy: Participation and Opposition.* New Haven, NJ: Yale University Press.

Dalton, Russell J. (1996). *Citizen Politics*, 2nd edn. Chatham, NJ: Chatham House.

——(1999). 'Political support in advanced industrial democracies'. In Pippa Norris (ed.). *Critical citizens.* Oxford: Oxford University Press.

——(2005). *Citizen politics: Public Opinion and Political Parties in Advanced Industrial Democracies*, 4th edn. Washington, DC: CQ Press.

——and Martin P. Wattenberg (1993). 'The not so simple act of voting'. In Ada Finifter (ed.). *Political Science: The State of the Discipline II.* Washington, DC: American Political Science Association, 193–218.

————(eds.) (2000). *Parties Without Partisans.* Oxford: Oxford University Press.

——Scott C. Flanagan and Paul Allen Beck (eds.) (1984). *Electoral Change in Advanced Industrial Democracies: Realignment or Dealigment?* Princeton NJ: Princeton University Press.

Doorenspleet, Renske (2001). *The Fourth Wave of Democratization, Identification and Explanation.* University of Leiden: PhD Thesis.

Downs, Anthony (1957). *An Economic Theory of Democracy*. New York: Harper and Row.

Duverger, Maurice (1951). *Les Partis Politiques*. Paris: A. Colin.

——(1954). *Political Parties*. New York: Wiley.

Easton, David (1965). *A Systems Analysis of Political Life*. New York: Wiley.

——(1975). 'A re-assessment of the concept of political support', *British Journal of Political Science* 5: 435–57.

Eijk, Cees van der (2001). 'Measuring agreement in ordered rating scales', *Quality and Quantity* 35: 325–41.

——and Kees Niemöller (1983). *Electoral Change in the Netherlands*. Amsterdam: CT Press.

——, Mark N. Franklin and Erik Oppenhuis (1996). 'The strategic context: Party choice'. In Cees van der Eijk and Mark N. Franklin (eds.). *Choosing Europe? The European Electorate and National Politics in Face of a Union*. Ann Arbor, MI: Michigan University Press, 332–65.

————and Cees van der Brug (1999). 'Policy preferences and party choice'. In Hermann Schmitt and Jacques Thomassen (eds.). *Political Representation and Legitimacy in the European Union*. Oxford: Oxford University Press.

——and Mark N. Franklin (eds.) (1996). *Choosing Europe? The European Electorate and National Politics in the Face of Union*. Ann Arbor: University of Michigan Press.

——and Erik V. Oppenhuis (1990). 'Turnout and second-order effects in the European elections of June 1989: Evidence from the Netherlands', *Acta Politica* 25: 67–94.

Enelow, James M. and Melvin J. Hinich (1984). *The Spatial Theory of Voting: An introduction*. Cambridge: Cambridge University Press.

Erikson, Robert S., Michael B. MacKuen and James A. Stimson (2000). 'Bankers or peasants revisited: Economic expectations and presidential approval', *Electoral Studies* 19: 295–312.

Esaiasson, Peter and Knut Heidar (eds.) (2000). *Beyond Westminster and Congress: The Nordic Experience*. Columbus: Ohio State University Press.

Farrell, David (1997). *Comparing Electoral Systems*. Englewood Cliffs, NJ: Prentice Hall.

——and Ian McAllister (2006). 'Voter satisfaction and electoral systems: Does preferential voting in candidate-centered systems make a difference?', *European Journal of Political Research* 45: 723–49.

Feldman, Stanley (1982). 'Economic self-interest and political behavior', *American Journal of Political Science* 26: 446–66.

——(1988). 'Structure and consistency in public opinion: The role of core beliefs and values', *American Journal of Political Science* 32: 416–40.

Ferrara, Federico, Erik. S. Herron, and Misa Nishikawa (2005). *Mixed Electoral Systems. Contamination and its Consequences*. New York: Palgrave.

Festinger, Leon (1957). *A Theory of Cognitive Dissonance*. Stanford, CA: Stanford University Press.

Fidrmuc, Jan (2000). 'Economics of voting in post-communist countries', *Electoral Studies* 19: 199–217.

Fiorina, Morris P. (1981). *Retrospective Voting in American National Elections*. New Haven: Yale University Press.

——(1990). 'Information and rationality in elections'. In John A. Ferejohn and James H. Kuklinski (eds.). *Information and Democratic Processes*. Urbana, IL: University of Illinois Press.

Fischer, Alastair J. (1996). 'A further experimental study of expressive voting', *Public Choice* 88: 171–84.

Fisher, Stephen D. (2004). 'Definition and measurement of tactical voting: The role of rational choice', *British Journal of Political Science* 34: 152–66.

Fiske, Susan T. and Shelley E. Taylor (1991). *Social Cognition*. New York: McGraw-Hill.

Forgas, Joseph P. and Stephanie J. Moylan (1987). 'After the movies: Transient mood and social judgments', *Personality and Social Psychology Bulletin* 13: 467–77.

Fowler, Floyd J. (1984). *Applied Social Science Research Methods Series: Survey Research Methods*. Beverly Hills, CA: Sage Publications.

Fox, John (1997). *Applied Regression Analysis, Linear Models, and Related Methods*. Thousand Oaks, CA: Sage Publications.

——(1984). 'Issue preferences, socialization, and the evolution of party identification', *American Journal of Political Science* 28: 459–78.

——and John E. Jackson (1983). 'The dynamics of party identification', *American Political Science Review* 77: 957–73.

Franklin, Mark N. (1996). 'Electoral participation'. In Laurence LeDuc, Richard G. Niemi, and Pippa Norris (eds.). *Comparing Democracies: Elections and Voting in Global Perspective*. Thousand Oaks, CA: Sage, 216–35.

——Tom Mackie and Henry Valen (eds.) (1992). *Electoral Change. Response to Evolving Social and Attitudinal Structures in Western Countries*. Cambridge: Cambridge University Press.

——with Cees van der Eijk, Diana Evans, Michael Fotos, Wolfgang Hirczy de Mino, Michael Marsh and Bernard Weßels (2004). *Voter Turnout and the Dynamics of Electoral Competition in Established Democracies since 1945*. New York: Cambridge University Press.

Franzese, Robert J. Jr. (2005). 'Empirical strategies for various manifestations of multilevel data', *Political Analysis* 13: 430–46.

Frey, Bruno S. and Alois Stutzer (2000). 'Happiness, economy and institutions', *Economic Journal* 110: 918–38.

Friedrich, Robert J. (1982). 'In defense of multiplicative terms in multiple regression equations', *American Journal of Political Science* 26: 797–833.

Fuchs, Dieter (1989). *Die Unterstützung des Politischen Systems der Bundesrepublik Deutschland*. Opladen: Westdeutscher Verlag.

Fuchs, Dieter and Hans-Dieter Klingemann (1990). 'The left-right schema'. In M. Kent Jennings, Jan Van Deth, Samuel H. Barnes, Felix J. Heunks, Ronald

Inglehart, Max Kaase, Hans-Dieter Klingemann and Jacques J. Thomassen. *Continuities in Political Action*. Berlin: deGruyter, 203–34.

——and Steffen Kühnel (1994). 'Wählen als rationales Handeln'. In Hans-Dieter Klingemann and Max Kaase (eds.). *Wahlen und Wähler—Analysen aus Anlass der Bundestagswahl 1990*. Opladen: Westdeutscher Verlag, 305–64.

——and Edeltraud Roller (1998). 'Cultural conditions of transition to liberal democracy in Central and Eastern Europe'. In Samuel H. Barnes and János Simon (eds.). *The Postcommunist Citizen*. Budapest: Erasmus Foundation.

Fukuyama, Francis (1989). 'The end of history?', *The National Interest*, 16: 3–16.

——(1992). *The End of History or the Last Man*. New York: Free Press.

Gallagher, Michael (1992). 'Comparing proportional representation electoral systems: Quotas, thresholds, paradoxes, and majorities', *British Journal of Political Science* 22: 469–96.

Gilljam, Mikael and Sören Holmberg (1995). *Väljarnas Val*. Stockholm: Norstedts Juridik.

Glasgow, Garrett (2001). 'Mixed logit models for multiparty elections', *Political Analysis* 9: 116–36.

Glass, David (1985). 'Evaluating presidential candidates: Who focuses on their personal attributes?', *Public Opinion Quarterly* 49: 517–34.

Golder, Sona N. (2006). 'Pre-electoral coalition formation in parliamentary democracies', *British Journal of Political Science* 36: 193–212.

Golosov, Grigorii V. (2005). 'Political parties and independent candidates in the Duma election'. In Vladimir Gel'man, Grigorii V. Golosov, and Elena Meleshkina (eds.). *The 1999–2000 National Elections in Russia. Analyses, Documents and Data*. Berlin: Sigma, 36–58.

Gomez, Brad and J. Matthew Wilson (2001). 'Political sophistication and economic voting in the American electorate: A theory of heterogeneous attribution', *American Journal of Political Science* 45: 899–914.

Goodhart, Charles A. E. and Rajendra J. Bhansali. (1970). 'Political economy', *Political Studies* 18: 43–106.

Greene, William H. (2000). *Econometric Analysis*, 4th edn. Upper Saddle River, NJ: Prentice-Hall.

Gschwend, Thomas and Marc Hooghe (2004). *Strategic Voting in Mixed Electoral Systems*. Reutlingen: SFG-Elsevier.

——(2007). 'Institutional incentives for strategic voting and party system change in Portugal', *Portuguese Journal of Social Science* 6: 15–31.

——and Marc Hooghe (2008). 'Should I stay or should I go? An experimental study on voter responses to pre-electoral coalitions in Belgium', *European Journal of Political Research* 47: 566–77.

Gunther, Richard (1989). 'Electoral laws, party systems, and elites: The case of Spain', *American Political Science Review* 83: 835–59.

Guttman, Joel M., Naftali Hilger, and Yochanan Schachmurove (1994). 'Voting as investment vs. voting as consumption: New evidence', *Kyklos* 47: 197–207.

Halman, Loek, Ruud Luijkx, and Marga van Zunder (2005). *Atlas of European Values*. Amsterdam: Brill Academic Publishers.

Heberlin, Thomas A. and Robert M. Baumgartner (1978). 'Factors affecting response rates to mailed questionnaires: A quantitative analysis of published literature', *American Sociological Review* 43: 447–62.

Herron, Erik S. and Misa Nishikawa (2001). 'Contamination effects and the number of parties in mixed-superposition electoral systems', *Electoral Studies* 20: 63–86.

Holmberg, Sören (1999). 'Down and down we go: Political trust in Sweden'. In Pippa Norris, (ed.). *Critical Citizens*. Oxford: Oxford University Press.

——and Tommy Möller (eds.) (1999). *Premiär för personval*. Stockholm: SOU 1999:92.

House, James S. and William M. Mason (1975). 'Political alienation in America', *American Sociological Review* 40: 123–47.

Huber, John D. and G. Bingham Powell, Jr. (1994). 'Congruence between citizens and policymakers in two visions of liberal democracy', *World Politics* 46: 291–326.

Huntington, Samuel (1991). *The Third Wave: Democratization in the Late Twentieth century*. London: University of Oklahoma Press.

Huseby, Beate (1999). 'Government economic performance and political support'. In Hanne-Marthe Narud and Toril Aalberg (eds.). *Challenges to Representative Democracy: Parties, Voters and Public Opinion*. Bergen: Fagbokforlaget.

Inglehart, Ronald (1990). *Culture Shift in Advanced Industrial Society*. Princeton, NJ: Princeton University Press.

IDEA (1997). *The International IDEA Handbook of Electoral System Design*. Stockholm: IDEA.

Iversen, Torben (1994). 'Political leadership and representation in West European democracies: A test of three models of voting', *American Journal of Political Science* 38: 45–74.

Jackman, Robert W. (1987). 'Political institutions and voter turnout in the industrial democracies', *American Political Science Review* 81: 405–23.

——and Ross A. Miller (1995). 'Voter turnout in the industrial democracies during the 1980s', *Comparative Political Studies* 27: 467–92.

Jacobson, Gary C. (1997). *The Politics of Congressional Elections*. New York: Harper Collins.

Jacoby, William G. (1986). 'Levels of conceptualization and reliance on the liberal-conservative continuum', *Journal of Politics* 48: 423–31.

Jones, Bradford S. and Marco R. Steenbergen (1997). 'Modeling multilevel data structures'. Paper prepared for the 14th annual meeting of the Political Methodology Society, Columbus, OH, July 25, 1997.

Kaase, Max and Kenneth Newton (1995). *Beliefs in Government*. Oxford: Oxford University Press.

Kalton, Graham and Howard Schumann (1982). 'The effect of the question on survey responses: A review', *Journal of the Royal Statistical Society Series A (General)* 145: 42–73.

Kan, Kamhon and Cheng-Chen Yang (2001). 'On expressive voting: Evidence from the 1988 U.S. presidential election', *Public Choice* 108: 295–312.

Kaplan, Abraham (1964). *The Conduct of Inquiry: Methodology for Behavioral Science*. Scranton, PA: Chandler.

Karp, Jeffrey A. and Susan A. Banducci (2008). 'Political efficacy and participation in twenty seven democracies: How electoral systems shape political behavior', *British Journal of Political Science*, 38(2): 311–34.

——(1999). 'The impact of proportional representation on turnout: Evidence from New Zealand', *Australian Journal of Political Science* 34: 363–77.

—— and David Brockington (2005). 'Social desirability and response validity: A comparative analysis of over-reporting voter turnout in five countries', *Journal of Politics* 67: 825–40.

——and Shaun Bowler (2001). 'Coalition government and satisfaction with democracy: An analysis of New Zealand's reaction to proportional representation', *European Journal of Political Research* 40: 57–79.

——Jack Vowles, Susan A. Banducci, and Todd Donovan (2002). 'Strategic voting, party activity, and candidate effects: Testing explanations for split voting in New Zealand's new mixed system', *Electoral Studies* 21: 1–22.

Katz, Richard S. (1980). *A Theory of Parties and Electoral Systems*. Baltimore, MD: Johns Hopkins University Press.

——(1997). *Democracy and Elections*. New York: Oxford University Press.

Keeter, Scott, Carolyn Miller, Andrew Kohut, Robert M. Groves, and Stanley Presser (2000). 'Consequences of reducing non-response in a national telephone survey', *Public Opinion Quarterly* 64: 125–48.

Kelley Jr., Stanley and Thad W. Mirer (1974). 'The simple act of voting', *American Political Science Review* 68: 572–91.

Key, Vladimer O., Jr. (1966). *The Responsible Electorate: Rationality in Presidential Voting, 1936–1960*. Cambridge, MA: Harvard University Press.

Kiewiet, D. Roderick (1983). *Macroeconomics and Micropolitics: The Electoral Effects of Economic Issues*. Chicago: University of Chicago Press.

——(2000). 'Economic retrospective voting and incentives for policymaking', *Electoral Studies* 19: 427–44.

——and Douglas Rivers (1984). 'A retrospective on retrospective voting', *Political Behavior* 6: 369–93.

Kinder, Donald R. (1983). 'Diversity and complexity in American public opinion'. In Ada W. Finifter (ed.). *Political Science: The State of the Discipline*. Washington, DC: American Political Science Association, 389–425.

——Gordon Adams and Paul Gronke (1989). 'Economics and politics in the 1984 American presidential election', *American Journal of Political Science* 33: 491–515.

——and Roderick D. Kiewiet (1981). 'Sociotropic politics: The American case', *British Journal of Political Science* 11: 129–61.

Kirchheimer, Otto (1965). 'Der Wandel des westeuropäischen Parteiensystems', *Politische Vierteljahresschrift* 6: 20–41.

Kish, Leslie (1965). *Survey Sampling*. New York: John Wiley and Sons.

Kleppner, Paul (1982). *Who Voted? The Dynamics of Electoral Turnout, 1870–1980*. New York: Praeger.

Klingemann, Hans-Dieter (1979). 'Measuring ideological conceptualizations'. In Samuel H. Barnes, Max Kaase et al. *Political Action: Mass Participation in Five Western Democracies*. Beverly Hills, CA: Sage, 215–54.

——(1999). 'Mapping political support in the 1990s: A global analysis'. In Pippa Norris (ed.). *Critical Citizens*. Oxford: Oxford University Press.

——(2005). 'Political Parties and Party Systems'. In Jacques Thomassen (ed.) *The European Voter*. Oxford: Oxford University Press, 267–308.

——and Dieter Fuchs (eds.) (1995). *Citizens and the state*. Oxford: Oxford University Press.

——and Bernhard Wessels (2001). 'The political consequences of Germany's mixed-member system: Personalization at the grass roots?' In Matthew Soberg Shugart and Martin Wattenberg (eds.). *Mixed-member Electoral Systems: The Best of Both Worlds*? Oxford: Oxford University Press, 279–96.

Kramer, Gerald H. (1971). 'Short-term fluctuations in U.S. voting behavior, 1896–1964', *American Political Science Review* 65: 131–43.

——(1983). 'The ecological fallacy revisited: Aggregate- versus individual-level findings on economics and elections, and sociotropic voting', *American Political Science Review* 77: 92–111.

Kroh, Martin (2003). *Parties, Politicians, and Policies: Orientations of Vote Choice across Voters and Contexts*. Amsterdam: Universiteit van Amsterdam (Academisch Proefschrift).

——(2006). 'Taking don't knows as valid responses: A complete random imputation of missing data', *Quality and Quantity* 40: 225–44.

Laakso, Markku and Rein Taagepera (1979). 'Effective number of parties: A measure with applications to Western Europe', *Comparative Political Studies* 12: 3–27.

Ladner, Andrea and Henry Milner (1999). 'Do voters turn out more under proportional than majoritarian systems? The evidence from Swiss communal elections', *Electoral Studies* 18: 235–50.

Lane, Jan-Erik and Svante Ersson (1990). 'Macro and micro understanding in political science: What explains electoral participation?' *European Journal of Political Research* 18: 457–65.

Lau, Richard R. and David P. Redlawsk (2001). 'Advantages and disadvantages of cognitive heuristics in political decision making', *American Journal of Political Science* 45: 951–71.

Laver, Michael J. and Ian Budge (1992). *Party, Policy, and Government Coalitions*. London: Macmillan.

Lazarsfeld, Paul F., Bernard R. Berelson, and Hazel Gaudet (1944). *The People's Choice: How the Voter Makes up his Mind in a Presidential Campaign*. New York: Columbia University Press.

Leighley, Jan E. (1990). 'Social interaction and contextual influences on political participation', *American Politics Quarterly* 18(4): 459–75.

Lewis-Beck, Michael S. (1988). *Economics and Elections: The Major Western Democracies*. Ann Arbor, MI: University of Michigan Press.

——and Martin Paldam (2000). 'Economic voting: An introduction', *Electoral Studies* 19: 113–21.

Leyden, Kevin M. and Stephen A. Borrelli (1995). 'The effect of state economic conditions on gubernatorial elections: Does unified government make a difference?', *Political Research Quarterly* 48: 275–90.

Leys, Colin (1959). 'Models, theories and the theory of political parties', *Political Studies* 7: 127–46.

Lijphart, Arend (1968). *The Politics of Accomodation: Pluralism and Democracy in the Netherlands*. Berkeley, CA: University of California Press.

——(1984). *Democracies: Patterns of Majoritarian and Consensus Government in Twenty-one Countries*. New Haven, CT: Yale University Press.

——(ed.) (1992). *Parliamentary versus Presidential Government*. Oxford: Oxford University Press.

——(1994). *Electoral Systems and Party Systems: A Study of Twenty-seven Democracies, 1945–1990*. Oxford: Oxford University Press.

——(1997). 'Unequal participation: Democracy's unresolved dilemma. Presidential address, American Political Science Association, 1996', *American Political Science Review* 91: 1–14.

——(1999). *Patterns of Democracy: Government Forms and Performance in Thirty-six Countries*. New Haven, CT: Yale University Press.

——and Carlos H. Waisman (eds.) (1996). *Institutional Design in New Democracies*. Boulder, CO: Westview.

Lipset, Seymour Martin (1959; 1966). *Political Man*. London: Mercury Books.

Listhaug, Ola (1995). 'The dynamics of trust in politicians'. In Hans-Dieter Klingemann and Dieter Fuchs (eds.). *Citizens and the State*. Oxford: Oxford University Press.

——and Kristen Ringdal (2004). 'Civic morality in stable, new and half-hearted democracies'. In Wil Aarts and Loek Halman (eds.). *European Values at the Turn of the Millenium*. Leiden: Brill.

——and Matti Wiberg (1995). 'Confidence in political and private institutions'. In Hans-Dieter Klingemann and Dieter Fuchs (eds.). *Citizens and the state*. Oxford: Oxford University Press.

Long Jusko, Karen and Phillips W. Shively (2005). 'Applying a two-step strategy to the analysis of cross-national public opinion data', *Political Analysis* 13: 327–44.

Lowry, Robert C., James E. Alt, and Karen E. Ferree (1998). 'Fiscal policy outcomes and electoral accountability in American states', *American Political Science Review* 92: 759–74.

Luebbert, Gregory M. (1986). *Comparative Democracy: Policy Making and Governing Coalitions in Europe and Israel.* New York: Columbia University Press.

Lupia, Arthur, Mathew D. McCubbins, and Samuel L. Popkin (eds.) (2000). *Elements of Reason: Cognition, Choice, and the Bounds of Rationality.* Cambridge: Cambridge University Press.

Luttberg, Norman R. and Michael M. Gant (1985). 'The failure of liberal/conservative ideology as a cognitive structure', *Public Opinion Quarterly* 49: 80–93.

Lynn, Peter and Bridget Taylor (1995). 'On the bias and variance of samples of individuals: A comparison of the electoral registers and postcode address file as sampling frames', *Statistician* 44: 173–94.

McAllister, Ian and Martin P. Wattenberg (1995). 'Measuring levels of party identification: Does question order matter?', *Public Opinion Quarterly* 59: 259–68.

MacDonald, Stuart E., George Rabinowitz, and Ola Listhaug (1995). 'Political sophistication and models of issue voting', *British Journal of Political Science* 25: 453–83.

McFadden, Daniel (1974). 'Conditional logit analysis of qualitative behavior'. In P. Zarembka, (ed.). *Frontiers in Econometrics.* New York: Academic Press, 105–42.

MacKuen, Michael B., Robert S. Erikson, and James A. Stimson (1989). 'Macropartisanship', *American Political Science Review* 83: 1125–42.

Markus, Gregory B. (1988). 'The impact of personal and national economic conditions on the presidential vote: A pooled cross-sectional analysis', *American Journal of Political Science* 32: 137–54.

Marsh, Michael (2000). 'Candidate centred but party wrapped: Campaigning in Ireland under STV'. In S. Bowler and Bernie Grofman (eds.). *Elections in Australia, Ireland and Malta Under the Single Transferable Vote: Reflections on an Embedded Institution.* Ann Arbor, MI: University of Michigan Press.

Martin, Elisabeth (1983). 'Surveys as social indicators: Problems in monitoring trends'. In Peter H. Rossi, James D. Wright, and Andy B. Anderson (eds.). *Handbook of Survey Research.* New York: Academic Press.

Merrill, Samuel III and Bernard Grofman (1999). *A Unified Theory of Voting: Directional and Proximity Spatial Models.* Cambridge: Cambridge University Press.

Milbrath, Lester W. and M. L. Goel (1977). *Political Participation.* Lanham, MD: University Press of America.

Miller, Arthur H. and Ola Listhaug (1990). 'Political parties and confidence in government: A comparison of Norway, Sweden and the United States', *British Journal of Political Science* 20: 357–86.

————(1998). 'Policy preferences and political trust: A comparison of Norway, Sweden and the United States', *Scandinavian Political Studies* 21: 161–87.

Miller, Arthur H. and Martin P. Wattenberg (1984). 'Politics and the pulpit: Religiosity and the 1980 elections', *Public Opinion Quarterly* 48: 301–17.

Miller, Warren, Roy Pierce, Jacques Thomassen, Richard Herrera, Sören Holmberg, Peter Esaiasson, and Bernhard Weßels (1999). *Policy Representation in Western Democracies*. Oxford: Oxford University Press.

Miller, Warren E., Arthur H. Miller, and Edward J. Schneider (1980). *American National Election Studies Data Sourcebook, 1952–1978*. Cambridge, MA: Harvard University Press.

Mishler, William and Richard Rose (1994). 'Support for parliaments and regimes in the transition toward democracy', *Legislative Studies Quarterly* 19: 5–32.

—— —— (1999). 'Five years after the fall: Trajectories of support for democracy in post-communist Europe'. In Pippa Norris (ed.). *Critical Citizens*. Oxford: Oxford University Press.

Mokken, Robert J. (1971). *A Theory and Procedure of Scale Analysis*. The Hague: Mouton.

Monroe, Burt L. and Amanda G. Rose (2002). 'Electoral systems and unimagined consequences: Partisan effects of districted proportional representation', *American Journal of Political Science* 46: 67–89.

Moulton, Brent R. (1986). 'Random group effects and the precision of regression estimates', *Journal of Econometrics* 32: 385–97.

—— (1987). 'Diagnostics for group effects in regression analysis', *Journal of Business & Economic Statistics* 5: 275–82.

—— (1990). 'An illustration of a pitfall in estimating the effects of aggregate variables on micro units', *Review of Economics and Statistics* 72: 334–38.

Mozaffar, Shaheen, James R. Scarritt, and Glen Galaich (2003). 'Electoral institutions, ethnopolitical cleavages and party systems in Africa's emerging democracies', *American Political Science Review* 97: 379–90.

Mueller, Dennis C. (1989). *Public Choice II*. Cambridge: Cambridge University Press.

Mueller, John. (1970). 'Presidential popularity from Truman to Johnson', *American Political Science Review* 64: 18–34.

Nannestad, Peter and Martin Paldam (1994). 'The vp-function: A survey of the literature on vote and popularity functions after 25 years', *Public Choice* 79: 213–45.

Nie, Norman. H., J. Junn, and K. Stehlik-Barry (1996). *Education and Democratic Citizenship in America*. Chicago: University of Chicago Press.

—— Sidney Verba and John R. Petrocik (1976). *The Changing American Voter*. Cambridge, MA: Harvard University Press.

Niemi, Richard G. and Joel D. Barkan (1987). 'Age and turnout in new electorates and peasant societies', *American Political Science Review* 81: 582–88.

—— Stephen C. Craig and Franco Mattei (1991). 'Measuring internal political efficacy in the 1988 National Election Study', *American Political Science Review* 85: 1407–13.

Nohlen, Dieter, Florian Grotz, and Christof Hartmann (eds.) (2001). *Elections in Asia and the Pacific*. Oxford: Oxford University Press.

Norpoth, Helmut, Michael S. Lewis-Beck, and Jean-Dominique Lafay (eds.) (1991). *Economics and Politics: The Calculus of Support*. Ann Arbor, MI: University of Michigan Press.

Norris, Pippa (1991). 'Gender differences in political participation in Britain: traditional, radical and revisionist models', *Government and Opposition* 26: 1–56.

——(1999a). *Critical Citizens: Global Support for Democratic Governance*. Oxford: Oxford University Press.

——(1999b). 'Introduction: The growth of critical citizens?'. In Pippa Norris (ed.). *Critical Citizens*. Oxford: Oxford University Press.

——(1999c). 'Institutional explanations for political support'. In Pippa Norris (ed.). *Critical Citizens*. Oxford: Oxford University Press.

——(2001). 'The twilight of Westminster? Electoral reform and its consequences', *Political Studies* 49: 877–900.

——(2004). *Electoral Engineering: Voting Rules and Political Behavior*. New York: Cambridge University Press.

North, Douglass C. (1990). *Institutions, Institutional Change and Economic Performance*. Cambridge: Cambridge University Press.

Oppenhuis, Erik (1995). *Voting Behavior in Europe. A Comparative Analysis of Electoral Participation and Party Choice*. Amsterdam: Het Spinhuis.

Ordeshook, Peter C. and Olga V. Shevetsova (1994). 'Ethnic heterogeneity, district magnitude, and the number of parties', *American Journal of Political Science* 38: 100–23.

Pacek, Alexander C. and Benjamin Radcliff (1995). 'Economic voting and the welfare state: A cross-national analysis', *Journal of Politics* 57: 44–61.

Page, Benjamin I. and Calvin C. Jones (1979). 'Reciprocal effects of policy preferences, party loyalties and the vote', *American Political Science Review* 73: 1071–89.

Paldam, Martin (1981). 'A preliminary survey of the theories and findings on vote and popularity functions', *European Journal of Political Research* 9: 181–99.

——(1991). 'How robust is the vote function?'. In Helmut Norpoth, Michael S. Lewis-Beck, and J. D. Lafay (eds.). *Economics and Politics: The Calculus of Support*. Ann Arbor, MI: University of Michigan Press, 9–31.

Palfrey, Thomas and Keith Poole (1987). 'The relationship between information, ideology, and voting behavior', *American Journal of Political Science* 31: 511–30.

Papke, Leslie E. and Jeffrey M. Wooldridge (1996). 'Econometric methods for fractional response variables with an application to 401(k) plan participation rates', *Journal of Applied Econometrics* 11: 619–32.

Pappi, Franz Urban (1996). 'Political behavior: Reasoning voters and multi-party systems'. In Robert E. Goodin and Hans-Dieter Klingemann (eds.). *A New Handbook of Political Science*. Oxford: Oxford University Press.

——and Hermann Schmitt (1994). *Parteien, Parlamente und Wahlen in Skandinavien*. Frankfur: Campus.

Paskeviciute, Aida and Christopher J. Anderson (2003). Political party behavior and political trust in contemporary democracies. Paper prepared for presentation at the Annual Meeting of the American Political Science Association, Philadelphia, PA, August 28–31.

Pattie, Charles J. and Ron J. Johnston (2001). 'Routes to party choice: Ideology, economic evaluations and voting at the 1997 British general election', *European Journal of Political Research* 39: 373–89.

Pollock, Philip H., III (1982). 'Organizations as agents of mobilization: How does group activity affect political participation?', *American Journal of Political Science* 26: 485–503.

Popkin, Samuel L. (1991). *The Reasoning Voter: Communication and Persuasion in Presidential Elections*. Chicago: University of Chicago Press.

Powell, G. Bingham, Jr. (1982). *Contemporary Democracies: Participation, Stability and Violence*. Cambridge, MA: Harvard University Press.

——(1986). 'American voter turnout in comparative perspective', *American Political Science Review* 80: 17–44.

——(2000). *Elections as Instruments of Democracy: Majoritarian and Proportional Visions*. New Haven, CT: Yale University Press.

——and Guy D. Whitten (1993). 'A cross-national analysis of economic voting: Taking account of the political context', *American Journal of Political Science* 37: 391–414.

Przeworski, Adam, M. E. Alvarez, J. A. Cheibub, and F. Limongi (2000). *Democracy and Development: Political Institutions and Well-being in the World, 1950–1990*. Cambridge: Cambridge University Press.

——and Henry Teune (1970). *The Logic of Comparative Social Inquiry*. New York: Wiley.

Rabinowitz, George and Stuart E. MacDonald (1989). 'A directional theory of issue voting', *American Political Science Review* 83: 93–121.

Rahn, Wendy M., Jon A. Krosnick, and Marijke Breuning (1994). 'Rationalization and derivation processes in survey studies of political candidate evaluation', *American Journal of Political Science* 38: 582–600.

Reed, Steven R. (1997). 'The 1996 Japanese general election', *Electoral Studies* 16: 121–5.

Reif, Karlheinz and Hermann Schmitt (1980). 'Nine second-order national elections. A conceptual framework for the analysis of European election results', *European Journal for Political Research* 8: 3–44.

RePass, David E. (1971). 'Issue salience and party choice', *American Political Science Review* 65: 389–400.

Richman, Wendy L., Sara Kiesler, Suzanne Weisband, and Fritz Drasgow (1999). 'A meta-analytic study of social desirability distortion in computer-administered questionnaires, traditional questionnaires, and interviews', *Journal of Applied Psychology* 84: 754–75.

Riker, William H. and Peter C. Ordeshook (1968). 'A theory of the calculus of voting', *American Political Science Review* 62: 25–42.

Rivers, Douglas (1988). 'Heterogeneity in models of electoral choice', *American Political Science Review* 32: 737–57.

Rogers, Diane Lim, Kenney H. Barb, and Gordon L. Bultena (1975). 'Voluntary association membership and political participation: An exploration of the mobilization hypothesis', *Sociological Quarterly* 16: 305–18.

Rosenberg, Shawn, Lisa Bohan, Patrick McCaffery, and Kevin Harris (1986). 'The image and the vote: The effect of candidate presentation on voter preference', *American Journal of Political Science* 30: 108–27.

Rosenstone, Steven, John M. Hansen, and Donald R. Kinder (1986). 'Measuring change in personal economic well-being', *Public Opinion Quarterly* 50: 176–92.

Rudolph, Thomas J. and J. Tobin Grant. (2002). 'An attributional model of economic voting: Evidence from the 2000 presidential election', *Political Research Quarterly* 55: 805–23.

Sanders, Elisabeth (1980). 'On the costs, utilities and simple joys of voting', *Journal of Politics* 42: 854–63.

Sartori, Giovanni (1968). 'Political development and political engineering'. In John D. Montgomery and Albert O. Hirschman (eds.). *Public Policy*. Cambridge: Cambridge University Press, 261–98.

——(1976). *Parties and Party Systems*. Cambridge: Cambridge University Press.

——(1986). 'The influence of electoral systems: Faulty laws or faulty methods?' In Bernard Grofman and Arend Lijphart (eds.). *Electoral Laws and Their Consequences*. New York: Agathon Press, 43–68.

Schmitt, Hermann (1998). 'Issue-Kompetenz oder Policy-Distanz?' In Max Kaase and Hans-Dieter Klingemann (eds.). *Wahlen und Wähler*. Opladen: Westdeutscher Verlag.

——(2000). 'Zur vergleichenden Analyse des Einflusses gesellschaftlicher Faktoren auf das Wahlverhalten: Forschungsfragen, Analysestrategien und einige Ergebnisse'. In Hans-Dieter Klingemann and Max Kaase (eds.). *Wahlen und Wähler*. Opladen: Westdeutscher Verlag.

——(2001). *Politische Repräsentation in Europa*. Frankfurt: Campus.

——and Jacques Thomassen (1999). *Political Representation and Legitimacy in the European Union*. Oxford: Oxford University Press.

Schuessler, Alexander A. (2000). *The Logic of Expressive Choice*. Princeton, NJ: Princeton University Press.

Schumann, Howard and Graham Kalton (1985). 'Survey methods'. In L. Gardner and Elliot Aronson (eds.). *Handbook of Social Psychology: Theory and Method*. New York: Random House.

Schumpeter, Joseph A. (1942; 1976). *Capitalism, Socialism and Democracy*, 5th edn. London: Allen & Unwin.

Shugart, Matthew Soberg (1993). 'Of presidents and parliaments', *East European Constitutional Review* 2: 30–2.

Shugart, Matthew Soberg (2001). 'Electoral "efficiency" and the move to mixed-member systems', *Electoral Studies* 20: 173–93.

—— and John M. Carey (1992). *Presidents and Assemblies: Constitutional Design and Electoral Dynamics*. Cambridge: Cambridge University Press.

—— and Stephan Haggard (2001). 'Institutions and public policy in presidential systems'. In Stephan Haggard and Mathew D. McCubbins (eds.). *Presidents, Parliaments, and Policy*. Cambridge: Cambridge University Press, 64–102.

—— and Martin P. Wattenberg (eds.) (2001*a*). *Mixed-member Electoral Systems: The Best of Both Worlds?* Oxford: Oxford University Press.

—— —— (2001*b*). 'Mixed-member electoral systems: A definition and typology'. In Matthew Soberg Shugart and Martin P. Wattenberg (eds.). *Mixed-member Electoral Systems: The Best of Both Worlds?* Oxford: Oxford University Press, 9–24.

Sigelman, Lee and William D. Berry (1982). 'Cost and the calculus of voting', *Political Behavior* 4: 419–28.

—— and Syng N. Yough (1978). 'Left-right polarization in national party systems: A cross-national analysis', *Comparative Political Studies* 11: 355–79.

Simon, Herbert A. (1957). *Models of Man*. New York: Wiley.

Singer, Eleanor, Robert Groves, and Amy Corning (1999). 'Differential incentives: Beliefs about practices, perceptions of equity, and effects on survey participation', *Public Opinion Quarterly* 63: 251–60.

Sniderman, Paul M. (1993). 'The new look in public opinion research'. In Ada W. Finifter (ed.). *Political Science: The State of the Discipline II*. Washington DC: American Political Science Association, 219–43.

—— and Richard A. Brody, and Philip E. Tetlock (1993). *Reasoning and Choice: Explorations in Political Psychology*. Cambridge: Cambridge University Press.

Snijders, Tom and Roel Bosker (1999). *Multilevel Analysis: An Introduction to Basic and Advanced Multilevel Modeling*. Thousand Oaks, CA: Sage Publications.

Steenbergen, Marco R. and Bradford S. Jones (2002). 'Modeling multilevel data structures', *American Journal of Political Science* 46: 218–37.

Stokes, Donald E. (1963). 'Spatial models of party competition', *American Political Science Review* 57: 368–77.

Strøm, Kaare (1999). 'Voter sovereignty and parliamentary democracy'. In Hanne Marthe Narud and Toril Aalberg (eds.). *Challenges to Representative Democracy: Parties, Voters and Public Opinion*. Bergen: Fagbokforlaget.

Taagepera, Rein and Mathew Soberg Shugart (1989). *Seats and Votes: The Effects and Determinants of Electoral Systems*. New Haven, CT: Yale University Press.

Tanur, Judith (1983–4). 'Methods for large-scale surveys and experiments', *Sociological Methodology* 14: 1–71.

Teixiera, Ruy A. (1992). *The Disappearing American Voter*. Washington, DC: Brookings Institute.

Thomassen, Jacques (1976). 'Party identification as a cross-national concept: It's meaning in the Netherlands'. In Ian Budge et al. (eds.). *Party Identification and Beyond*. London: John Wiley.

—— (2005). *The European Voter*. Oxford: Oxford University Press.

Tillie, Jean (1995). *Party Utility and Voting Behaviour*. Amsterdam: Het Spinhuis.

Tilly, Charles (ed.) (1975). *The Formation of National States in Western Europe.* Princeton, NJ: Princeton University Press.

Tóka, Gábor (1995). 'Political support in East-Central Europe'. In Hans-Dieter Klingemann and Dieter Fuchs (eds.). *Citizens and the State.* Oxford: Oxford University Press, 354–82.

Topf, Richard (1995). 'Electoral participation'. In Hans-Dieter Klingemann and Dieter Fuchs (eds.). *Citizens and the State.* Oxford: Oxford University Press, 27–51.

Tourangeau, Roger, Lance J. Rips, and Kenneth A. Rasinski (2000). *The Psychology of Survey Responses.* Cambridge: Cambridge University Press.

Traugott, Michael W. (1987). 'The importance of persistence in respondent selection for pre-election surveys', *Public Opinion Quarterly* 51: 48–57.

Tsebelis, George (1995). 'Decision-making in political systems: Veto players in presidentialism, parliamentarism, multicameralism and multiplaryism', *British Journal of Political Science* 25: 289–325.

Tullock, Gordon (1971). 'The charity of the uncharitable', *Economic Inquiry* 9: 379–92.

Vanhanen, Tatu (1997). *Prospects of Democracy. A Study of 172 Countries.* London: Routledge.

Verba, Sidney (1995*a*). 'The citizen as respondent: Sample surveys and American democracy. Presidential address, American Political Science Association, 1995', *American Political Science Review* 90: 1–7.

—— (1995*b*). 'Beyond SES: A resource model of participation', *American Political Science Review* 89: 271–94.

—— and Norman Nie (1972). *Participation in America: Political Democracy and Social Equality.* New York: Harper and Row.

—— —— and Jae-On Kim (1978). *Participation and Political Equality: A Seven-Nation Comparison.* Cambridge: Cambridge University Press.

—— Kay L. Schlozman, and Henry E. Brady (1995). *Voice and Equality: Civic Volunteerism in American Politics.* Cambridge, MA: Harvard University Press.

Vetter, Angelika and Oscar W. Gabriel (1998). 'Candidate evaluations and party choice in Germany, 1972–1994: Do candidates matter?' In Christian J. Anderson and Carsten Zelle (eds.). *Stability and Change in German Elections: How Electorates Merge, Converge, or Collide.* Westport, CT: Praeger, 71–98.

Vowles, Jack, Peter Aimer, Susan Banducci, and Jeffrey Karp (eds.) (1998). *Voter's Victory? New Zealand's First Election Under Proportional Representation.* Auckland: Auckland University Press.

Wängnerud, Lena (1993). 'Kvinnliga riksdagskandidater—vem lägger märke till att de finns?' In Jörgen Westerståhl (ed.). *Person och Parti.* Stockholm: SOU.

Weil, Frederick D. (1989). 'The sources and structure of legitimation in Western democracies', *American Sociological Review* 54: 682–706.

Wenzel, James P., Shaun Bowler, and David J. Lanoue (2000). 'Citizen opinion and constitutional choices: The case of the UK', *Political Behavior* 22:

241–65.

Weßels, Bernhard (1991). *Erosion des Wachstumsparadigmas: Neue Konfliktstrukturen im politischen System der Bundesrepublik?* Opladen: Westdeutscher Verlag.

——(2004). 'Sachfragen, generalisierte politische Positionen und Leistungsbewertungen: Zur Konditionierung präferenzorientierten Wählens'. In Frank Brettschneider, Jan van Deth und Edeltraud Roller (eds.). *Die Bundestagswahl 2002. Analysen der Wahlergebnisse und des Wahlkampfes.* Wiesbaden: VS Verlag, 143–66.

West, Darrell (1995). 'Television advertising in election campaigns', *Political Science Quarterly* 109: 789–810.

White, Stephen, Richard Rose, and Ian McAllister (1997). *How Russia Votes.* Chatham, NJ: Chatham House.

Whiteley, Paul F. (1988). 'The causal relationships between issues, candidate evaluations, party identification, and vote choice—the view from "rolling thunder"', *Journal of Politics* 50: 961–84.

Wielhouwer, Peter W. and Brad Lockerbie (1994). 'Party contacting and political participation, 1952–90', *American Journal of Political Science* 38: 211–29.

Wolfinger, Raymond and Steven Rosenstone (1980). *Who Votes?* New Haven, CT: Yale University Press.

Woodall, Brian (2000). 'The politics of reform in Japan's Lower House electoral system'. In B. Grofman, S. C. Lee, E. Winckler, and B. Woodull (eds.). *Elections in Japan, Korea, and Taiwan Under the Single Non-transferable Vote.* Ann Arbor, MI: University of Michigan Press.

Worcester, Robert M. (1983). 'The polls: Britain at the polls 1945–83', *Public Opinion Quarterly* 48: 824–33.

Yammarino, Francis J., Steven J. Skinner, and Terry L. Childers (1991). 'Understanding mail survey response behavior', *Public Opinion Quarterly* 55: 613–19.

Zuckerman, Alan S. (ed.) (2005). *The Social Logic of Partisanship.* Philadelphia, PA: Temple.

I. Technical Reports (American National Election Studies)

Bartels, Larry (2000). *Question Order and Declining Faith in Elections*, National Election Studies Technical Reports, No. 60.

Bowers, Jake and Michael J. Ensley (2003). *Issues in Analyzing Data from the Dual-Mode 2000 American National Election Study.* American National Election Studies Technical Reports, No. 64.

Green, Melanie. C., Jon A. Krosnick, and Allyson L. Holbrook (2001). *The Survey Response Process in Telephone and Face-to-Face Surveys: Differences in Respondent Satisficing and Social Desirability Response Bias.* American National Election Studies Technical Reports, No. 62.

Sapiro, Virginia and W. Philips Shively (2002). *Comparative Study of Electoral Systems, Module 1: 1996–2001.* Codebook. Center for Political Studies, Institute for

Social Research, University of Michigan, ICPSR Archive Number 2683.

Wessel, Christina, Wendy Rahn, and Tom Rudolf (2000). *An Analysis of the 1998 NES Mixed-Mode Design.* American National Election Studies Technical Reports, No. 57.

II. CSES Documents

The Comparative Study of Electoral Systems (CSES), general information: http://www.cses.org

The Comparative Study of Electoral Systems (1999). *CSES Module 1 Advance Release (dataset).* Ann Arbor, MI: University of Michigan, Center for Political Studies (producer and distributor).

CSES Planning Committee (1996). *The Comparative Study of Electoral Systems: Final Report of the 1995-1996 Planning Committee.* http://www.cses.org/plancom/module1/95rpt2.htm – accessed March 28, 2008.

Schmitt, Hermann and Bernhard Weßels (2005). 'Meaningful choices. Under which conditions do general elections provide a meaningful choice-set, and what happens if they don't?' Stimulus paper for the Third Wave of the Comparative Study of Electoral Systems, to be conducted from 2006 through 2010. http://www.cses.org

Shively, W. Phillips and Nancy E. Burns (2001). 'Political science research infrastructure: Comparative Study of Electoral Systems'. Proposal to the National Science Foundation. Award reference number SES-0112029. The University of Minnesota and University of Michigan

Thomassen, Jacques, Steven J. Rosenstone, Hans-Dieter Klingemann, and John Curtice (1994). 'The Comparative Study of Electoral Systems' (Stimulus Paper). http://www.cses.org/plancom/module1/stimulus.htm – accessed March 26, 2008.

III. Other Internet-based Sources

Eurobarometer, general information: http://ec.europa.eu/public_opinion or http://www.gesis.org/eurobarometer

Central and Eastern Euro-Barometer 2: 'Current Affairs and the Media. 1991'. http://www.gesis.org/en/data_service/eurobarometer/ceeb/topics.htm

Eurobarometer: 'Trend File'. http://gesis.org/en/data_service/eurobarometer/standard_ eb_trend/trendfile.htm

Public Opinion Analysis Sector of the European Commission. http://ec.europa.eu/public_opinion

European Election Study, general information: http://www.europeanelectionstudies.net

Commission of the European Communities (1989). Euro-Barometer 31A: 'European elections, 1989. Technical Documentation'.

European Election Study Research Group (1994). 'Abstract'. http://www. europeanelectionstudies.net

European Election Study Research Group. 'Technical documentation'. http://www. europeanelectionstudies.net

European Values Study (EVS), general information: http://www. europeanvalues.nl>

European Values Study (EVS): http://www.europeanvalues.nl

Freedom House, general information and dataset: http://www. freedomhouse.org

Freedom House (1999). 'Freedom in the world. The annual survey of political rights and civil liberties 1998–1999'. http://www.freedomhouse.org/survey99

International Institute for Democracy and Electoral Assistance (International IDEA), general information: http://www.idea.int

IDEA (1997). 'Voter turnout from 1945–1997: A global report on political participation'. http://www.idea.int/publications/voterturnout.html

International Social Survey Program (ISSP), general information: http://www. issp.org

International Social Survey Program (ISPP): http://www.issp.org

Inter-Parliamentary Union, general information: http://www.ipu.org

Inter-Parliamentary Union. 'Women in national parliaments' (situation as of 5 December 2001). http://www.ipu.org

Lijphart's Election Archive: http://dodgson.ucsd.edu/lij

Lijphart Elections Archive, University of California, San Diego. http://dodgson. ucsd.edu/lij

STATA, general information: http://www.stata.com

Sribney, W. (1998). 'What are the advantages of using the robust variance estimator over the standard maximum-likelihood variance estimator in logistic regression?' STAT FAQ at http://www.stata.com/support/faqs/stat/robust_var.html

STATA (1985–99). *User's Guide, Release* 6. College Station, Texas: Stat Press. http://www.stata.com

World Values Survey (WVS), general information: http://www. worldvaluessurvey.org

World Values Survey (WVS): http://www.worldvaluessurvey.org

Index